Singapore in the Global System

This book tracks the phases of Singapore's economic and political development, arguing that its success was always dependent upon the territories links with the surrounding region and the wider global system, and suggests that managing these links today will be the key to the country's future. Singapore has followed a distinctive historical development trajectory. It was one of a number of cities which provided bases for the expansion of the British empire in the East. But the Pacific War provided local elites with their chance to secure independence. In Singapore the elite disciplined and mobilized their population and built successfully on their colonial inheritance. Today, the city-state prospers in the context of its regional and global networks, and sustaining and nurturing these are the keys to its future. But there are clouds on the elite's horizons; domestically, the population is restive with inequality, migration and surplus-repression causing concern; and internationally, the strategy of constructing a business-hub economy is being widely copied and both Hong Kong and Shanghai are significant competitors. *Singapore in the Global System* discusses these issues and argues that although success is likely to characterize Singapore's future, the elite will have to address these significant domestic and international problems.

Peter Preston is a member of the Department of Government and Public Administration of the Chinese University of Hong Kong. His research interests revolve around the issue of complex change, which he has pursued in the contexts of Third World development theory, questions of English identity and the political economy of change in East Asia. His recent publications include: *Understanding Modern Japan: A Political Economy of Development, Culture and Global Power* (2000); *Political Change in East Asia* (2003); and *Relocating England: Englishness in the New Europe* (2004).

Routledge Contemporary Southeast Asia Series

1 **Land Tenure, Conservation and Development in Southeast Asia**
Peter Eaton

2 **The Politics of Indonesia–Malaysia Relations**
One kin, two nations
Joseph Chinyong Liow

3 **Governance and Civil Society in Myanmar**
Education, health and environment
Helen James

4 **Regionalism in Post-Suharto Indonesia**
Edited by Maribeth Erb, Priyambudi Sulistiyanto and Carole Faucher

5 **Living with Transition in Laos**
Market integration in Southeast Asia
Jonathan Rigg

6 **Christianity, Islam and Nationalism in Indonesia**
Charles E. Farhadian

7 **Violent Conflicts in Indonesia**
Analysis, representation, resolution
Edited by Charles A. Coppel

8 **Revolution, Reform and Regionalism in Southeast Asia**
Cambodia, Laos and Vietnam
Ronald Bruce St John

9 **The Politics of Tyranny in Singapore and Burma**
Aristotle and the rhetoric of benevolent despotism
Stephen McCarthy

10 **Ageing in Singapore**
Service needs and the state
Peggy Teo, Kalyani Mehta, Leng Leng Thang and Angelique Chan

11 **Security and Sustainable Development in Myanmar**
Helen James

12 **Expressions of Cambodia**
The politics of tradition, identity and change
Edited by Leakthina Chau-Pech Ollier and Tim Winter

13 **Financial Fragility and Instability in Indonesia**
Yasuyuki Matsumoto

14 **The Revival of Tradition in Indonesian Politics**
The deployment of *adat* from colonialism to indigenism
Edited by Jamie S. Davidson and David Henley

15 **Communal Violence and Democratization in Indonesia**
Small town wars
Gerry van Klinken

16 **Singapore in the Global System**
Relationship, structure and change
Peter Preston

Singapore in the Global System
Relationship, structure and change

Peter Preston

LONDON AND NEW YORK

First published 2007
by Routledge
2 Park Square, Milton Park, Abingdon, Oxon OX14 4RN

Simultaneously published in the USA and Canada
by Routledge
711 Third Ave, New York, NY 10017

Routledge is an imprint of the Taylor & Francis Group, an informa business

First issued in paperback 2012

© 2007 Peter Preston

Typeset in Times New Roman by
Taylor & Francis Books

All rights reserved. No part of this book may be reprinted or reproduced or utilised in any form or by any electronic, mechanical, or other means, now known or hereafter invented, including photocopying and recording, or in any information storage or retrieval system, without permission in writing from the publishers.

British Library Cataloguing in Publication Data
A catalogue record for this book is available from the British Library

Library of Congress Cataloging in Publication Data
Preston, P. W. (Peter Wallace), 1949-
Singapore in the global system : relationship, structure, and change / Peter Preston.
p. cm. – (Routledge contemporary Southeast Asia series; 16)
Includes bibliographical references and index.
1. Social change – Singapore. 2. Globalization – Singapore. 3. Elite (Social sciences) – Singapore. 4. Singapore – Economic conditions – 21st century. 5. Singapore – Social conditions – 21st century. I. Title.
HN800.67.A8P74 2007
327.1095957 – dc22
2007021674

ISBN13: 978-0-415-33190-6 (hbk)
ISBN13: 978-0-415-54219-7(pbk)
ISBN13: 978-0-203-39807-4 (ebk)

To the memory of my mother

Contents

	List of photographs	viii
	Preface	ix
	Acknowledgements	x
1	Singapore contexts	1
2	Complex change	12
3	Impact and reply	40
4	General crisis	58
5	New trajectories	79
6	Locating Singapore	100
7	Trading cities	160
8	Unfolding trajectories	197
	Notes	216
	Bibliography	263
	Index	275

Photographs

1	Singapore, Boat Quay	145
2	Singapore, Yishun North Point Shopping Centre	146
3	Singapore, Holland Avenue	147
4	Singapore, upgraded apartment blocks, Holland Avenue	148
5	Singapore, hawker centre, Yishun	149
6	Hong Kong, Argyle Street, Kowloon	168
7	Hong Kong, Shatin Village, New Territories	169
8	Hong Kong, Shatin New Town, New Territories	170
9	Hong Kong, Ma On Shan, New Territories	171
10	Hong Kong, Tolo Harbour, New Territories	172
11	Bangkok, downtown skyline	183
12	Bangkok, Ramkamhaeng, suburban street scene	183
13	Bangkok, Ramkamhaeng, informal housing area	184
14	Bangkok, Ramkamhaeng Road	185
15	Bangkok, coffee Shop, Ramkamhaeng	186

Preface

According to a familiar version of the history of Singapore, development began in 1965; earlier years were merely precursors to the achievements of the contemporary elite; and the sweep of the island's history could be summarized as the evolutionary attainment of the crowning achievement of successful rugged independence. It is a nationalist history. A different reading of the historical development experience of Singapore can be presented; the materials are readily available as the territory has been the subject of a wealth of scholarship. Singapore can be placed in context. This text puts Singapore back into its own history; it puts it back into its own geography; and it puts it back into those local, regional and global structures which have been its sustaining environment. There is no one Singapore; there is only the currently recoverable history of the succession of polities which have embraced the island. Contemporary Singapore is the contingent outturn of a contested elite political project; it is novel in that territory and polity coincide in the form of an island city-state; but there have been other projects in the past; there will be others in the future.

Acknowledgements

I first travelled to Singapore in 1982. It was my first experience of living and working outside England. It was a delight. Over the years it has been my good fortune to be able to live and work in several other countries in Asia and Europe. This book took preliminary shape whilst I was living in Germany, some of the ideas about development in Singapore were written up whilst I was living and working in Tokyo and the current version has taken shape whilst I have been working in Hong Kong. The text of this book has followed me around Europe and Asia. It has taken too long to write but there never seemed to be much of a hurry, for not only were the various places in which I found myself absorbingly interesting but also Singapore itself was a regular stopping-off point. The current book is one result of these travels and I should like to record my thanks to colleagues, students and friends scattered around these two continents.

1 Singapore contexts

There is no one Singapore; there is only the currently recoverable history of the succession of polities whose particular geographical extents have encompassed the island. The ancient history is lost in myth[1] but the modern history begins with the expansion of the British Empire, where global trading interests required bases.[2] The process drew in and remade existing sub-regional polities with multiple agents involved in complex exchanges. The shifting economics and politics of the colonial era lodged these territories firmly within the modern world but the general crises of the twentieth century radically reconfigured colonial patterns and as replacement elites sought to define and pursue their own political projects their actions shaped the postcolonial trajectories of the territories they now controlled. These processes were contingent; multiple agents animated shifting patterns of change; contemporary patterns are the outcome of these processes. They are contingent. Patterns of life in Southeast Asia in the modern period have been made and remade; these changes have enfolded the island of Singapore; they have shaped the lives of the various denizens of that island; and they have made and remade the polities whose territories have embraced the island.

After the British seizure of the South Asian sub-continent, Calcutta and Madras on the eastern coast were the stepping-off places for further expansions; George Town, Malacca and then Singapore were occupied in order to control the Straits of Malacca and protect the route to China. In the British sphere in East Asia, Singapore and Hong Kong became crucial colonial ports; they were links in a global system; they facilitated access to their local hinterlands within the Malay world of Southeast Asia and southern China; later the ports of the informal empire[3] extended British influence, and Bangkok and Shanghai drew in Siam and the central regions of China. The history of these four cities records their participation in a series of polities: from the mandala states of Southeast Asia,[4] the feudal states of Indo-China and China, and the various colonial states, through to, more recently, a city-state, two great provincial capitals and the primate city of an independent nation-state. The modern history of these cities reflects the turbulent progress of the unfolding shift to the modern world; trading exchanges; colonial rule; the catastrophe of East Asia's general crisis;

2 *Singapore contexts*

decolonization; cold war; and more recently deepening economic, social and political progress within the confines of the region of East Asia.[5] Their modern history reveals an interlinked set of discrete historical trajectories, unfolding routes to the modern world.

In the early nineteenth century Singapore island lay at the intersection of a series of circles of practice/ideas: the cultural realm of modernity; the British trading empire; the South Asian sphere; the Malay sphere of the archipelago; and the Chinese-centred trading sphere of the Nanyang. These flows of practice/ideas enfolded Singapore island. Singapore island has been home to a number of polities and the extent of these polities overlapped with the geographical territory in different ways as the British looked to a global trading empire, the Malays to the archipelago and the Chinese to their motherland. The weight of these spheres in the minds of successive Singapore-based elites has altered; a number of histories are available; as the power of particular players has changed, rising or falling, so too has one history been favoured over another. The elite of the contemporary city-state tell a quite particular tale; they present a national past;[6] it is a nationalist past, which celebrates the putative evolutionary achievement of a rugged independence. But the historical record is more complex; so too the present day, where contemporary Singapore is located within a number of spheres – Association of Southeast Asian Nations (ASEAN), East Asia and the global trading sphere – which the elite must manage as they plot a route to the future. The current polity is not separate from the modern world; it is firmly and deeply lodged within that world. The present pattern is the contingent outcome of dynamics of change, and change continues to unfold.

The dynamics of complex change

The interpretive critical elucidation of the dynamics of complex change in the ongoing shift to the modern world lies at the heart of the classical European tradition of social theorizing.[7] This preoccupation has animated the work of diverse theorists: eighteenth-century Enlightenment thinkers; nineteenth-century classical political economists; and recently the work of general theorists, development analysts and international political economists. An elaborate conceptual vocabulary is available:[8] it centres on the contingent social dynamics which underpin the social world and create particular societies; it grants a key role to elites, who must read enfolding structures, mobilize their domestic populations and order their political projects; it addresses the historical trajectories of societies which are marked out by these exchanges; it considers the intermingled patterns created via interactions with the paths followed by other communities; and it maps the resulting contingent domestic and international patterns of relationships. These processes are contingent; there is no simple logic to events; there is no single system; rather, a contingent global (non)system;[9] the currently available pattern of changing relationships.

Global capitalism had its origins in sixteenth-century Europe; domestic intensification and international expansion marked its development; exchanges with other cultures entailed their reconstruction; capitalism was reproduced in diverse forms in exchanges with extant civilizations.[10] Three cultural spheres were implicated in the reconstruction of East Asia: the diverse principalities of South Asia; the multiplicity of local powers in Southeast Asia; and the ordered empire of the Chinese in East Asia; these three cultural spheres shared extensive trade links along which goods, people and ideas moved. European incursions plus later American and Japanese activities remade East Asia: the incomers were buoyed by the vigour of their commercial capitalist system; they manoeuvred against each other and against local country powers; spheres of influence were carved out of the patterns of relationships which had constituted East Asian civilizations. Geographically, British incursions into Asia from the seventeenth century were centred on the South Asian sub-continent, running down an arc of territory through Burma and the Malay peninsula to Singapore,[11] thereafter extending to Siam, encompassing northern Borneo, taking in the island of Hong Kong and finally reaching through Shanghai into the valley of the Yangtze river and hence the interior of China. The British Empire came to comprise both formally colonized territories and a wide arc of informal empire[12] holdings; trade was the driver, not acquisition of territory; the line of advance was dictated by contingent events;[13] the political institutional key was the creation of a network of colonial port cities:[14] Calcutta and Madras; Penang, Malacca and Singapore; Hong Kong; plus the informal empire port cities of Bangkok[15] and Shanghai.[16]

The shift to the modern world

The macro-history of East Asia can be grasped in terms of a quartet of phases: first, the patterns of life of the indigenous civilizations; second, the incursions of the Europeans and Americans and the variety of local responses; third, the twentieth-century sequence of interlinked crises; and, fourth, the subsequent continuing period of strong post-colonial national development.[17] In each phase distinctive patterns of life can be identified: an economic system, a social system, a cultural system and, running through it all, a pattern of political relationships of power.

East Asia prior to the arrival of European and, later, American traders was home to a number of rich, successful long-established civilizations: there was a Chinese cultural sphere comprising China, the Korean peninsula, the Japanese islands and the Indo-Chinese polity of Vietnam; a Malay cultural sphere comprising a number of polities in mainland Indo-China and a multiplicity of shifting maritime empires in the archipelago to the south;[18] and, finally, an influential South Asian cultural sphere centred on the sub-continent comprising dozens of princely territories that maintained trade and cultural links with eastern neighbours. These three cultural spheres were distinctive, sophisticated, economically advanced and linked by extensive trading networks which carried goods, people and ideas; contemporary scholars treat this broad Asian sphere as the core area of the global system prior to the emergence of Europe and America.[19]

European and, later, American traders[20] began to participate in these established networks of trade from the sixteenth century onwards. At first they were only minor figures: a few ships, a few people, visiting a few ports in order to exchange a limited spread of goods. Their impact grew on the back of the development within Europe of the political economic system called capitalism; a dynamic system which routinely increased its domestic efficiency and expanded externally. European and American traders began to have a deeper impact on East Asia, and slowly, as they were joined by missionaries, adventurers, soldiers, administrators and so on, they began to remake East Asia. They were participants within an existing system; indigenous agents responded in a multiplicity of ways; power-holders faced major problems of accommodating the demands of the outsiders, some adjusting, others collapsing, others coming into being;[21] merchants found new opportunities and competitors; and the social world had new ideas, practices and opportunities to absorb. The extant peoples of East Asia were not passive victims; they adjusted: some prospered, some did not. The agents of empire were also diverse, though their empires had similar characteristics: empires were run from metropolitan centres; the nationals of these centres were privileged; there was a subtle exchange with extant political, economic and social power structures; often there was a racial divide; and the whole system was legitimated with ideas of the superior civilization of the colonizers. The region was slowly reordered in line with the demands of European and American governments and traders, and a series of empires and spheres of influence were established. In the late nineteenth century the Japanese also established an empire in Northeast Asia.[22]

The system expanded until the early years of the twentieth century; but it was unsustainable, a matter of demographics,[23] metropolitan critics plus local leaders who had come to understand the modern world and were determined to become participants. The system fell into decay and a general crisis[24] developed: economic, social and political confusion attended by extended military conflicts. The crisis can be dated[25] from the Chinese Revolution of 1911, which marked the first rejection of colonialism in favour of active equal participation in the modern world, through to 1975, when the reunification of Vietnam signalled the end of colonialism. The crisis unfolded at different times within the territories of the region but the descent into chaos in China was the first symptom; thereafter Imperial Japanese aggression ensured the crisis had regional scope; the collapse of the European and American empires followed; the post-war struggles for independence and clarity in respect of national development generated further confusions; but in time a series domestic elites coalesced and thereafter shaped the post-war regional world.

A series of national elites emerged. Their political projects initially centred on survival. In places such task were long drawn out. However, slowly elites came to affirm the pursuit of national development; that is, packages of economic, social, cultural and political reform oriented to the needs of the domestic populations. There was great success in Japan, the Asian Tigers and later more patchily in Southeast Asia. Indo-China remained mired in war. In China an autarchic state socialism advanced slowly at great cost to the population until its 1978 reorientation. By the middle of the 1980s the economic advance of the region was apparent to everyone: there were large industries; extensive scientific research; major universities; a growing middle class; there were deepening economic, social, cultural and political linkages throughout the area; and the area generated a strengthening flow of manufactured exports. The idea of an East Asian region emerged. It has been suggested that the global system now comprises three key regions: East Asia, Europe and North America. The countries of East Asia continue to develop; these matters continue to be debated.[26]

British involvement: India, the Malay archipelago and China

British involvement in Asia was not concerned with settlement; it was driven by trade and shaped by multiple conflicts with contending European and local country powers. The process was haphazard in terms of the actual accumulation of particular bases and territory, but it was also guided by the overarching concern for trade; the resultant process of expansion was both resolutely instrumental-rational and buttressed by ideological celebrations of the culture of the traders and claims for the broad value and inevitability of trade. It was also shaped by geography: the traders entered from the west; the Indian sub-continent was the first area of activity; later they operated in the archipelago; and finally they moved northeast assembling an informal empire in Siam and China. These holdings were secured by force and guile, held by armies made up largely of locals and linked to the metropolitan centre by colonial trading ports – Calcutta, Madras, Georgetown, Malacca, Singapore, Hong Kong, Bangkok and Shanghai. Trading was not restricted to delimited empire spheres; trading between the territories of the colonial empires was extensive; other colonial port cities figured in the overall pattern: Batavia, Saigon and Manila plus the cities of the Chinese coast and later those of Japan.

The East India Company, founded in 1657,[27] was the organizational vehicle for English expansion in the Asian region. It began in the seventeenth century; it deepened in the eighteenth;[28] it became more important after the loss of the American colonies; and the related inauguration of the project of the British Empire[29] underscored the importance of the region. The Indian sub-continent was the key possession. The Company slowly infiltrated the patchwork of sub-continental princely states: trade links, military alliances, co-options and annexations. It was an irregular expansion, filled with risk, suffused with violence and driven by the intermingled demands of trade, imperial competition and individual opportunism.[30] The British fought around fifty wars in the period 1610–1857 to subjugate the sub-continent;[31] it required three wars in the nineteenth century to conquer the Burmese.[32] The sub-continent was secured against competition from indigenous princely states and the competing claims of the Dutch, Portuguese and French only through multiple wars, diplomatic manoeuvring and the establishment of trading settlements. Colonial empire generated riches for some, advancement for others and failures for many;[33] it overturned extant elites in the sub-continent. However, the Company's role was terminated by the 1857 Indian Mutiny; thereafter the British government assumed control. The colonial trading cities of Calcutta and Madras[34] linked the sub-continent to the metropolitan centre; they also provided bases for expansion to the east.

The Southeast Asian Malay world was made up of local powers which traded throughout the archipelago and maintained links with the Indian sub-continent and China. It was a coherent region.[35] The Europeans entered seeking trade. Their activities remade the region as a series of discrete colonial spheres of influence. Indigenous patterns of livelihood were overlaid with newer activities serving the demands of the wider system: novel local trade goods; later commercial primary products; a dependent capitalist pattern. Trade was the driver, colonial ports the keys; these complex settlements drew the peoples of the region into the global capitalist system. It was a destructive business: the Dutch overwhelmed the extant powers of the archipelago in a series of wars; the French invaded and seized control of Indo-China; whilst the British, here preferring guile to warfare, established three trading ports on the Malay peninsula which formed the crucial links in a chain that was to run to the overriding goal of China.

Francis Light established the port of George Town in 1786; Stamford Raffles established the port of Singapore in 1818; George Elliot established the port of Hong Kong in 1841.[36] The former fell quickly out of favour as it was sited at a point remote from the archipelago and China. Singapore and Hong Kong, in contrast, quickly became important colonial and global cities. In the informal sphere of empire, the Bowring Treaty of 1855 drew Bangkok into the global system,[37] and the Opium War of 1839–42 and the Arrow War 1856–60 drew China into the system as a series of trading ports were opened. George Balfour established a trading settlement in Shanghai in the autumn of 1843; trade grew and in time an informal British sphere extended along the valley of the Yangtze river into inland China.[38] The British trading houses exported Chinese luxury products, tea and, later, migrants to America and the Nanyang; the traders brought manufactured goods and later opium.[39] This process of incursion and mutual accommodation was repeated by the other European, American and later Japanese colonial powers. It was in this manner that East Asia was drawn into the modern world. However, empire was not sustainable; collapse was inevitable, and, with it, an extensive and dramatic reordering of economies, societies and polities.

General crisis; the opening for national development

The British Empire in East Asia was assembled over some 300 or so years. In the years following the Great War there was some talk of reform but little was accomplished. The consensus amongst celebrants and critics seems to have been that the empire would for a while endure; in the event, it was overturned in the space of a few months in late 1941 and early 1942.[40] The irruption of the armed forces of the Imperial Japanese destroyed the established patterns of trade, politics and military power within East Asia. British holdings in China, Hong Kong, Malaya, Singapore and Burma were physically overrun; Indo-China was controlled by the Japanese and was out of reach; and the situation in India was parlous in the extreme, with domestic unrest and hostile armies close to the eastern border.[41] The European war impoverished the colonial centres, and the hitherto economically powerful British, Dutch and French were for a period dependent upon American credits and aid packages, which made the costs of any attempts at recolonization problematic; at the same time, domestic reformers urged decolonization, the Atlantic Charter celebrated democracy and local elites, having made their colonial pilgrimages, looked for change. The end of the Pacific War offered little real chance for the re-establishment of colonial territories, and against varying levels of metropolitan resistance the colonial national elites took their chance. The British returned only to preside over the final dissolution of the empire. In the formal colonial sphere, Burma, India and Malaysia were quickly independent, Singapore a little later, and only in Hong Kong was colonial withdrawal delayed. In the informal sphere, elites simply moved out of the British orbit: Thailand moved into the cold war Indo-Chinese sphere of the Americans; China briefly resumed its civil war before establishing the People's Republic; and so neither Bangkok nor Shanghai had any place for the erstwhile colonial power of Britain.

Shaping national trajectories: Singapore, Hong Kong and the informal periphery

Singapore, Hong Kong and the cities of the informal periphery, Bangkok and Shanghai, moved through dissimilar trajectories both in the period of strong colonial influence and in the post-colonial period of locally determined trajectories. The four cities were drawn into the modern world through their contact with British imperialism and moved through very different trajectories, particularly after the general crisis which allowed local elites to move to the fore and determine lines of advance according to local concerns and agendas.

Singapore island was a possession of the British East India Company from 1818 to 1867; many in the region regard it as one more Malay-style trading city – hence its early success – but its economic role was as a transhipment point. Goods moved from the archipelago outward, manufactures

8   *Singapore contexts*

inwards and crucial passing trade linked Britain and China; business serviced the port and the masses provided labour. Local politics reflected the situation: power lay with civil servants in India and the colony, whilst the local expatriate business elite manoeuvred for influence; local business grew more important and was co-opted, whilst the masses of migrants organized themselves; a pervasive ethnic division in economic and political life was reflected in spatial divisions in settlement. In 1867–1941 the territory became a formal colony: a governor was appointed; civil servants in London and the island were key power-holders; powerful expatriate business was joined by local Chinese business. In the late nineteenth century the west coast of Malaya was drawn into the colonial sphere and Singapore prospered as established trading activities were supplemented by a globally significant primary product export business.[42] The1941–45 period of Imperial Japanese control was confused with the occupation forces deploying repression and calls for cooperative reform, but the exigencies of war overrode other considerations and from 1943 onwards the condition of the territory declined sharply, producing economic collapse and great hardship for the population.[43] The post-war period saw a rapid sequence of changes: the1945–58 period encompassed recovery from war damage and the pursuit of independence; in 1959 internal self-government was established; in 1963 there was union with Malaysia; and, finally, in 1965 came an unexpected independence.

Singapore has been ruled by the People's Action Party (PAP) since independence;[44] there has been continuity in the overall project of national development. The starting point was a colonial port cut off from its natural hinterland; the government mobilized the population; an ideology of vulnerability, self-reliance and continual upgrading was affirmed; there was repression of political opponents and co-option of unions; a development bank was formed, along with planning apparatus and the systematic encouragement of multinationals; local entrepreneurs were rather left to their own devices and moved into retail and services. The deal for the population has been acquiescence in exchange for material welfare: housing, schooling, medicine, pensions (via a forced saving scheme that funnels savings into economic investment), leisure facilities; and stability.

In the parallel case of Hong Kong, the island was extracted by war from the Chinese sphere in 1842; the state asserted itself and the colony was organized through a mix of co-option and repression of the local people. The focus was the China trade; it was also a base for the Pearl river trade; it quickly became a successful trading port. The ideology of laissez-faire justified the pattern of activity of the state. The focus was on traders. It justified neglect of other economic activities, yet by1900 there was significant Chinese-funded light industry. In the inter-war period of 1918–41 British and Chinese capital was invested at similar levels, industry developed; it was Chinese, a large employer and did not get any direct help or acknowledgement from colonial rulers. A type of dual-sector economy developed:

trade/commerce and industry, where the former was the preserve of colonialists and allies and the latter was organized by Chinese. The Imperial Preferences system did give Chinese business access to a wider market; in the depression era there was mercantilist competition, but local traders argued against protecting local industry.

The 1941–45 occupation was a disaster and the population fell from 1,500,000 to 500,000. Subsequent rebuilding was initially rapid; the 1949 inauguration of the People's Republic of China (PRC) plus the cold war resulted in a UN embargo on trade with China; there was also US hostility and restrictions; flight capital also came in as Shanghai textile industrialists relocated to Hong Kong; incoming capitalists linked up with local banks and other light manufactures developed/recovered; as before the war, there were multiple small firms which adapted quickly in plastics, toys, electrical goods, watches and textiles; labour was cheap, organized labour fragmented (Kuomintang(KMT)/Chinese Communist Party(CCP)) and it suffered from colonial restrictions so the labour market was very competitive.

The role of the colonial government has been debated; it affirmed an ideal of laissez-faire in the nineteenth century; later, in the 1960s, as domestic problems mounted it was revised to 'positive non-intervention' whereby the government paid minimum attention to monetary, financial and social services whilst offering information/training encouragements to industry. Theorists debated matters: on the one hand neo-classical thinkers saw Hong Kong as close to a free market with a minimum state and business finding comparative advantage in an open marketplace; whilst political economists saw a system centred on a business–state alliance exercised via the administrative state. In terms of structural constraints and elite projects, the state project has not been national development; rather, it has served the local business elites. The 1997 handover has not evidently altered matters.

Singapore and Hong Kong were central to the project of empire. There was also an informal empire. It marked the furthest reach of the colonial powers. It too had its cities. British influence was extended in Asia through the informal empire cities of Bangkok and Shanghai. In Bangkok a royal elite sought to ward off the demands of the British and the French by ordering their own modernization from above; it was successful. Some of the elements of a modern state were put in place. The 1932 *coup d'état* removed the absolute monarchy and ushered in a long period of bureaucratic/military rule; the demands of the Imperial Japanese were managed; British and European influence severely restricted; the dynamics of the end of the Pacific War plus the rapidly established cold war moved the Thai elite into the American sphere. A further period of bureaucratic/military rule only ended in 1992. Announcements of the status of the fifth Asian Tiger proved premature; the country recovered from the financial crisis only to fall into a political crisis in 2006. Nonetheless Thailand is a key country within Southeast Asia.

10 *Singapore contexts*

Shanghai developed through the nineteenth century around the International Settlement. The city was caught up in the general crisis in China. An early centre for Communist Party activity, it was the site of a Kuomintang-inspired massacre of local leftists. It eclipsed Hong Kong in the 1930s as a centre for economics, politics and culture. The Imperial Japanese invasion of China in 1937 ruined the city. Further confusions followed in the resumed civil war and it fell out of the global capitalist trading system. In Maoist China it figured as a base for the Great Proletarian Cultural Revolution. Development resumed after Deng Xiaoping's accession to power and it is now a key trading city in East Asia, cited as a competitor to Hong Kong.

Contemporary trajectories: Singapore and Hong Kong

The Singapore economy now comprises port, oil processing, multinational corporation (MNC) manufacturing, some science-based high-tech, a service sector and a growing financial sector. The deal remains in place: the population offers support and the state provides material welfare in what is now an extensively middle-class society. The stated political-economic goal is to become a regional service hub; a critical variant speaks of the hotel Singapore, whilst a related critical political comment speaks of an air-conditioned nation. The future is debated. There are paradoxes of success: the city has a global role, the local form of life is comfortable but doubts, which revolve around the nature of the incumbent elite, are expressed about the longer term. A number of scenarios can be identified:

- Scenario 1, Muddle Through Alone: the PAP party-state continues unreformed whilst the elite endeavours to replicate the recipe of earlier success.
- Scenario 2, Globalization (American Sphere): the PAP party-state elite endeavours to replicate earlier success, with a particular focus on East Asian newly industrialized countries, Japan and the USA.
- Scenario 3, Globalization (General): the PAP party-state elite endeavours to replicate earlier success, insisting that business opportunities can be exploited around the globe.
- Scenario 4, Regional Hub (East Asia): the PAP party-state is partially reformed as the elite turns to the local East Asian region.
- Scenario 5, Hotel Singapore: the PAP continues to run Singapore and the island is made into a business hub, with local people either withdrawing to the heartlands or becoming expatriates.[45]

Turning to Hong Kong, the economy is similar to that of Singapore: a major port plus a vigorous logistics industry serving the Pearl River Delta; a financial centre of global stature; extensive commercial activities; extensive manufacturing interests located in China. The city is rich. However there are post-1997 questions relating to the local political situation and the

Singapore contexts 11

intentions of Beijing. Commentators express doubts about the longer term. A number of scenarios can be constructed:

- Scenario 1, Securing the Continuation of the Present Model: the Hong Kong elite manage Beijing as they managed the British[46] and the territory maintains its global role.
- Scenario 2, Adoption of the Singapore Model: Hong Kong's elite seek to compete energetically within the global system and follow Singapore[47] in upgrading Hong Kong's global economic niche.
- Scenario 3, Deep Integration:[48] Hong Kong becomes the key element of an integrated forward-looking Pearl River Delta region.
- Scenario 4, Slow Dissolve: Hong Kong becomes just another Pearl River Delta town and experiences long-term relative decline.[49]
- Scenario 5, Rational Authoritarianism Hong Kong: the Beijing authorities draw Hong Kong into their project for China's peaceful rise.[50]

In general, elites must read and react to enfolding structural change: successive decisions, those intended, coupled to those made by default, plot a course, unpack a project; the course marks out an historical development trajectory. British engagement with Asia reoriented the trajectories of numerous country powers, absorbing them, one way or another, within the embrace of a system of empire; the period drew these occupied territories into the modern world; European civil war coupled to the dynamics of the general crisis in East Asia offered local national elites their chance; they took it, establishing thereby a number of new nation-states; the sometime British sphere fragmented – Burma, India, Malaysia, Singapore, Brunei and Hong Kong all emerged from the colonial wreckage. The two sea ports – both servants of the China trade – have pursued parallel trajectories, Singapore lodged within Southeast Asia, Hong Kong within the Pearl River Delta.

The trajectories recall their pasts; they inform their presents; they are the starting point for the unfolding business of reading and reacting to enfolding change.

The unfolding dynamics of the ongoing shift to the modern world

The European irruption into the settled pre-modern East Asian world occasioned profound change; existing forms of life were radically remade; extant civilizations gave way to colonial empires, which thereafter dissolved away leaving the contemporary pattern of nation-states. The history reveals a multiplicity of routes to the modern world; a series of discrete trajectories; and a resultant spread of particular forms of life. It is within this intellectual frame – endlessly shifting patterns of relationships – that the historical development trajectories of Singapore, Hong Kong and the sometime informal empire cities can be placed.

2 Complex change

The classical European tradition of social theorizing centres on the analysis of complex change:[1] nineteenth-century work was legislative;[2] contemporary analysis is oriented towards the reflexive elucidation of the dynamics of change;[3] definitive positions are eschewed; provisional statements are available; so too dialogic exchanges with denizens of other cultures and/or intellectual traditions; theorizing change is contested.[4] Substantively, complex change embraces systematic change in all areas of the social world: political-economic, social-institutional and cultural. One received strand of work, one expression of this preoccupation, is the material of political economy; the approach offers an holistic analysis of change; cast in economic terms in the nineteenth century, dismissed by mainstream economics in the marginalist revolution, it has found continuing expression in the Marxist tradition, development theory and recently international political economy.[5] Shifting patterns of change can be grasped in terms of the crucial agents and their projects, the contexts which shaped phases of development, the breaks marking abrupt redirections and the slow shifts of power within regional and global systems.

At the outset, the projects of agents animate historical development trajectories; there are various major actors (state regimes, multinationals, commercial operations and international organisations) and thereafter the multiplicity of social groups making up the peoples of the region (established economic power-holders, the newly prosperous, the marginal and so on). East Asia entered the modern world through the episode of colonial rule (traders, financiers, administrators and soldiers); indigenous elites responded actively; ordinary people adjusted; forms of life were remade over the generations; colonial pilgrimages introduced the novel ideas that informed national movements. In the confusions of the Pacific War nationalist groups secured independence; thereafter state regimes mobilized their populations in pursuit of national development strategies. Multiple intra-regional and extra-regional successes followed. Elite groups are becoming more conscious of the region's identity, power and future. Then, second, phases mark the historical development experience of communities. Any particular region will have periods of relative stability and episodes of more or less rapid complex change. Development is discontinuous. Internal dynamics and links to the relevant wider system will shape any particular phase, producing a specific continuing pattern of economic, social and cultural life, a more or less settled way of doing things; the people of the territory make their ordinary lives, pursue their projects and elaborate their cultural self-understandings; and when these patterns are disturbed, orchestrating coherent responses is difficult and the resultant period of complex change can be traumatic. East Asia has experienced relatively long periods of relative stability as extant patterns of life continued down the years. The period before the arrival of the Europeans saw the rise and fall of a succession of polities; thereafter the territories of the region were reordered in line with the demands of the expanding global industrial-capitalist economy; a later reordering established the post-colonial pursuit of national development; a regionally ordered phase is in prospect. Third, breaks redirect the trajectories of communities. The shift to the modern world has been achieved in a discontinuous episodic fashion. The breaks marking the transition of a particular territory have been accompanied by conflict; in East Asia social discontinuities have been diverse and the patterns of conflict complex; the modern period was shaped by the invasive growth of industrial-capitalism. The earliest contacts were made in Southeast Asia; the early demands of the European traders were sustainable; however, as the pace of economic advance within the metropolitan core accelerated the demands made upon the territories of Southeast Asia increased; in the absence of any coherent response by local elites these areas were eventually absorbed; a little later Chinese ruling elites made the mistake of underestimating the dynamism of the capitalist system which carried the European traders, and the country became a quasi-colony. It was only in Japan that an indigenous Asian elite managed to contrive a coherent response, and by the end of the century, after a modernization self-consciously ordered by the elite, the Japanese had become a powerful industrial society. Finally, intra-regional and extra-regional relationships will shift as individual trajectories advance unevenly; the historical development experience of a particular territory is always lodged within the contexts offered by the wider region and global system; global structures of power are not regular and different territories will advance, or retreat, at different rates.[6] East Asia since the Pacific War has undergone a period of rapid relative advance within the global system; particular countries have advanced quickly; the core is Japan, there are a series of vibrant peripheral territories in the Tiger economies and Southeast Asia; China is rapidly developing and its peaceful rise[7] will further transform the region.

The classical tradition offers theoretical machineries which inform substantive work that in turn carries a definite discourse: the unfolding dynamics of the shift to the modern world. The modern world has been shaped by industrial capitalism; its historical occasion has been debated;[8] the novel system prospered; the innovative dynamic was not restricted to the

14 *Complex change*

domestic sphere; from the sixteenth century the system expanded; and for many cultures the impetus to radical change came with shifting patterns within the global system. Change was impressed upon many cultures; new patterns of structural circumstances implied new lines of activity. Routes to the modern world have been shaped by the responses of local elites/masses.[9] The irruption of European capitalism precipitated a sequence of reorderings of forms of life in East Asia: accommodation, crisis, collapse and the pursuit of national development.

Identifying East Asia is problematic. In the long period prior to the invasive spread of industrial-capitalism the region was Sino-centric; subsequently it was absorbed into the system of colonial empires; during the Pacific War it was subsumed within the Greater East Asian Co-Prosperity Sphere; thereafter, it was divided by cold war alliances; the Western-focused group were subject to the hegemony of the USA; however, the beginnings of a political-economic and cultural emancipation from the hegemony of the USA can be identified; the countries of the socialist block spent decades following autarchic development trajectories but are now opening up to the global system. The end of the cold war in Asia has prompted debate about the future of the region.[10] A series of positions can be identified: American, Japanese and Chinese. The US view is shaped by cold war thinking: a 1990s relocation of anxieties from geo-strategy to geo-economics (ordering the economies of the otherwise threatening region around Asia Pacific Economic Cooperation (APEC));[11] and a 2000s rehearsal of security concerns (China). The Japanese view has been ordered around the image of flying geese (the newly industrialized countries (NICs) slot in behind the leader and ASEAN brings up the rear of the formation); and lately, nationalism has been reasserted (ideas of a normal nation, rearmament and political conflict with China). The Chinese look to rapid growth, nationalist assertion and deepening participation in regional and global networks. East Asian regionalism is developing slowly; it will develop in its own fashion – slow networking rather than formal institutional mechanisms. Debate is ongoing.

Macro-phases

In East Asia there were three macro-phases in the shift to the modern world: the 1786–1911 period of European and American expansion; the 1911–75 period of general crisis; and the subsequent continuing period of national development. East Asian patterns of life were extensively reconstructed; industrial-capitalist practices displaced available agrarian, commercial and trading forms of life. Various agents were involved: in phase one, indigenous elites, indigenous masses, the traders, missionaries and soldiers who ordered the expansion and the people in power in the metropolitan centres who, with greater or lesser understanding[12] of their actions, orchestrated the process; in phase two, the revolutionary nationalists, military expansionists, warlords, gangsters, politicians and their myriad victims, whose collective chaotic efforts dragged the region forwards; and, in phase three, the administrators, businessmen, political leaders and disciplined citizens whose collective projects created modern nation-states in East Asia.

Singapore and Hong Kong were crucial to the European/British involvement in East Asia. The settlements were located at the intersection of European, Malay and Chinese spheres. They were complex settlements linking local, regional and global structures, and their elites read and reacted to shifting circumstances fostering distinctive historical trajectories, Singapore embracing national development, Hong Kong an ambiguous status within a Chinese nation-state.

Change phase one: impacts and responses

The area had a number of centres: China, Northeast Asia, Indo-China and Southeast Asia. Relationships were longstanding; local economies were strong; it was the global centre prior to the emergence of the modern world in Europe. At the centre was the Chinese polity, ordered around an emperor by a centralized bureaucratic state. The economic base of the system revolved around peasant agriculture; society was ordered around family, kin network, clan group and language group; culture celebrated family and ancestors and had religious expression in the traditions of Confucianism, Buddhism and Islam. The system was established in the second century BC. It had wide influence within the region; the cultural pattern extended to Korea, Japan and Indo-China; it was involved in extensive trade networks throughout East Asia until the mid-sixteenth-century decision to withdraw from trade and turn inwards; the decision which coincided with the European expansion; in the nineteenth century these incursions overturned extant forms of life and lodged China in a disadvantaged position within the developing global industrial-capitalist system. To the south, Indo-China polities experienced considerable influence from the Chinese Empire. Vietnam emerged from the shifting kingdoms of the region and the suzerainty of the Chinese around 1000 AD, and an agrarian bureaucratic system was sustained until the nineteenth-century incursions of the French. Elsewhere in the sub-region the pattern of life resembled that of the wide Malay sphere, with a shifting pattern of empires centred on the charismatic and material success of a leading royal family; these empires succeeded one another as local centres of power ran through the sequence of advance and retreat; there were major civilizations in Cambodia, Thailand and Burma. The entire area was formally colonized by Europeans, with the exception of Thailand, whose elite exploited their position between competing colonial powers to order their shift to the modern world. And finally in the archipelago there were Malay maritime trading empires; a royal family controlling a key port would attract followers and traders from the region; they rose quickly; they were shifting and fluid; patterns of trade could reconfigure; the empires traded across great distances within the archipelago and the economy revolved around small-scale agriculture, fishing and trade. They traded with Arabia, the Indian sub-continent and China. The earliest European contacts were in the sixteenth century, and by the end of the nineteenth century the area had been largely absorbed into European and American colonial systems.

Pre-contact East Asia comprised sophisticated polities; in the fifteenth to seventeenth centuries regional trading linkages were well developed.[13] East Asia centred upon agrarian feudal China; in Korea the agrarian feudal pattern was repeated; so too in Japan. Chinese influence in Indo-China was extensive, particularly in Vietnam. Elsewhere the pattern of life resembled the Malay sphere. In the archipelago of Southeast Asia a shifting series of Malay maritime trading empires developed around a royal family and a key port; patterns of loyalty were personal; these empires traded throughout the archipelago and beyond with linkages to China, India and Arabia.[14]

The modern world can be understood as a particular cultural form;[15] modernity embraces human reason, affirms natural science and is dominated by industrial-capitalism; a dynamic system; domestic intensification and international expansion have entailed asymmetric exchanges with other cultures which have been absorbed and remade. Yet up to the late eighteenth century European and American influence was slight: the traders were minor players in a large diverse region. The industrial revolution changed the relationship as new schedules of demands, coupled to technological advances in communications, plus the military-technological superiority of Europeans and Americans provided the impetus to greater involvement. The progressive reconstruction of local forms of life eventually finds expression in formal colonial empires; indigenous forms of life are slowly absorbed within the various empire structures of the global industrial-capitalist system; elite/mass reaction is overborne, agents adjust; by the late nineteenth and early twentieth centuries there are stirrings of anti-colonial nationalism.

The European, American and Japanese empires expanded rapidly in the late nineteenth and early twentieth centuries.[16] Dutch, British, French and American traders manoeuvred against each other and local country powers in three major spheres: the India trade, the archipelago spice trade and the China trade. The vehicles of early European expansion were the trading companies – authorized by their governments to act as quasi-states, waging war, making treaties and annexing territories.[17] In 1611 the Dutch East Indies Company (VOC, formed in 1602) opened a factory at Batavia in the Bantam Sultanate,[18] thereby laying claim to the spice. The British East India Company was established in 1657; the French also looked for advantage but were not generally successful.[19] The European wars of the late eighteenth and early nineteenth centuries altered trading patterns within the East Indies: the Napoleonic Wars saw the French defeated, and the British and Dutch divided Southeast Asia and India;[20] thereafter, as European engagement deepened, the trading companies were replaced as the full apparatus of the colonial state was deployed.

The Dutch sphere comprised most of the islands of archipelagic Southeast Asia along with trading concessions in China. The Dutch began their slow expansion through the islands in the seventeenth century and took control through a series of wars against local sultanates. The Dutch expanded from their base in Batavia; Bantam was subjugated in 1664; most of Java by 1777; Jogjakarta and Surakarta by1830. In the archipelago Malacca was Dutch in 1641; Macassar by 1667; Tidore by 1667; Ternate by 1683; Palembang by 1825; Bali by 1854; Banjarmassin by 1860; Aceh by 1899; Flores by 1907; and western New Guinea in the late 1920s.[21] The Dutch controlled the existing trade in spices by holding the key ports; the 1830–70 Cultivation System raised production by requiring villages to supply government monopolies; in 1870 a nominally free labour system was introduced; agricultural activities centred on plantation agriculture dealing in sugar and rubber, effectively destroying the indigenous agricultural economy. The Dutch authorities devolved significant power to Batavia; colonial rule was indirect, working through local rulers.[22] Anti-colonial opposition produced the ethical policy, a half-hearted compromise between humanitarian progressivism and economic interests;[23] pursued for two decades, it fell away in the 1930s[24] as local nationalist movements emerged.[25] Serekat Islam was active in the period 1912–26; elements formed the Indonesian Communist Party and launched a failed revolt in 1923; however, the idea of national independence took root, blending Islam and Marxist ideas together with an ideal of 'Indonesia'.[26] The colonial authorities responded with repression; the Imperial Japanese were well received;[27] nationalists were shortly to seize their moment.

The British sphere comprised Burma, the Malay peninsula, the northern coast of Borneo, islands in the Pacific and trading concessions in China. Expansion was conducted under the aegis of the ideology of liberal free trade, although nominal commitments were eventually made to colonial development/independence. The Burmese kings were pushed aside, inward migration followed and minority groups were acknowledged. The traditional Malay maritime trading empires, expanding and contracting with the ebb and flow of the power of the sultanate, with patterns of loyalty personal rather than formalized,[28] and ordered in an extensive network of sea-borne trade, were pushed to one side as the colonial power moved to develop the territory by opening up mines and plantations and facilitating inward migration. Expansion and rule in the colonies were shaped by changes in the metropolitan centres; colonial rule constituted a particular route to the modern world. The British occupied Penang in 1786, Francis Light[29] having secured the agreement of the local sultan, and further bases were sought at Singapore in 1819, and later in Malacca in 1824; the British had a route to China and an early trading base became active at Canton around 1715,[30] and in Hong Kong in 1842.[31] The Malay peninsula was occupied from 1874; British officials administered the affairs of the sultans, who were absorbed within the late-Victorian empire. Links were also established in the north with Siam. Positioned between expanding British[32] and French territories, the Siamese elite managed the demands of the colonial powers whilst pursing development. King Mongkut initiated the strategy, continued by King Chulalongkorn,[33] and whilst the Siamese had to cede territory in the south to the British and in the east to the French, the 1896 Anglo-French agreement guarantied the country's autonomy, freeing the leadership to pursue development,[34] in a bureaucratic capitalism.[35] After the Pacific War Thailand prospered and the British Empire disappeared.

The French sphere comprised Vietnam, Laos and Cambodia. Commercial interests sought to block the expansion of the British and secure a route to southern China.[36] A series of wars established their power in Vietnam and Indo-China in 1862, 1867 and 1873 and they established a protectorate in 1883. Colonial economic reordering was extensive, with light industries, commercial undertakings and the infrastructure of a modern society being slowly put in place. In rural areas there was land reclamation and the development of commercial rice farming and rubber plantations. Development, exploitation and the mission to civilize commingled. Colonial theory vacillated between assimilation and association, but in practice neither were used as the key remained control; the administration of the colony was inflexible.[37] The Imperial Japanese absorbed the territories in 1941. Local nationalists organized; and notwithstanding post-war French attempts to restore the status quo ante, they were ejected in 1956. A divided Vietnam was left to the cold war attentions of the USA, finally securing its territory in 1975.

The Americans came late to the business of overseas colonial expansion, having pursued the task of securing the continental USA in a process of internal colonization as Native Americans were pushed aside and having resolved the issue of the appropriate route to the future for the USA through civil war. Late in the nineteenth century the USA established a colony in the Philippines, looked to secure wider influence in East Asia and maintained concessions in China. The American sphere in East Asia centred on the Philippines. The islands became part of the Spanish Empire in1565. The area had many micro-states but attained coherence through colonial rule, although influence amongst the Muslim sultanates in the southern islands was limited.[38] The colonial-sponsored shift to the modern world produced an agrarian feudal society with deep class, ethnic and religious[39] divisions. An indigenous nationalist movement established itself in the later part of the nineteenth century and promulgated the notion of a Filipino identity. Independence was achieved in 1898. However, at the moment of success America invaded. The interests of the US government were strategic,[40] but the goal of independence was affirmed.[41] Colonial rule secured the power of large landholders, and a rich Filipino elite developed along with an impoverished peasant mass. The economy evidenced a mix of colonial forms, with large Spanish-style landed estates running commercial plantations as the territory became an economic adjunct of the USA. After the Pacific War returning Americans confirmed the power of the local elites.

European and American contact entailed the extensive reconfiguration of extant forms of life in East Asia to meet the demands of metropolitan capital,[42] with the key link of the local area and global system being provided by colonial primate cities.[43] The linkages of these areas to each other were extensive but controlled, as the empires were mercantilist, liberal and later protectionist.[44] The high tide of empire occurred in the early twentieth century; tensions in Europe precipitated a global crisis, reordering Europe and East Asia.

Change phase two: general crisis

The Great War marked the start of a general crisis[45] in the global capitalist heartlands of Europe, where the collapse of pre-modern empires led to widespread economic, social and political breakdown; a similar collapse convulsed East Asia; China in 1911–78; Japan in 1931–51; Southeast Asia in 1941–65; change undermined the old order; colonialism was transient; matters were clarified only with the emergence of local independent nationalist elites.

Colonial relationships introduced new economic activities (infrastructure, industries, consumption), new social activities (rural to urban migration, new patterns of livelihood, new patterns of family/community) and new patterns of political thinking; received expectations and authorities were undercut; novel forms of life were available for some and new ideas were available for some; but change was slow. Tensions accumulated over time: elites and masses variously acquiesced, collaborated or resisted. Some prospered (the Malay sultanates); others saw opportunity (migrant Chinese workers moving into the Nanyang); others saw their patterns of life destroyed (the Malay 'pirates' removed from Johor–Riau by the Royal Navy). Arguments for colonization were common in the nineteenth century; arguments for reform appeared in the early twentieth century; empires were not stable and legitimating claims to cultural superiority were undermined by the industrialized slaughter of the Great War; indigenous political groupings formed and arguments for national independence and development were presented.[46] The breakdown occurred in China. East Asia experienced a sequence of interlinked crises between 1911 and 1975 involving China, Japan, the USA and the Europeans. It was an interlinked overlapping sequence: there were multiple wars; each was different, involved different participants, had different effects and has been remembered differently; together they constitute a general crisis.

The sequence of intermingled intersecting wars in China in the period 1911–78[47] involved a multiplicity of actors, some foreign, most domestic.[48] Following the immediate conflicts of the revolutionary period warlords emerge: these regimes control an army/territory, have fluid internal loyalties, shifting alliances, engage in multiple wars and enter various alliances with the Kuomintang and the Imperial Japanese. There are two overarching struggles: the Civil War and the Sino-Japanese War. The Kuomintang and Communist Party emerge after the revolution with programmes for national development; the Kuomintang draws support from landlords, bourgeoisie and gangsters, the Communists from urban/peasant masses, but under Chiang Kai-Shek the Kuomintang declines into warlordism[49] and cooperative relationships collapse into the 1927–49 civil war, which is interrupted by the 1931–45 Sino-Japanese War. In the final phase the USA is involved, part mediator, part arms supplier to the Kuomintang. After a lull the fighting resumes and the Kuomintang makes advances, but the Communist Party inherits Japanese weapons in a Manchuria vacated by the USSR and secures military victory, inaugurating the People's Republic in 1949, whilst the USA sustains the Chiang dictatorship in Taiwan. The latter's situation is assimilated by US cold war warriors to the broad struggle against communism. Chinese support for North Korea during the 1950–53 Korean War entails subsequent cold war competition with the USA. However, domestic conflicts continued; the Cultural Revolution is one countrywide conflict. Matters only stabilize in 1978 when Deng Xiaoping begins market-oriented reforms and a coherent strategy of national development begins to take shape.

The Japanese elite embraced late industrialization and late imperialism, securing trading concessions in China and confronting both China and Russia for influence in the Korean peninsula, where wars in 1894–95 and 1904–05 culminated in the 1911 annexation of Korea. Elite support for Britain, France and the USA in the Great War was ill rewarded at Versailles when the League of Nations charter did not include the requested clause renouncing racial discrimination. Japanese relations with European powers, the USA and China declined, domestic politics were factionalized and violent and Japanese army adventurism drifted into war. The Japanese sought to extend their influence in China by invading Manchuria; adjacent to their Korean colony and further developed as Manchuko, it provided a base for further advances into northern China until the 1937 Sino-Japanese War begins. The general crisis of 1931–51 resulted in military defeat and occupation.

The involvement of the USA in the period 1941–75 revolved around a series of wars: 1941–45 Pacific War; 1946–51 Huk Rebellion; 1950–53 Korean War; 1965–75 Second Indo-China War. There were also wars related to the Indo-China War in Laos and Cambodia. Over the period of these conflicts the position of the USA within East Asia was radically recast. The USA had extensive commercial interests in China. Conflict in China meant that the US relationship with Imperial Japan deteriorated slowly during 1930s, and whilst the US was an active player, not a passive victim, the outbreak of the Pacific War was nonetheless a shock to the elite/population. The authorities were not inclined to fight in China, or to help re-establish European colonies, but they were hostile to 'international communism', against which they were happy to recruit cold war allies. The outcome of the Chinese civil war was a shock to the US elites/masses and it encouraged the US to assist in the division of Korea, where the outbreak of war confirmed the worst fears of the US elite. A cold war now runs in East Asia. The Korean War enters US mythology and ends the reform experiment in Japan, as the country becomes a cold war ally, as does the Chiang dictatorship. The cold war serves to embroil the Americans in a number of regional conflicts. The American elite read the Huk Rebellion of 1946–51 in cold war terms – communist, inconvenient – and they aided the Philippines elite in suppressing rebellion. More catastrophically, after the First Indo-China War of 1946–54 saw the country divided pending elections, the USA moved in to support the anti-communist South Vietnamese. The war restarted, with the US moving a large army into Vietnam in 1965. The Second Indo-China War ran from 1965 to 1975, devastating Vietnam, Laos and Cambodia.

The European involvements encompassed imperial collapse, failed recovery of empire and decolonization: 1941–45 Pacific War; 1946–54 First Indo-China War (France); 1945–50 Indonesian Revolution (Holland); 1948–60 Malayan Emergency (British). The European empires in East Asia were swept away by the Imperial Japanese armed forces: French Indo-China was occupied in the 1940s, with the Vichy regime only able to acquiesce in Japanese demands, and the military campaign of late 1941 and early 1942 destroyed the British, Dutch and American empires in Asia in a matter of a few weeks. The British army repelled a Japanese attack towards India and thereafter reoccupied parts of Burma; Australian forces occupied parts of Papua New Guinea; American forces reoccupied the Philippines, but the American strategy relied on naval forces. An island-hopping advance on Japan and the capture of Saipan Island in 1944 brought the Japanese home islands within range of aircraft and the war was ended via naval advance and air power. In Indo-China and Southeast Asia there were intact Imperial Japanese armies in place at the end of the Pacific War. In a confused situation involving Japanese armies, nationalist guerrillas, politicians plus Allied armies and returning colonial powers, the Europeans and Americans attempted to re-establish their positions but they were variously unsuccessful. The Dutch returned to their colonial territory and there were conflicts with nationalists, and after two brief wars plus other local conflicts in the period 1945–50 the Republic of Indonesia was established and the Dutch withdrew. The French attempted to re-establish their control, but Vietnamese nationalists contested this and after a year of futile negotiations a war began which continued until the French lost a strategic battle and a UN-brokered settlement allowed the French to withdraw. The British returned to their colonial holdings in Malaya and began negotiations about decolonization, but their wartime ally the Malayan Communist Party began an armed struggle and eventually the British withdrew.

The sequence of interlinked wars in East Asia that ran from 1911 to 1975 evidenced a deep-seated general crisis centred on the way in which East Asia was to be ordered and lodged within the global industrial-capitalist

22 Complex change

system; peripheral colonialism was replaced by the pursuit of national development. As in the case of Europe, the collapse of one system was not followed directly by its replacement; it took time. In Europe the wars of 1914–45 resulted in the occupation and division of the continent and recovery was initiated in context of block-time.[50] In East Asia the 1911–75 crisis was resolved in Japan under US occupation, in the Tigers in the context of the cold war, in Southeast Asia in the context of a post-colonial cold war-influenced pursuit of regional identity and in China via the belated 1978 decision to integrate with the global industrial-capitalist system. In brief, it was not until the late 1970s that the drive for national development was established in all the countries of East Asia.[51]

Change phase three: national development

The dissolution of colonial empires was confused, intermittently violent and marked the start of the current phase in the ongoing shift to the modern world in East Asia; in this process the underlying demands of the industrial-capitalist system for access first expressed in colonial form were remade in the guise of new nation-states, the model long adopted in the core. The general crisis gave indigenous elites their chance; they sought mass political support in exchange for promises of material progress and elites turned the machineries of their states to the pursuit of national development.[52] The task was one of managing change within shifting structural contexts, and a series of projects of national development were pursued, each different as elites read global, regional and local structural logics and formulated projects; together there are many overlaps and similarities, an East Asian model.

In Japan the occupation authorities supported the rise of a conservative business-dominated elite committed to economic recovery and the alliance with the USA; the iron triangle of bureaucracy, business and politicians took responsibility for the family of Japanese people who in turn affirmed the ideal of harmony.[53] In 1945 some 35 per cent of accumulated Japanese wealth had been destroyed; the period 1945–50 was difficult; the Korean War of 1950–53 was a major help as local industry was given a massive injection of cash and the conservative financial system, along with planning and repression of labour, ushered in a state-centred business-dominated system oriented to production and exports; and expansion ran through the 1950 and 1960s, the miracle economy. In the 1970s the economy grew more slowly; nevertheless Japan emerged as a major economy and in the 1980s industry moved to higher value-added activities. In 1985 the Plaza Accord revalued the yen against the dollar and delivered a complex shock to the system, producing domestic inflation and land speculation. A bubble economy developed. There was also external relocation of Japanese productive activity to other areas in East Asia where operating costs were reduced and exports to the USA continued. There was some evidence of domestic hollowing out and some structural unemployment, but aid, trade and foreign direct investment patterns established a production network throughout East Asia. The domestic bubble burst in 1991 and there was a long golden recession with nil or very low economic growth, continued stability and general prosperity. There was much pressure for liberalization, which was resisted in the main, and by the early 2000s the economy seemed to have recovered. The old pattern of political economy seemed intact but there were new anxieties about relations with the USA and the region. There was particular concern about the implications of the rise of China. In Japan post-war economic policy reveals a series of phases but there is a distinctive pattern of state-directed, business-friendly, socially disciplined and export-oriented development; the model is successful and in the four Tigers – South Korea,[54] Taiwan,[55] Hong Kong and Singapore – similar trajectories unfold.

In Southeast Asia the colonial empires of Europeans cut across the existing regional unity as the colonialists made a series of separate territories. However, as the colonial system collapsed nationalist groups moved to seize their moment and modern nation-state projects were pursued. Slowly nation-states developed. They did so in the context of regional anxieties about borders, minorities, economic resources and outside influences. The replacement elites faced difficulties in establishing themselves within their territories, difficulties in agreeing borders between new countries within the region and difficulties in securing regional stability within the context of the cold war. The solution was the regional organization ASEAN. It was begun in 1967 with six members and by 1999 had ten member countries covering the whole of Southeast Asia.[56] The organization was dedicated to stability and economic growth, and whilst it has had a mixed record in respect of growth it has had an excellent record in respect of stability. The organization has helped countries and region to define themselves; to establish identities. ASEAN is now a well-regarded success as a regional organization. It has pursued policies with regard to security and economic growth. It is widely seen as a successful security organization. However, it is seen as less successful with regard to economics, where the member countries tend to have similar economies, with much primary production in largely rural agrarian economies. Many have relatively low-tech manufacturing or MNC industry which competes rather than cooperates, plus industry which looks outside the region rather than inside it. However, recent free trade agreements and regional growth areas are viewed optimistically. The ASEAN countries can be grouped according to their respective historical trajectories:[57] Malaysia, Thailand, Brunei and Singapore; Vietnam, the Philippines and Indonesia; and Cambodia, Laos and Myanmar. The ASEAN organization has provided a framework within which countries have defined themselves and their region. It has been a vehicle for the establishment of identities in the context of dissolving colonial empires.[58]

After the confusions of the Maoist period the Chinese elite has pursued national development. In the first phase, 1978–84, there were agricultural reforms and the establishment of special economic zones (SEZs). The reforms in rural agriculture were successful and production rapidly advanced, but reforms in urban areas were more difficult. In the second phase, 1984–87, industry and finance were reformed and industrial enterprises were given more autonomy and moved towards commercial market operation. There were questions of divestiture, questions of finance and questions of performance. Specialist banks were established and moved towards commercial market operation and there were questions of performance. The third phase begins with Deng's 1992 Southern Tour, which reaffirmed the importance of the reform programme: the socialist market economy. It is ambitious. The state socialist system was distinctive. The party/state broadly directed all aspects of the economy and citizens' lives. There was much scope for flexibility in the translation of theory into practice and many inefficiencies and resistances. The state was intermingled with the economy and disentangling the two was difficult. This involved creating a marketplace with laws, firms and consumers. It involved creating social welfare systems covering health, education and housing. It also implies creating a political system to order/legitimate these new arrangements. These reforms borrow from the experience of East Asia with its preoccupation with the state-directed pursuit of national development. It is export-oriented industrialization and the economy has grown rapidly. There are many achievements. There are now some 300 million middle-class citizens. There are multiple problems: incoherence of planning between the capital and provinces; weak rule of law; slow state-owned enterprise (SOE) reforms; a weak banking system; corruption in business and the state machine; inequality between coastal and inland China; rural/urban migration; inequality in urban areas; crime in urban areas; and catastrophic environmental degradation. The economic reforms and consequent social impacts and reforms have continued, but there have been few political reforms. But, more positively, China has joined the World Trade Organization (WTO) and this will create jobs; it is advancing rapidly with reforms to the economy; the growth of export industries continues; Chinese industry is climbing up the technology ladder; the domestic consumer market continues to grow; the growth of the affluent middle class provides a support base for government; and cities across China are being rebuilt. China now engages extensively with the East Asian region and on a wider scale has deepening relationships with the USA and the European Union.

East Asia entered the modern world through the particular experience of colonialism (either direct or indirect). The experience produced a spread of new nation-states. It also left quite distinctive residues: there are remnants of ancient civilizations coupled to the more recent memories of the long colonial episode. Replacement elites sought national development and this in turn produced the distinctive developmental state. The years following the Pacific War have seen success; the drive for national development continues; but there are domestic and international tensions surrounding domestic equity and global system economic balances. It has been suggested that East Asia might reasonably move beyond its characteristic concern for growth,[59] but this seems unlikely.

Unfolding trajectories and contingent patterns

East Asia experienced significant impacts from the expanding colonial-ordered industrial-capitalist system; the extant forms of life were all more or less extensively reconfigured to meet the demands of metropolitan capital;[60] the colonial primate cities were the key links between local area and global systems.[61] The modern period is dominated by its cities. Great cities were present in agrarian forms of life and played key roles in the political, commercial, religious and trading spheres. In the years before the arrival of the Europeans cities such as Tokyo, Bangkok, Canton and Shanghai were major settlements. However, the shift to the modern world[62] both revolved around urbanization and remade cities: commercial relations became capitalist market relations; established strategies of ordering labour power became labour markets; and elites became measured according to their material success or democratic credentials or both. Cities became centres of scientific advance; cities also grew dramatically; these cities aggregated populations and they linked these populations with wider networks. Great cities have typically been trading cities. In the period of the shift to the modern world in East Asia existing settlements were remade or settlements were founded anew. A number of new colonial port cities emerged.[63] They were crucial links in global industrial-capitalist networks. They were crucial intermediaries linking peripheral territories to the global networks. The European empires in East Asia expanded through such urban networks. The British founded trading cities and these, rather than territory, were crucial to empire. The British Empire in Asia centred on the South Asian sub-continent, secured through numerous wars against local and European opponents; in the east Calcutta and Madras were major centres; further east Singapore and Hong Kong provided access to the archipelago and southern China; the informal empire cities of Bangkok and Shanghai accessed parts of Indo-China and the central heartland areas of China.

The colonial spheres progressed unevenly until the empires were finally swept away.[64] Patterns of structural relationships, global, regional and local, are contingent; social groups inhabit particular niches within complex sets of structures; agent groups read and react to their circumstances and plot routes to imagined futures; and state regimes order political projects. East Asian elites have operated within environments shaped by indigenous civilizations, incoming colonial powers, general crisis and more recently the contested world of liberal industrial capitalism. East Asia's position within the global system has changed; powers have risen or fallen within the region; and novel nation-state units have emerged, with their elites pursuing projects of national development. The contemporary pattern within in East

26 *Complex change*

Asia is the outturn of these processes; it is contingent and the macro-process of the shift to the modern world continues to unfold.

Singapore in the global system

The island of Singapore has been home to a number of discrete polities. The people living within these polities have made their livelihoods, ordered their societies and managed their politics in similarly discrete ways as elites and masses have read and reacted to enfolding structural circumstances. A sequence of patterns of life can be retrospectively identified; this records a series of ways in which the people based on the island have made their lives within the world that they inhabited. Against the recently fashionable theorists of globalization who urge the novelty of systemic change, it can be asserted that change is not atypical; it is given.

The historical development experience of Singapore in Southeast Asia

A conventional history of Singapore might begin by noting that in 1819 T. S. Raffles established a trading port which quickly became successful, drew in people from around the region and provided the base from which the independent government of Singapore moved on to create further economic, social and political success. Modern Singapore is thus the direct legatee of Raffles. However, this version of the development history of Singapore is misleading. The territory has played a number of roles within wider encompassing systems. The local state has mediated the relationship of domestic sphere and trans-state structures of power. There has not been one state form in Singapore; rather, there have been several. Each of these can be seen to represent a particular occasion of the integration of the population of the island into the wider embracing system. Each of these occasions of integration can be seen to have characteristic economic, social and cultural forms. And between the identifiable configurations we can posit not evolutionary change but discontinuity, with the relatively abrupt changes signalling the achievement of a new relationship with the embracing system, and internally, so to say, a new arrangement of politics, economy and culture.

The pre-contact Malay world was characterized by the rise and fall of a succession of maritime trading empires. The economies of these maritime empires were in the main based on sea-borne trade, and extensive networks of trade were established. The internal politics of these sultanates were beset with intra-familial manoeuvrings for power in a fluid political system ordered around the person of the sultan, with patterns of loyalty personalized rather than formalized. Thereafter the political extraction of the island itself from the Johor–Riau sultanate's grasp by the British involved a period of intense political manoeuvring which centred on inventing a sultan of Singapore by promoting a weak member of the ruling family. The newly invented sultan signs an agreement with Raffles that gives the British a claim against both the indigenous ruler in Riau and the Dutch. Thereafter, on a wider stage the survival of this new polity is dependent on an argument between Penang, the East India Company (EIC), London and the Dutch. Then, as the nineteenth century drew towards its close, a crucial change took place within the capitalist heartlands of Europe with the rise of industrial production and a mass market for consumption goods. The impact upon Southeast Asia was in terms of a new schedule of goods demanded, a movement away from agricultural specialist crops and miscellaneous handicrafts towards those goods required by an industrial mass economy: tin, rubber, sugar, oil and so on. There were related new political arrangements both in the peninsula and on the island of Singapore itself. And the post-Second World War period has seen two main episodes: the early attempt to submerge Singapore within a federation with the peninsula and the subsequent effective establishment of a dependent capitalist form of life.

The original ideological commitments of the PAP core group of English-educated professionals, all of whom had made what have been called colonial pilgrimages, are best regarded as social democratic; thus their early programme embraced demands for an end to colonial rule, the formation of a unitary Malayan state and the pursuit of development. The circumstances and future of a peripheral capitalist formation are theorized by a group of English-educated professionals, and the shift to independence thus entails a very significant measure of intellectual as well as political-economic continuity. Commentators have stressed the role of the local state machine in fashioning contemporary Singapore. The state has been very active in fashioning the particular pattern of economic, social and cultural development in the wake of independence. Having come to power in alliance with a Chinese-speaking socialist mass movement, the technocratic, professional English-educated core of the PAP then ran a series of battles with the mass elements in order to secure total control of local politics. Their control was complete very early on and has remained free from effective challenge ever since. The support of the masses was sought and achieved via economic development policies that relied on inviting in the MNCs and supplying the basics of a welfare state in the form of housing, schooling and health. It is an extensively interventionist system. Decisions are made at the top and passed down. Internal democracy has a distinct form; thus if one thinks of a very attenuated Fabian-type democratic socialism this gives the overall flavour of the economy and polity. Local commentators have spoken of depoliticization, or an administrative society or, recently, an Asian communitarianism.[65] The PAP has used an interventionist state machine to make the population and resources of the state maximally involved in the wider currents of the global capitalist market.

The elite have used the machineries of the state to lodge the territory within the global system. The current pattern or state form is but the latest in a long sequence. In the case of Singapore there has been not one state form but several. Each state form articulates a different role within the wider embracing system. Each has its own self-understanding: thus for the island of Singapore we move from Malay maritime empire, where political and cultural life centred on the person of the Sultan, through the construction of a formal colony, to a dependent capitalist state which vigorously promotes a notion of nation-statehood even as it operates within the increasingly Japan-dominated East Asian region of the global system. There is no one Singapore; there is, rather, the currently recoverable history of a succession of discrete ways in which the island has lodged itself within the wider economic systems enfolding it: each successive phase has been articulated by a particular state machinery, each a way of ordering internal forces so as to interact effectively with global-system structures of power.

The shifting patterns of structural power which enfold the Singaporean polity have been reconfigured in recent years. It has been argued that a Japanese economic sphere within the global economy is now in the process of formation and it could therefore be argued that one possible future for Singapore is as a part of a Japan-centred yen zone within the global capitalist system. It is now clear that the context within which Singapore operates is sub-regional (ASEAN), regional (East Asia, centred on Japan) and thereafter global. This is the given pattern of structural circumstances to which agents must necessarily respond. It may be said that these are old problems. It might also be said that the state regime is offering familiar solutions to its schedule of contemporary problems: read and respond to enfolding structural circumstances; adjust intelligently; and adjust prospectively. The state regime's response to the dynamic of globalization and regionalization has been expressed in the popular slogan 'going global' and a slew of policy initiatives summarized as the goal of becoming a regional hub economy.

A number of scenarios sketching possible futures can be presented:

- Scenario 1, Muddle Through Alone: the PAP unreformed party-state affirms that vulnerability requires economic advance, which in turn demands a disciplined population and endeavours to repeat the recipe of earlier success, so the territory is presented as a base for global capitalist business, where this entails upgraded labour, administration, fiscal incentives, government-linked companies plus state investment in key industries and state investment in key service sectors. This is a mutedly optimistic scenario in which the lack of domestic political/cultural reform militates against domestically generated new initiatives and the multiplicity of external competitors shrinks the field of possible opportunities.
- Scenario 2, Globalization (American Sphere): the PAP unreformed party-state elite affirms that vulnerability requires economic advance but also security linkages, and as the desired ally is the USA the East Asian network of the USA becomes attractive as a location for Singapore as the elite endeavours to repeat the recipe of earlier success with a particular focus on East Asian Tigers, Japan and the USA. This is a mutedly optimistic scenario.

- Scenario 3, Globalization (General): the PAP unformed party-state elite endeavours to repeat the recipe of earlier success, but grants that the global system is extensively integrated and therefore business opportunities exist around the globe and these can be exploited so that the Singapore footprint is reworked and the territory's niche within global capitalist system dispersed and deepened. This is a mutedly optimistic scenario.
- Scenario 4, Regional Hub (East Asia): the PAP partially reformed party-state elite reads and reacts to changing enfolding circumstances and the elite discontinues its habit of defining itself against its neighbours, decides that it cannot compete with low/medium-technology Chinese production, notes that Japan and the USA are remote partners, recalls that the local area was the environment within which Singapore prospered prior to 1965 and determines that a new partnership could be forged. This is a tentatively optimistic scenario.
- Scenario 5, Hotel Singapore: the partially reformed party-state looks to upgrade Singapore as a world-class business hub; members of the local population withdraw into the heartlands or become expatriates. Optimistically, the island prospers as a world-class business hub; pessimistically, it becomes merely a hotel for those who work there or pass through.

Hong Kong in the global system

The geographical territory of Hong Kong has been lodged within various economic and political spheres: it was an obscure part of the southern Pearl River Delta region of the Qing Empire, home to a few thousand farming and fishing communities; it was a major colonial trading port linking, in particular, the empires of China and Britain; it was a crucial link within East Asian and trans-regional networks; during the cold war it was a conduit linking the People's Republic to the global system; lately it has become an NIC; commentators report that it has been its own place since the late nineteenth century.[66]

The Qing period

Early nineteenth-century Hong Kong had a population of several thousand farmers, fishermen and local traders. It was not a significant site; it was not a significant settlement; it was a remote part of the southern realms of the Qing empire. It was not underdeveloped;[67] in preceding centuries China had been a major economic power within the global system;[68] in the early nineteenth century the empire was still strong.

Qing Empire Hong Kong was a remote territory; the resident population numbered several thousand; there were numerous villages, many long established. The social pattern was that of rural China: family, clan and language group; temples, clan halls and perhaps schools provided institutional structures for these communities; the local economy revolved around

30 *Complex change*

farming and fishing; there was a quarrying industry; the island communities exported stone and preserved fish; the economy mixed subsistence and trade; the island communities had a recognized absentee landlord; the island communities were taxed by the local Qing official. These were settled ordered established communities.[69] Around 7,500 people lived on Hong Kong island when the British took control in 1841;[70] there was a rapid inflow of migrants and the population reached 22,000 in 1847 and 85,000 in 1859; 1,600 non-Chinese were present in 1859.[71]

The period of impacts and responses (1842–1941)

Colonial incomers worked at the edge of empire; they were sojourners, they came for trade; local agents were not passive;[72] the nominally colonial holding developed through extensive collaboration between incoming British and the elites who formed within the rapidly expanding Chinese population. British and Chinese newcomers quickly outnumbered the established local population;[73] the creation of a commercial nexus within the global system ensured that Hong Kong quickly took on a distinctive character.

Hong Kong was extracted from the Qing Empire to serve as a port for British trading interests; there was a complex exchange between the local population, inward migrants and the British; the local population were active players; and it produced an economy operating in local, regional and global spheres. The colony received migrants from mainland China; the territory was divided by race, with a small resident European population plus a rapidly growing Chinese population. It was at first a colonial trading port but later it became a key commercial city within the global economy and an established colony. Success rested upon the development of global capitalism and an outflow of people from unsettled China produced the migrant or coolie trade and made an obscure port linking two empires into a global commercial nexus. The British faced resistance to their rule, particularly after the acquisition of the New Territories, but the British and Chinese elites collaborated in order to build a prosperous settlement. Stability did not mean an absence of political conflict;[74] a local balance was maintained; it was its own place.[75] In the 1918–41 inter-war period Chinese capital invested was equal to British;[76] the territory was secondary to Shanghai in the 1930s; but the Japanese invasion of China underscored its vulnerability, as the territory was not militarily defensible; in the event extant patterns of life were engulfed by the confusions of the Pacific War.

The period of general crisis (1941–67)

The general crisis in East Asia can be dated from the Chinese Revolution of 1911 through to the final liberation from colonialism of Vietnam in 1975. In this period economic, social and political patterns dissolved into confusion. The experience of collapse differed: China endured civil war and invasion;

Hong Kong largely escaped the upheavals of the mainland. But mainland politics spilled over into Hong Kong from 1911 to 1941 and the colonial authorities and local Chinese elites managed the problems.[77] However received certainties collapsed with the Imperial Japanese invasion of 1941. The territory was occupied within a few days. The city was re-Asianized; names were changed; the currency was changed and the population reduced. Foreign nationals were interred and the locals adapted.[78]

The colonial power rushed to reoccupy the territory in 1945. The recolonization in 1945 was attended by confusions. The civil war in China provided a space for the reoccupation. The war in China produced a flow of refugees. The population quickly recovered and surpassed pre-war levels. The victorious Communist Party did not challenge the status quo with regard to Hong Kong, but the cold war in East Asia added further problems as the outbreak of the Korean War in 1950 led to United Nations sanctions against China and Hong Kong became a link between China and the global system, with a covert trade with the People's Republic and flows of immigrants.

Thereafter, the city developed rapidly. The cold war division of East Asia had direct implications for Hong Kong. Its links with China were reworked as the trading role diminished whilst manufacturing prospered with American war expenditures. American policy benefited the region, for example by permitting access to US domestic markets, and these also helped Hong Kong.[79] The territory became one of the four Asian Tigers. Up until 1967 these developments were ad hoc, but in 1967 the Cultural Revolution spilled over into Hong Kong, with riots and bombings. However, the local population rallied to the colonial government and the trouble was managed, whilst reforms were instigated[80] in the economic, social and political spheres. A distinctive Hong Kong form of life began to emerge,[81] the rise of a popular idea of Hong Kong.[82]

The (first) period of national development (1967–97)

A local elite formed in the late nineteenth century through collaborations with the colonial power. The territory became rich. The state did not explicitly systematize the pursuit of development because an elite oligarchy pursued a project centred on commerce and trade. The British were sojourners. The Chinese elite focused on commerce, whilst the local Chinese population used family, relatives and clan networks to order their lives. The local population maintained links with China, and prior to the Pacific War there were more or less open borders. But politics intervened and the border was closed because of the cold war and the inward flows of refugees. In the 1950s, in the context of the cold war, restrictions were imposed and the Hong Kong population became settled. Those who were born and raised locally had no experience of the mainland and they came to understand themselves in local terms.[83] The local situation contrasted with that of the mainland. Mao's policies were erratic and after the failure of the Great

Leap Forward he sought to redeem his position by inaugurating the Cultural Revolution. It proved to be important in Hong Kong. In 1967 there were PRC/Maoist-inspired riots and a bombing campaign in Hong Kong. Local Hong Kong residents supported the colonial government and it responded by modernizing itself, becoming less evidently colonial and more a city government. The pace of welfare reforms accelerated, endemic corruption was addressed, illegal migration was curbed and there was localization of jobs. A local Hong Kong form of life took shape and residents began to think of themselves as Hong Kongers.

Hong Kong emerges as an East Asian NIC. Economic take-off had begun in the 1950s[84] when existing small-scale industries were joined by migrant textile entrepreneurs and local manufacturing became an important economic sector. The American cold war expenditures and policies helped the economy[85] and the 1967 Cultural Revolution spillover produced local reforms. There were broad economic/social advances and these advances accelerated with mainland reforms. Hong Kong entrepreneurs became the major investors in mainland export-processing zones and relations with the mainland deepened. In 1984 the Sino-British Joint Declaration outlined the future status of Hong Kong within China and linkages deepened further in the long run-up to reunification in 1997. This was the first period of quasi-national development. It also saw more evident difficulties in the relationship between Hong Kong and China.

The (second) period of national development (1997 onwards)

The 1997 reversion of sovereignty to China was accomplished by the British and Chinese governments. The population of Hong Kong were not consulted nor were they official participants in the reversion talks. One colonial power handed the territory to a successor colonial power. A long period of mutual adjustment began between Hong Kong and Beijing, but locally national development continues. Hong Kong became a Special Administrative Region (SAR) of China. The Sino-British Joint Declaration of 1984 was enshrined in the Basic Law, which is the mini-constitution provided for Hong Kong by Beijing, the outcome of Deng Xiaoping's 'one country, two systems' formula. A process of mutual adjustment unfolds: local elites are split with respect to their relationship with Beijing and unclear about lines of development for Hong Kong. Beijing's views are unformed: no to local public politics; otherwise unclear. The first post-handover administration of Tung Chee Hwa (1997–2005) faced considerable difficulties (the Asian financial crisis, international terrorism, Severe Acute Respiratory Syndrome (SARS) and a series of local disputes about development policies) and was widely judged a failure. The second post-handover administration of Donald Tsang (2005–) was both more popular and luckier as there were no external crises, but lack of clarity with respect to the political future of the territory continued. The issue of domestic politics is intertwined with questions of relationships with Beijing and the attitudes of mainland elite leaders, and estimations of how these issues might be resolved colour the expectations commentators have for the future.

Hong Kong's historical development trajectory has been shaped by global, regional and sub-regional factors. The same will be true of the future. A number of scenarios sketching possible lines of development can be mentioned:

- Scenario 1, Securing Continuation of the Present Model: a revised elite take power and manage Beijing as they managed the British.[86] The territory maintains its global role, deepens its linkages with the mainland (economic, social and political), maintains its special status (juridical, administrative and political) and continues much as it has been in recent years, that is, as a sophisticated, prosperous trading city. This is an optimistic scenario requiring that Beijing does not interfere.
- Scenario 2, Adoption of the Singapore Model: there is effective local leadership and rapid economic advance but no popular politics.[87] The territory maintains its special status but the local leadership moves to compete energetically within the global system by seeking to follow Singapore in upgrading its global footprint or niche. This is an optimistic scenario requiring an absence of interference from Beijing.
- Scenario 3, Deep Integration:[88] Hong Kong becomes a key element in the Pearl River Delta region and there is deep economic integration, with cross-border investment, trade and flows of people; such integration extends not merely to immediate neighbour cities but throughout the delta region, and the deepening integration is complemented by further delta region coordination (for example major infrastructural development or environmental regulation). In all this Hong Kong keeps its juridical, administrative and political independence and it thus sustains global role. This is a fairly optimistic scenario requiring some cooperation from Beijing and significant cooperation from southern Chinese power-holders.
- Scenario 4, Slow Dissolve: Hong Kong's trajectory is shaped by Beijing's anxieties and local elite short-termism; there is deeper integration but it neglects to maintain juridical, administrative and political independence; mainland practices are imported; there is ineffective instruction from Beijing coupled with extensive corruption; Hong Kong becomes just another Pearl River Delta town with long-term relative decline, but the territory continues to be just as prosperous as the rest of delta region – now a global manufacturing site. This is a pessimistic scenario.
- Scenario 5, Rational Authoritarianism Hong Kong: the territory is slowly absorbed within mainland economic, social and cultural structures but the distinctive mix of Beijing's rational authoritarianism, the local elite's opportunism and the discipline of the local people produces a distinctive mix – orderly, non-democratic and prosperous. This is a restrictedly optimistic scenario.

Hong Kong island has played a number of distinctive roles within the wider international economy, at first a remote rural territory of the Qing Empire, thereafter a colonial trading port and then a relative backwater in the 1930s. Hong Kong emerged as an NIC in the cold war era. Its commercial role grows along with deepening investment linkages with the Pearl River Delta. Its future as Hong Kong SAR remains open; it is difficult to see failure; perhaps reorientation; but the key issue is the precise nature of any reorientation.

Cities of the informal empire: Bangkok and Shanghai

Human social interactions constitute the social world, formal institutions order these relationships and the habit of reification presents such institutions as fixed, solid and thing-like. The exchange of social relationships and institutions is inverted, with the later taken to determine the former, but the truth of the matter is that social relations are primary; human social life is thoroughgoingly social. Empire has been read in this reified fashion; empire figured in formal discourse as an institutional apparatus ordering a defined geographical territory; thereafter professional and informal discourses of empire would unfold: orientalist scholarship,[89] informal stereotypes, experiences and daydreams.[90] But this inverts the reality: empire was accumulated piecemeal; it was acquired by war, manoeuvre and elite-level accommodations; it was untidy; the extent of territorial holdings was always in flux; and the reach of any formal colonial apparatus within the peoples nominally controlled was always contested.

Read institutionally/geographically, for simplicity, a distinction can be made between formal empire and informal empire,[91] the later pointing to those areas of colonial-style activity which were pursued for one reason or another without the construction of the formal apparatus. But the key was trade; the trading relationships established with local groups were crucial (country power elites, official servants, merchants and maybe villagers or other small local groups). These relationships constituted the trade. It was trade that underpinned the colonial empires; trade volumes were significant and trading links were ordered. Treaties set up trading settlements and these settlements drew the surrounding areas into the modern world; these were the cities of the informal empire.

Siam/Bangkok

In 1822 John Crawfurd travelled from recently acquired Singapore to - Bangkok and sought trade links with Siam. But he was not successful. A little later the 1826 Gurney Treaty delineated the British and Siamese spheres in the Malay peninsula; it granted British trading rights in a number of northern Malay states.[92] Then in 1855 John Bowring signed a treaty with the Siamese monarch Mongkut.[93] The treaty governed trade, it granted the British extra-territorial rights and it allowed the importation of opium. The new relationship was successful; the British advanced their trading interests and the new linkage reoriented Siamese elite thinking away from China towards the incoming Europeans. The exchange between the incoming Europeans, whose presence was supported by the resources and machineries of the modern world, and the rulers/peoples of the Siamese mandala state remade the extant society: economic change, social change, cultural change and political change. Over time local elite groups made Thailand.

The trajectory of Siamese/Thai development is distinctive. Siam was a long-established polity prior to the intrusions of the Europeans. The Siamese kings ruled a dispersed fluctuating territory around the valley of the Chaophrya river; the pre-modern mandala state sought allegiances from a number of groups peripheral to the centre based on the river. The pre-modern world was not an arcadia: there were numerous bloody wars; empires rose and fell. At the time of Bowring's mission the Siamese elite were established in Bangkok and they responded to the insistent demands of the foreigners by accommodating their wishes with respect to trade whilst looking to reform their own holdings. The shift to the modern world in Siam was a top-down affair; the elite borrowed colonial models as they sought to establish borders, nationality and a rational central administration. The shift to the modern world made Siam a colony of the Bangkok elite, but development was successful: the central elite asserted themselves in traditional peripheral areas; early versions of national community were fashioned from the intellectual and moral resources of Buddhist and royal institutions; and the central control came to revolve around the royal household, the army, elite factions, and these confronted a passive demobilized mass.

There were a series of influential kings: Mongkut ruled in the mid-nineteenth century and inaugurated change; he was succeeded by the greatest reformer, Chulalongkorn, who created an elite bureaucracy in order to better pursue modernization from above. Subsquent kings presided variously over further reforms until the mid-twentieth century. The country began to coalesce and advance. The absolute monarchy came to look anachronistic. In 1932 there was a confused double coup and army reformers removed the absolute monarchy: to make the break with the old regime entirely clear, in 1939 the country was renamed Thailand. The wider regional and global context was unpropitious: in the early 1930s there was civil war in China; the Imperial Japanese armies were beginning their invasions in the north of China; European colonial powers were distracted by gathering war on their home continent; and in various ways corporatist ideologies of hierarchy, discipline, nation, war and expansion were in vogue. General Phibun was influenced by these ideas and initiated a war with France whilst cooperating with Imperial Japan. In the event it was a poor choice and as the Pacific War came to an end, Phibun withdrew as the Americans became a key force within Bangkok. The reorientation towards

America stayed in place throughout the subsequent decades of cold war, military rule and half-hearted development projects.

In the 1950s and 1960s there were a number of military rulers; various import-substituting industrialization programmes were followed; American influence remained strong; and theorists spoke of a bureaucratic capitalist system. General Phibun returned to power. In the 1970s the economic strategy continued; there were also further military coups, a brief experiment in liberal democracy, communist rebellions and the continued spillover of the American wars in Indo-China. Thailand was a frontline state. The end of the cold war brought some relief; the 1980s saw a marginal democratization; the 1990s saw a further failed coup and a period of civilian politics and economic advance. The economy grew rapidly until the disaster of the Asian financial crisis swept through the region. The impact was severe – currency market speculations spilled over into local stock markets, banks tightened credit, firms failed, banks in turn failed, the economy slumped, urban–rural migration developed as the out of work returned to their villages and, finally, the political system was overturned in a period of new constitution writing.

The 1997 crisis attracted a series of explanations: Washington Consensus, institutional economics and political economy. Pasuk Phongpaichit offers a political economy explanation of the Thai crisis and the explanation focuses on social groups, their interests and their access to policy making. It is an explanation that looks to social processes as groups within the country respond to changing circumstances. The Thai economy from 1959 to 1976 saw growth in gross domestic product (GDP) average 7 per cent. It was not a direct Thai version of Japan but a local version of the East Asian focus on national development, with local banks using high savings to fund informal lending. Many Thai corporate groups developed; there was little state direction and they used cheap rural labour, foreign direct investment (FDI) from Japan and adopted largely an import-substituting industrialization (ISI) approach. The turning point came in the mid-1980s. A small economic/financial crisis generated four consequences: the expansion of the role of technocrats; financial liberalization; the reorientation of Thai conglomerates; and the rise of new business groups. There was also democratization. A powerful informal coalition emerged involving technocrats, new business groups, reoriented conglomerates and Washington and the upshot was the drive to liberalize and develop rapidly. Liberalization was begun by the technocrats, supported by Washington, enjoyed by new business groups, reoriented conglomerates and newly influential politicians (urban and rural bosses), but unfortunately the process ran out of control. The currency became attractive to speculative attack. Once the currency had been devalued many local businesses and banks could not support their debts – a downward spiral began. One upshot was a rewritten constitution.

The political system is distinctive: the king is an active influential player; the bureaucracy created by Chulalongkorn is an elite group; the army ruled

Complex change 37

for fifty years and remains influential; the Buddhist church is influential; metropolitan business groups are linked to the state and to parties; provincial business groups are linked to parties; metropolitan civil society is vigorous; and rural areas have many development non-governmental organizations (NGOs). The substantive record of the elite is weak; recently it is stronger; it has sketched out a distinctive route to the modern world. The most recent phase saw a provincial tycoon, Thaksin Shinawatara, organize a new party and successfully contest elections in 2001; the party pursued a national development strategy; it was re-elected in 2005. Public demonstrations led to a further election; an opportunistic opposition boycott resulted in the election – won handsomely by Thaksin – being voided, and rescheduled elections which commentators expected the prime minister to win were aborted by a military coup in late 2006.

China/Shanghai

The Treaty of Nanking of 1842 meant that five treaty ports were open to Europeans and Americans; Shanghai was one; George Balfour arrived in Shanghai in November 1843 and began the process of building what was to become the international settlement.[94]

Shanghai was an established city prior to the arrival of Europeans. Local merchants in the city had begun some trade with Europeans before 1842, and thus the city was known to the Europeans. The British official Balfour rented a house to serve as a consulate inside the city walls, with the intention of being close to the centres of administration; however, the location was poor and the consulate was later relocated outside the city walls.[95] The British settlement was built on land outside the city leased after laborious negotiations from local peasant landowners. A grid of streets was laid out and individual firms constructed their own buildings. At the same time certain collective facilities were also laid out (wharves, the Bund, cemeteries and so on; later a race course was added). The British brought Cantonese compradors with them, so their links to the local people were at first somewhat limited. Balfour worked closely with the local city authorities to establish agreed procedures for trade. In this he was giving practical effect to the Treaty of Nanking. The new settlement prospered, with the British thinking in terms of a quasi-colony and the local Chinese thinking in terms of the familiar pattern of the trading guild.[96] Thus the first moves in Shanghai's shift to the modern world were read by local authorities in terms of long-established practices where Confucian officials ruled and merchants followed these rules.[97]

The treaty port of Shanghai was successful.[98] Chinese merchants came to the city and so did foreign traders. There were successes in exporting tea and silk but there were also disappointments with regard to imports of cotton and woollen piece goods, which the Chinese regarded as inferior to local textiles. The new trading economy played a wide-ranging role and it

38 *Complex change*

served foreigners, local merchants and the chains of suppliers/distributors along the Yangtze river. The new trading economy interacted with the existing economy and it created winners and losers. As the trading role developed a key trade good was opium. It was an unofficial trade but it was intimately related to the growth of the banking industry, as it required lines of credit,[99] and it was crucial to British trade in the east.[100] It was not a British monopoly; rather it was carried out in China in the company of local producers and distributors.[101]

As the British settlement prospered other traders came, in particular from France and America. These two countries both established settlements, and whilst the French Concession remained separate, in time the British settlement embraced American interests and it became known as the International Settlement in 1852.[102] The settlement prospered and developed into a quasi-colonial enclave. The port developed a significant role within the empires of the incomers. Much of the development was secured in agreement with local Chinese authorities; indeed, its prosperity depended upon collaborative activity. The early settlement boasted a population of around 100 incomers, whilst the city of Shanghai had grown to 250,000. It was a complex situation, with foreign traders, local traders, traders from other parts of China and the Qing officials. In 1853–55 the city was occupied by Small Sword rebels,[103] and as the wider Taiping Rebellion continued its course through the period 1851–64, trade in Shanghai advanced. It was a dual city, made up of foreigners and locals.[104]

The period 1864–1911 was the high tide of the imperialist advance. The collapse of Qing gave full reign to Chinese nationalism and a general crisis engulfed China from 1911 to 1978. Shanghai was shaped by these wider events. After 1864 the city grew. The trading role continued. A local textile industry developed. After the 1894–05 Sino-Japanese War foreign investment was allowed,[105] and it flowed in so that the city grew again. The politics of the city were always complex and after 1911 local ruling networks mixed KMT, CCP, local merchants, gangsters and elements of the locally based foreigners. After 1920 Shanghai was a major industrial and commercial city. After 1927 it had no communists because Chiang Kai-Shek's Northern Expedition advanced towards Shanghai in early 1927 and sympathizers confronted and massacred local Communist Party members. As a result, the civil war began and at first the Communist Party was defeated and withdrew to remote rural areas. Shanghai from 1927 to 1937 was a key city in nationalist China; successful and fashionable, it eclipsed Hong Kong. The Imperial Japanese invasion in 1937 brought war and a confused period of semi-collaboration in pursuit of survival. The Japanese surrendered in 1945 and the civil war was resumed; against common expectations the KMT was defeated. Mao proclaimed the People's Republic in 1949. After the communist takeover the city's links with the outside world were severed; capital flight had taken place; most foreigners left; and Hong Kong received some inward textile industry resources. The party made the city a major industrial centre and redistributed the resources generated throughout the country. It controlled inward migration and encouraged outward relocation so the city grew slowly.[106] The city did not regain its pre-communist role as a trading port. Shanghai's development was redirected once again after 1978. The city was not at fist an SEZ but it was granted open port status in 1984; it has been successful; the Pudong area developed from 1990 as a new trading centre and there has been much subsequent rapid growth.

Unfolding change

Agents must read and react to enfolding change; the demands made upon local country powers by the incoming Europeans and Americans were severe. These were not just one more group of traders; rather they came with the support of all the power of the growing metropolitan industrial-capitalist system. European and American incursions within East Asia remade the region; there were multiple exchanges with local groups; local groups were active, not passive, and they reacted in a multiplicity of different ways. British imperial involvement was driven by trade. Great colonial trading cities constituted a global network. Each both sustained the network and drew its immediate hinterland into the system: Singapore linked British India to China and facilitated the exploitation and development of the Malay peninsula; Hong Kong linked Singapore and India to northern Chinese trading ports and opened up the hinterland of the Pearl River Delta; Bangkok opened up the basin of the Chaophrya river and central Siam; Shanghai gave the British, Europeans and Americans access to central China. The cities were keys to the networks of empire and their collections of local hinterlands. Singapore and Hong Kong had long histories as colonial cities. Their historical development trajectories were shaped by those formative experiences; the marks are visible today. In contrast, Bangkok and Shanghai had rather different routes to the modern world but both ran through an exchange with British and other Europeans and Americans. Today both cities are embedded in the modern world and the colonialists are merely a remote part of their history.

It was the colonial episode that brought the modern world to East Asia. Economic, social and political change flowed through the region. The collapse of the colonial empires gave local elites their change; reading and reacting to unfolding structural change they plotted new routes to the future built around the demands of national development. The constituent nation-states of the region embraced new projects; they sketched out new trajectories and the region as a whole was reconfigured, as was the wider global system. The region is now part of the modern world – independent, distinctive, active.

3 Impact and reply

The modern world impacted Asia over some three hundred and fifty years; the newcomers interacted with existing forms of life (economic, social and cultural systems); industrial capitalism[1] was vigorous and so too were the cultures of Asia. These exchanges were contingent; they were sometimes violent;[2] the outcome was not given; the patterns assumed by these exchanges varied from place to place and from time to time. It was a fluid evolving interaction; there were multiple agents involved; there were multiple institutions (country powers, companies and states). These exchanges generated distinctive patterns (territories, states, spheres of influence); these patterns deepened into distinctive empire spheres, formal and informal; these in turn ran until overwhelmed by the general crisis in East Asia. The Europeans came to Asia in the sixteenth century as their home civilization picked up its energies:[3] first the Portuguese, thereafter the Dutch, British and French. Their expansion was marked by intra-European wars and a multiplicity of alliances and wars with and against local 'country powers'. Local elites and peoples were active; they read and reacted to change; they learned the lessons of the modern world and many prospered. In time, as global circumstances shifted, aspirant replacement elites emerged; the long twentieth-century general crisis gave them their chance; and systems of empire first were reconfigured and then dissolved away.

An active exchange

The overall shape of the exchange between Europeans and local peoples can be characterized variously: in terms of power, the peoples of Asia were at first overborne by the demands of the carriers of the modern world but later seized their chance to expel the outsiders; in terms of learning, the peoples of Asia discovered how the modern world worked and took their place within that world; in terms of complex change, neither Asia nor Europe is a fixed entity and the interactions contributed to making and remaking both Asia and Europe, with multiple agents adjusting to changing structural circumstances (and with variously located social scientists telling multiple subsequent tales). The European impact was uneven; in some places; at some times; for various reasons; using differing institutional vehicles; and each exchange produced a particular synthesis of European/Asian forms of life; particular trajectories were set in motion, these in turn informing subsequent exchanges.

The incoming powers included the Dutch, French, Americans and British.[4] Amongst the Europeans, with regard to the early impact/response, the British secured bases in the South Asian sub-continent through the eighteenth century and these were used for subsequent eastern expansion. In Malaya the British acquired ports: George Town in 1786 and Malacca in 1824. The sultanates continued; there was an inflow of migrants; local wars provided the British with a pretext for intervention in the peninsula in 1874. The sultanate system was fixed in place within the system of empire. The Malays remained relatively uninvolved. A further inflow of migrants fed the labour needs of the growing economy; there was the usual mix of colonial development/exploitation until the regional general crisis unfolded in the territory through the period 1941–57. The main settlement in British Malaya was Singapore. The British acquired Singapore in 1818. It was sparsely inhabited, with a rapid inflow of migrants, many sojourners and thus a fluid population. The city grew as a colonial sea port, prosperous until it was caught up in the regional general crisis of 1941–65. Eventual independence saw these problems resolved. If Singapore was the main settlement in Malaya, its clearest role was as a link in the empire chain that reached into China. The British acquired Hong Kong in 1842; treaties signed following a short war secured its extraction from China; the territory received large inward flows of migrants; it became a prosperous colonial sea port; and its colonial status insulated it from the conflicts in China. It was occupied during the Pacific War and then in a curiously unseemly episode recolonized.[5] The regional general crisis impacted Hong Kong tangentially but there was some spillover from conflicts in China: there were flows of refugees and in the 1960s the Cultural Revolution brought bombing and riots to the territory, but these had the effect of solidifying a sense of Hong Kong not as an independent country but rather as its own place within an empire frame now long out of date. Local reforms advance in the economic, social and cultural spheres but the politics remains unreformed. In the 1980s talks began about the lease of the New Territories and the result was the Anglo-Chinese Joint Declaration of 1984, pledging retrocession to China. The territory is transferred to Beijing and now the crisis does arrive: Hong Kong is a small global trading city, whereas China is a state socialist behemoth.[6] Hong Kong now has to settle its domestic arrangements, reach a modus vivendi with Beijing and protect its place in the regional/global system.

The informal empire added to these territories: in Siam and China. The British moved north from Singapore and the peninsula to contact the Siamese court in Bangkok; and the mandala state adjusted; and Mongkut began modernization from above in 1851. The British colonial model was copied.

42 Impact and reply

Bangkok colonized the territory that would become the modern nation-state of Thailand. Chulalongkorn continued and deepened a royal absolutism which prospered until the crisis 1932–45. Thailand emerged as an American protégé.[7] The informal empire grew in southern and central China; Hong Kong was joined by the port of Shanghai;[8] the International Settlement functioned as a colony within a city; the city became a key centre of outward-focused development; it linked a sophisticated local economy to the wider industrial-capitalist global system. The Qing Dynasty attempted to accommodate the demands of the incoming foreigners and failed. General crisis engulfed China – and the city – from 1911 to 1949.

The British impact – economic, social and political – rippled through the region. The incoming power intermeshed with extant forms of life (which continued much as before); it interacted with extant forms of life (thereby changing both) and where interaction was institutionalized novel forms of life took root, which were liable thereafter to further exchange/change. The process of colonial expansion was dynamic; there was no plan; the British came for trade and all else was secondary. Singapore and Hong Kong were constructed within the context of these processes.

The incoming peoples, local agents and complex exchanges

The historical centre of the global economy was Asia;[9] a trading system linked East Asia, Southeast Asia and South Asia. The European traders[10] began to participate in Asian trade from the sixteenth century onwards; at first minor figures, a few ships, a few people, their impact grew as they were joined by missionaries, adventurers, soldiers, administrators. Indigenous agents responded in a multiplicity of ways; power-holders faced problems of accommodating the demands of the outsiders, some adjusting, others collapsing, others coming into being;[11] merchants found new opportunities and competitors; and the social world had new possibilities/problems to absorb. There were no passive victims; groups adjusted; some prospered, some did not.

Money and credit fuelled the expansion of Europe. Spanish and Portuguese sixteenth-century colonization in Latin America produced exports of precious metals; these funded colonial expansion across the Pacific; the Spanish colonized the Philippines in the sixteenth century and joined in the Asian circuits of trade/money. The early traders sought specialist products, silks, ceramics and spices. At first they came in small numbers, eventually setting up trading factories, and the existing patterns of East Asian trade could accommodate these demands. The rise of industrial capitalism occasioned changes; European demands shifted to the output of mines and plantations and they sought larger markets for their own manufactures. As their economic impact deepened so did their political demands: factories turned into treaty ports; seasonal trading (monsoon winds) turned into all-year trading; and they began to change the local economy with new imports, new exports and new trading partners. The region was slowly subordinated to the wishes of the European traders and governments and a series of empires were established. The empires were run from metropolitan centres; they comprised formal and informal areas;[12] the nationals of these centres were privileged; there was a subtle exchange with extant political, economic and social power structures; often there was a racial divide; and the whole system was legitimated with ideas of the superior civilization of the colonizers.

Colonial political economies served the interests of metropolitan capital. A number of changes were made: commercial law was introduced; metropolitan ideas and law with regard to land ownership were introduced; commercial agriculture in the form of plantations was begun; mines dug; roads and railways built; and taxation systems were established to fund colonial rule. A number of colonial port cities were built; typically there was residential segregation of races; and there was heavy inward migration from surrounding areas. The confused pattern led to subtle exchanges between various agents' groups.[13] In colonial Malaya, for example, economic behaviour could be segregated according to ethnic group: British financial institutions; British trading houses; British-owned plantations; Chinese petty traders in towns; Chinese tin miners in rural areas; Chinese coolie labourers; Indian plantation labour; Malay smallholders in rural areas; Chinese merchants and financiers; Indian professionals; and Malay landlords.[14] Of course, such economic differentiation could provide the seeds for social/ political conflicts and the political exchanges were also subtle: the British were focused on trade sectors; the British used local people as traders and labourers; the Chinese controlled the opium retail trade; the Chinese traders controlled the inflow of labourers from Southern China; the Straits Chinese were a privileged group; Indians became a privileged group; the Malay Royals were co-opted into the Empire, receiving large pensions; and the Malay peasantry remained rural.

Colonial economies cut across the established economic patterns in Southeast Asia;[15] a long-established regional trade network was disrupted by colonial mercantile spheres of interest, Dutch, British, French and American. The impact of the newcomers generated a complex pattern of economic activity. It can be envisioned as a series of layers of economic and trade activity: the lowest layer would be traditional products for local consumption; the next layer traditional products still traded across colonial boundaries along old established regional trade routes; the next layer would bring people and goods into the region from the surrounding areas; and the final layer linked the colonial sphere to the global economy through colonial port cities to the metropolitan core. The example of the opium trade illuminates the complexity of the exchanges between the various agents:[16] a valuable crop grown in India, where it displaced peasant food production, it was exported via Southeast Asia to southern China; it became a major trade good generating large revenues; it created a large industry involving many people (producers, transporters, wholesale markets, retail distributors, opium shopkeepers and customers); and, finally, the industry was organized and provided a key social institution and crucial tax revenues.

The years before the Great War were the high tide of the European and American empires in East Asia: original cultures had been irrevocably altered, foreign dominance seemed established and critical voices were few; in the event, a general crisis developed in Europe and in East Asia. The Chinese Revolution of 1911 was the first in an interlinked sequence of regional conflicts that ran until 1975; the Pacific War was a decisive moment. Formal empires were swept away and indigenous nationalist groups seized their chance; a host of new nations emerged and, whilst the economies of East Asia were deeply embedded in the modern global industrial-capitalist system, the war had caused extensive damage and pessimistic experts looked to a future of agriculture and low-tech manufactures. This was the starting point for the leaders of the new nations, the legacy of their colonial route to the modern world. It was made more difficult by the onset of the cold war.[17] Overall, it was the structural pattern the replacement elites had to deal with once they took power and began the task of national development.

The British in Southeast Asia; great arc, peninsula, archipelago and China

The British East India Company[18] was the organizational vehicle for English expansion in the Asian region. The eastern expansion of British trade interests began in the seventeenth century, deepened in the eighteenth[19] and reached its furthest extent in the nineteenth. The Company infiltrated the patchwork of sub-continental princely states with trade links, military alliances, co-options and annexations; such expansion was accompanied with competition with Portuguese, Dutch and French traders. It was an irregular expansion, filled with risk, suffused with violence; advance was secured against local powers and other Europeans. The loss of the American colonies underscored the importance of the region; it was crucial to the British Empire.[20] The sub-continent was the base for further expansion: Francis Light established the port of George Town in 1786; Stamford Raffles established the port of Singapore in 1818; George Elliot established the port of Hong Kong in 1841;[21] the British fought three wars to conquer the Burmese;[22] the Opium War of 1839–42 and the Arrow War of 1856–60 secured Chinese compliance with European and American demands for trading rights; a series of ports were opened; the country was informally divided; George Balfour in 1842 began constructing what would become the International Settlement in Shanghai and in time the British sphere extended along the valley of the Yangtze. In 1855 John Bowring secured the agreement of the Siamese king for trading operations in Bangkok. The 1857 Indian Mutiny marked the end of the company's role; after that date expansion was a matter for the British government.

Singapore and Hong Kong were key trading ports. First Singapore was extracted from the wider Johor–Riau sultanate; a peripheral royal figure was acknowledged as Sultan of Singapore; a treaty was signed; a British claim on the territory secured. Neither the East India Company in India nor the Dutch in Riau was happy, but the territory survived. It prospered; at first taken by local traders as a the key port in a standard Malay maritime empire, it was a Malay–British condominium; inward migration altered the domestic balance of power; elements of the Malay elite turned their attention to Johor; and the Chinese became a third powerful group. The territory was embedded within the British sphere of Southeast Asia as a key trading nexus; multiple groups used the port, local, European and American; it prospered until overwhelmed by war in 1941. Second, the British acquired Hong Kong in 1842; it was extracted by war from China; an indigenous population was mostly ignored; the territory prospered as a colonial sea port; inward Chinese migration built the population over the nineteenth century; by 1900 Chinese capital was equivalent to British; the inter-war period saw Shanghai as a fashionable centre; wartime occupation was devastating. In both cases, reconstruction followed the Pacific War; thereafter further changes ensued.

Active exchange and contingent patterns

Against the familiar histories of colonial expansion, the process was neither organized nor straightforward: the European empires were accumulated piecemeal; initiatives were sometimes local, sometimes initiated by the imperial centre. The incomers were drawn by the lure of trade; they were carried, so to say, on the back of a powerful form of life, and as they extended their reach they did so with the benefits of asymmetries of power – intellectual, technical and organizational – which let them insert themselves within local political systems and on occasion simply override local opposition. The local country powers were not passive; they accommodated the incomers, now resisting, now acquiescing and always learning. Against the equally familiar nationalist histories of colonial expansion (and retreat), the process was neither one-sided nor wholly exploitative. The business of empire – its acquisition and loss – escapes these simplicities; the historical record is more interesting. As regards empire, the pattern is contingent; there were multiple shifts and changes; trajectories were established but they shifted and changed; the colonial era mediated the shift to the modern world; it was not a smooth evolutionary process; it is a broken history; the general crisis of 1911–75 ensured the emergence of a variety of national development projects.

Civilizations of Asia: impacts and patterns of response

Prior to the arrival of European and, later, American traders, East Asia comprised a number of sophisticated cultures:[23] a Chinese cultural sphere,

46 *Impact and reply*

including modern China, Korea, Japan and Vietnam; a Malay cultural sphere, encompassing mainland Indo-China and the archipelago to the south;[24] and a South Asian cultural sphere centred on the sub-continent and embracing modern-day India, Bangladesh and Sri Lanka. These three cultural spheres were distinctive, sophisticated and economically advanced; they were linked by extensive trading networks, which were sustained by numerous trading ports. In the fifteenth to seventeenth centuries the trading linkages within the region were particularly well developed[25] but linkages to the wider global system were minimal. Yet it was the core area of the global system prior to the emergence of Europe and America.[26] The historical core of the region was China. The Sino-centric system collapsed in the nineteenth century. Japan responded quickly; it sought to accommodate the modern world, develop quickly and fulfil the role once played by China.

Forms of life in Asia

The modern world can be understood as a particular cultural form, a way of organizing relationships between people and nature;[27] the cultural form of modernity comprises the celebration of the power of human reason, the extensive development of natural science and the pursuit of livelihood through science-based industrial capitalism. The cultural form originated in Europe; it is dynamic (intensification/expansion); it has encompassed much of the world; and in this continuing process local cultures have been drawn into the system and their patterns of life remade. In East Asia European traders arrived in small numbers from the sixteenth century; they traded manufactures for small quantities of exotic and luxury products; European involvement grew; the dynamics of industrial-capitalism in the nineteenth century produced new raw materials requirements and expanded flows of manufactures; colonial regimes were imposed; the territories of the region were drawn deeply into the global industrial-capitalist system. The exchange with East Asia extended over several centuries. The period of settled high colonialism was brief (late nineteenth to mid-twentieth century). Various indigenous groups adopted the intellectual resources from the colonizers; indigenous nationalist groups turned the political resources against the colonizers;[28] overall the episode moved the peoples of East Asia unevenly into the modern world.[29] Trade was the driver.

There were three major trading arenas: the India trade, the spice trade and the China trade. Europeans joined existing trading networks; there were multiple actors; European powers manoeuvred in shifting alliances for position and advantage;[30] there was no uniform market; trade was distinguished by geography, ethnicity and marketplace.[31] The major vehicles of European expansion were the trading companies.[32] The Amsterdam Company sponsored its first voyage to Bantam in 1596–97; the East Indies Company (VOC) was formed in 1602 and sought a monopoly of trade beyond the Cape of Good Hope; the Dutch government authorized it to wage war, make treaties and build fortresses; the Dutch opened a factory at Jakarta in 1611.[33] The East India Company (EIC) was established in 1657; the English government allocated similar powers. Europeans manoeuvred for advantage on the Indian coast: the Dutch seized Sri Lanka in 1658 and Malacca in 1641; the English gained territory in India; the French also looked for advantage but were not generally successful.[34] Later, the nineteenth century saw changes within the sphere of metropolitan capital and consequent changes in the demands placed upon the region by the European traders; the depth of European involvement increased; the India trade grew (manufactures/opium), the archipelago trade was reworked (archipelago goods joined by plantations and mines) and the China trade grew (manufactures, tea, silks and other specialist products and opium). Southeast Asia was colonized; China became a quasi-colony; and Japan became a participant in colonial expansion.

European incursions

Europeans and Americans reached Southeast Asia from the sixteenth century onwards, and here they made the most rapid deep impacts. Mainland Southeast Asia has a number of great river valleys: the Irawadi, Chaophrya, Mekong and Red. A number of civilizations flourished in these areas, in time coalescing as the Burmese, Thai, Khmer and Vietnamese. They practiced wet-rice cultivation; followed Confucian and Buddhist great traditions; established a number of great cities; traded extensively; fought numerous highly destructive wars; and produced fluid shifting pre-modern polities.[35] After 1800 the Europeans began to move into the area. The British moved into Burma and the southern Malay peninsula; the French moved into Vietnam, Laos and Cambodia; Siam[36] escaped direct colonization as it served as a buffer state between colonial spheres. However, the influence of the British and French was extensive. Siam colonized its own hinterland and adopted modern forms in order to minimize the risk of colonization. In the area as a whole traditional forms of life slowly retreated; the complex mixture of colonial exploitation and development drew the territories into the modern world. Similarly, Southeast Asia was characterized by mandala states;[37] the area comprised numerous shifting polities;[38] maritime empires developed; trading networks were extensive; a regional sphere was constituted.[39] European incursions from the seventeenth century remade the polities and region. The early impact of the Europeans was slight; they were simply one more trading group. The nineteenth century industrial revolution generated new economic demands; a system of colonial empires slowly absorbed indigenous polities; traditional forms of life declined; the hitherto integrated region resolved into discrete colonial spheres, each remade in concert with its contingent of foreigners.

48 *Impact and reply*

The goal: China

Europeans and Americans sought to reach China,[40] the desired destination of trading links, long resisted; the Chinese economy was powerful both domestically and internationally; it did not need the incomers; it resisted them; it was only the drive of the capitalist and later industrial-capitalist system that overbore the Qing, which, having replaced the Ming Dynasty in 1681, itself collapsed in 1911.

China[41] was predominantly agricultural; the economy rested on the labour of peasant farmers;[42] the political centre provided law and administration. The household was the basic unit; the family was hierarchical and patriarchal; it was a site for production and consumption. Lineage was a way of organizing the life of the village; the family was the centre of social life and individuals found their existence within its confines. Family membership included ancestors whose status required ritual acknowledgement in folk religious practice. Buddhism and Taoism flourished; Confucianism served as a legitimating philosophy; the Confucian scholar became the rational bureaucrat of the empire. The Qing Dynasty faced problems; internally, a rising population, stagnating economy and a complacent elite;[43] there was widespread popular dissent; the use of regional armies created potential alternate centres of power; and externally European traders became a threat. They had been a growing presence in the eighteenth century, when trade had been primarily agricultural exports in exchange for silver. An imbalance of trade resulted. Opium became a valuable trade good; the Chinese authorities objected;[44] the British launched the Opium Wars of 1840–42. The Chinese government acquiesced in greater trade linkages; the Chinese ceded Hong Kong; other treaty ports were established. The combination of internal decay and external conflicts led to debate amongst the Chinese elite with respect to learning from the foreigners in order to modernize the country. The proponents of the status quo proved the more influential. The country avoided outright colonization only when the Europeans and Americans agreed that all should be allowed to trade. In practice, quasi-colonial spheres of influence developed; final collapse came in the revolution of 1911.[45]

The Chinese economy was the core of the pre-modern global system.[46] Chinese had traded in East Asia for centuries.[47] European and American demands for trading rights unsettled the ruling elite; there was little grasp of the challenge posed.[48] Decline accelerated in the wake of the Opium Wars; the treaty-port system established the European and American trading presence; and the resistance of the 1899 Boxer Rebellion was quickly suppressed by a combined expedition of Europeans, Americans and Japanese. The Qing Dynasty was incapable of formulating a response to the incursions of the expanding industrial-capitalist system; the incapacity lay in the balance of social forces.[49] The equilibrium of the system was fatally disturbed by the arrival of Western traders. The hitherto weak Chinese traders now had access to a powerful trading partner in the European and American trading companies. After the Opium Wars of 1842 the Chinese merchant groups began to prosper, in particular along the coasts, where they traded as compradors with the Europeans and Americans.

The dynastic centre's response to the incursions of the West was wholly inappropriate to the threat which it posed. There was no centrally sponsored attempt to learn the lessons of the West and modernize. There was little attempt to improve agriculture, as there was no landlord interest in pursuing such development. The system stagnated and was unable to respond. There were some regionally based attempts at modernization, and these typically centred on armaments technologies. Overall, the dynasty was unable to read and react to the developing demands of the global system in the nineteenth century – and slowly it decayed as regional authorities became more powerful and as the European and American presence (and later the Japanese) coupled with the rise of Chinese comprador traders shifted the economy away from the quasi-feudal agrarian system towards an industrial-capitalist system. In the early years of the twentieth century the Qing Dynasty finally began a programme of reforms: constitutional, administrative, financial, military and educational; in 1909 provincial assemblies were elected, in 1910 a National Assembly was convened (half elected and half appointed by the imperial court). This was too little; it failed.

Sun Yat-sen built up the Revolutionary Alliance and between 1906 and 1911 staged a series of failed armed uprisings. In 1911 the Qing Dynasty central government experienced one more crisis (over railway construction) and there was a widespread revolt amongst the provincial gentry and two-thirds of the country quickly fell into the hands of Sun Yat-sen's revolutionaries, who declared him president in the provincial city of Nanjing. However, the Qing authorities asked General Yuan to suppress the rebels and in the ensuing confusion both the dynasty and the newly established republic gave way first to the brief rule of General Yaun and thereafter to a series of regional warlords. Political power was widely dispersed; there were multiple conflicts; there were many warlords. The CCP was formed in 1921; Sun Yat-sen died in 1925; Chiang Kai-Shek inherited power in the KMT, and a military authoritarian government was set up in Nanjing in 1927. The KMT government was tainted by landlordism, gangsterism, opportunistic commercial factions, backward-looking nationalism and militarism; it was an East Asian variant of fascism.[50] And in addition the effective collapse of central authority left the country open to the demands of foreign powers. The colonial powers expanded their spheres of influence; the Japanese became involved and in 1937 began open warfare.

Opening Japan

The Japanese home islands were comparatively remote from the main arenas of European activity. American expansion across the Pacific in the nineteenth century brought the Americans into contact with both China and Japan.[51] It was American activity that precipitated change in Japan and drew the country into the modern world.

The Japanese islands were home to agrarian societies in the sixth century.[52] A rich agricultural economy flourished; urban centres grew; trade links with the Korean peninsula were established; later links with China. The key resource is land; it is around its control that politics revolves. Medieval Japanese society advanced. It also generated warfare and a system of military government emerged. The confusions of an increasingly fractious polity ended with the Battle of Sekigahara; Tokugawa Ieyasu defeated other regional lords and established the Tokugawa Shogunate, the first period of peace for some three hundred years. The Tokugawa Shogunate was feudal:[53] landholdings funded government; the shogun ruled in Edo; the daimyo regional lords ruled landed territories, controlled by the alternate attendance system, pledges of allegiance, dynastic marriages, restrictions on local forces and expensive public works; samurai warrior-bureaucrats administered and policed the system. The economy was agricultural; the population rose from 18 million in 1600 to 30 million in 1850; Edo had a population of one million in the early 1700s. Commercial development advanced as farmers produced for the market and basic transport systems, distribution systems and credit facilities were developed.[54] The social system derived from Confucian models and was hierarchical; each person owed allegiance and obedience to his or her superior. The lives of common people centred on the continuing family; the family owned property and worked as a group within which the rights and duties of individual members were specified. But the system was flawed; success made it unstable; rising agricultural production improved the prospects of farmers; increasing domestic trade helped the situation of artisan craft producers and urban merchants. The samurai were embroiled in maladministration and debt; the daimyo and shogun were able to defend their own positions, but tensions became uncontrollable faced with the demands of foreign traders.[55] Japan had adopted a closed-country policy in 1633; external trade links were controlled; Nagasaki was the point of access for Chinese and Dutch traders; foreign ideas entered. Dutch learning included natural science, medicine and military equipment; knowledge spread slowly, resisted by patriots as moral decline. European and American movement into the region gathered pace, the Chinese government was forced to open trading ports in the mid-nineteenth century; colonial traders looked to Japan; the moribund shogunate could deal neither with internal problems nor with the demands of the traders. Commodore Perry signed a trade treaty in 1854; European powers also secured treaties. The Japanese called them unequal treaties and regarded them as a national disgrace; the political elite were split, there was pressure for resistance and there was some small-scale violent conflict; eventually the episode precipitated crisis and the Meiji Restoration of 1868.

As the European and American powers extended their influence in China through the nineteenth century, the attention of traders began to turn towards Japan; this was the high watermark of European and American imperial advance; the inability of the old Tokugawa Shogunate to formulate a coherent response to the demands of the Western powers led to the Meji Restoration in 1868. The Meiji state borrowed from the model of the West and restructured Japanese political-economic, social-institutional and cultural patterns; however, changes in patterns of authority were held to a minimum in a state-sponsored authoritarian modernization from above.[56] In the late nineteenth and early twentieth centuries the political-economic development of Japan was rapid. The pursuit of economic development drew heavily on the available model of the West. The Meiji pursuit of development came to involve early diplomatic conflict with the Great Powers in Europe and the USA, particularly with respect to Japanese colonial activities. During this period the European powers and the USA were extensively involved in China. It was the period of spheres of influence and trading ports. And in the nineteenth century nation-states still had routine recourse to war in order to settle disputes and so Japan pursued its concern for security using an available strategy. As the Meiji state secured a measure of industrial modernization it sought further security in the form of the establishment of a sphere of influence in East Asia. In the process of expansion there was early Japanese activity in the area of the Russian Far East, in the Korean peninsula and in China. The Sino-Japanese war of 1894–95 lasted nine months, in which time the Japanese armed forces expelled the Chinese from Korea and captured Port Arthur and the Liao-tung peninsula. The peace treaty also ceded Taiwan to Japan. Conflict with Russia for influence in Manchuria and Korea led to the Russo-Japanese war of 1904–05; Japanese success increased Japan's influence in Manchuria and Korea (protectorate in 1905, annexed in 1910); the European and American powers acquiesced. The naval victory over the Russian navy gained approval from Asians[57] and Japan began to make demands on China a few years later. Western sympathy faded. In the 1930s the Japanese invaded China; the USA was critical and the Pacific War followed.

East Asia: impact, resistance and crisis

East Asia was home to distinctive forms of life. European incursions drew these peoples into the global industrial-capitalist system; indigenous elites and peoples responded; it was an active response and there were winners and losers; however, the exchange was asymmetric; the Europeans and Americans were buoyed by the power of the industrial-capitalist system and in time existing patterns of life were overborne.[58] A number of foreign empires were established: Portuguese, Dutch, French and later American. In the eighteenth and nineteenth centuries foremost amongst these was the British Empire; as the incomers moved to secure their trading interests,

52 *Impact and reply*

the long-established regional centre, China, collapsed, and in the confusion of changing regional relationships Japan sought to take its place.[59] Further conflicts ensued. Overall, the expansion of the modern world was disruptive. The exchange between incomers and local communities was complex. However, local people were not replaced; they did not disappear, but adapted; and they were significant contributors to the process of making the modern world in East Asia.

Reactions and responses in the British sphere

European and later American incursions were incremental. Early contacts were made with Indian sultanates; later the Spice Islands. The expansion drew in territories throughout Southeast Asia and the Americans replaced the Spanish in the Philippines. China was the goal of later expansion; later still Japan and Northeast Asia were drawn into the industrial capitalist networks of trade. East Asia was overwhelmed; local agents interacted with incomers in the process of establishing a pattern of colonial territories. The impact of industrial capitalism ordered through colonial regimes was severe; extant forms of life were extensively reconfigured; the key linkages between the local area and the global system were provided by the major colonial port cities:[60] Singapore, Batavia, Manila, Bangkok, Hong Kong and Shanghai. Within the general framework of European and American expansion, the British carved out an empire in East Asia.

British Singapore

Singapore island was selected within the context of Anglo-Dutch manoeuvring as a base for the projection of British mercantile power.[61] This required the political extraction of the island from the locally power-ful[62]Johor–Riau Sultanate;[63] after intense political manoeuvring, a newly invented sultan of Singapore signed an agreement with Raffles that gave the British a claim against both the indigenous ruler in Riau and the Dutch.[64] In 1823 the power struggle between British and Malay rulers was resolved in favour of the British. In 1835 the Temmengong's successor Ibrahim agreed to throw in his lot with the British and assist in the suppression of piracy; the old maritime pattern declined, the seafarers disappeared and the Malays turned their attention to Johor.[65] In Singapore by mid-century the Chinese population was the largest single group; they serviced the manpower needs of the trading centre and through the tax farm on opium they furnished the larger part of the settlement's revenue.[66] The period from 1819 to the early 1870s can be taken as the phase of the projection and establishment of British mercantile capitalist power on Singapore island and within the surrounding archipelago. The formal shift to colonial status for Singapore took place in 1867; the British advance into the Malay peninsula began with the 1874 Pangkor Engagement.

In Singapore there was a coincidence of economic interests between European and Chinese merchant classes; in the early years of the nineteenth century the key institution around which the political and economic life of the Chinese population revolved was the opium tax farm coupled to clan and secret society groups. The relationship was formalized with the establishment of the Chinese Protectorate in 1877 and the establishment of the Chinese Advisory Board in 1889; later prominent Chinese joined the colonial government machinery. Singapore then became a major nexus in the British-centred sphere of the world industrial-capitalist system and a link in the chain to China. Singapore also served to link British India, the Malay peninsula and Hong Kong with the southern British possessions of Australia,[67] New Zealand and assorted Pacific Islands.[68]

In the Malayan peninsula the British traded from a base in Penang established by Francis Light in the last years of the eighteenth century;[69] later Malacca; after the Pangkor Engagement the British slowly increased their influence with the local sultanates. As the colony solidified, so too did the system of sultanates and indirect rule whereby the British concerned themselves with development and the traditional rulers with their peoples. The Malay community existed in relative tranquillity for many years; development drew in immigrants and the territory became multi-ethnic, encouraging the first expressions of Malay nationalism. The beginnings of political activity were in the 1920s, the earliest influences coming through Islam both from the Middle East via religious revival and from Indonesia with the influence of Serekat Islam.[70] In Malay communities nationalism grew; in the Chinese communities in the 1920s and 1930s communists and the KMT competed for support; the Indian community also organized; however, its internal caste distinctions hindered effective action. Overall, this nascent activity did not crystallize as a coherent nationalism; rather, it ran along ethnic lines.[71] Yet all this was changed by the wartime occupation; the Japanese interlude reinforced ethnic lines and these concerns flowed into the politics of independence.

British Hong Kong

In the early nineteenth century British and other Western trading interests sought a reliable base in the area of the Pearl River Delta; the region was a frontier between the Qing Empire, the peoples of Southeast Asia and the empires of the Europeans; it was also home to a significant indigenous population – Cantonese-speaking in the main – southern Chinese, often summarily characterized as distinct from their northern compatriots. It was a border area; it was the site of a clash between the growing forces of the modern world and the Qing Empire, at this time both powerful and conservative. The island was acquired as a base following the Opium War; further territory was added in subsequent years; it provided access to south China; later it was supplanted by Shanghai. The British sought to establish a trading centre, which could not be created by them alone; success required the participation of local Chinese traders. The relationship was a species of collaboration; the core exchanges were economic. The formal apparatus of colonial rule excluded or disregarded the local Chinese; they built parallel structures and they worked the structures they found and made their own spaces; local Chinese had a sense of themselves as distinct, as Hong Kongers, by the late nineteenth century. The two sets of institutions slowly intertwined; Hong Kong emerged as its own place. Reasons for this success have been debated; a crucial aspect of it is the territory's separation from China.[72]

Hong Kong's history involves the incoming colonial agents and the local Chinese; the local bourgeoisie, the business elite, understood themselves as a distinctive group, committed to China yet able to work within the British Empire; local popular groups were more oppositional; the exchange between the colonial elite, local elite and mainland elites is complex; it is out of this mix that Hong Kong emerges as its own place.[73] In the early years of the colony few Chinese traders settled; there were problems of security (local pirates/entrepreneurs); there was no significant economic advantage (Chinese merchants remained based in other Pearl River towns); and there was Qing Empire official hostility. Hong Kong gathered up the less reputable elements amongst the trading community. Advances came with European and American capitalist growth and social conflict in China.[74] Western economic growth disrupted established trading patterns. Hong Kong-based traders had new opportunities; the mid-nineteenth-century abolition of slavery created a demand for migrant workers – the coolie trade – and Hong Kong was the major transhipment point for workers bound for North America and later Southeast Asia. The trade was run by Chinese. The Taiping Rebellion produced a flow of recruits for the trade. Where Hong Kong had been an obscure outpost linking the British and Chinese empires, it was now a key link in an important international trade network, a major commercial centre;[75] it became its own place as the machineries of foreign empire provided a space for a Chinese elite to coalesce and prosper.[76]

The Chinese business elite used social and political spaces made available by their distinctive location; as the formal apparatus of British colonial rule developed, the local Chinese elite built a Chinese Hong Kong in parallel – slowly the two institutional spheres interacted. The British had minimal intentions for Hong Kong; they were sojourners. The Chinese elite settled; they built institutions – Man Mo Temple in 1847, District Watch Force in 1866 (acknowledged and 'officialized' in 1891), Tung Wah Hospital in 1872,[77] the Chinese Chamber of Commerce in 1896 and the Bank of East Asia in 1919.[78] Other commercial and social organizations developed. The Qing Empire now spoke of overseas Chinese rather than traitors. Complex networks developed within Hong Kong, between Hong Kong and the mainland, and between Hong Kong and Chinese communities in Southeast

Asia and North America. The Chinese business elite came to view themselves as a local – that is, Hong Kong – elite; the colonial government concurred; a subtle race-inflected interchange between colonial British and local Chinese produced a distinctive society; local elites were aware of Hong Kong's failings as well as its success, sympathetic to the ideal of modernized China[79] and willing if necessary to defend the colonial system in Hong Kong.[80]

Hong Kong lay at the ragged edge of two empires:[81] British and Qing; as the industrial-capitalist system extended and intensified its reach, Hong Kong became a key commercial centre. Local elites had complex linkages with the mainland and overseas; the people in Hong Kong – sojourners and settlers – made a distinctive place.[82]

British influence in Siam

Siam avoided formal colonization by virtue of its position between British and French domains. Neither power asserted itself; both were content with the existence of a buffer state; and both adjusted that state's borders in line with their own interests, the British taking territory in the southern Siamese realms, the French removing large areas of the eastern Siamese realms.[83] However, the Siamese were ordered around an energetic reforming domestic political elite; the elite were neither conservative nor passive nor overwhelmed, and they actively sought progress. In the mid-nineteenth century King Mongkut agreed trading links and initiated reforms; in the later nineteenth and early twentieth centuries King Chulalongkorn continued these reforms and constructed an absolutist modern state and nation. In the regional context, the Anglo-French agreement of 1896 guaranteed Siam's autonomy, freeing the leadership to pursue development.[84] The elite looked to the models provided by the neighbouring colonial rulers, British and French. The former had established a powerful economic and cultural presence in Bangkok following the Bowring Treaty; and this accelerated drives for reform.[85]

The Thai bureaucracy was reformed; paid officials replaced local royal rulers and a modern army was built up. These state-building activities began in the central region and were extended over the whole traditional Siamese territory; the outline of a bounded, ordered nation-state was created. These modernizing reforms continued, in time creating a distinctive bureaucratic capitalism.[86] The economy had been rapidly modernized, with three key changes: the establishment of an independent peasantry with a rural economy centred on rice growing, a key export commodity, along with rubber, tin and teak; the rapid development of a Chinese business network within the country and acting as compradors for foreign business, thereby linking the rural Siamese to the global economy; and the generation of substantial tax revenues which funded the development of the state.

King Chulalongkorn died in 1910 and his successors were neither effective nor popular. The army took over in 1932; thereafter the three key institutions have been the army, the bureaucracy and the monarchy. Inevitable wartime collaboration with the Imperial Japanese was followed by absorption within the American cold war sphere.[87] From 1945 until the early 1990s a variety of military dictatorships oversaw a haphazardly successful development trajectory.[88]

The British influence in Shanghai

British power in India was extended during the eighteenth century. The Dutch East Indies Company continued to trade in the archipelago but restrictive monopoly trading practices had the effect of redirecting trade to the more liberal British. Later in the century the Napoleonic revolutionary wars found local expression. European conflicts drew in country powers; the French were defeated and the British and Dutch divided the territories of Southeast Asia and India.[89] The British occupied Penang in 1786, Singapore in 1819 and Malacca in 1824; the Malay peninsula was occupied piecemeal starting in 1874. The China trade linked metropolitan Britain, British India and the territories of the Qing Empire.[90] The trade quickly became crucial to the British Empire. The British had a base at Canton around 1715. The China trade became imbalanced as the British bought tea, silks and other specialist goods with the local regional currency whilst the Chinese bought very little in return. The British found one product which they could sell – opium – but the Beijing authorities decided to suppress the trade; the British eventually insisted that the Chinese authorities relax their restrictions on imports and following the Opium Wars of 1839–42 and 1856–60 a series of treaty ports were opened, including Hong Kong and Shanghai.

The British Empire in East Asia was centred on the informal empire in China. The goal was trade. The key bases were Hong Kong, which accessed the Pearl River Delta, and Shanghai, which allowed access to central China. In Shanghai, the British established a base, later the International Settlement, adjacent to the existing large Chinese city; as with other European and American colonial trading ports it drew in local traders, who interacted with the outsiders. The port drew central China into the modern global industrial-capitalist system.

From impact and response to general crisis

Indigenous elites endeavoured to deal with the novel demands of European and American incursions. Sometimes they failed; sometimes they were successful. It was a complex process of accommodation. The colonial era drew the territories of East Asia into the modern world. The colonies themselves evidenced the familiar mix of exploitation and development. The peoples of the region were active; the process of drawing the region into the colonial systems and thereby the modern world could not advance without their participation. The numbers of foreigners in the region during this period was low and the incomers were always and everywhere a small minority. The British, like other colonial rulers, created novel economic, social and political spaces within which local merchants and other actors could operate. In Shanghai, Hong Kong and Singapore Chinese merchants were active and prospered. They added primary product exploitation to their portfolios, they created industries and they established powerful banks. These merchants became influential; they built hospitals and schools and in time they were co-opted to the formal apparatus of colonial rule; these three were 'Chinese cities' long before the British finally left. The pattern was replicated elsewhere; other groups prospered. Southern Johor was developed by Malay princes; the system of princes was assisted by the system of indirect rule favoured by the colonial power. In Siam there were similar exercises in economic, social and political rebalancing. Standard metropolitan images of active colonialists and passively adjusting subjects are false; so too the standard nationalist inversion whereby aggressive incomers overwhelm successful locals. The shift to the modern world was powered by an elaborate exchange of people, goods, finance and ideas.

Empire was, however, unsustainable over anything but the relative short term; the exchange of goods, finance and ideas drew East Asia into the modern world, but once there it was the local people who were going to determine its course. The lessons of modernity were brought to Asia by foreigners but they were put to use in Asia by Asian people. The transition was awkward; just as colonial expansion was haphazard, sometimes violent and involved multiple alliances whereby the characteristic exploitation and development could be secured, so too was the withdrawal. Reconfiguring the East Asian region was not simple or straightforward. The tensions inherent in the system of empire began to make themselves evident from the mid-nineteenth century; the 1857 Indian Mutiny was but an early instance of multiple resistances. The Chinese Revolution of 1911 inaugurated a long general crisis which included civil breakdown, conflicts and modern industrial-scale warfare, and it was the latter which finally shattered the colonial system. The desire of the Imperial Japanese to participate as equals in the contemporary global system led them to accumulate territory in Korea, Manchuria, China and later Indo-China and Southeast Asia; the general war that ensued destroyed both their empire and those of the Europeans and Americans. As the system of empire dissolved in confusion, local aspirant replacement elites took their chance; numerous wars unfolded throughout East Asia; different wars; different participants; different memories; and different timings; however, as the fighting died down replacement elites moved to declare the independence of new nation-states; some further confusions ensued, made worse by cold war, but the episode did finally issue in the inauguration of various projects centred around national development.

4 General crisis

The collapse of empire was inevitable as these political structures were unsustainable; they were always going to be transient phenomena. Demographics was key; foreigners were always a small minority;[1] learning was another key as the elites and masses of the colonized territories learned how the modern world worked (the economics, the social organizations and the politics). Sweeping imposed change was another key; as extant forms of life were turned upside down it could only provoke a reaction.[2] The project of empire was challenged with anti-foreigner movements, religious cults/revivals, mutinies, uprisings, nationalist movements and metropolitan reformers.[3] The old system, as modified in the phase of impact/response to modernity, fell apart: economic breakdown, social breakdown and political breakdown. It was not clear how the social world was to be ordered,[4] but it was clear that extant patterns were illegitimate. The unfolding general crisis was marked by a series of interlinked wars: overlapping participants, different experiences and different memories. The collapse began in China;[5] at the start of the sequence East Asia was dominated by competing European, Japanese and American empires and China was divided; at the end of the sequence the European, Japanese and American empires were gone and a number of new or radically remade countries had been established. The transformation was attained at great cost; total casualties numbered in the tens of millions.

The scale of the crisis: breakdown, confusion and war

The general crisis began[6] with the progressive rejection of colonialism embodied in the Chinese Revolution; nationalist elites sought an equal participation in the modern world; it was not until the end of the Vietnamese war that foreign aspirations to colonial rule were finally quietened in East Asia; a number of interrelated problems accumulated in the early years of the twentieth century, economic, social, political and security, until finally systemic collapse ushered in general crisis.

Economic change involved intra-regional rebalancing and extra-regional competitions. Intra-regional reorganization revolved around the emergence of the economic power of Japan; the 1868 Meiji Restoration enabled the elite to pursue national development and by the turn of the twentieth century Japan was a major industrial and military power; it defeated China and Russia in wars, acquired colonial territory and continued to advance its industrial development. As Japan became a significant economic power within East Asia, its rise disturbed extant patterns.[7] At the same time, extra-regional changes were occurring; the economic development of the USA was proceeding rapidly and by the turn of the century it was a global economic power; it was significant economic power within East Asia and its links were long established.[8] The deepening of this established economic power produced further pressures for change in East Asia; the relative decline of formerly important European empires[9] also contributed to pressures for rebalancing. In China development advanced in the coastal cities where the areas were linked to overseas colonial powers;[10] overseas Chinese diasporas linked the mainland to Southeast Asia and North America. Extra-regional problems also contributed; the 1930s Great Depression was precipitated[11] in the USA and its effects rippled through the global capitalist sphere.

Social change reworked established social relationships and the apparently settled social relations of colonial empire were thrown into question; the phase of impact/response had seen local elites respond actively,[12] with the masses of population relatively untouched; the early phases of colonial rule had seen relatively small numbers of foreigners and relatively slow changes to established patterns of life; however, economic advances in the global capitalist sphere led to much deeper impacts on local society and the second industrial revolution of late nineteenth century, which saw natural scientific advances informing industrial production, gave rise to new demands for raw materials, markets and patterns of order. New demands were made for informal rule to be replaced by organized colonial holdings, in particular ordered polities with law and appropriate social reordering. Plantation systems and extractive industries were established; land and labour were needed; existing customary land rights were disturbed and colonial legal systems established; land was alienated and labour was coerced or imported. New distribution systems were needed; new ports, railways and roads; and new financial systems. Further, contrary to liberal market ideologies, schedules of needs/wants are social and new demands and new products disturbed existing social practices; some benefited; others did not. Increasing disruption plus elite inability to deal with incomers favoured radical action.

Political change swept through the empires. Empire brought legitimating ideologies, claims to the superiority of modern civilization. It was a complex exchange with mutual learning and mutual misunderstanding; it produced Orientalist discourses, racial ideologies and various Social Darwinist ideologies. There was discrimination and inequality within colonial holdings; the exchanges were not all of a piece with elite figures, state civil servants, professional and subalterns; the mix was thoroughly complex; the scope for collaboration/dissent similarly complex. The claims to legitimacy of empire were sustained in the nineteenth century, but they faltered after the Great War as claims to European cultural superiority became unsustainable and criticism began to accumulate. Domestic European or American criticisms focused on welfare issues (such as slavery, recreational drug use and prostitution) and there were calls for political reform. There were calls for the eventual independence implied in legitimating ideologies of empire. Nationalist criticism developed as elements of local elites learned the political vocabulary of nation and state; they argued for independence; many nationalisms were proposed, usually with ethnicity as a base; some succeeded and some did not. Pan-Asianist ideologies were presented, some influential. Religious traditions were invoked, some influential.[13] All through the 1920s and 1930s these criticisms were heard, and as systemic tensions accumulated these alternate readings gained influence.

Security change occurred as accumulated systemic tensions disposed critics to violence; a series of outbreaks of insurrectionary violence occured. The break was made in China; the southern revolutionary forces launched one more insurrection and this time it was successful; Imperial China collapsed. However, contrary to the intentions of the insurrectionists, violence became endemic; there were a succession of wars, including civil wars, interstate wars, colonial wars, wars of colonial succession, cold wars, peasant-based guerrilla wars and state terrorist wars. The violence was indiscriminate; it embraced whole peoples. The sequence came to an end with the re-unification of Vietnam; there are ongoing problems with residual issues from civil wars, residual issues from the Pacific War and residual issues from the cold war; whilst these are serious, the general crisis has passed.

The crisis unfolded at different times within the territories of the region: the descent into chaos in China; Imperial Japanese aggression; the collapse of the European and American empires; the widespread chaos of the Pacific War;[14] the post-war struggles for independence; and the sequence of cold war proxy conflicts. The establishment of regimes definitively oriented towards national development marked the end of the crisis; they secured an equal autonomous participation in the modern world; the aspiration which had presaged collapse.

The onset/resolution of the crisis has various dates:

- Region 1911–75
- Singapore 1941–65
- Hong Kong 1941–67/97
- Malaysia 1941–57
- Thailand 1932–45/92
- Japan 1931–52
- China 1911–78

The dating is inevitably somewhat arbitrary; that there was a crisis is clear. Individual country experiences varied: in Singapore, colonial rule collapsed with war and independence began only in 1965, a crisis period of twenty-plus years; in Hong Kong, colonial rule collapsed in 1941, was resumed in 1945 and ran on until 1967, when contemporary Hong Kong took shape, a period of thirty-plus years; Malaysia too was occupied in 1941 but attained independence in 1957; Japan's crisis ran from the descent into war through to the resumption of sovereignty; China, which led the region into crisis, began the process of recoverery only with the reform programmes of 1978, a period of more than sixty years. Overall, the general crisis of the region ran from 1911 to 1975, some sixty-four years. The dates of other countries could be noted; the crisis was long drawn out in places; and there are unresolved problems, residuals, both in the form of direct issues in Korea and Taiwan and in the guise of more subtle questions of self-understanding and official memory in Japan, China and the USA. The immediate British sphere involved Singapore and Hong Kong; more broadly, the formal empire and the informal territories based around Bangkok and Shanghai.

The crisis engulfed the region; the process of collapse/recovery was not confined within juridical borders; nor was the process of collapse/recovery confined within the borders of extant socio-cultural units; the process of collapse/recovery remade existing juridical and socio-cultural territories; the process made nation-states; the contemporary regional pattern of nation-states emerged from this general crisis; elites embraced projects of national development; they secured an equal autonomous place in the modern world.

The general crisis in East Asia unfolded through a sequence of inter-related wars. The social dislocation, economic destruction and human loss were very great; East Asia rehearsed the experience of early twentieth-century Europe with regard to the scale of the general crisis. Social breakdown, political ambition and assorted dreams of territorial aggrandizement precipitated a broad collapse into warfare; once the downward spiral of war had begun it proved difficult to stop: the early phase involved Chinese insurrectionary violence, the 1911 Revolution, warlordism and an extended civil war; a subsequent phase involved a Sino-Japanese war, chaotic at the time, incomprehensible in retrospect; the third phase assimilated the Pacific War to the wider Second World War; thereafter a series of wars of colonial retreat were made more intractable by their assimilation into the putative logic of cold war; until, finally, nation-states began one by one to emerge from the crisis and establish their own projects of national development.

The sequence involved multiple conflicts:

- 1911–14 Chinese Revolution;
- 1914–16 Yuan Shikai Interval;
- 1916–26 Warlord Era;

62 *General crisis*

- 1918–41 Anti-Colonial Movements;
- 1926–28 Northern Expedition;
- 1927–37 First Chinese Civil War;
- 1931–34 Jiangxi Soviet;
- 1931–32 Japanese invasion of Manchuria;
- 1932–37 Japanese expansion in Northern China;
- 1937–45 Sino-Japanese War;
- 1941–45 Pacific War;
- 1945–50 Indonesian Revolution;
- 1946–51 Huk Rebellion;[15]
- 1946–49 Second Chinese Civil War;
- 1946–54 First Indo-China War;
- 1948–60 Malayan Emergency;
- 1950–53 Korean War;
- 1963–66 Konfrontasi;
- 1965–68 Indonesian coup/regime change;
- 1966–69 Cultural Revolution;
- 1953–93 Cambodian wars;
- 1953–75 Laos conflicts;
- 1954–75 Second Indo-China War;
- 1978–91 Third Indo-China War.

These conflicts included civil strife, interstate warfare, anti-colonial struggles, class-based insurrections and numerous cold war proxy exchanges.[16] They were fought using modern weapons; they were fought at great cost to civilian populations; they often involved outsiders as either interested allies or simple invaders; and these wars radically disrupted extant forms of life. The costs of this sequence of interlinked conflicts were very high; not only were there multiple interlinked conflicts but warfare had become more destructive. In the pre-modern period fighting usually involved only armies, with cities and peoples regarded as valuable prizes, but in the modern period new technology meant better killing rates[17] and an appreciation of the importance of industrial resources, which now became targets; analysts spoke of total war. Pre-modern wars recorded high casualty rates amongst the military, whereas modern wars record high casualty rates amongst both the military and civilians.[18] In the later phases of the crisis air power was been a particular contributor to civilian deaths; in Europe, from Guernica to Dresden; in East Asia, from numerous Chinese cities through to Hiroshima, Nagasaki and the peoples of Korea and Indo-China.

Some idea of scale can be gained from the numbers; the casualties were high:[19]

- Warlords and civil war   1916–37   4,000,000
- Chinese civil war   1945–49   2,500,000

- Sino-Japanese and Pacific War   12,600,000
- Southeast Asia Occupations   5,000,000
- Korean War   800,000
- First Indo-China War   1945–54   600,000
- Second Indo-China War   1960–75   2,700,000
- Indonesian Regime Change   1965   500,000
- Third Indo-China War   1978–91   1,500,000
                                     Total: 31,200,000

The general crisis marked the collapse of elite/mass efforts to accommodate the demands of the modern world; there was systemic collapse; elites knew neither how to order their communities nor where to direct their aspirations; a spiral of conflict dragged entire societies into ruinous wars; however, the general crisis also undermined the empires of the colonial powers and as a matter of report the recovery of local autonomy was achieved through the experience of radical collapse. The scale of the collapse is difficult to grasp in retrospect, for whilst the post-Second World War years have seen many small wars there has been no general conflagration on the scale of the early twentieth-century crises. The general crisis was the environment within which subsequently familiar figures made their first moves within their political realms.[20]

Unfolding general crisis

A number of conflicts marked the general crisis; established political balances collapsed; China collapsed into revolutionary violence, warlord-ism and civil war; Imperial Japan engaged in aggressive war against its neighbours; and European powers were confronted with Japanese aggression, colonial revolt and wars of colonial withdrawal. The dissolution of empire required the establishment of successor political units; nation-states formed; however, as a semblance of order was restored the region was enveloped in the multiple coils of the cold war. The cold war in East Asia has its occasion in American geo-strategic competition with the USSR and, somewhat later, the People's Republic of China. In the last stages of the Second World War opinion within US political elites shifted decisively in favour of competition rather than cooperation with the Soviets; in Northeast Asia, notwithstanding agreements made at Yalta there was a desire to end the fighting before the Soviet armies could become involved, and similarly there was a desire on the part of the Soviets to get their troops involved before the Japanese defeat.[21] Thereafter the competition moved to the Korean peninsula and as a result of the open warfare the USA extended its cold war operations throughout the region. It was within these very difficult circumstances that the new nation-states of East Asia made their appearance and began their post-war drives for national development.

64 *General crisis*

Revolutionary conflicts, warlordism (1911–26) and civil war (1927–37)

The final years of Imperial China are chaotic.[22] The Qing regime inaugurated some top-down governance reforms in 1909 as it tried to create a strong central bureaucracy; this would have been the key mechanism in a drive to secure modernization from above; however, there was no social base available to support such reforms, so they were too little too late.[23] At this time there were numerous revolutionary groups which agitated, organized and attempted armed uprisings. The power of the central authorities was dissolving away, with local figures seeking to take control; some were reactionary, others pragmatic, whilst others looked to a novel future for China. Sun Yat-sen was a key figure in the anti-Manchu Revolutionary Alliance, based in the south with links outside China amongst the diasporas in Hong Kong and the Nanyang. Sun spent much time travelling, seeking support and financing. After numerous failed rebellions, one gathered support amongst the elites in fifteen provinces, at which point the Imperial Court asked General Yuan Shikai to assist, and after negotiations the Court agreed to abdicate: the Qing empire was dissolved and in principle a republic was established. However, the confusions continued. Yuan was named as first president in 1911 but attempts to establish republic foundered. A parliament was convened in 1913 with the Nationalist Party (the successor to the Revolutionary Alliance) as the dominant group, but Yuan ignored it. In 1913 the Second Revolution against Yuan failed and from 1913–16 Yuan headed a military dictatorship, at one point declaring himself emperor. Matters did not improve with Yuan's death as his rule was succeeded by the general disintegration of the warlord period of 1916–28.[24] The warlord groups were constituted by any local group with military power, including ex-generals, gangsters, governors of provinces, local strongmen and bandit groups (producing in response local village defence units). The country was radically insecure. There were two main groups of warlords, northern and southern, with further sub-groupings: the northern group had Anfu Clique and Chihli Clique, plus a third major northern warlord was backed by the Japanese in Manchuria. There were continually shifting alliances between these and smaller warlords and they generated multiple local-level wars. It was in this environment that the Nationalist Party and the Communist Party sought to collaborate in the task of reconstructing China. The alliance was short lived and from 1927 the two parties were the key players in a long-running civil war.

The Nationalist Party was established in 1912. After the rise of Yuan the party was one more relatively weak group; however, it was organized and it sought to unify the country. At the same time factions within the party viewed the numerically small but increasingly influential communists with suspicion. The party had two wings, each with different social bases: left leaning (reformers, with a base among peasants and urban radicals) and right leaning (conservative, with a base among landowners, the gentry and urban industrialists). The environment was one of political and intellectual change: in 1915 there was the New Culture Movement, with intellectuals/ students; on 4 May 1919 there were student protests against Versailles Treaty discussions awarding Shandong to Japan; and from 1917 there was growing interest in Marxism–Leninism. There were also some reactions reaffirming traditional China. The overall concern was for the future; the common goal was a China free from feudalism, imperialism and violence, but multiple factions manoeuvred for power. Sun died in 1925. Chiang Kai-Shek established a base in the military and manoeuvred for power within Kuomintang, which he controlled by 1926.[25] Chiang was a conservative authoritarian; the New Life Movement was established in 1934; modelled on European fascisms (leadership and moral example), it adopted an ambiguous stance towards the cultural package of modernity; Chiang was an effective warlord.[26]

The Communist Party was established in 1921. The Soviet Union offered support and Comintern agents travelled to China; ambiguous advice mixed rational analysis of the Chinese situation (a rural, agrarian, largely peasant population with few modern cities and fewer proletarians) with the requirements of Soviet foreign policy (protect the Soviet Union). The latter was central when the Second World War commenced. Overall, it was a positive relationship, albeit with some significant tensions.[27] One strand of advice related to the nationalists; the Soviet Union urged cooperation. The first United Front was formed in 1924 and the intention was to defeat the warlords and to unify China; the Soviet Union encouraged doubtful communists. The two parties had intermingled memberships and ideologies but they had different sources of support within the population communists from the poor, nationalists from the better-off – and their elites manoeuvred for position. In the event the relationship did not develop well for the communists; the break came with the Northern Expedition.

Chiang begins the Northern Expedition in 1926. It is a joint nationalist and communist military advance designed to suppress local warlords and unify the country. It is successful and the armies sweep northwards from their southern bases, gathering support along the way. However, there are latent tensions amongst these nominal allies; in rural areas communists have opposed landowners and in urban areas they have been organizing unions and strikes; the groups that bear the burdens of these attacks are the reform-minded bourgeoisie, who support the nationalists. Chiang's allies amongst landowners and industrialists are decidedly unhappy. Chiang decides to break with the communists. In April 1927 in Shanghai Chiang's allies attack the local communist groups. The episode is violent and the Communist Party in Shanghai is largely destroyed. The anti-communist suppression continues throughout the territories controlled by the nationalists. The nationalists are successful; they make a series of deals with local warlords and manage to unify the country in 1928. Their capital is Nanjing and the period 1927–37 sees economic advance. Shanghai becomes a key city in China, a link in a global chain of trading cities.

66 *General crisis*

The defeated Communist Party retreats to a number of rural base areas;[28] these are located in places remote from the main centres of population and provide a place where the communists can both recover and regroup. In central southern China the Jianxi Soviet (1931–34) is developed along communist lines. However, the nationalist government looks to suppress the experiment and begins a series of nationalist military encirclement actions designed to extirpate this remnant of the Communist Party. The nationalists launch five campaigns – which bring great destruction to the area – before forcing the Communist Party to retreat. The 1934–35 Long March records the efforts of the remnant communists to escape and regroup. A march of several thousand miles brings the communist army to the north of the country. The Yan'an base area in Shaanxi Province is established. The nationalists plan to attack but in late 1936 Chiang Kai-Shek is obliged[29] to enter a second United Front. The intention is to resist the Japanese; however, as the Imperial Japanese invade there is little cooperation and after initial nationalist defeats at the hands of the Imperial Japanese there is little resistance; Chiang and Mao both realize that with the USA and Soviet Union embroiled in war it is only a matter of time until Imperial Japan is defeated; the Pacific War years become, in effect, a pause in the Chinese civil war.

Japan, Northeast Asia, China and the Pacific War

The Japanese response to the practical demands of the modern industrial-capitalist world mixed adoption and rejection plus a defensive insistence upon the particularity of the Japanese.[30] The elite noted the fate of China and initiated a drive for development; a related set of concerns grew in respect of the other countries of East Asia; the elite reasoned that the old tributary relationships with China which had ordered East Asia for centuries were no longer appropriate to the new global system; the Japanese embraced an imagined responsibility.[31] In the event, the interests of three governments came into conflict in respect of Korea: Japanese, Chinese and Russian. The hostilities which began in Korea drew in Taiwan and came to involve Manchuria. In Korea the elite had shown only intermittent interest in the activities of incoming Europeans and Americans; the kingdom turned inwards; extra-regional and regional powers were anxious to end this isolation; as pressure mounted in the nineteenth century the local Yi Dynasty collapsed into rival groups; internal confusion meant that the elite was unable to resist outside pressures; Koreans became pawns in the manoeuvres of their neighbours. The Japanese movement into Korea, which had traditionally had tributary relations with China,[32] began in the late nineteenth century as an attempt to prize the territory away from the influence of China whilst at the same time blocking the advance of Russian influence. Japan imposed unequal treaties on Korea in 1876; the Japanese struggled with the Chinese for dominance; both governments stationed troops in the country from 1882. These concerns issued in war against China in 1894–95. In the Sino-Japanese War the Japanese defeated the Chinese;[33] after the war the Japanese sought to pursue development. However, conflicts with Russia also broke out; the Russo-Japanese war of 1904–05 resulted in a significant naval victory for the Japanese but there was a costly stalemate in the ground war; after negotiations the Japanese prevailed; Korea became a protectorate in 1905 and was annexed in 1910; the Japanese also enhanced their position in Manchuria; as Japan became a recognized power, late development was complemented by late imperialism.[34]

The Imperial Japanese empire in Northeast Asia comprised the three territories of Korea, Taiwan and Manchuria. In Korea the subsequent development can be analysed in terms of shifting patterns of class-based production; colonial exploitation and development; and some industrialization, particularly in the north, but it was not until the 1930s that the production demands of rearmament generated significant industrial development.[35] However, the occupation also acted to undermine established Korean culture as Japanese models of education, language and family names were imposed. The colonial regime drew protests; the March First Movement 1919 was repressed;[36] exploitation and oppression reached a peak during the Pacific War. A similar trajectory encompassed Taiwan. The island had been a remote territory of the Chinese Empire for centuries; it began to attract mainland immigration in the seventeenth century when the Dutch established a trading base in the southern part of the island; the territory was absorbed within the Chinese sphere in 1683 by the Qing Dynasty; the island remained a backwater; following the Sino-Japanese war of 1894–05 the island was ceded to the Japanese. The Japanese inaugurated a development programme in Taiwan; the Japanese built infrastructure, reformed landholdings and introduced agricultural extension services; exports to Japan grew; later in the 1930s there was a measure of industrialization; the territory developed within the colonial system; a modest prosperity developed. Such modest prosperity was also secured in the final area of the new empire, Manchuria. The territory had been poor and relatively sparsely populated; it became an area of concern in the later years of the nineteenth century; it was the heartland of the Manchu Dynasty, which has displaced the Ming; the territory abutted the lands of the Russian Empire, which had expanded eastwards over the nineteenth century and looked to the territory of Manchuria as a route to the warmer, more southern seas; the Japanese looked to Manchuria as an element of a sphere of control and stability surrounding the home islands. After the Japanese victory over the Russian empire in 1904–05 the Japanese increased their involvement in Manchuria; the South Manchurian Railway Company was important; the Japanese slowly displaced the influence of the Chinese and Russians; the area became a major centre of influence and concern for the Japanese army; the area was extensively developed and eventually was given a nominal independence in 1932 as the state of Manchukuo.

68 *General crisis*

The Great War provided the Japanese government with an opportunity for expansion by taking over German interests in China and certain Pacific islands. At the same time the various Japanese concerns with China were summarized in the guise of the 1915 'Twenty-One Demands' in respect of privileging Japanese interests in China. After the war the Versailles Treaty left the Japanese with their gains, although not with full Western approval. In the 1920s Japan joined in the discussions of the Great Powers and was party to decisions designed to stabilize the situation in East Asia. However, also in the 1920s and 1930s there were new domestic developments as the Meiji oligarchs and their immediate successors slowly left the political scene. This had the effect of removing an important source of ideas in respect of the appropriate trajectory of development for Japan. There was a measure of democratization in the Taisho period and the beginnings of more extensive party political activity but the Great Depression of the 1930s had severe consequences for Japan; it effectively destroyed the Taisho democracy. The collapse in world trade effectively extracted the Japanese from the international system within which they had operated and propelled them into a self-contained East Asian yen block. At the same time the economic slump created a mass of unemployed in Japan, with strikes in urban areas and widespread poverty in rural areas, and the proponents of ultra-nationalism found support in these areas. In this environment of political confusion the nationalist and militarist right wing came to the fore. The drift towards military rule in Japan began early in the century; there was the success of the Meij Era's victorious wars against China and Russia; and continuing intermittent conflict with China encouraged the military to assume a greater role within the polity; in the 1930s the military had very great power; by the late 1930s Imperial Japan was in effect a military dictatorship.[37]

The regime drifted into an all-out war against China in 1937; the Imperial Japanese engagement with China began in the late nineteenth century;[38] it gathered pace thereafter, issuing in invasion in the late 1930s. Japan's shift to the modern world had been informed by the quasi-colonization of the hitherto regional centre, China, and by the positive example of the Europeans and Americans;[39] elite desires for success co-mingled development[40] and empire.[41] Tanaka[42] identifies Japan's Orient: as the core power of East Asia was ruined, Japan was obliged to take up the burden of leadership. A colonial sphere was constructed in the Korean peninsula, Manchuria, the Ryukyu Islands, the Kurile Islands, Sakhalin, Formosa, certain islands in the Pacific and China. The campaigns in China began in the north in Manchuria and then slowly extended towards Beijing. With full-scale war the Japanese armies conquered the northern part of China and moved inland along the Yangtze river. The nationalists were defeated in battle around Shanghai and they began a long retreat to what became their wartime capital in Chongqing. They received supplies from the British and Americans. The American forces also offered military advice. The Japanese also captured large areas in southern China, in particular the coastal areas, including Hong Kong.[43] The Japanese military advance was steady, albeit somewhat directionless.[44] Notwithstanding military reverses elsewhere, there were further Japanese advances in 1944 until virtually most of the eastern part of the country was occupied.

Japanese involvement in China had heightened international tensions;[45] European governments were weak and exposed, offering muted protests; the American government progressively sanctioned the Japanese with restrictions on trade: problems accumulated. The diplomatic exchanges of the American and the Japanese failed to resolve matters. Southeast Asia and large areas of the Pacific were drawn into the conflict when the Japanese armed forces launched a series of attacks across the northern Pacific area; the 1941–45 Pacific War ensued.

The Pacific War

As the general crisis unfolded a number of conflicts came to overlap: the Chinese Civil War, the Sino-Japanese War and the Pacific War ran into one another and the result was a general war in East Asia. The trigger for the wider encompassing conflict was the clash between Imperial Japan and the USA in respect of the actions of the former country in China. A schedule of American economic sanctions – in regarding particular oil and scrap iron – put intense pressure upon the Japanese elite as both materials were vital for war making; in particular, the oil embargo placed the Japanese naval fleet in jeopardy, as with no fuel oil it would be unable to operate. There were debates amongst the military and political elite as to the appropriate response; war was canvassed, with two options considered – a drive towards the south to capture the resources of Southeast Asia and a move towards the north to confront the Soviet Union. The Imperial Japanese elite did not want to add war with the Soviet Union and the USA plus Europeans to their existing war in China. The option of discontinuing their war in China and seeking a rapprochement with the USA was rejected.[46] There was significant confusion in Japanese thinking; in the event the Japanese launched a war against the American and European holdings in the Pacific region. In the space of six months they drove the Americans out of the Philippines, the Dutch out of the Dutch East Indies, the British out of Hong Kong, Malaya and Burma;[47] they neutralized the French in Indo-China, found allies in Thailand[48] and all European and American holdings in China were seized. It was a dazzling military victory.

The military campaigns of the Pacific War comprised several main elements: there was a rapid Japanese advance over a vast area of territory in Southeast Asia and the Pacific secured by naval and air force power; these holdings were additional to the vast land territories seized in Northeast Asia and China. At the height of their expansion the Japanese controlled Korea, Manchuria, most of China, Indo-China, Southeast Asia and a spread of islands in the Central and South Pacific. The expansion destroyed the European empires and their armed forces in the region; the British fought on the Indian/Burmese border;[49] Australians fought in the South Pacific and in China both the nationalists and the communists fought intermittent campaigns; however, the main response to Japanese aggression was made by the United States. In early 1942 the Japanese decided to extend their Pacific Ocean perimeter by seizing the island of Midway; this resulted in a catastrophic naval defeat at the hands of the American fleet; it meant that after around six months of war the military initiative in the Pacific passed to the Americans. The American advanced along two axes – they moved along the Solomon Islands chain towards the Philippines and along a string of Central Pacific islands directly towards Japan. It was a naval and air force campaign. The fighting was severe but in contrast to other war theatres produced relatively low casualty rates. The Americans invaded the Philippines in 1944 and destroyed the bulk of the remaining Japanese navy. In the Central Pacific American forces advanced island by island, and when the island of Saipan was captured in 1944 the Japanese home islands were in range of heavy bomber aircraft.[50] At this point the American military forces had overwhelmed the Japanese naval and air forces and the result of the conflict was now an inevitable crushing defeat for the Japanese; the American air force proceeded to systematically destroy the cities of Japan, whilst at the same time the remnants of the Japanese navy and merchant marine were destroyed.

The final stages of the military campaign brought the political aspect of war to the forefront as the Americans, Soviets, Europeans and Japanese looked to the nature of the inevitable defeat and the subsequent trajectory of Japan. There were mixed motives amongst the participants of these exchanges: the USA sought to protect its key position; the Soviet Union sought to secure promises made at Yalta; Chinese factions sought advantage ahead of their renewed civil war; Europeans looked to recover their empire holdings; whilst the Japanese elite were faced with accommodating national catastrophe. The end of the Pacific War flowed into renewed civil war and the nascent cold war. A particular competition for influence in Northeast Asia developed between the Americans and the Soviet Union. The Japanese nursed hopes that the Soviets would not participate in the war; however, Soviet involvement had been agreed at Yalta; Soviet invasions of Japanese-held Manchuria removed the last futile hopes of the Japanese elite that they might somehow escape defeat.[51] In August 1945 the Japanese government surrendered unconditionally; the American-dominated Supreme Commander for the Allied Powers (SCAP) authorities occupied Japan; the country was subject to enforced reform.[52] And the Japanese empire was dismantled. Overall East Asian casualties were around 20 million; the war caused extensive damage; cities in Japan, China, Indo-China and Southeast Asia were destroyed; the economic base of the countries was weakened; established economic linkages were disrupted. There was social and political disruption;[53] established order broke down;[54] military rule was established; new political groups sought power; colonial territories were reoccupied; these moves were opposed by local national leaderships, and there were a number of wars of colonial retreat.

The wars of colonial retreat

In the years following the end of the Pacific War the SCAP authorities repatriated Japanese troops and stripped the Japanese of their empire. European and American colonial empires also dissolved. In many cases withdrawal from the territories of colonial empires was attended by violence and in some cases by foreign intervention.

Indonesian independence was secured after a confused exchange involving the British, Dutch and local groups. The occupying Japanese had encouraged nascent Indonesian nationalism and a youth movement came to provide the core of an Indonesian army. As the war ended, a small group of nationalist leaders proclaimed the independence of the putative country Indonesia. The Dutch tried to recover their colony and they received help from the British whilst they were opposed by the Indonesian nationalists. There was a confused period of manoeuvring and there were two short wars. The Indonesians received international sympathy (in particular, the Americans were not disposed to help the Dutch) and the Dutch withdrew.[55] The Republic of Indonesia was formed but that was not the end of the conflicts as there were disputes with neighbours about related political projects; in particular, the Indonesian government was unsympathetic to the British plans to make a federation of their territories in the Malay peninsula and northern Borneo; a low-level guerrilla war followed before the Indonesian elite finally acquiesced in the pattern of British withdrawal.

The British military advanced from India into Burma and thence at the war's end to Malaya, Singapore and Hong Kong, along the arc[56] of their Southeast Asian empire. The British withdrawal from Burma left a civil war in progress amongst the Burmese and between the Burmese and minority ethic groups; later British withdrawal from India overlapped with partition and there were population exchanges and conflict. In Malaya they tried to recover their colony as it had been a major dollar earner in pre-war days. They had some ambiguous success; the Malay elite were not averse to the British presence in the context of an ethnically divided population and nor were the Chinese, who had acted as resistance allies of the British during the war. However, the British quickly realized that colonialism was untenable and they manoeuvred to put in place a conservative Malay successor elite. The ethnic tensions plus the nascent cold war added complications and their erstwhile Malayan Communist Party ally unexpectedly opted for military revolt.[57] A guerrilla campaign began and the British organized a successful counter-insurgency campaign. The conflict ran for twelve years until the preferred conservative Malay group secured power. The British also had to deal with the Indonesian government's policy of konfrontasi – a low-level

72 *General crisis*

guerrilla war which ran on until 1965. And in the midst of these confusions, ethnic tensions led to riots in Singapore and the ejection of that territory from a unified Malaysia. Subsequent conflicts were domestic as the Malaysian and Singaporean governments established their respective rule in the face of assorted dissenters.

Matters followed a not dissimilar trajectory in the Philippines. The American military recaptured the islands in late 1944; there was inevitably considerable damage and loss of life. The Americans return the landed elite to power; independence was organized; elections were manipulated so as to exclude opposition groups. Subsequent rebellions by impoverished peasants were inconvenient to the elite and were read in cold war terms; the Americans involved themselves in their suppression and a long drawn-out low-level war ensued;[58] these conflicts continued intermittently for decades.

Finally, colonial withdrawal issued in two long drawn-out wars, and in both cases the exercise of the dissolution of empire was confused by the logic of cold war and foreign intervention: Korea and Indo-China. The former followed Japanese withdrawal so can be treated as a product of the cold war; the later involved both colonial and cold wars. The British occupied Vietnam after the Japanese surrender; they were met by local nationalists; however, the British allowed the French to return.[59] The French attempted to re-establish their colony; the British assisted; local nationalists offered resistance; political discussions dragged on for around a year but French intransigence proved unhelpful. Eventually, fighting broke out and the French attempted to re-conquer the territory. However, it slowly became clear that their colonial rule was unsustainable and in seeking advantageous terms for peace negotiations they contrived a military engagement at Dien Bein Phu; it was a debacle; the French withdrawal thereafter was rapid. However, the war was now read by the Americans in cold war terms; they replaced the French and installed a puppet government which they armed – sustaining thereby a second lengthy war.

The Chinese Civil War (1946–49)

The developing cold war was given impetus by the result of the civil war in China. After the Pacific War the USA continued to finance and arm Chiang Kai-Shek; Hong Kong[60] was a transit point for Chiang's best troops as they were resupplied by Americans and moved north; the Communist Party came into possession of large stocks of weapons captured by Soviet forces in Manchuria; there was a lull in the fighting; Chiang Kai-Shek's forces then advanced into Manchuria. The nationalists had superior material and this underpinned an expectation of rapid victory. However, the better organized and highly motivated Red Army defeated them quickly. The Red Army quickly advanced south and Mao declared the People's Republic in 1949. The defeated nationalists fled to Taiwan; the local Taiwanese were violently suppressed and the island population was divided. Chiang ruled as a

US-backed military dictator until his death in 1975. Thereafter there were political reforms; however, the tensions across the Taiwan Straits continue down to the present.

The American political establishment reacted badly to the defeat of the nationalists, Chiang Kai-Shek had been seen as a modernizing figure; Madame Chiang was a well-connected figure in Washington; domestic American political conflicts were fuelled by the conflicts in China; the episode was drawn into burgeoning anti-communist sentiment.[61] The American determination to reorder the post-Second World War world (in politics via the United Nations and in economics via the machinery of Bretton Woods) became skewed; an originally universal intention was restricted; the realm of state socialism was denied political legitimacy and so far as was possible excluded from the new global settlement. The apparatus of the cold war was constructed; the cold war began; in East Asia it cut across the attempts of post-colonial governments to chart paths to the future; in East Asia it also included a series of brutal unnecessary wars.

Cold Wars: The Korean War

The USA provided military and financial aid to the Chinese nationalist forces during the Pacific War;[62] domestic American anti-communism disposed them to read the establishment of the People's Republic in hostile terms; American right-wingers spoke of 'losing China;' and it was seen as one more instance of the international communist threat. American involvement in Korea embraced the same logic and the Korean War became a key cold war myth; it is understood as a partial victory against expansionist international communism. But the reality is different. Korea had been an unequal feudal society; Japanese colonialism had mixed exploitation, repression and development but the country remained unequal and largely agrarian. There were deep-rooted class conflicts.[63] As the Pacific War ended, the Japanese handed power to local Korean groups, who assumed power in the process of grass-roots national liberation. However, outside forces had become interested in the fate of the peninsula. At Yalta, Korea had been placed in the Soviet sphere but the US changed their minds, the Soviets acquiesced and a division was imposed along the 38th parallel. As American forces moved into the south they were met with open rebellions; in the north a communist government was more subtly established. Two states were formed[64] and the foreign powers withdrew; however, there were further local-level provocations until the north invaded the south. The war drew in the Americans and in turn their actions invited Chinese intervention. This futile war killed millions of Koreans and ended in stalemate; the north became an inward-looking authoritarian communist state, while the south enjoyed a series of US-backed cold war military dictators, embracing democracy only in the late 1990s.[65]

The establishment of the People's Republic of China, plus the Korean War, confirmed for the home-grown US anti-communists that their Manichean

74 *General crisis*

views were correct; the cold war came to East Asia, and once the apparatus of cold war was in place it reached throughout the region and local nationalists or reformers were routinely characterized by their domestic opponents as communist and either they were attacked directly or local elites were supported by the Americans in their strategies of repression.[66]

Cold Wars: First Indo-China War (1946–54)

The French endeavoured to reoccupy Vietnam;[67] the Vietnamese resisted. The French persuaded the Americans that their war was an anti-communist struggle; they received support. The war dragged on. The French sought to strengthen their position ahead of talks with a projected decisive battle at Dien Bien Phu; after military defeat they acknowledged their position was untenable and sought to withdraw. In 1954 in Geneva there were peace discussions; the country was divided in advance of elections and reunification. The American involvement deepened; disregarding the terms of the Geneva agreement, they established a puppet state in south Vietnam; American activities drew in other Indo-Chinese countries; Thailand became a key base area for US operations, which were permitted by the military regime in power.[68]

Cold Wars: Second Indo-China War (1960–75)

After the Geneva agreements, the US sought to block the influence of the communist party in South Vietnam; however, local communists were backed by the north and eventually they resumed fighting. The South Vietnamese forces could not control the situation. The Americans had had military advisors in Vietnam since the mid-1950s but in 1965 as the security situation deteriorated the American army was deployed and extensive military operations followed. The American forces were confident, but there was domestic US opposition and the 1968 Tet Offensive launched by the southern allies of the north Vietnamese persuaded Americans that a military victory was unattainable. The Americans began the slow process of disengagement; the Americans withdrew in 1973; fighting intensified; the war ended in 1975.

Cold Wars: Third Indo-China War (1978–91)

The war in Vietnam had wider repercussions; there had been US-sponsored interference in the domestic politics of Cambodia, Laos and Thailand. In Cambodia the Khmer Rouge came to power in Phnom Penh in the confusions of American defeat. It was a peasant movement inspired in part by Maoist celebrations of peasant activism. Urban populations were relocated to the countryside; the process was accompanied by extensive violence; domestic violence spilled over the border and there were clashes with

Cambodia's erstwhile socialist neighbour Vietnam; finally, in 1978, the Vietnamese army invaded, removed the Khmer Rouge and installed a new government. The Americans took the opportunity for revenge on the Vietnamese and backed the Pol Pot regime; and so too did China; so too did ASEAN. The Thai military made their border territory available for a collection of guerrilla groups as the Khmer Rouge were joined by others and as the Americans and their supporters sought to make their interference minimally respectable. The Vietnamese withdrew in 1991 paving the way for a UN-supervised election; this returned the Vietnamese favourite to power; however, by this time the Americans and Chinese were no longer anxious to punish Vietnam; the countries of Indo-China joined ASEAN. The achievement of a fragile peace in Cambodia marked the end of some forty-five years of warfare in Indo-China, much of it sustained by outsiders for their own usually ignoble purposes.

Crisis, memory and recovery

The general crisis,[69] in particular the wars, has been read into official and popular memory in a number of ways; predictably, there are multiple official national pasts; internationally they are occasions for conflict;[70] domestically they are areas of continuing debate;[71] and any simple resolution in either sphere is unlikely.[72] Memories do not subsist outside social relationships;[73] memories are constructed and reconstructed; and agents located variously within the social sphere produce, disseminate and consume more or less critically these memories. In considering the social locations available, schematically one might speak of three interrelated scales, macro, meso and micro: first, the macro scale concerns empires and states, and they produce national pasts and adopt official positions; second, the meso scale concerns organizations and groups, and they too adopt official positions and keep official records; and, third, the micro scale concerns groups and individuals, and they sustain folk memory, plus individuals have their own memories.

The general crisis marked the rejection of colonial-era mediated modernity; local elites sought novel routes to the future; a multiplicity of social groups fashioned numerous local responses; and a lengthy period of confusion followed. This can be seen to have had a number of substantive centres of activity, and around these memories have accumulated: the Chinese Civil War; Imperial Japanese wars; the fall of the European empires;[74] and the engagements of the USA. These activities/memories have fed into the post-imperial phase of East Asian modernity: first, when replacement elites took power, the contexts in which they operated were bequeathed by the outcomes of the various wars; and, second, the ways of reading and reacting to their circumstances were given in part by extant memories. The later provided a complex set of ideas: agreements as to what had happened; agreements as to what needed to be learned; agreements as to which directions polities could reasonably advance in; and clear views as to which directions

76 *General crisis*

were closed. There were winners and losers. There were many losers: the destroyed empires; losers in civil wars; defeated rebellions; and suppressed political movements. There were many winners: new elites; newly powerful social groups; and regional powers. The winners tend to be remembered, losers forgotten; however, they too might be embraced in scholarly reflection.

The wars in China left domestic residues. A general view of the modern period labels the episode 'the century of humiliation'. There are the residues of an unfinished civil war. In respect of the Sino-Japanese conflicts there is bitterness against the aggressors and a disposition towards nationalist/racist hostility towards the Japanese. This is convenient to the elite, save when it becomes too popular and too energetically pursued. The Mao period has an ambiguous place; there were achievements in war, failures in development projects and a catastrophe in the late politics of cultural revolution. Meanwhile, outside China foreigners blamed the victim: China was seen as disorganized, corrupt, tragic and exciting.[75] Chiang's regime was seen as deeply corrupt.[76] Mao's regime was seen as unpalatable. The cold war imagery was negative but later the post-cold war imagery changed, with elite-level distrust (use of convenient stereotypical memory), corporate-world enthusiasm for trade and popular-level interest in cultural exchange (tourism, students, media, etc.). In recent years, the domestic and international imagery has slowly shifted with the idea of China's peaceful rise. Similarly, the Japanese wars left residues. Inside Japan there are multiple memories: Japanese nationalists (for whom Yasakuni Shrine is key symbolic site); the Japanese peace movement (for whom Hiroshima is key symbolic site); and the ordinary Japanese, who are not engaged. And outside Japan there are multiple memories. There is extensive Korean hostility. There is Chinese hostility. In Southeast Asia there are multiple ambiguous memories: harsh rule, in particular towards the Chinese, plus encouragement for independence movements. At the same time, many now look at Japan and see a rich, high-tech and peaceful country.[77] And the fall of the European empires in Southeast Asia produced residues: European generations that had known empire were bereft, whilst later generations did not notice. Externally, Europeans entered a new phase of history; America was now the global power; the European tasks outstanding were the dissolution of empire and the reconstruction of their own shattered continent. In the former territories of empire there were various memories: in Malaysia and Singapore, empire fell away into the background; in Indo-China the rule of the French was forgotten in years of cold war; in Indonesia there is an official memory of a victorious war of colonial liberation. And the final sometime colonial power is the USA, and here too there are accretions of memory. However, unlike the other colonial powers, it is still present in the region. Inside America[78] there was pre-war talk of a special relationship with China; the Pacific War was seen as a virtuous war resulting in a just victory; cold war engagement was seen as virtuous; and then later Japan became an ally, the cold war faded slowly and China was granted recognition.

Outside America, the Japanese see an ally, the Chinese a hegemonist competitor, and others a stabilizing security force and a crucial trading partner.

It might be noted, finally, that whilst the general crisis produced great disruption, a post-colonial modernity took shape; recovery has proceeded apace; and whilst development is uneven, the region is rich.

Uneven routes to the modern world

East Asia was drawn into the modern world through the experience of colonial rule, a mix of exploitation and development; it was a transient phenomenon.[79] European and American empires became unsustainable: demographics implied change;[80] metropolitan critics and indigenous nationalist elites urged change; as consent ebbed away the system declined; an agreed clear replacement order was unavailable; and the region dissolved into general crisis.[81] The general crisis involved numerous wars; there was extensive economic, social and political collapse; the resolution of these multiple interlinked problems extended over decades and it was not until the end of the Pacific War that effective action began in parts of the region. When action began it was clouded by cold war division: the American sphere was governed by the ideas of liberal markets, trade and liberal democracy; the former colonial area was governed by the ideas of national development (variant forms of liberal markets and liberal democracies); and China and its fellow socialist states turned to state-socialist national development. The long episode has left numerous residues – multiple memories, official, organizational, communal and individual. These ideas have in part shaped post-colonial modernities; elite understandings of already experience historical trajectories feed directly into the search for routes to the future.

Individual post-colonial elites pursued various projects. The core concern in all cases was with elite survival. In Japan economic nationalism drove recovery; in South Korea a nationalistic state development project began; in Taiwan national development was clouded by civil war and cold war as a military dictatorship laid futile plans to return to the mainland and built a developmental state incidentally; and in Hong Kong recolonization ensured continued prosperity and arrested development. In Southeast Asia a variety of projects were pursued: Thai military dictatorship; Filipino cleptocracy; Indonesian guided democracy followed by developmentalism; in Malaysia a corporate development; and in Singapore outward-directed development. Subsequent reform programmes in China confirmed the general pursuit of national development;[82] and the strategy was embraced in Indo-China. Recovery from general crisis was slow; but eventually most states pursued national development in some form or other.

The general crisis impacted Singapore and Hong Kong relatively late: in Singapore the period 1941–65 saw the chaos of war, the confusions of decolonization, the further confusions of federation and unexpected independence in 1965; in Singapore matters were clarified but in Hong Kong the relationship with China added further ambiguities to the situation. First, in Singapore the nature of the crisis was determined by the collapse of the empire; its wider system environment collapsed; a new direction was inevitable and its need quite obvious, and the type of direction eventually clear. The British had favoured federations in other parts of their disintegrating empire in a process of lumping together otherwise disparate bits of territory into something that looked like a state and maybe potentially a nation. In Southeast Asia the Malay peninsula, territories in northern Borneo and Singapore were slated for federation, but debates about constitutions made this awkward. Malaysia gained independence first, and Singapore asked for membership but the experiment failed and finally independent nation-statehood was embraced in the absence of alternatives. The elite pursued national development but later came to face problems attendant upon their success; external competitors responded to their economic success and local people sought alternatives to the government's disciplined focus on economic growth. And then in Hong Kong the nature of the crisis was different. It ran over the period 1941–67/97. At first, the collapse of empire then recolonization was accomplished, and the status quo ante was restored and subsequently maintained. There was elite-level collaboration between colonialists and local leaders;[83] there were some reforms locally and the population rallied to Hong Kong in 1967[84] and a quasi-national development project unfolded. In 1984 the Sino-British Joint Declaration was signed and the crisis was extended, as the reversion of the territory to China is problematical. It is a juridical quasi status quo ante,[85] a retrocession of territory to the successor state of the original treaty/lease maker, but substantively it is a development mismatch.[86] It is within these unusual structural circumstances that the elite of Hong Kong must fashion a route to the future. The local elite comprises factions; the local population evidences divergent political opinions; the territory has an absent political centre. Fashioning a route to the future in these circumstances could be difficult. Finally, it might be added that the sometime informal periphery – Bangkok and Shanghai – suffered during the general crisis. Shanghai was invaded by the Imperial Japanese and Bangkok was obliged to accommodate the Japanese. The crisis was resolved differently for these cities and both were permanently and definitively removed from the informal empire of the British. Thailand became an American-sponsored military dictatorship and a base for America's Indo-China wars, whereas Shanghai was absorbed into the Maoist socialist system of China.

5 New trajectories

At the outset, the incoming modern world made contact with extant forms of life only at the margin, as one more small group of traders in the environment of the local port of the local country power; however, as these exchanges deepened the colonial system came to be superimposed on extant patterns of life. It generated its own logic, centred on the contested compromises achieved by the multiplicity of players involved. It undermined extant patterns of life and, in time, provoked extensive change, as the apparatus of superimposed colonial rule was never going to be able to hold the system by force. Systemic crisis unfolded; the general crisis precipitated the Pacific War; the conflict swept away the empires; indeed, the global system of empires fragmented. The construction of a replacement of empire was not simple; local elites aspired to rule; local peoples had hopes of better material lives; and the former colonial powers – plus the now dominant power of the USA – required continuing access to those economic resources and networks which had brought them into empire making in the first place. The available model of political order embraced ideas of nation-states and a global community of states, ordered, imperfectly, for the moment, around the machineries of the United Nations and Bretton Woods. In this environment, local elites took their chance. The collapse of the colonial systems ushered in a domestic elite concern for active self-directed participation in the modern world. The institutional inheritance of the colonial era was reworked; a number of variants of corporate states served the projects of the elites. The broad pattern was the pursuit of national development; but there were multiple projects; there were multiple diverse trajectories; and each was delineated through shifting exchanges within the regional structures and beyond.[1] Change ran through East Asia; in the space of a few decades, patterns of political organization which had been put in place over centuries were overturned, and the familiar contemporary pattern of mostly new nation-states was constructed.

Changing circumstances, novel projects

As the general crisis receded new elites began the pursuit of new projects; a contingent sequence unfolded: in Japan an economic nationalist project

80 *New trajectories*

took hold[2] and prospered within the ambit of American cold war anti-communism; the former Japanese colonies of South Korea and Taiwan combined domestic anti-communist developmentally minded dictatorships with American cold war-inspired tutelage; in Indo-China, collapsing empires, local nationalism, available strongmen and American anti-communism combined to generate twenty-five years of warfare which ruined the area and long delayed the emergence of a species of national development project; in related areas of Southeast Asia, problems associated with decolonization, intra-regional tensions plus further American-sponsored cold war interventions and the creation of ASEAN combined to shape the emergence of various elite projects, including simple survival, spectacular theft, national development and a measure of nascent regional integration; and in China an autarchic peasant-centred development trajectory was established until it was sharply redirected along lines by now familiar within the East Asian region.

The disintegrating apparatus of the colonial era provided the resources and starting point for new elites; novel projects were perforce shaped by these starting points; domestic struggles and international relations further shaped their development; as individual domestic projects unfolded, their manifold interactions combined to create a regional pattern, at first disfigured by cold war, later underpinned by extensive economic based networks. It is this shifting and difficult environment which has shaped the development of Hong Kong and Singapore; it is this environment which shaped the development trajectory of the hitherto British peripheral colonial trading city Bangkok; it is this environment which shapes the rather different trajectory of the sometime outward-looking trading city of Shanghai.

Japanese elite economic nationalism

The Japanese elite-directed pursuit of national development after the Pacific War had a number of key features:[3]

- it was bureaucrat directed;
- it was business friendly;
- the politicians were subordinate but active participants;
- the population was highly disciplined;
- the focus of the efforts was to create a 'first class economy'.

The occupation authorities were led by General MacArthur (Supreme Commander Allied Powers). SCAP had several thousand Tokyo-based officials; they were divided into optimistic New Deal reformers and conservative realists. The reformers had the upper hand at first and sought to create a liberal-democratic Japan:

New trajectories 81

- the military were repatriated, demobilized and disbanded;
- the higher levels of bureaucracy were purged;
- the official state-Shinto religion was abolished;
- a programme was begun to break up big conglomerates (zaibatsu);
- a new constitution was promulgated and sovereignty was vested in the people;
- the continuing family was abolished;
- the emperor renounced his divine status and became a constitutional monarch;
- a bicameral parliament (lower/upper) with a cabinet system was established;
- a new education system was established, modelled on the US system;
- new labour laws were introduced (unions and strikes were allowed);
- new land laws redistributed land from landlords to family owner-farmers.

The occupation authorities' expectations of recovery were modest but the Japanese elite reaffirmed the goal sought since Meiji of a first-class economy. The period 1945–50 was very difficult:[4] there were many shortages of plant, materials, people and goods; the USA helped with money and food supplies; the USA hindered progress with some ill-considered economic reforms such as dismantling conglomerates and enforcing financially restrictive economic policies on an already weak economy; other reforms were ambiguous, as with free trades unions, but some reforms were helpful, for example land reform. The SCAP-mandated reforms continued until 1947 when the start of the cold war ensured that all attempts to reform Japan were abandoned as the country became an anti-communist ally of the USA. The Korean War of 1950–53 was a major help to the Japanese recovery:[5] the reforms of the economy were stopped and the key expectation now was production; Japan became a key base for the US army; local industry was given a massive injection of cash; and the conservative financial system, planning and repression of labour ushered in a state-centred business-dominated system oriented to production and exports.[6]

The economy recovered rapidly. The early phase of expansion ran through the 1950 and 1960s and was dominated by heavy industry; integrated steel mills were constructed on the coast, ships were built using mass production techniques and new chemical industries were established. A dual economy developed, with large conglomerates (salarymen running export-oriented high-tech industry) and small firms (family-based conglomerate suppliers, agriculture and services). The next phase in the 1970s was dominated by machinery, cars and consumer goods; there were problems of pollution, poor welfare services and the global oil shocks were recognized and addressed. The next phase, in the 1980s, involved higher-value-added science-based high-tech such as electronics, specialist steels, chemicals and new materials. A new problem emerged: the Japanese ran a large trade surplus on their American trade and they were accused of unfairly focusing on exporting whilst restricting access to their home market. The 1985 Plaza Accord revalued the yen against the dollar; it was anticipated that this would reduce the trade imbalance; in the event it provided a complex shock to the system as various agents responded to the new circumstances: domestic inflation and speculation in land created a bubble economy; the external relocation of Japanese productive activity plus aid, trade and foreign direct investment patterns established a production network throughout East Asia; there was some hollowing out and structural unemployment; and as the operating costs of industry were reduced, exports continued. Japanese government attempts to curb the expansion punctured the bubble economy in 1991 and there was a long 'golden recession' with low economic growth, a high rate of unemployment (for Japan), continued bad loan problems plus continued stability and prosperity. By the early 2000s the economy had recovered; the old pattern of political economy seemed intact but there were new anxieties about relations with the USA, the region and the implications of the rise of China.

The record has been much debated: the politics,[7] the economy[8] and the culture.[9] In terms of managing complex change, reading enfolding structures in order to formulate a political project, the Japanese elite have been consistent since the time of Meiji – they want a first-class economy and a place within the modern world.

South Korea and Taiwan

The Japanese experience inspired other East Asian elites, each constructing a distinctive variant. In each the state has been a key factor; so too the role of the USA.

The Japanese experience was influential in a number of interrelated ways:

- the importance of elite commitment to national development;
- the importance of working pragmatically within the existing global system;
- the importance of export-oriented development as a strategy of participation and upgrading;
- the importance of a disciplined domestic economic nationalism;
- the importance of clear domestic benefits from the elite-sponsored project.

The Americans contributed in a number of interrelated ways:

- by providing aid (financial, military, technical);
- by opening their domestic markets to receive exports;
- by providing an expanding global marketplace into which the Tigers could expand – the fruit of the Bretton Woods system – by virtue of its own vigorous domestic economic growth.

The pattern was reproduced in an initial quartet of countries: South Korea, Taiwan, Hong Kong and Singapore. The first two had entered the modern world through the experience of Japanese colonialism, which offered a variant of the familiar mix of exploitation and development, whereas the later two entered the modern world via the experience of British colonialism, which, in the case of these two cities, was overwhelmingly concerned with trade and not the development of the territories. The experiences of the quartet were further distinguished in the post-war years: the sometime Japanese territories became embroiled in wars – actual, experienced and threatened – whereas the territories associated with Britain were able to continue a long-established preoccupation with trade with much less disruption.

Korea was internally divided following the withdrawal of Japanese forces: class division was sharp; ideological conflict was sharp; domestic tensions spilled over; two states were formed; the country became the site of an early proxy war between the state-socialist bloc, with its uneasy linkage of the Soviet Union and the People's Republic with the liberal trading bloc, centred on the USA.[10] In the north, Kim Il-sung ruled an autocratic Stalinist state-socialist country until his death in 1994, when he was succeeded by his son Kim Jong-Il; the elite mobilized the population; the official ideology of *juche* demanded self-reliance and pursued heavy industrialization with much plant built underground after the experience of war. The country has been largely closed off to the outside world; the country remains inward looking and poor. In the south, Syngman Rhee's chaotic nationalist regime ruled from 1948 to 1960; American assistance provided a large percentage of the state budget and the government was involved in rent seeking as business and the state machine looked for favours to gain access to aid flows; Rhee was ousted in a popular uprising/coup. Park Chung Hee's 1961–79 dictatorship embraced the Japanese model in the *Yushin* policy of state-led national economic development and laid the foundations of the contemporary South Korean economy: the state is in charge, technocrats have become influential and the state controls credit and licences for investment. The economy is developing, with large firms – chaebol – which have close relations to the state and the nationalized banks, as well as wide interests, and are concerned to expand market share.

Park was assassinated but Chun Doo Hwan and Roh Tae Woo seized power; the elite project continued but domestic pressure for reform – democratization – built. In 1987 Chun was forced from office and Roh Tae Woo took over; a dual programme of reforms was pursued. First came economic reforms – there was liberalization, credit became more freely available, chaebols were targeted for reform (so they looked more like 'normal liberal-market' conglomerates) and the privileged position of the chaebols was weakened – but overall with limited success. There was also a second tranche of political reforms, which led leads to freely elected presidents – Kim Young Sam was elected in 1992 and the Korean military returned to their barracks. Korea continued with a democratic system; the

84 *New trajectories*

Asian financial crisis had a severe impact and overall direction was not too clear; however, now Korea has a very sophisticated modern high-tech economy in a nationalist and democratic country.

Taiwan was formally handed to the Chinese nationalists at the end of 1945; at end of civil war the Republic of China (ROC) dictatorship relocated to Taiwan. Sharp conflicts lead the indigenous Taiwanese to retreat from political life; the economy was divided, with some sectors KMT, some Taiwanese. The KMT state took central role and accepted American advice; this allowed the technocrats to plan as the state determined to build a successful economy and secure local legitimacy after the fiasco on the mainland; the economy recovered its 1939 levels by 1952. In the period 1950–60 a strategy of import-substituting industrialization was followed. The KMT state allocated foreign exchange, set tariffs and maintained an overvalued currency. Industrialization advanced rapidly in textiles, petroleum and metals; problems emerged by 1954 with KMT business involvement, corruption and the small domestic market. The USA encouraged economic reforms; the KMT was pressured by both the US and local, often US-trained, technocrats to shift to export-oriented industrialization. From 1960 to 1973 the new strategy was followed; small firms were encouraged to cooperate in order to be able to compete in export markets; the policy mix on taxes, credit and tariffs encouraged production for export whilst protecting the domestic marketplace; certain sectors were encouraged and there was a boom in exports in textiles, light electrical goods and electronic components plus a boom in savings (available for investment); the state was heavily involved. A secondary import-substituting industrialization programme ran from 1973 to 1980; it was a strategy of industrial deepening. The oil shock suggested vulnerability; US rapprochement with China was also difficult; and the KMT state developed heavy industry in steel, ships and petrochemicals. As the state sector was strengthened in strategic areas, it was also strengthened against local Taiwanese business. The state has been central in Taiwan's development. The later phases from 1980 onwards have seen a high-tech economy emerge; the state was an early practitioner of upgrading (moving the economy to higher-tech goods and up the value-added chain); from 1987 the economy became more internationalized but always controlled; there were burgeoning investments in China and Southeast Asia; and there were inhibitions to economic advance due to the difficult political relationship with Beijing.

The ASEAN countries of Southeast Asia

European colonial empires created discrete spheres within the Southeast Asian region,[11] as the colonial system collapsed nationalist groups seized their moment; diverse projects were pursued,[12] centred on security, only intermittently running with elite rhetorics of national development; however, nation-states coalesced in the context of regional anxieties (borders, minorities, economic resources) and outside influences (power asymmetries within the global system and in particular the demands of ex-colonial powers and the cold war). ASEAN has been an important vehicle for ordering the interactions of local regional elites, establishing the identities[13] of their countries and the region; it has pursued policies with regard to security and economic growth; it is a successful security organization but has been less successful with regard to economics, where the members tend to have similar economies with extensive agrarian primary production, significant underdevelopment,[14] low-tech manufacturing and extra-regionally oriented multinational corporation plants which compete rather than cooperate; however, recent free trade agreements and regional growth areas are viewed optimistically.

Acharya[15] argues that ASEAN has been crucial in managing the process of decolonization in Southeast Asia; it has helped elites and populations formulate their identities. ASEAN has grown to encompass all the countries within Southeast Asia:[16]

- 1967 ASEAN 5, Malaysia, Singapore, Indonesia, Thailand, the Philippines;
- 1984 ASEAN 6, Brunei;
- 1995 ASEAN 7, Vietnam;
- 1997 ASEAN 9, Laos and Myanmar;
- 1999 ASEAN 10, Cambodia.

ASEAN now comprises ten countries.[17] They are not all the same; the set can be unpacked. The ASEAN countries evidence three rather different types of trajectories; distinctive dialectics of structure and elite agent in the unfolding shift to the modern world of the countries of Southeast Asia. Quantitative[18] and qualitative strategies can be envisaged, and using the latter the ASEAN countries can be analysed substantively in terms of historical trajectories: first, the process of colonization/decolonization (how the countries entered the modern world); second, the interlinked episodes of war, decolonization and cold war (the circumstances in which elites came to power); and, third, the nature of their pursuit (or not) of national development. The ASEAN countries can be grouped in terms of a simple summation of their historical development trajectories: more or less peaceful and more or less pro-development:[19] Group 1, Malaysia, Singapore, Brunei and Thailand, where decolonization was mostly peaceful, the global system situation clear and relatively undamaging, there was mostly domestic stability and where pursuit of development has been more or less continuous; Group 2, Vietnam, Indonesia and the Philippines, where decolonization was troubled or violent and relations within the global system were difficult, that is, the countries were caught up in the cold war, which generated significant domestic problems which interrupted the pursuit of development; and Group 3, Cambodia, Laos and Myanmar, where decolonization was relatively unproblematic but the global situation was relatively poor, with two

86 *New trajectories*

caught directly in the cold war and one withdrawn into an autarchic strategy, producing severe domestic problems and an interrupted pursuit of development.

The historical role of ASEAN is distinctive. Acharya[20] characterizes the pre-contact pattern of life in Southeast Asia as dispersed micro-polities; trading empires; little regional coherence; however, commerce did integrate the region and linked it to China and India. Colonialism reworked the pattern: segments linked up with metropolitan centres; the regional pattern was disrupted; empire spheres developed. Decolonization was not a clean break: colonial patterns endured; cold war conflicts further militated against change; regional organizations were formed and failed. ASEAN emerged from these unpropitious circumstances; the organization carried numerous domestic anxieties; it was oriented towards economic and political cooperation; there were problems; the end of war in Vietnam helped; war in Cambodia did not; by 1997 ASEAN membership encompassed all Southeast Asian nations; the region was reintegrated (after a fashion). ASEAN is a significant regional diplomatic organization; it has accumulated various dialogue partners; yet the 1997 financial crisis underscored its weakness. Acharya notes that the organization has helped solidify a Southeast Asian regional identity; the organization has helped individual countries settle differences and construct national identities within the context of the region and the inheritances of the colonial era (extra-regional links, state boundaries and domestic populations).

The five founding members of ASEAN established the organization in 1967. Offers of membership were made at the time to the countries of Indo-China and to Burma but these countries decided not to participate, the latter viewing the organization as too closely linked to the Western bloc powers. Thereafter, the 1960s and 1970s were difficult decades in Southeast Asia. However, in the 1980s there were significant changes. The end of the cold war was crucial. The Vietnamese occupation of Cambodia was also brought to an end. The American presence in the region was scaled down. China began to undertake reforms and engage with the region. All these improvements in security were complemented by a general rise in prosperity within East Asia. Local elites took the view that the time was ripe for ASEAN to re-engage positively with the non-members in order to bring all Southeast Asian countries within the single organization – a process understood as meaning that in some sense Southeast Asia would be completed. After some discussion the Indo-China countries and Myanmar joined, and by 1997 there were ten members of ASEAN 10. The members of ASEAN claim that one key reason for the organization's success is 'the ASEAN way', and this points not merely to the way in which the organization works – that is, with a minimal formal bureaucratic structure and lots and lots of meetings – but also to the organization's intrinsic Asian-ness, that is, the ASEAN way is regarded as distinctively Asian (in contrast to 'Western'). The ASEAN way has a series of key principles which govern its work: (1) non-interference in each other's domestic affairs; (2) a cooperative style in meetings; (3) decisions reached by consensus. However, ASEAN now faces challenges: the 1997 financial crisis was a major problem but ASEAN's ability to respond was slight; the accession of Myanmar has been problematical; and revising the ASEAN way has been mooted and debates about the future direction of the organization and its members continue.

The record of the organization has been subject to extensive commentary. ASEAN is approaching its fortieth anniversary and many commentators have said that its long life is itself a triumph but ASEAN has achieved more than simple survival. The economic record of ASEAN is not impressive. The economies of the ASEAN countries are linked with the outside world rather than each other and the economies of the ASEAN countries tend to produce a similar range of primary and low-tech industrial products. Nonetheless, there has been cooperation in enhancing intra-ASEAN trade and in working together in various world bodies to advance the common interests of ASEAN and in recent years there has been a renewed interest in advancing economic cooperation. In contrast, the political record of ASEAN is impressive. The organization was constructed at a very difficult time within the region when there was considerable scope for damaging conflict; it has helped members to resolve bilateral problems; it has helped the region formulate a common position with respect to the Vietnamese invasion of Cambodia; it has helped the region formulate a more coherent stance with regard to China; it has allowed regional political elites to meet each other quite routinely in a variety of meeting places; and it has helped to foster something of a sense of regional identity amongst elite players.

Group 1: Malaysia, Thailand, Singapore and Brunei

The group one quartet of trajectories cannot be assimilated to one model but they do have some overall similarities: there has been successful national development; their elites have generally been committed to that goal; domestic circumstances have been propitious; and external circumstances have been generally encouraging.

Malaysian elites, following independence in 1957, have pursued national development; progress has not always been smooth. The Malaysian elite are committed to national economic growth but constrained by domestic politics; there is ethnic/economic/political division (Malay/Chinese) and religious divisions within Malays; the United Malay National Organization (UMNO) elite is coherent (internal competition), accesses the resources of the state and has mobilized the Malays; it has links with the Malaysian Chinese Association (MCA) and the Malaysian Indian Congress (MIC) in Barisan Nasional (the National Front). Prior to 1969 the state pursued an import-substituting industrialization policy designed to broaden the existing primary product economy (plantations and mines). Inter-ethnic riots in 1969 made this slow strategy unacceptable politically; the 1972 New Economic

Policy (NEP) aimed to industrialize the country by lifting up the Malay population so that the country did not have an ethnic, economic and political divide; a series of pro-Malay policies were implemented in education, employment and the economy; there was broad success (along with all problems associated with 'positive discrimination programmes'). Mahathir in the 1980s pursued policies of 'look East' and 'twenty-twenty vision' in order to learn from Japan and become a developed economy by 2020. This has generated a critical Malay middle class, an Islamist reaction from the Partai Islam Se-Malaysia (PAS) and cross-ethnic parties such as the Democratic Action Party (DAP). The 1997 Asian financial crisis produced external global-market problems (crisis plus the imposition of exchange controls) and internal political problems (Anwar Ibrahim); Mahathir survives and the country continues successfully. The leadership transition was organized in 2003 when Abdullah Badawi took over, maybe leading to a more relaxed leadership. The country has a vigorous political life, with an intermittently repressive central government and rapid development over the last twenty years.

Thailand is home to a number of crucial elites groups: the military (which has ruled Thailand for fifty years) and its factions/coups; the bureaucracy, created by Chulalongkorn, separated off from society, an elite group; the business world, including Bangkok conglomerates, regional business groups and liberal business groups. There is elite disunity; they are never united, always manoeuvring. In the period 1950–60 there was strong American influence, a half-hearted import-substituting industrialization programme and army rule from Phibun/Sarit. In the 1970s there was ISI plus democracy, cold war spillovers, radical students, an elected parliament, army coups and resistance guerrillas. In the 1980s there was ISI plus democracy plus EOI under General Prem. In the 1990s there was EOI plus liberalization plus a bubble economy plus democracy again, with unimpressive prime ministers, Chatchai, Chuan, Banharn and Chavalit. Until quite recently the elite were committed to their own continuation; social forces include a sceptical, demobilized mass which was rural and is now more urban. An ideology of 'Thai-ness' (place, religion and king) aids integration. A number of regime outcomes can be noted: 1947–70 unstable authoritarian; 1975–76 unstable democratic; 1976 to mid-1980s semi-democratic; and mid-1980s fuller democracy.[21] The 1997 crisis produced a new constitution and the election of Prime Minister Thaksin, re-elected in 2005; a Thai pursuit of national development was apparently in place, but in 2006 elite-level conflict resumed.

Singapore, as noted below, has an elite committed to national economic growth. The state has been deployed to mobilize the population. The colonial inheritance was a major trading port, and diversification and upgrading has been key. The country is now a manufacturing centre, a financial centre, a science centre and is looking to become a commercial leisure centre. There is a strong elite commitment to national growth. The

New trajectories 89

country is a key player within ASEAN. Finally, Brunei is an absolute monarchy, with the elite committed to their own continuance; an oil economy provides large financial flows to distribute to population.

Group 2: Vietnam, Indonesia and the Philippines

The elites of the group two countries have pursued national development intermittently and in circumstances disturbed by violence.

Vietnam was ruined by wars against France and the USA during the period 1945–75; the country secured its independence in 1975. After reunification a state-socialist strategy was deployed. The political system is state socialist: the party/state rules. The task of reconstruction and recovery from war was begun within the ideological framework of socialist central state planning, peasant communes and urban state industry. It was not successful. A sharp change of direction in 1986 – *Doi Moi* – embraced market-oriented reforms and policy pragmatism; it has had some success. The USA ended its embargo in 1994 and the country joined ASEAN the following year. Concern is for socialist national development. The country now faces problems of domestic reform – economic and political.

Indonesian independence was declared by Sukarno in 1945; it was secured after a series of short conflicts in 1949. The first constitution was organicist and affirmed the doctrine of *Pancasila* (God, unity, humanitarianism, the sovereignty of the people and social justice); the later 1950 constitution was more democratic. The 1955 elections involved a series of parties representing a bureaucratic line, a Muslim line, an outer island line and a communist line – a confused political situation. Then in 1957 Guided Democracy was established on the basis of the revived 1945 constitution in a system that balanced the army, Communist Party and regional groups. Suharto's 1965 coup established the 1945 constitution-based New Order regime; the global rise in the price of oil in the early 1970s produced large revenues; Suharto dispensed patronage to the army, bureaucracy, business (Chinese) and civil society groups in a Javanese elite-controlled corporatist mobilization for development; there was a primary product economy plus oil, coupled with attempts to upgrade the economy through labour intensive manufacturing and high-tech industries. The Asian financial crisis destroyed the elite balance; Suharto fell. Habibie took over in 1998, followed by Wahid, Megawati Sukarnoputri and Susilo Yudhoyono; politics are not settled, but the stability of the country is maintained; continued stability and slow economic recovery are a significant achievement.

The Philippines archipelago was a colony of Spain; an indigenous independence movement was successful at end of the nineteenth century; US colonial invaders suppressed the movement. The economic pattern established under Spanish rule centred on landed estates; landowners plus peasants; patron/client relations. The US colonial authorities reinforced the pattern and added an American-style electoral system. The elites can look to land; businesses were built thereafter. American-style electoral competition was a route to office and plunder. Politics involve an elite and a mass; there is elite coherence and a demobilized mass; the public sphere is emotive; key is patronage; in rural areas there are patrons and in urban areas boss-ism. Political life is dominated by elite families, lately laced with recycled media celebrities. The Philippines elite are often characterized as committed to their own interests; the elite control large landed estates and these provide financial backing for some manufacturing industry; but the economy is primary product, a labour exporter, with low-level manufactures and tourism; and much is underdeveloped.

Group 3: Cambodia, Laos and Myanmar

The countries of group three have not pursued national development; domestic and international violence have supervened; elites have attended to the dictates of the pursuit of security.

Cambodia became independent from France in 1953 and in the 1960s was engulfed by the Vietnam War. The Khmer Rouge seized power in 1975 and pursued an agrarian socialism; a disaster unfolded. The Vietnamese intervened in 1978/89; an unholy alliance linking China, Western countries and regional powers (Singapore) rallied to the support of the Khmer Rouge regime; a UN-sponsored peace agreement led to elections in 1993; Hun Sen took power, retaining it into the new century. Cambodia joined ASEAN in 1999 but as the economy remains largely agrarian, reconstruction and development proceed slowly. And Laos gained independence from France in 1953. The Vietnam War spilled over into the country and the communist Pathet Lao seized power in 1975. A state-socialist political system orders an agrarian economy. There have been reforms since the late 1980s and Laos joined ASEAN in 1997.

In Burma Aung San established the Independence Army then National Army in 1943 as Japanese granted nominal independence; later the Anti-Fascist People's Freedom League (AFPFL) sought independence. Aung San was killed in 1947; in 1948 there was formal independence, then civil war between central Rangoon forces and peripheral ethnic states plus the Burmese Communist Party. Rangoon slowly asserted its control; there was elite conflict. Semi-civil war became the normal situation, the army (Tatmadaw) the key institution in political life. In 1962 Ne Win took power and established from 1962 to 1974 the Burmese Way to Socialism; this consisted of socialism plus Buddhism and was anti-Western, extreme nationalist and authoritarian; rule was via the Revolutionary Council. The country was poor. In 1974 there was a new constitution. The Burma Socialist Programme Party ruled until 1988 – Ne Win plus the army. The economy was nationalized; there were co-ops and Indian and Chinese business left. The country remained inward looking and very poor. In June 1988 there were riots, Ne Win resigned and elections were announced. In September 1988 an army coop established the State Law and Order Restoration Council (SLORC) but elections were held in May 1990. Aung San Suu Kyi's National League for Democracy won a massive majority, the army ignored the election result and SLORC renamed itself the State Peace and Development Council (SPDC). The army/party elite control the country; it is a military dictatorship and remains very poor; there is ongoing fighting in border areas, there are refugees in Thailand and the ordinary people live their lives as best they may. The country joined ASEAN in 1997; the motivation of existing members were not clear, speculations mentioning anxieties about Chinese influence, 'completing Southeast Asia' and maybe some commercial opportunism. Myanmar is an embarrassment to ASEAN.

Problems of Southeast Asian countries

After taking power, replacement elites confront two sorts of problems: domestic, the business of security, order and development; and the international, how to deal with regional neighbours and the demands of the global system.

There were domestic problems. The countries of Southeast Asia had intermingled post-colonial trajectories; they faced similar problems: (1) security, where agreed external borders (neighbours) had to be set and internal stability (minorities) settled; (2) order, where law, citizenship, political system and national identity all had to be engineered; and (3) development, where economic growth, linking the local to the global system, and development, with welfare benefits to the population (health, schooling and better material lives), had to be achieved. The elites had to deal with given structures and make projects (and a key concern was establishing themselves in power). In the late 1940s there were a series of available ideas/theories: from the first world there were ideas of development and modernization; from the second world there were ideas of socialism; and from the third world there were ideas of independence and non-alignment. The general record is uneven. Elites in Southeast Asia had many problems in adjusting to each other and the global system, but in time ASEAN turned out to be a useful regional organization, and as ideas of socialism and non-alignment fell away, debates came to revolve around development (a general idea) and modernization (a more specific idea reflecting US influence, that is, liberal democracy and free markets).[22]

There were international problems. The recently fashionable theory of globalization points to the putative global integration of economic activity,[23] but critics reject the claims as metropolitan pro-market propaganda and note that to the extent there is economic integration it seems to be regional.[24] In Southeast Asia there has been a measure of regional integration and openness to the wider global system. There are benefits in economic, social, cultural and political linkages. But there are also dis-benefits, such as uneven development, migration flows, transnational crime (drugs, weapons, people traffickers), environmental problems and financial-sector instability (with all the consequent problems).

At the end of the Pacific War the dissolution of the European/American colonial empires was quite rapid – sometimes relatively peaceful, sometimes violent. The replacement elites faced difficulties in establishing themselves within their territories, difficulties in agreeing borders between new countries within the region and difficulties in securing regional stability within the context of the cold war. The solution was a regional organization, ASEAN. It has contributed to regional stability and therefore growth; the region was integrated through commerce prior to colonization; colonial empires cut across established linkages; the region is reconstituting but within a radically different context; current problems are many; the region has been successful in the past and whilst the current situation is difficult it is going forwards.[25]

Unfolding trajectories in China

The collapse of the European, American and Japanese empires in East Asia ushered in several decades of sweeping change as hitherto relatively marginal and poor areas within the global industrial-capitalist system remade themselves by upgrading their economies, reforming their societies and – neglecting usually their politics – secured much more powerful niches within that global system. At first, China took a different route; the legacies of Qing Dynasty inequality, quasi-colonial exploitation and development, invasion and years of civil war presented the victorious communist forces with an impoverished and ruined country and it was from this point perforce that they had to move forwards. Communist doctrine and Moscow's advice pointed towards urban heavy industry as the route, but the country was mostly rural and its people mainly peasant farmers. Maoist socialism looked to the countryside; it was here that the first moves towards development were begun.

The early period of Mao's rule was successful; there was economic development in the countryside and new industrial facilities and cities were built. The record was good. China became something of a model for development in economies dominated by peasant farming. Thereafter, Mao's variant of communism, which stressed not merely the class importance of the peasantry but also the power of their mass mobilization – a sort of peasant vitalism – led him to propose ever more grandiose development projects. There were severe failures. Mao's rule declined through the Hundred Flowers movement, the Great Leap Forward and the Cultural Revolution into the clique-ridden confusions of the last years of the chairman's life.[26] In 1978 Deng Xiaoping inaugurated a long period of piecemeal accumulative market-oriented reforms. These were sustained over twenty-five years and recorded great success, albeit around the turn of the twenty-first century with significant social and environmental distress.

Deng Xiaoping began pragmatic market-oriented reforms in 1978. The new leadership in the period 1978–2005[27] stressed learning from West; knowledge and technology were embraced and reforms inaugurated to copy the East Asian development model; the programme was technocratic, piecemeal, developmental and national; the state/party system was maintained along with class demobilization, market mobilization and all the concomitant stresses and strains of headlong catch-up growth. In the period 1978–84 there were agricultural reforms and the establishment of special economic zones; the reforms in rural agriculture were successful and production rapidly advanced; and the special economic zones were successful. In the period 1984–87 industry and finance were reformed and these proved more problematical: industrial enterprises were given more autonomy and moved towards commercial market operation and there were questions of divestiture, questions of finance and questions of performance; and specialist banks were established and moved towards commercial market operation and there were questions of performance. Deng's Southern Tour in 1992 reaffirmed the importance of the reform programme, with the slogan of constructing a 'socialist market economy'. The reform programme was very ambitious; the state-socialist system was distinctive as the party/state broadly directed all aspects of the economy and citizens' lives; there was much scope for flexibility in translation of theory into practice and many inefficiencies and resistances; the state was intermingled with the economy and disentangling the two was difficult; it involved creating a marketplace with law, firms and consumers; it involved creating social welfare systems with health, education and housing; it involved creating a political system to order/legitimate the new arrangements. The economic reforms and consequent social impacts/reforms have continued under Deng's successors but there have been few political reforms.[28]

China is now regarded as a major power as its economic weight is rapidly growing and its political power is also growing. What is true of China is also true of the region. East Asia is now one of the three major regions within the global economy and along with the European Union and the United States of America (plus its North American Free Trade Agreement (NAFTA) partners) dominates world industrial production and trade. The modern world in East Asia evidenced in the days of colonialism is long gone; the disintegration of empire has produced an interrelated set of dynamic country trajectories. East Asia is not playing catch-up and nor is it copying some ideal-typical West (itself an increasingly passé confection); it has lodged itself on its own terms with the modern world. And that modern world continues to unfold. It is also the environment within which Singapore, Hong Kong and the cities of the sometime informal empire now operate and which they help shape.

Singapore, Hong Kong and the informal empire

The two cities have had intermingled but different historical trajectories: occupation, crisis and national development. Both were extracted from

94 *New trajectories*

wider polities, Singapore from the Johor–Riau Sultanate and Hong Kong from Qing Dynasty China. Both prospered as colonial entrepots linking local to regional/global networks. Both experienced East Asian general crisis: in Singapore from 1941 to 1965 with war/occupation, decolonization and a failed merger; in Hong Kong from 1941 to 1967/97 with war/occupation, a second colonization and skewed development. From 1965 onwards the indigenous Singaporean elite pursued national development; from 1997 the indigenous Hong Kong elite sought to locate themselves within a Beijing-centred[29] project of national development. In both cities indigenous elites must read and react to enfolding structural circumstances; their situations are similar (both are trading/manufacturing cities located within local regional and global networks (the one ASEAN/global the other Greater China/global)), their capacity for action dissimilar (the one elite autonomous, the other not), their likely trajectories divergent.

In Singapore the 1945–58 recovery from war damage parallels the political pursuit of independence: in 1959 internal self-government; in 1963 union with Malaysia; and finally in 1965 independence. The PAP ruled Singapore; there was continuity in the overall project of the pursuit of national development. The starting point was as a colonial port, now cut off from its natural hinterland; the government mobilized the population; there was an ideology of vulnerability, self-reliance and continual upgrading; there was repression of political opponents and co-option of unions; formation of a development bank, setting up of planning apparatus and encouragement of multinationals; local entrepreneurs were rather left to their own devices and could not compete so moved into retail and services; the economy had port functions and the government encouraged light industry, oil processing, tourism, and high-tech industry; the government routinely intervened in the economy, encouraged the business sector and upgraded people as it upgraded other aspects of the economy. The deal for the population was material welfare: housing, schooling, medicine, pensions (via a forced saving scheme that funnelled savings into economic investment), leisure facilities and stability. The government's concern for economic growth has been unpacked as policy pragmatism and a related concern to upgrade the economies facilities, including people. In the early twenty-first century the economy comprises the port, oil processing, multinational corporation manufacturing, some science-based high-tech, service sector and a growing financial sector. The deal remains in place: the elite requires obedience; the population offers support and the state provides material welfare in what is now an extensively middle-class society; the stated political-economic goals are to become a regional service hub; a critical variant speaks of the hotel Singapore, whilst a related critical political comment speaks of an air-conditioned nation;[30] the future is debated.

In Hong Kong after recolonization in 1945 recovery was positive; the 1949 inauguration of the People's Republic coupled with the cold war resulted in a UN embargo on trade with China; there was US hostility and restrictions, but flight capital also came in as Shanghai textile industrialists relocated to Hong Kong; incoming capitalists linked up with local banks and other light manufactures developed/recovered; as before the war there were multiple small firms which adapted quickly in plastics, toys, electrical goods, watches and textiles; labour was cheap, organized labour was fragmented (KMT/CCP) and suffered from colonial restrictions so the labour market was very competitive. The role of colonial government was debated; they affirmed an ideal of laissez faire in the nineteenth century; later in the 1960s as domestic problems mounted this was revised to 'positive non-intervention', whereby the government paid minimum attention to monetary, financial, social services and information/training encouragements to industry. Theorists debate matters: on the one hand neo-classical thinkers see Hong Kong as close to a free market with a minimum state and business finding comparative advantage in an open marketplace; on the other political economists see a system that centres on a business/state alliance exercised via the administrative state; but the state is central; the state project has not been national development; rather, it has been the servant of a colonial/local business elite; since the 1997 handover, there has been no clear sign of an agreed route to the future; there is neither domestic Hong Kong clarity nor surety about Beijing's understanding and intentions.

The informal empire of the British dissolved away in the years following the Pacific War; the wartime years destroyed the British commercial presence in both Bangkok and Shanghai. First, Bangkok and Thailand were taken into the orbit of the Americans; their cold war commitments created both a preference for development (after Rostow, communism thrives on poverty) and an amiable tolerance of military dictatorships, presented in some commentary as the most reliable partners of development; Bangkok was remade; American bases and associated expenditures and aid packages fuelled Thai elite corruption but also a modest development; it is not until the 1990s that democracy makes a partial appearance; but the nature of Thai elite commitments in respect of political projects remains somewhat cloudy. Second, Shanghai was removed from all foreign reach by the civil war victory of the Communist Party; the city was not favoured during the long years of Mao; it recovered in the post-1978 period; by the turn of the twenty-first century foreign business had returned, but now to a city firmly controlled by local elites.

Unfolding dynamics of change

East Asia has been remade in the years since the end of the Pacific War; change has swept through the region; but change is a given and elites must read and react to its demands; such reactions in turn shape the unfolding structural pattern; new circumstances take shape and so new demands are made of elites.

Cold war, crisis and changing regional patterns

A number of events have impacted Southeast Asian politics: the end of the cold war; the financial crisis; the emergence of terrorist problems; and disease epidemics. A number of wider structural changes are in process: the rise of China; the emergence of Japan as a regional power; the relative decline of the USA; and the return of European influence in the guise of the European Union.

In East Asia the cold war began in Northeast Asia. In Japan the American occupation authorities were divided between New Dealers and Republicans. The New Dealers were at first the leaders and they began to reconstruct Japan on the model of the USA, but when the conservatives in the US occupation authorities took control they argued that Japan should be made into a strong ally of the US. Shortly thereafter in Korea, where a difficult background of colonialism and Great Power manoeuvring led to the country being divided, the North invaded the South, precipitating a major regional war in which first the Americans joined and then the Chinese. South Korea joined Japan within the US sphere and the wider division of East Asia rapidly followed. Taiwan became an American ally, Hong Kong fell into the US sphere and Southeast Asia was drawn into the US sphere. Indo-China experienced catastrophic wars and joined the socialist block. The cold war engagement of the USA entailed not merely ideological/military aggression but also extensive economic and social cooperation. The USA ordered a Western liberal market-oriented sphere within East Asia and in doing so it provided the broad security/policy environment within which diverse national elites pursued national development strategies,[31] creating, in time, the Asian miracle. The end of the cold war in East Asia has been slow: Deng Xiaoping's market reform programme was inaugurated in 1978; the 1985 Plaza Accord encouraged Japanese investment in East Asia and by 1989–91 theorists were already speaking of the East Asian region and the East Asian miracle economies. But there are residual problems: North/South Korea; Taipei/Beijing; and the nature of the relationship of the USA, China and Japan, where the end of the cold war calls into question old certainties as cold war allies have become vigorous economic competitors.

The Asian financial crisis unrolled through the region and caused extensive damage. It began with currency speculation, forced devaluations and International Monetary Fund (IMF) bailouts. It created social and political problems. It also generated extensive debates about explanations and cures: the Washington Consensus view specified 'crony capitalism', whereas critical international political economists took the view that it flowed from too rapid liberalization linked to global liberalization. Within the region, the crises led to a loss of trust in the USA (which was seen not as helping, but as looking after itself) and a loss of trust in the IMF/World Bank (which was seen as too sympathetic to Washington). There were new anxieties about Japan's continuing recession; there were anxieties about China's rapid growth, with China seen variously as competitor, cooperator, regional leader or aspirant hegemon. At the same time, there was talk of regional financial cooperation (including the exchange of economic data for early warning, cooperation with financial back-up packages if currencies attacked again and in the future an Asian bond market (local use of local saving) and speculatively an Asian Monetary Fund. In all this there have been downstream consequences: Linda Weiss[32] has reviewed the role of states in the pursuit of development and made it clear that the stronger the state in East Asia the quicker the response, and the more oriented to the East Asian model the quicker the recovery; but, at the same time, in respect of large parts of the region the episode offers a useful reminder of status: urban, rich and developed (some); rural, poor and not so developed (most).

The Japanese economic bubble was pricked in 1991. The Japanese economy began a long recession where production remains stagnant, the banks have bad debts and unemployment has risen. Commentators worry that Japan has entered a deflationary spiral (where prices fall, so people delay spending, thus reducing demand, so prices fall further – and as prices fall, business contracts). The Japanese government received much advice from Western economists and politicians all oriented towards a liberalized economy in line with the Washington Consensus, but the Japanese were never likely to abandon goals of security and growth that had been established by Meiji. One potential solution lies in Japan taking a bigger role within a somewhat more integrated East Asia regional sphere, but elites are uneasy about Japanese leadership, as there are still unresolved issues and memories of the Pacific War.[33]

The ambiguities of current development trajectories are evident in China. The country has emerged as an East Asian regional power; it has somewhat uneasy relations with Japan; it has very uneasy relations with Taiwan; it has reasonable relations with Southeast Asia (except for tricky issue of South China Sea); and in the recent Asian financial crisis the Chinese government acted to support regional economies, winning praise. It is an increasingly significant regional power. However, at the same time, much of China is rural and poor, plus in recent years outbreaks of violence directed at the state or local power-holders have increased and these are often read as evidence of widespread social distress. On a wider scale, the USA has had an internal debate about how to deal with China; some spoke of containment and some of engagement. Recently some have spoken of both together – 'congagement'. We can note two things: from the US perspective, China is a regional security competitor and also an increasingly important trading partner; from the Chinese perspective, the trade and technology transfers are valuable but the Chinese are deeply suspicious of US security intentions, speaking of 'hegemonism'.

There are now extensive debates about the role of the USA: the economic role – the decline of the Bretton Woods system, the rise of the neo-liberal

Washington Consensus and the role of the World Trade Organization (WTO); and the political role – will the USA act alone or within the network of international laws. All these debates are also involved in debates about the political, security and cultural position of the USA: in East Asia the political/cultural role of the USA has been resisted in recent years, where this is the burden of all the talk about Asian Values; in Europe the political/cultural role of the USA has found an institutional rejection, and this is the burden of the development of the European Union. It has been noted that the USA has an extensive global deployment of military forces. The reason for these deployments is debated: to protect vital interests (but Europe and Japan do not deploy forces around the globe); to organize global security (but this is rarely a military matter, usually economic and political – matters for bilateral and multilateral diplomacy); or to secure its empire hegemony (and whilst this is a rather strange argument, as the USA does not look much like an empire, Chalmers Johnson argues that the US military itself has quasi-empire aspirations).

Finally, a broad shift is in process in the global system: the Pacific War destroyed European influence in East Asia; however, European power was not merely removed, the overall pattern of power was changed as the USA became the key outside economic and security power. However, over the years since the Pacific War various European countries have slowly rebuilt their connections with East Asia. The European Union now has an activist directory or bureaucracy, a parliament and most recently a currency. It is beginning to look like a federal political system. In the global context the European Union is now a major economic player, something of a political/diplomatic player (but rather weak) and it is beginning to develop an integrated defence identity. The European Union is clearly determined to encourage links between Europe and East Asia, and recently the elites of both regions invented the Asia Europe Meeting (ASEM), an international organization designed to foster these links.

The pursuit of national development in East Asia

The sequence of macro-historical phases sketched here on the basis of an available wealth of scholarship offers numerous insights: first, the expansion of European and American power derived from the contingent creation of capitalism, which was a very dynamic expansionary system; second, the impact of European and American expansion was slow to gather pace and was articulated via subtle exchanges with extant peoples concerned with their own interests until it finally became overwhelming; third, distinctive intellectual and political discourses emerged because the colonial world was distinctive – it was not unitary and diverse strands of opinion/analysis emerged amongst colonial groups, subject groups and amongst aspiring domestic elite modernists; fourth, the colonial system was superimposed on extant patterns of life and so the colonial system generated its own logic through the contested compromises achieved by the multiplicity of players, and it also undermined the extant patterns of life and provoked extensive changes – as the apparatus of superimposed colonial rule was never going to be able to hold the system by force, systemic crisis unfolded; and, fifth, the collapse of the colonial systems ushered in a domestic elite concern for new trajectories, an active self-directed participation in the modern world secured through variants of corporate states producing overall diverse trajectories, each delineated through shifting exchanges within the regional structures and beyond.[34] And, finally, it is clear that this macro-sequence frames the development experiences of Singapore, Hong Kong and the other territories whose shift into the modern world was mediated by the experience of British colonialism.

6   Locating Singapore

Singapore island has been lodged within a number of wider encompassing systems; the island has been a site where multiple systems intersected; these co-existing intersecting systems (each a complex social pattern) have secured particular political relationships, allowing the participants to secure their diverse objectives. Singapore island has been lodged within these wider systems in a series of ways and has played a number of different roles in line with dominant elite interests: Malay, British and Chinese. In each set of structures there were different actors and institutions; and between agents within each sphere there were complex exchanges. These forms of life have interacted on Singapore island; at any one time a particular mix of elements could be found, ordered according to shifting political relationships. There is no one Singapore; there is only the tale told now of the trajectory sketched out by successive elite accommodations to changing unfolding circumstances; contemporary arrangements are contingent; the trajectory could have been different; elites could have acted otherwise; the future is open.[1]

British traders, moving eastwards from their bases in India, advancing towards the goal of China, entered the extant Malay world; they encountered an established form of life, a coherent civilization, a regional economy.[2] The Malay world comprised numerous maritime trading empires; their economies were based on seaborne trade; there were extensive networks of trade; political power and authority rested upon control of a key port; politics were ordered around the person of the sultan. European traders participated in an existing trading system; the networks were complex, so too the politics; country powers and traders manoeuvred for advantage; foreign encroachment was persistent. The British manoeuvred against the Dutch and local country powers; the episode is complex as there were multiple agents; the British slowly displaced Malays and migrants flowed into the settlement; the island was embedded within three spheres, British, Malay and Chinese, and was a mechanism for discrete and interlinked trade flows; Singapore island was a local and regional trade nexus.[3] The late nineteenth-century industrial production and mass consumer markets within the European capitalist heartlands placed new demands on Southeast

Asian economies for tin, rubber, sugar, oil and so on; Singapore became a conduit for the extraction of tropical agricultural, mineral and primary products and for the introduction of European manufactures; the new economic relationship was mediated by the establishment of new political arrangements both in the peninsula and in Singapore island as the colonial power asserted control; a formal colonial system was established to order a global trading role. The colonial system endured until it was destroyed by the Imperial Japanese advance into Southeast Asia; the end of the Pacific War saw the colonial power returning; however, at this time the idea of empire was untenable; an uneasy process of colonial retreat followed. After independence in 1965 the Singapore state regime, centred on the PAP, presided over a major reorientation of the economy and society: inviting in the multinational corporations and making a dependent capitalist economy, a global trading hub.[4]

The sequence of changes underpins contemporary Singapore. The elite must read and react to the manifold demands of unfolding change; these contingent dynamics underpin contemporary Singaporean forms of life. The elite project moves ahead; the dynamic of the elite project has unfolded down the years; it has not been a simple process and has often been contested; it now drives deep into the lives of the ordinary people; its broader expression is the discrete 'footprint' or 'state form' occupied within the modern world by Singapore. The current polity is a contingent achievement; the state regime is wedded to material advance; it looks to upgrade its niche within the global division of labour; the population has been made available to agents within the global capitalist system; the state regime has actively sought out these linkages; the rewards for the domestic population have been great – growth and welfare;[5] however, the paradox is that as the state looks to upgrade its role it becomes ever more dependent upon that global system; the elite goal is characterized as becoming a regional business hub; the paradoxical elite-sponsored deconstruction of Singapore continues apace.

State forms: contexts and actions

State, nation and nation-state are cultural artefacts created over time;[6] elites use these ideas and institutions to secure order and legitimacy and lodge territories within the global system; each instance will have a specific character, a distinctive mix of elements, a state form; any extant state form represents the way in which local agents have read and reacted to these trans-state patterns of power.

Singapore island has been lodged within several state forms; each articulates a different role within the wider embracing system: Malay maritime empire, formal colony and key nexus in the contemporary global system; each has its own self-understanding; each successive phase has been articulated by a particular state machinery, each a way of ordering internal forces so as to interact effectively with global system power structures; each phase displays the understandings held by the relevant constituent groupings; and between configurations there has been discontinuity; changes signal the achievement of a new relationship within the systems and novel domestic arrangements of economics, culture and politics. There is no one Singapore; there is, rather, the currently recoverable history of a succession of discrete ways in which the island has lodged itself within the wider systems enfolding it.

These patterns of structural power have been reconfigured in recent years; the context within which Singapore operates is sub-regional (ASEAN), regional (East Asia) and thereafter global; it is the given pattern of structural circumstances to which agents must necessarily respond. These are old problems and the state regime is offering familiar solutions: read and respond intelligently and prospectively to unfolding structural circumstances; the state regime's response to globalization and regionalization have been expressed in the slogan 'going global' and a slew of policy initiatives have been summed up as the goal of becoming a 'regional hub economy'.

Pre-contact forms of life

A succession of maritime trading empires characterized the pre-contact Malay world;[7] geographically fluid, ordered around the person of the sultan and structured by bonds of loyalty, they expanded/contracted alongside the power of the central sultanate. Their economies were based on seaborne trade; the goods traded involved agricultural products and craft goods and extensive networks were established; control of a trading port was crucial.

The archipelago supported a regional network of trade;[8] the incursions of the Europeans slowly subordinated the area to the needs of metropolitan industrial capitalism, with its political expression in colonial empire; the process was lengthy; incoming Europeans engaged in extant regional politics, one further set of players. The Portuguese, Dutch, British and French sought trade links: the Portuguese captured Malacca in 1511; the Dutch seized territory in Java in 1619; the British occupied Penang in 1786; and the French moved into Indo-China in 1862.[9] The politics of the subordination of the Johor–Riau sultanate were complex:[10] there were conflicts between the established Malay and Bugis inhabitants; and Chinese settlers had established gambier plantations in the Linga, Johor and Riau areas;[11] these formed the context for intra-European conflicts.

The Johor–Riau Sultanate occupied the Riau–Lingga archipelago to the south of the Malay peninsula; the polity was the successor to Malacca, which had been seized by the Portuguese and later the Dutch; its rulers looked to the sea peoples of the archipelago and the major trade route running through the Straits of Malacca;[12] a trading port on Bintan island was the heart of the polity,[13] with control and authority stretched out in a fragile network.[14] The patterns of trade involved Chinese goods coming in from the east, archipelago goods, local Chinese agricultural goods and European/Indian goods coming in from the west. Singapore island was a part of the Johor–Riau sultanate.

As the eighteenth century drew to its close the sultanate was unable to sustain its coherence in the face of the incursions of the Europeans with their quite particular schedule of economic and political demands, and in time the sultanate was displaced. The political competition for control involved local agents, Dutch and British; the sultanate was slowly overwhelmed by the demands of the European powers. Anglo-Dutch conflict framed the movement of the British into the area; the key was the occupation of Singapore island; it was extracted from the political grasp of the sultanate through manoeuvring centred locally on recognizing a weak member of the ruling family as sultan of Singapore, which gave the British a claim against both the Johor–Riau sultan and the Dutch. The survival of the new settlement further depended on exchanges between the authorities in Penang, the EIC, London and the Dutch.[15] The Malay elite might have expected to rule a settlement resembling a Malay maritime port in concert with the British; the immediate power struggle came to a head in 1823, was resolved in favour of the British, yet the Malay practice of exacting tribute from passing shipping continued. Matters were settled in 1835 as local elites agreed the suppression of piracy, thereby ending the old form of life on Singapore island. The Malay economy and society were reoriented;[16] the traditional pattern focused on seaborne trade, required a key port and available seafarers, but now activity centred on the expansion of agriculture in Johor.[17] The British and Malays dominated early Singapore but Chinese migration altered the pattern; Chinese formed the largest population group by mid-century, provided the trading centre manpower and through the social institution of the opium tax farm contributing a large part of the settlement's revenue.[18]

Reorienting the territory

The island of Singapore was selected as a base for British mercantile capitalist power;[19] the political extraction of the island from the Johor–Riau sultanate involved manoeuvring against the sultan and the Dutch;[20] the British promoted a weak member of the ruling family as sultan of Singapore; agreements were signed in 1818; a claim against the indigenous ruler in Bintan and the Dutch was secured; thereafter, the survival of the new polity depended upon arguments between Penang, the East India Company, London and the Dutch.[21] In the event the territory prospered,[22] but Malay patterns of life were reordered.

A power struggle followed; the Malay pattern of life revolved around seaborne trade and required control of a key port and the presence of available seafarers; it came to an end when the British asserted themselves against the sultan and Temmengong in 1823; the Temmengong's successor, Ibrahim, agreed to throw in his lot with the British and assist in the suppression of piracy; this marked the reorientation of Malay economy and society.[23] The sultanate dwindled away and the Temmengong turned to the peninsula; economy and society were reoriented; the Malays developed an agricultural economy in Johor;[24] the British settlement became a key port within a global trading network.

Johor at this time had a small population, comprised of Chinese agriculturalists displaced from Singapore island. There was a wider agricultural network; the Chinese agricultural economy was based on gambier, which was grown throughout the Lingga and Riau archipelagos; it took in Singapore island; but as the British consolidated their hold the Chinese came to play the roles of labourers and middlemen.[25] The process was not smooth; the displacement of the extant agricultural system by British controlled free trade economic interests provoked conflicts amongst local Chinese in 1851, 1854 and 1857.[26] The class system comprised European traders,[27] Chinese merchants, petty merchants not directly involved in port activities, craft workers, labourers and the inhabitants of the contracting agricultural sphere.[28] The British and Malays controlled Singapore till the mid-1840s; however, by mid-century the Chinese population had become the largest single group. These migrants provided labour for the port; they also provided the greater part of the settlement's revenues through the opium tax farm, itself a major social institution;[29] and they displaced the earlier agricultural economy in what, in time, became an ordered migrant society; a crucial part of the trading city.

The period from 1819 to the early 1870s can be taken as the phase of the projection and establishment of British mercantile capitalist power on Singapore island and within the surrounding archipelago;[30] this power was projected in the context of much manoeuvring with and against both the Dutch and the various indigenous groupings – Malays and an extant Chinese agricultural grouping.[31] The island became a nexus within local/international trade patterns. Multiple actors were engaged; many prospered but some did not. There was significant continuity of economy and society in the early period as the British slowly displaced Malays as the pre-eminent group; thereafter both accommodated the Chinese, who provided labour power, tax income and in time the main body of the local population. Carl Trocki[32] argues that the economy and society on Singapore island up to the 1880s was a continuation of the familiar pattern of a Malay trading empire; in the earlier years a Malay–British condominium; the later shift to tripartite rule is driven by demography because by mid-century the Chinese population was the largest single group; they serviced the manpower needs of the trading centre, and through the tax farm on opium they furnished the larger part of the settlement's revenue; the opium farm was also the major social structural institution for the Chinese population. However, the role of the territory was changing; the British industrial-capitalist system was global in its reach; Singapore was an important trade centre; yet it is only late on in the nineteenth century that tripartite rule over a successful mercantile centre gave way to British predominance over an element of an industrial-capitalist world system.

The shift towards formal colonial rule

The late nineteenth-century rise of industrial production[33] and with it a mass market for consumption goods in Europe impacted upon Southeast Asia; the goods required were no longer agricultural crops or handicrafts, but the tin, rubber and oil required by industrial economies; dispositions to restrict trade were reinforced by the formation of colonies; and relatively open trade was reordered as industrial capitalism advanced along empire lines.[34] In the archipelago there was routine competition between the British and Dutch; yet the trade grew, facilitated by the 1869 opening of the Suez Canal.

The British moved into the Malay peninsula; new trading opportunities developed. These compensated Singapore for the contraction of its archipelago trade, producing a more ordered, extensive colonial/capitalist exploitation, with new economic relationships mediated by new political arrangements. The detail here is complex: reordering was not smooth; the 1857 Indian Mutiny resulted in the government of India and the Straits Settlements being moved to London; in 1858 the EIC was dissolved; in 1867 after much confusion and lobbying the Straits Settlements became a Crown Colony; the 1874 Pangkor Engagement marked the start of the colonization of Malaya; Singapore was the hub around which the colonial system of British Malaya was constructed. Within this context, the manner of the articulation of effective colonial power required the slow extension of the machineries of administration and government within the area of Singapore itself and in the Malay peninsula; dominance by the colonial power. The Malays were involved in the creation of modern Johor; initially the establishment of agricultural operations; later a model territory within the British-made system of sultanates; the expanded British interest in the peninsula resulted in the 1896 establishment of the Federated Malay States Protectorate, and in 1909 the Un-federated Malay States Protectorate. The construction of the formal colony was a mixture of cooperation and control; the base was the economic interests of the Europeans, Chinese and Malays; development, class and ethnicity commingled from the earliest period of the history of Singapore.

In Singapore the interests of Malay, Chinese and colonial elites were reconciled; the interests of the Malay elites now coincided with the colonialists; the Temenggong and sultan ordered the lives of the Malays; similar coincidence of economic interests linked colonial and Chinese merchant classes; again, life was ordered. Early in the nineteenth century Chinese society was organized around the opium tax farm, clan and secret society

106 *Locating Singapore*

groups. Later, the colonial power was more assertive. The Chinese Protectorate was established in 1877 in order to regulate the coolie traffic and brothels; the Chinese Advisory Board was formed in 1889 to regulate secret societies.[35] The establishment of these bodies formalized British and Chinese relations. The Europeans established and controlled the colonial state. Singapore had become a major nexus in the British-centred sphere of the world industrial-capitalist system, a conduit for the extraction of tropical agricultural, mineral and primary products, and for the introduction of European manufactures; it was a coolie town,[36] supervised by an ethnically plural elite.

Colonial withdrawal, federation and independent statehood

The Pacific War radically undermined the system of empires. The British could not sustain their colonial holdings in Asia.[37] Dissolution was rapid; the process allowed indigenous elites to assume power, but the peninsular states and Singapore moved in constitutionally separate directions. Two constitutions were written for Malaya;[38] agreement was enshrined in the Federation of Malaya with formal independence in 1957. From 1946 the island of Singapore remained a Crown Colony and internal self-government advanced. An independent Singapore emerged; there were three phases: internal self-government, federation with the peninsula and the establishment of a dependent capitalist economy and society.

The process of establishing internal self-government was convoluted. Anti-colonial guerrilla warfare began in the peninsula in 1948; dissolution of empire overlapped with cold war; conflict marked politics in Singapore; the British were intent on maintaining a military base and an economic foothold; local political groups variously wanted power. The British envisioned a continuing linkage between Singapore and Malaya and there was a merger in 1963–65. The familiar explanation of its failure points to ethnicity; however, the merger tried to link a neo-colonial primary product unit with a major trade nexus oriented to the world system. The colonial era priority of Singapore was resisted but the implied subordinate incorporation of the island within the new unit would have required the reorientation of its economy/role from global trade nexus to merely the major port for a primary product exporter;[39] the merger failed. Independent Singapore was remade by inviting in the multinational corporations; the government broadened the economic base, co-opted the population and established a dependent capitalism; the process ran through several phases,[40] generating a richer exchange with the global system.

Independence involved a measure of intellectual as well as political-economic continuity; the elite was made up of English-educated professionals who had made their colonial pilgrimages[41] and their early programme embraced demands for an end to colonial rule, the formation of a unitary Malayan state and the pursuit of economic and social development. The

Singaporean elite argued that the country was exposed, vulnerable, devoid of natural resources and had to rely on its hardworking people; these claims were repeated routinely, seemingly widely accepted and in large measure false as they did not inherit a weak resource-less island, rather a key trade nexus within the global system whose immediate neighbour Malaysia had been for the preceding century or so part of the same empire territory.[42] Nonetheless, the territory was lodged within the global industrial-capitalist system; change runs through that system and local elites must respond. A number of political battles from 1954 to 1968 secured PAP control: independence, where it was clear that the colonial power was leaving, less clear to whom they would bequeath control;[43] domestic power,[44] where local rivals were subdued;[45] and orientation, with the goal of an outward-directed national development settled.

Singapore was lodged within regional and global structures. A developmental state mobilized the civil service, armed forces, community organizations and media in order to secure economic, socio-cultural and political goals. Growth and welfare were pursued through economic diversification[46] and the provision of health care, schooling, housing and jobs. The state was active in fashioning economic, social and cultural development in the wake of independence; having come to power in alliance with a Chinese mass movement, the technocratic professional English-educated PAP elite demobilized their erstwhile allies to secure control of local politics; the support of the masses was achieved with development policies that invited in multinational companies and provided health care, schooling, housing and jobs. It was an extensively interventionist system; decisions were made at the top and passed down, with internal democracy at a minimum but not absent; local commentators spoke of elite-fostered technical-pragmatic development,[47] a depoliticized administrative society[48] or recently communitarian democracy.[49] The state read external structures of power and ordered internal relations to secure a particular goal: the state regime embedded the domestic economy within wider regional and global structures. The upshot was an inegalitarian externally oriented economy and society; the elite made the local population available to multinationals[50] and the territory is secure, rich and deeply embedded within the global capitalist system. Yet the contemporary Singaporean development trajectory has been variously contextualized;[51] the discrete episodes of decolonization, Japanese-centred regionalism and recently 'China Rising' underscore the givens of unfolding systemic change; the elite must read and react to change; current patterns are inevitably contingent.

Singapore has an activist state committed to the pursuit of growth and welfare; the record is one of great success: the elite have invited in the multinational corporations and via labour laws and welfare/education programmes made their population available; economic prosperity has been secured; so too welfare benefits.[52] The population has borne the cost of cultural reconstruction and is superficially depoliticized, docile and consumerist.

108 *Locating Singapore*

Singapore: first moves after independence

The original political commitments of the replacement elite were social-democratic;[53] their early programme embraced demands for an end to colonial rule, the formation of a unitary Malayan state and economic development;[54] independence involved a significant measure of continuity;[55] subsequently, the political orientation of the PAP underwent changes as the new nation-state responded to events in the global system.

The official ideology insists that Singapore is vulnerable, having no natural resources, only the resources of its people. The image of vulnerability flowing from location, size and paucity of natural resources is an unsubtle misdirection of attention; Singapore is lodged within a broader system, but so too are all states; the Singaporean state machine is an institutional power-articulating membrane whereby global system flows can be controlled to a greater or lesser extent. Constraint and opportunity, the logical givens of the notion of structure, offer occasions for action, elite-ordered action in the first instance; other groups act insofar as they may. In the nearly three decades since independence external and internal events bear upon the Singapore state/government, which having begun life wedded to social-democratic goals slides towards a technocratic-authoritarian mode of securing the integration within the global capitalist system of Singapore's economy/society.

Over the early period 1954–68 the PAP ran through a series of overlapping and cross-cutting political battles to secure independence, domestic power and mobilize the population. In securing independence these political battles were ostensibly against the British but the detail reveals a more tangled situation. Crucially the British were leaving anyway, and through the late 1940s and early 1950s the only issue was how and to whom would power be bequeathed. It was quickly made clear that the communist members of the anti-Japanese resistance were not going to inherit power, and the resultant Malayan Emergency fixed this decision in place. General notions of federation, which seem to have been popular with the British, were discussed and latent Malay nationalism awakened. Malaysian independence with Malay rights entrenched came in August 1957. In Singapore the PAP, under the leadership of Lee, forged an alliance with left-wing trades unions and Chinese students. Seemingly regarded with fear by the local establishment, the PAP achieved internal self-government in 1959 with their indigenized programme of social democracy. And thereafter securing the hegemony of the PAP was a similarly complex and drawn-out matter. In the run-up to the 1959 election the PAP fought against other pro-independence parties and distinguished itself by making a successful alliance with the left-wing unions and Chinese students. After securing internal power there was a confused interval that involved two areas of manoeuvre: the Malaysian Federation issue and the PAP elite's struggle with its erstwhile allies, the unions/students. The battle against the left unions/students, which had taken institutional form with the establishment in 1962 of Barisan Socialis, was tilted firmly in the direction of the PAP by the expedient of Operation Cold Store, the detention of some one hundred political opponents. The union with Malaysia lasted from September 1963 to August 1965. After separation Barisan Socialis withdrew its remaining members from parliament and the PAP hegemony was established; the PAP project then unfolded.[56]

In establishing the early mobilizing state PAP used the civil service, armed forces, community organizations, media and so on to secure its economic, political and socio-cultural goals. The PAP's socio-cultural mobilization followed on from this recruitment/co-option of the population in general, which later became straightforward social engineering, and entailed the dissemination of PAP official ideology through many channels: media, unions, community-level organizations, schools, parliament and formal state occasions. The pursuit of growth and welfare was central to the political project of the PAP, and this programme was vigorously pursued through efforts to diversify the economic base of the country, to industrialize and to provide minimum welfare services in the shape of health care, schooling, housing and jobs. Goh Keng Swee's growth policies involved fiscal incentives and infrastructural development; after independence there was a shift from ISI to EOI strategies so as to address the problems of withdrawal from Malaysia, Singapore's established trade area. One key strategy for economic growth and social welfare has been the Central Provident Fund (CPF), which is an important saving and welfare mechanism with its forced saving for old age.[57]

The state has been vigorously developmentalist in rhetoric and action. Much has been done; Singapore has been ever more tightly fixed into the global capitalist system. The paradox of the state regime's ideology and action is that of undoubted success entailing apparent failure; as Singapore ever more successfully achieves national development it becomes ever more deeply enmeshed within the wider global industrial-capitalist system.

The goal changes; the elite commitment to a version of social democracy declines; the model becomes technocratic and authoritarian; not just the inherent logic of social democracy[58] but the exposed position which their policies engender, a response to realized relative weakness; and whilst the masses enjoy economic growth, there is a cultural/political price to pay. Critical Singaporeans regard the authoritarianism as unnecessary; the goal is questioned in critical labels such as 'hotel Singapore' and 'air-conditioned nation'.[59]

Industrial-capitalist development in Singapore

The state has been active in fashioning economic, social and cultural development; having dismissed its opponents in the period of the dissolution of empire in alliance with a Chinese-speaking socialist mass movement, the technocratic, professional English-educated core of the PAP then struggled to secure total control; it has remained free from effective challenge. The support of the masses was secured through development policies that relied on inviting in the multinationals and ensuring welfare in the form of employment, housing, schooling and health care. It is an interventionist system; decisions are made at the top and passed down; democracy is at a minimum but not absent; local commentators speak of depoliticization or an administrative society. What is clear is that the rule of the PAP has to be seen in terms of an interventionist state machine being used to make population and resources (geography and the history of linkages to the capitalist centres) maximally involved with the wider currents of the world capitalist system.[60] The upshot is an externally focused economy and society.

In the 1980s Heyzer[61] revealed how the local population has been made available by the PAP state regime to the multinationals; an inegalitarian pattern of development that could manifest pressures for change, a point also made by Chan.[62] The analysis anticipated the work of Yoshihara[63] in that it looked at the marginalization of local capital in construction, hotels and other local services. Yoshihara stressed the role of foreign capital in the economy and concluded that Singapore was merely a base in the region for overseas capital. Yet there is one very obvious problem with Yoshihara's model of capitalism, and it echoes the problems of the orthodoxy, and it is the focus on nation-state units: it is better to see states as membranes within wider flows of power, with power-holders being those who deploy the state machine to pursue a particular political project (which routinely, it seems, entails inventing a nation). The Singapore state has read flows of power and acted to secure a particular goal, in this instance a niche within the global economy. Rodan argued that 'a relatively autonomous political state has emerged with sufficient need and will to facilitate Singapore's incorporation into the emerging [New International Division of Labour] NIDL'.[64] It is clearly a quite particular strategy, one with benefits and costs. The resultant outward directedness is attended by risk (that the global system might alter its structure, altering in turn the niche occupied by Singapore) and high costs (to the population, who have been 'made available').[65]

However, for Singapore with its quite particular resource base, shifting into the world capitalist marketplace has meant a significant measure of externalization in the sense that active involvement brings greater dependency on forces wholly out of the control of the Singaporean people or state. Singapore is successful in major part because the economic, political and cultural structures of power within the global capitalist system run straight through it. Recalling the image of a bounded unit which is central to popular ideas of nation-statehood, it can be seen with the example of Singapore that reality is more complex: here the discrete unit is easily dissolved in the reality of complex transnational flows.

Possible regional spheres: ASEAN, East Asia

The circumstances whereby the four Asian Tigers were able to carve out an economic space within the rapidly growing global economy of the post-Second World War period involved the accidents of war whereby local elites replaced colonial powers; externally propitious circumstances, with global economic growth and the local effects of American wars in Korea and Vietnam; and elite commitment to national development.[66] Doubts about the future of the Asian Tigers have persisted; early arguments suggested that either propitious external circumstances would alter or local populations would recoil from the authoritarianism.[67] Others argued that the Asian Tigers operated within the Japanese sphere of the global economy;[68] again, it was suggested that Japanese success could not be expected to continue; renewed doubts were expressed as the Asian financial crisis unfolded.[69] In the event the crisis passed and Japanese success continued. Japanese success has been bound up with its trading role in Asia and the third world;[70] some have spoken of a new Japanese imperialism;[71] others caution attending to the constraining linkages to the USA;[72] reforms in China continue; the shape of an East Asian region is unclear.[73] Yet a Japanese economic sphere within the global economy has been identified; Japanese aid, trade and foreign direct investment have centred on East Asia;[74] one possible future for Singapore is as part of a Japan-centred region of East Asia.

The Plaza Accords of 1985 revalued the yen and encouraged Japanese business to relocate manufacturing plant in East Asia; this process coincided with accelerating development within China and the region entered a period of remarkable prosperity, interrupted only by the relatively brief confusions of the 1997 Asian financial crisis. The character of these regional interlinkages is debated; patterns of trade and the institutional vehicles of diplomatic exchanges are readily identifiable and whilst their precise character is unclear they do constitute a network of regional activities; a new aspect of those structural contexts with which states must deal.

A regional sphere in East Asia has been posited; the overall shift to the modern world has been achieved in a discontinuous and episodic fashion; the breaks marking the transition of a particular territory from one broad configuration of economy, society and culture to another have often been accompanied by conflict (either simply internal as domestic groups manoeuvre for advantage or also involving the incoming forces of global industrial capitalism); in the long process of the shift to the modern world in East Asia the lines of social discontinuity have been diverse and the patterns of conflict correspondingly complex. At the present time the post-cold war global industrial-capitalist system shows a number of cross-cutting tendencies: (1) to integration on a global scale, with a financial system that is integrated across the globe, and extensive increasingly denationalized multinational corporation operations; (2) to regionalization within the global system, with three key areas emerging where intra-regional linkages are deepening; and (3) to division on a global scale, with areas of the world apparently falling behind the regionalized global system. In East Asia the linkages of the region to the global system are very extensive and becoming more extensive. The linkages between the various parts of the region are also becoming extensive and deepening. The region has a core economy, extensive economic linkages, new political/trade mechanisms and a measure of cultural coherence. An integrated regional grouping can be taken to be in the process of formation (although the end point is most unclear and the extent of integration should not be overstated). Yet it is not a straightforward matter to identify a region as East Asia. It is clear that historically in the long period prior to the invasive spread of industrial capitalism the region was Sino-centric, and then with the expansion and deepening of the demands of industrial capitalism it was absorbed within colonial empires. In the period of the Pacific War the region formed part of the Greater East Asian Co-Prosperity Sphere that was centred upon Japan. Thereafter, most recently, it has been divided by cold war alliances into a Western sphere lodged within the US-centred Bretton Woods system and an inward-looking socialist sphere. The outward-directed group have been subject to the political-economic, political and cultural hegemony of the USA. However, the recent end of the cold war system has opened up the issue of the delimitation and future shape of the region. The outward-directed group is undergoing considerable change and in brief this may be summarized as the beginnings of a political-economic and cultural emancipation from the hegemony of the USA. At the same time the countries of the socialist block which spent decades following autarchic development trajectories are now opening up to regional and global systems. The regional project in East Asia is contested. The position of the USA is still shaped by cold war security thinking, with a significant relocation of anxieties from geo-strategy to geo-economics. The region is economically threatening and needs must be ordered according to US agendas, hence Asia-Pacific Economic Cooperation (APEC). In contrast the Japanese view is ordered around the image and programme of flying geese. The Tigers slot in just behind the leader, with their economies growing along with that of Japan, and ASEAN brings up the rear of the formation. And finally the Chinese view the regional arena within the frame of Greater China, or the China Circle. The growing economic power of China is taken to be expanding and drawing in the other powerful economies of the region. Overall, it can be said that regionalism within East Asia is only developing slowly and it will develop in its own fashion, with slow networking rather than decisive formal institutional shifts.

Many commentators have noted that a distinctive regional variant of industrial capitalism is in the process of construction.[75] In this perspective, the countries of East Asia can anticipate a prosperous future; the same would hold true for Singapore.

Official readings of the history of Singapore

The Singapore state regime[76] has been routinely interventionist; it has shaped the economy, society and thinking; it has promulgated an official ideology, both delimited-formal[77] and pervasive-informal.[78] The official ideology of the Lee period presents a characterization of Singapore, a complex of ideas which read the past, detail the present and sketch the future of Singapore. It comprises[79] the myth of a founder, the claim of evolutionary advance, the idea of vulnerability, the notion of multiracialism and the idea of pragmatism.

First, Raffles is said to have founded modern Singapore on an island unpopulated save for a few fishermen. This is misleading: the existence and history of the Johor–Riau Sultanate are elided; the politics of the extraction and absorption of the territory vanish; and contemporary Singapore is rooted in the early nineteenth century rather than located in the late twentieth. Then, second, modern Singapore is presented as developing in an evolutionary fashion. This is misleading: Singapore's political history is more plausibly read as discontinuous, but the ideological benefit to the state regime is that this presentation allows claims of novelty, fragility and voluntarism in respect of contemporary state form to be lodged. But novelty is only the novelty of the fifth incarnation, so to say, of Singapore. There is a depth to the history of Singapore which the official history denies. Again, the fragility is that of a territory that has successfully ridden the changes in the world system: Singapore, far from looking fragile, looks strong. And the voluntarism which stresses local endeavours, whilst not false, is misleading in that it disguises the extent to which Singapore's success is intimately bound to its role within the wider world capitalist system. Third, it is asserted that Singapore is highly vulnerable;[80] its environment is threatening; obedience is therefore required of the population, the New Singaporeans.[81] This is misleading: the historical record shows that Singapore island has been home to several state forms; successive populations have prospered; episodes of change have not uniquely impacted Singapore. And, fourth, Singapore is read as multiracial/multicultural.[82] This too is misleading: identity is read reductively; discipline is required; the state provides it; identities are officially specified; roots affirmed; and actual patterns of ordinary life left unremarked. It is a construct; it must be maintained; its boundaries policed.[83] Then, finally, the ideology of pragmatism[84] helps close the circle; the state regime is committed to economic growth; the goal dominates; it is presented as obvious/natural, demanded by the fragile position of the territory; counter-readings are blocked; criticism is either disruptive or pie-in-the-sky dreaming; political discourse reduces to the nature of economic growth; in these terms the record of the state regime is good. Within the circle it all makes sense.

How many Singapore state forms are there?

The development experience of Singapore has been widely discussed;[85] evolutionary descriptions and explanations of bounded national success are

114 *Locating Singapore*

available, official and scholarly; these familiar positions are misleading, as ideas and institutions are social constructs. The state should not to be seen as a solid unit, enclosing a nation and operating within a system comprising similar units, but as a membrane whereby trans-state political and economic flows within the world capitalist system are ordered. States are formal transmission mechanisms for the integration of a given population or territory into a wider system; states are directed by specific class coalitions; state regimes invent nations and nationalisms to buttress their control; state regimes pursue particular projects; the resultant general domestic or international pattern is a state form, the regime's footprint. The pattern of ideas promulgated in respect of state, nation and nation-state will be shaped by how the territory deals with the surrounding system. The institutional expressions of these sets of ideas are also social constructs; the practical apparatus of the state is the fluid and shifting, historically contingent expression of global, regional and local political dynamics. Any extant state form will represent the way in which local agents have read and reacted to these trans-state patterns of power and contrived their own sphere of effective legitimate control.

Singapore island has been home to several state forms; each articulates a different role within the wider embracing system; each represents a specific integration of the territory into a wider system; each has distinctive political, economic and cultural characteristics; each has a particular domestic class politics; and each has its own set of self-understandings. State forms have been reconfigured relatively quickly; each change inaugurates a new position within international relations and new domestic arrangements: Malay maritime empire, multi-ethnic trading port, formal colony and dependent capitalist city-state. The elite now promote nation-statehood whilst embedding the territory deeply within the Japan-centred East Asian sphere of the global system; the contemporary role is theorized as a regional hub. Change within the global system is normal; global patterns are contingent; state regimes read enfolding structures, order their populations and establish particular state forms; such state forms are fluid; domestic patterns are contingent. There is no single, continuous Singapore; rather, there is the currently recoverable history of a succession of discrete ways in which the island has lodged itself within the wider systems enfolding it: each successive phase has been articulated by a particular state machinery, each a way of ordering internal forces so as to interact effectively with global system flows of economic, social and political forces; each phase displays typical self-understandings, the ideas held by the relevant constituent groups.

Singapore: debating the newly industrialized countries in the 1980s

Development became an issue with the disintegration of European colonial empires; pressures for democratic reform were strong; the available economic theory was Keynesian; expectations of new political forms centred on nation-states; and replacement elites had the goal of effective nation-statehood irresistibly imputed to them.[86] Modernization theorists focused on national units at a time when the global system was becoming ever more interconnected; an available route to the future for these units was conceptualized by generalizing notions of progress specific to Americans and Europeans; dependency theory offered an alternative from the 1960s, with lines of argument calling attention to the disabling structural position of poor countries within the global capitalist system; recommendations were made for the pursuit of national development; comments were made on the necessity for reforms or changes to global power structures; expectations of change were modest.[87] The success of the newly industrialized countries (NICs) presented development theorists with difficulties; there were unpersuasive claims to vindication made by liberal-market theorists and initial dismissal by figures using dependency theory; the liberal-market position did not grasp the broad political nature of NIC success; patterns of interdependence within the global system were crucial; success was highly contingent; it became clear that the political project pursued by the elite in control of the state was crucial.[88]

A further area of debate cast doubt upon the record of the Asian NICs. In the late 1980s Bello and Rosenfeld[89] argued that the fortuitous structural circumstances attending NIC success were in the process of altering with American protectionism,[90] internal opposition to low-wage policies and the problem of shifting to high-tech high-value-added production; a retrogression to the third world was possible; and against the celebrations of liberal-market thinkers, replicating the pattern was unlikely. Yet in Southeast Asia the role of Japan was crucial: supplying capital and relocated manufacturing; lodging the NICs within its expanding economic space;[91] and linking elements within the region.[92] Singapore served as a bridgehead for Japanese (and other) capital coming into Southeast Asia,[93] in turn an element of wider regionalization;[94] and the Japanese success showed little sign of dissipating. Nonetheless, even here critics spoke of an inferior capitalism;[95] distinguishing subsistence, market and capitalist sectors, where the latter is the location of technologically innovative advanced industries, in Southeast Asia the economy centres on the market sector of small-scale low-technological firms, and these have financed state-inspired externally technologically based second-rate industrialization programmes – a Southeast Asian ersatz capitalism.

The debate continues;[96] for the moment it is enough to note that contemporary Singapore is the out-turn of a deeply political project; the elite have used the machinery of the state to further a self-conscious agenda of changes; an active state has read enfolding structures in order to fashion a distinctive niche within the global capitalist system, a dependent capitalist development; it has been theorized recently in terms of the idea of a 'global business hub'.

116 *Locating Singapore*

The development experience: the economy and the polity

Singaporean economists in the1980s considered the record: typically stability, continuity and the pursuit of economic growth were mentioned, the keys being 'political stability and economic policy'.[97] The intermixing of state and market were noted but not pursued; a government-supported free enterprise system was identified;[98] the role of key politicians was mentioned.[99] After the surprise of the mid-1980s economic downturn a report was prepared by Lee, H. L.:[100] problems identified comprised external matters (regional/global downturns) and internal matters (an overly rigid economy with a propensity to over-save (which savings had fuelled a local property boom/bust)); the intermixing of state and market was acknowledged; the report proposed further opening the economy; the rhetoric celebrated business and enterprise;[101] and underpinning the strategy were good government, efficient infrastructure, education, free enterprise and flexibility.[102] The government began a privatization programme and moved to encourage the local private sector.[103] However, others were more direct; political analysts identified the active role of the elite.[104] Linda Lim[105] pointed out that the state in Singapore plays a central role in shaping the economy: it provides infrastructure (utilities, telephone and post, port and airports, industrial estates, television, sanitation, all education, three-quarters of the housing, and medical services); it engages in production (state trading companies, airlines, shipping, shipyards, banking and many joint ventures); it holds 75 per cent of the land of the country and can acquire the rest; it is a major player in the capital markets (via the Central Provident Fund, the Development Bank of Singapore and the Monetary Authority of Singapore); it offers various incentives to guide private investment; and it shapes the labour market through regulation of conditions of work and control of labour.[106] Lim dismisses privatization;[107] the success of Singaporean capitalism is a matter of state direction.[108] The mainstream claim that markets made East Asia was questioned;[109] governments used the machineries of the state; attention turned to the politics of success.

As regards the development experience of the polity, modernization theory was presented in the geo-political context of cold war aid-donor competition, liberal democracy versus socialism;[110] the theory offered an apparently easy route to liberal market democracy; but concern for democracy decayed;[111] and metropolitan capitalist elites evidenced concern for order/access in their acquiescence to authoritarian governments.[112] Analysis was reoriented;[113] political analysis shifted from the ends of liberal democracy to the processes of political order; economics showed a preoccupation with growth rather than the broad recapitulation of Western development experience; concern increased for public policy making; and in East Asia the USA defended dictatorships. Modernization theory both interpreted and sought to guide the logic of peripheral capitalisms;[114] the modernization theory was deeply ideological; offering an idealized version of the putative goal of development coupled to an implausibly easy set of recipes for its realization;[115] the actual processes are best conceptualized in terms of continuing articulation of metropolitan capitalisms with local forms of life, the expansion of the capitalist system.[116] Singaporean politics were conditioned by the exchange of the commitment of the elite to national development and the structural condition of peripheral weakness; the elite demobilized their population, disciplined them and made them available to meet the needs of multinational manufacturing industries; the elite thereby sought to deepen their role within the global capitalist economic system.

The claim to an inherited underdevelopment is a part of the official ideology of the Singaporean elite. The claim is false: the island was never underdeveloped; it may have been poor in the years following the Pacific War, but so too was most of East Asia, Europe and the home territory of the British colonial power.[117] Castells argued that Singapore is a successfully planned developmental state;[118] orthodox economics are not helpful; the key is the role of the state because 'government intervention in the economy, in Singapore as elsewhere, is fundamentally a political process, aimed at implementing a political strategy toward the fulfilment of some overriding political goals'.[119] All agree the record is good: a 'patriarchal market socialism'[120] needing domestic reforms.[121] Castells also noted the emergence of 'new nodal points in the global economy',[122] where Singapore is one such and likely to become more important as the pattern of the global economy becomes more dispersed.[123]

Dependent capitalist development in Singapore

The role of the state regime in fashioning Singapore is crucial: having come to power in alliance with a Chinese-speaking socialist mass movement, the technocratic, professional English-educated core of the PAP then struggled with its erstwhile partners for control; the support of the masses was achieved via economic development policies that relied on inviting in the MNCs and supplying employment, housing, schooling, health care and leisure services. It is an extensively interventionist system; decisions are made at the top and passed down; internal democracy is at a minimum, but is not absent; local commentators speak of depoliticization or an administrative society.[124] The elite sought to make the territory maximally involved with the wider currents of the global capitalist market,[125] an externally oriented dependent capitalist development.

Critics argued that Singapore was not an NIC, merely a base for overseas capital with little local dynamism;[126] but elites read trans-state structures to inform projects; the Singapore state regime actively secured a niche in the global economy.[127] Rodan calls attention to state policies and the evolution of the global system:[128] (1) it is not enough to point to good policy as there had to be possibilities within the developing global system and these were forthcoming with the post-war long boom; (2) a favourable pattern of internal class relationships was necessary and the colonial power left the state relatively free to act to fashion a variety of corporatism; (3) the state committed itself to economic growth, engaged in extensive intervention[129] and organized extra-economic factors such as labour, schooling and welfare; (4) participation in the global system generates domestic demands; (5) and shifting role within the global system is not easy.[130] Success is contingent, the trajectory exposed; domestic costs are high.[131]

Actors and ideas: Lee Kuan Yew

Democratic elite theory[132] is derived from the elite theory of inter-war Europe: it was associated with both liberal theorists[133] and anti-democratic theorists;[134] more recently it has appeared in transitions theory;[135] it calls attention to the active role of elites and it is a useful supplement to more general discussions of structures/agents. The theory calls attention to the role of elites and their internal diversity (elite fractions), and helps uncover the internal dynamics of the various political systems. Singapore has been labelled a stable semi-democracy[136] but this can be disregarded in favour of looking directly at the multiple domestic actors involved. A narrow self-selecting elite governs Singapore; recently characterized as a core executive,[137] it comprises a few hundred people; it is the key group in Singapore.

The PAP inherited colonial Singapore: local elites had a deep knowledge of the ideas current within the modern world (pilgrimages); they had a deep knowledge of the anti-colonial political thinking current at that time (claims cast in terms learned on multiple elite pilgrimages); and they had a close acquaintance with forms of resistance to imported ideas (including Imperial Japanese official ideologies and grassroots communalism). They did not begin with an intellectual *tabula rasa*: they did not have recourse to inherited culturally carried ideas; rather, they utilized their inheritance of social democracy and borrowed contemporary political ideas or models. Down the years the borrowings have included the following:[138] first, during decolonization, in opposition, they adopted ideas from ideologies of the third world when they opposed the Suez invasion, supported Sukarno, granted that the India of Ghandi and Nehru offered a positive model and China's record was respected; second, at the time of separation new models were invoked, in particular Israel and (historical) Venice;[139] third, from the 1970s economically successful social-democratic models were invoked, thus Germany, Japan and Switzerland; and, recently, Singapore has itself been presented as a model of authoritarian and successful development which might be copied in other parts of East Asia.

These borrowings have been submerged in a National Past, a simplified official history of the polity detailing the achievement of a rugged independent society. The Singaporean National Past[140] revolves in significant measure around Lee Kuan Yew, who is presented as the animating figure of their success story; domestic commentary is often deferential to this National

Past and external commentary is also often deferential (either accepting the claims (hagiographic) or accepting the claims in order to protest (critical)), but the National Past is just that (an official ideology) and scholarship can usefully deconstruct these claims. Three issues are pursued here: first, disentangling Lee the PAP and the historical trajectory of Singapore; second, looking at Lee as the ideological capstone of the system; and, third, considering the implications of the specificity of historical trajectories and the idea of Asian Values.

Disentangling Lee Kuan Yew, the People's Action Party and the historical trajectory of Singapore

The official ideology of the state presents a narrative of the evolutionary achievement of a rugged independence most recently under the enlightened leadership of the PAP, which has been ably led by Lee Kuan Yew. But the official ideology is misleading; it is reductive; complex historical processes are reduced to matters of the leadership; it is further reductive in that one party leader is singled out. The various aspects of these processes must be disentangled: first, Lee Kuan Yew is not the PAP; second, the PAP is not Singapore; and third, Singapore's history is more than the era of PAP rule: The National Past must be deconstructed so as to get the scholarly tale straight.

The role of Lee has been widely discussed; there are many celebrants/critics of the man.[141] There are also discussions of the wider core group.[142] A related area of enquiry involves the exchanges within the core group and with opponents and other agents.[143] The crucial claim is that there was a core group, not one man. Lam and Tan[144] analyse the records/contributions of a dozen or so early PAP activists: organizational figures; economic/social architects; legalists; historians; Malay mobilizers; Chinese-educated vanguards; and one figure representative of the defeated. Lam and Tan recall that the period 1945–65 was filled with confusions: the slow collapse of European empires, including the British Empire; the cold war; the Malayan Emergency; the idea of non-alignment amongst newly independent nation-states; anti-colonial sentiment amongst other Southeast Asian elites and interference in the process of British withdrawal; debates amongst British administrators as to how to dissolve the empire (Malayan Union – Federation of Malaysia; Singapore as Crown Colony); debates amongst local political agents as to how independence should be organized (ideological, communalist and personality issues); negotiations between local and colonial leaders; and debates and activities amongst grassroots local agents (unionists, students), including strikes and riots. In this twenty-year period there were multiple voices: there were multiple projects for the future; the departing colonial power wanted continuing access for its commercial interests (the departing colonial power had signed up for cold war anti-communism – and fought the Malayan Emergency and later Konfrontasi);

Malay elites wanted power in any post-colonial arrangements (Malay nationalism was growing amongst the grass roots); Chinese minorities sought to assert themselves (noting the example the People's Republic, plus familiar Chinese chauvinism); and local agents educated in English sought non-communalist solutions in varieties of nominally left-wing socialism.

The PAP came to power in the context of the confusions following the Pacific War. A number of discrete phases issued in the emergence of an independent city-state: the formation of a Crown Colony (that is, institutional administrative separation from the Malay peninsula); the construction by steps of internal elective self-government; an assertion of a brief Singaporean independence; unification with Malaysia; and withdrawal from Malaysia in 1965 and independence. The domestic politics of each of these five steps/phases is filled with the confusion that attends the entire period; the general crisis in East Asia encompassed Singapore; there were multiple conflicts; shifting alliances; public violence; and elite fraction seizures of power (cold store). The island of Singapore was home to multiple groups; these groups remained; the victors order the population fragments – diversity is disciplined, the 'five Ms' – the victors also write the history; it is after 1965 that the familiar story of the achievement of a rugged independence under the visionary leadership of Lee and the PAP emerges; it is lodged in the public political culture of Singapore; it is a National Past.

A National Past is affirmed by the elite, which invokes the idea of underdevelopment;[145] the term was current at the time and has a particular logic;[146] a distinction is drawn between underdeveloped and developed and modernization is the process whereby a polity can move from the former condition to the later. It was very influential; and it was ideological. On the macro scale an idealized history of the present developed as an abstract general model for all other countries to follow; underdevelopment was read as an original condition; the history of the non-metropolitan countries was thus read out of the story; and the history that most had was one of extant civilizations subject to colonization. The micro-scale implication was that the actual history of ex-colonial territories could be disregarded; a *tabula rasa* was thereby invented; the pursuit of development began with independence and in the case of Singapore the PAP tackled underdevelopment; the colonial era was pushed into the background and was by implication a long period when foreign rule did not attend to the business of development. The tale is grossly misleading: Singapore became part of the modern world in 1818; it was constructed by the British; Singapore has a long history; and its history did not begin with independence or the PAP.

The National Past obscures the detail of the confusions of the 1945–65 period; there were multiple agents involved in fashioning the independence of Singapore; there were multiple projects; the PAP was only one organized agent; Lee was only one PAP leader; the outcome was contingent (it could have been otherwise). The National Past also obscures the deeper truth that the contemporary polity is lodged within regional and global structures of power; it is not separate; it is not autonomous; it needs must read and react to enfolding structural change; the contemporary polity is a contingent construction. The National Past reads out change; the manoeuvre is present in the abstract-general idea of 'vulnerability' (which must be combated) but there is no one fixed or essential Singapore; there is only the history of the successive locations of the territory within wider encompassing systems; change is routine, not atypical.

The Lee Kuan Yew myth

There is an available myth of Lee Kuan Yew which places him at the centre of the contemporary development trajectory of Singapore. In its unguarded positive versions the myth claims that Lee is responsible for the success of contemporary Singapore; substantively, the claim is false; the myth should be resisted; however, behind the myth there is a key political player; Lee's actions embody a coherent set of animating ideas; however ideas do not translate neatly into political practice – events, accidents and error also shape lines of action. The myth obscures matters; it has to be set aside in order to better grasp the unfolding dynamics of the Singaporean polity. The available myth of Lee Kuan Yew comes in positive and negative variants; there are celebrants and critics; they have it in common that they place Lee at the centre of the development history of Singapore; the claims contain both errors and elisions.

The claim contains multiple errors: historically Singapore was successful long before Lee; in the case of contemporary Singapore, Lee was one of a group of political leaders;[147] and in the case of contemporary Singapore, circumstances were propitious. First, historically, Singapore was successful from the early nineteenth century, there was a rapid inflow of population, rapid build-up of a trading role and the Suez canal and steam ships accelerated the development.[148] At the time of independence in 1965 Singapore was an established regional/global trading city; it was an established centre long before Lee Kuan Yew became political leader. Second, contemporary Singapore – positive and negative – is explained in significant measure in terms of the individual activity of one man, Lee Kuan Yew; however, he was only one of a group of core politicians; they were supported more widely amongst the community; and they were also supported by the outgoing colonial power. And, third, in terms of the prevailing circumstances, contemporary Singapore was a key nexus within regional and global trading networks; its success was underpinned and was also helped by events; the cold war in East Asia brought money flowing into the region – finance, aid, technology transfers, military support, diplomatic support and an open American market into which exports could be placed. After the Pacific War East Asia experienced a long period of prosperity. It was into this expanding economic environment that independent Singapore moved.[149]

122 *Locating Singapore*

The claim also contains untenable elisions of distinctions between the personal political career of Lee, the organizational record of the PAP and the development history of modern Singapore. The elisions are familiar; they are present in the commentaries; they are also promulgated by Lee, as in, for example, his claims to the vulnerability of Singapore and the judgement in recollection that 'we nearly didn't make it'. First, Lee's personal political trajectory might reasonably be characterized as fraught; the war years, end of empire and confusions of transitions to post-empire arrangements offered severe challenges and many opportunities for failure.[150] Second, the party political scene in Singapore during the end of empire was confused; parties presented themselves to restricted publics within an already small population; the disintegration of empire was not smooth; the cold war raised anxieties about communism; in the Malay peninsula there was a guerrilla war. The PAP was one more party; it had an English-educated leadership and could only prosper in a parasitic alliance with the mass movements of ordinary Chinese; once in control of the state it turned upon its erstwhile allies and destroyed them. To this extent the early career of the PAP was difficult; however, it did receive the active support of the departing colonial power; and from 1959 onwards the party was able to bend the machinery of the state to its will.[151] As regards Singapore – the third element in the familiar elision – it is enough to note that it had been successful since 1819, and there was no reason to suppose it could not continue to be successful. It was a key link in regional and global capitalist trading networks; its port serviced these links; it was powerful; it may also have been dilapidated after the war years; so too was most of East Asia and Europe.[152]

So, whilst Lee's trajectory, and that of the PAP, may have been fraught, Singapore was a well-established part of regional and global networks before either Lee or the PAP came onto the scene; these three should not be intellectually collapsed into one. Against this collapse it might be speculatively asserted that, given Singapore's powerful position within the global system, more or less any ruling elite could have made a success of the territory.

Nonetheless, Lee's actions embody a distinctive set of ideas/attitudes. Michael Barr identifies an elite conservative background, disturbed by the collapse of empire, which feeds into a determination to participate in anti-colonial struggles; thereafter a naïve celebration of the role of the elite matures into the pragmatic, ruthless opportunistic pursuit of power, and in turn a mature ideology develops comprising a trio of elements (progressivism, elitism and cultural evolutionism), which in recent years have been buttressed by a rediscovered Chinese heritage.[153]

Barr[154] records that Lee's family background was Baba; the family were Straits Chinese, a privileged minority in colonial society. The family provided an English and Malay language environment and an English-language education and Lee excelled. But the Japanese occupation shattered that world; Lee adjusted and found work with the occupation authorities;

thereafter he pursued his education in London and Cambridge, where he enjoyed a glittering academic career and mixed with adherents of the democratic socialism of the Fabians. Lee joined the Malayan Forum and discussed post-colonial political futures, specifically independence; he saw the returned students as a leadership elite which was naïve as it missed entirely the role of the Chinese masses. Lee returned to Singapore in 1950 and worked as a lawyer; he made his name whilst defending local unionists and opened links to the Chinese masses. The PAP was formed in 1954; thereafter local politics are labyrinthinely complex, the PAP won the 1959 election; the territory joined Malaysia in 1963; the politics were difficult,[155] the PAP aggressive;[156] Singapore withdrew in late 1965; Lee had a breakdown;[157] and independence was embraced. Lee became a city boss; opponents were repressed, economic advance and social welfare ruthlessly pursued – successfully. Barr's point is that the elite background plus family pressures fed into Lee's politics, but the issue is one of framing. Lee was talented, opportunistic, ruthless and successful but all this takes us in the direction of personalizing the development history of Singapore; it is a foolish move. Lee is not Singapore; Singapore was successful before Lee or the PAP came onto the scene.

Barr[158] argues that Lee's intellectual make-up comprises three key elements – progressivism, elitism and cultural evolutionism[159] – whereby elites can remake cultures, the better to secure progress. Progressivism is the dominant ethos of Lee's childhood (family, schooldays and university); it is an ideal of evolutionary accumulative progress – Europe was the model and an elite could shift Malaya towards that style of life. Elitism is a central strand of Lee's thought: inculcated by family, apparently confirmed by his own raw talent and expressed in a familiar elite conservative prejudice such that elites had achieved success by their own efforts and talent and thus deserved to be rich; the elite were, in some sense, above politics, naturally superior, although, in a somewhat contradictory fashion, in power Lee sought to expand the elite through co-option.[160] Cultural evolutionism, the final element, proposed that forms of life were malleable; they could be altered, engineered to be better, and the elite could specify the direction of requisite change.

As an ideological package or deep-seated set of prejudices it all hangs together; it is an entirely familiar elite conservative package.[161] It is further buttressed by reductive argument; elites are elites because their superiority is coded in their genes; and inequality cannot be overcome as it is in a sense a natural given. In its early forms the position is a species of technical expert socialism derived from the socialism of the Fabians; it recalls a widespread post-Second World War belief in the efficacy of rational planning. In its later guises there is a regrounding as Lee's elitism is recast as the paternalistic autocratic stance of a Confucian gentleman; Lee reinvents himself as Chinese; discarding his Straits-Chinese family background, he reinvents his past as a Hakka migrant.[162]

124 *Locating Singapore*

In brief, Lee was not the key to the success of Singapore. The territory was advantageously located within the global system and it is here that explanations for success are to be found. The PAP did not conjure success out of the air; its legacy was rich;[163] it built on that legacy; it built within propitious post-war circumstances;[164] and the developmentalist ideas did not originate with either Lee or the PAP as these ideas were widely available amongst political actors and experts at the time. The success of Singapore is evident, but buying into the myth of Lee Kuan Yew obscures matters. Independent Singapore is built on the legacy of a richly successful colonial trading city; it is the latest polity based on the island; and contemporary success flowed out of an extant historical trajectory.

Lee Kuan Yew: the ideological capstone of the system?

The political system in Singapore is variously characterized; there are celebrants, critics and interpreters. There are manifold cross-cutting debates but there are commonalities: there is an elite (a core group); it is elitist (the core group read themselves as a naturally scarce resource); it operates from the top down (the elite issue instructions and the masses are expected to fall into line); it is managerialist in style (claiming a neutral technical expertise that clothes the more raw exercise of power); it is intolerant of criticism (a description amenable to various readings – appropriate to the state's vulnerable situation, authoritarian and an expression of a distinctive non-Western ethos); and it reserves a particular place for leadership where the current long-serving leader is Lee Kuan Yew.

Political analyses of Singapore make great play with the leadership role of Lee, and some are hagiographic and some highly critical, but, as noted, Lee was only one key politician in early Singapore. Lee was one member of a wider elite group; Lee later dispensed with some of his early colleagues, whilst others seem to have been content to drift into the background, but Lee continues to be one politician amongst others. Nonetheless, Lee is the figure placed at the front; distinctions between the career of Lee, the activities of the PAP and the record of Singapore itself are elided. Lee becomes the public face of Singapore. Lee plays at least two roles: active political agent and official public face, the ideological capstone[165] of the regime/project.

The regime is curiously intolerant. Ideological and practical pressures dispose the PAP elite to this aggressiveness towards critics and competitors: in the first place, the elite self-understanding is cast in terms of their scarcity, expertise and disciplined commitment to the future of Singapore,[166] thus elections do not provide a mandate as in a liberal-democratic-type system; rather, they validate,[167] and high electoral scores indicate elite success, whilst low scores indicate failings; and then, in the second place, the majoritarian electoral system in Singapore is heavily rigged against the opposition but it routinely scores around 30–40 per cent support, and anything beyond 40 per cent of the vote starts to translate into seats in parliament.[168]

The peculiar intensity of PAP intolerance is more difficult to understand. However, some speculative explanations can be offered: first, psychological, it is down to Lee's personality; second, circumstantial, it is down to the context within which PAP came to power; third, situational, it is down to the contexts within which the PAP has perforce operated; fourth, project contingent, it is down to the functional requirements of PAP project, that is, making available a disciplined workforce to international multinational capitalism; fifth, city-state contingent, thus in a small place amongst elites, if politics is not consensual it will be factionalized and zero sum; and, sixth, cultural, thus the received historical trajectory of the Chinese has produced intellectual machineries which constitute families, relatives, clans and language groups rather than an abstract-general notion of society, hence particularistic thinking and networking (thus the give and take necessary for a democratic polity works with an abstract-general society, but it does not work where there is only my group and other groups). Finally, it might be noted that political institutional and cultural patterns are contingent; and authoritarian systems do change.[169]

The specificity of historical trajectories

The notion of world music calls attention to the rich diversity of local musical forms and suggests they be attended to directly rather than read in terms of their divergence from a taken-for-granted model exemplified by Western pop music; the notion of world politics calls attention to the rich diversity of local political forms and suggests they be attended to directly rather than read in terms of their divergence from a taken-for-granted model exemplified by Western liberal democracy. More formally, European-tradition social theorizing, alluded to earlier in this text, posits that local polities have distinctive trajectories and internal logics; historical comparative analysis interpretively/dialogically can grasp their unfolding logics. Politics has many forms. In the broad Chinese sphere there are four major polities: China; Hong Kong; Taiwan; and Singapore. China has a party/state system; Hong Kong has a species of post-colonial oligarchic rule; Taiwan has acquired the trappings of liberal democracy; and Singapore has produced a species of dominant party system. None of these looks like an American or European Union liberal democracy; each has its own trajectory and political logic. There are numerous strands to these debates; in Singapore notions of Asian Values and communitarianism have figured.

Chan[170] argues that the notion of democracy is not exhausted by the standard American model; indeed, the standard model cannot adequately grasp practices within America and Europe; against the familiar expectations associated with standard modernization or globalization theories,[171] economic change does entail social and political change, but historical experiences are particular; there are varieties of democracy. In Asia polities have evolved via particular historical experiences, notably colonialism, decolonization and the resultant urgent task of state building; many Asian experiences can be considered in this way; Singaporean politics has developed around one major party; it affirms clean administration and has delivered; it continues to develop. An Asian democracy can be discerned in a communitarian stress on the group, rather than the individual; a communitarian stress on the common good, rather than individual rights; an ingrained respect for authority and hierarchy; the presence of dominant parties, often emerging in the wake of the Pacific War; and the familiar model of a centralized bureaucracy and strong state, created in the context of the pursuit of development.

Chua recalls that the PAP came to power in 1959,[172] an elite group which ran its own project, holding power plus ideological hegemony through a clutch of ideas, including vulnerability, survival, the 'five Ms'[173] and pragmatism. But the PAP became a victim of its success; prosperity sits uneasily with the ideology of vulnerability; and material success in particular has invited individualism. The elite has made numerous adjustments in its public position:[174] an early response invoked Confucianism; a later response picked up from American neo-conservatives,[175] whose discussions of East Asia attributed stability and success to Confucianism. The PAP embraced these materials, arguing that Singapore was successful because of Asian Values. A communitarian ethic was identified – collectivist not individualist, with the state central not minimal. Chua[176] points out that a key issue is how the state functions and is legitimized; the PAP evades these issues by collapsing party, government and state;[177] but institutional structures are crucial[178] and mechanisms to construct a free consensus are lacking. In this light, a communitarian democracy in Singapore would require significant changes as the minimum conditions are clean elections and open debate; the former condition is (partially) met but the later is not.[179] Other institutional changes to the constitution and parliament are ambiguous,[180] attempts to protect Lee's legacy but perhaps also attempts to cultivate a middle ground.[181] Such reforms plus PAP's advertised commitment to democracy offer lines of immanent critique which are perhaps more useful than externally visioned complaint.

Lee Kuan Yew and Asian Values

There was a vigorous debate about global trends in the 1990s.[182] American elites in particular felt bullish: there had been a long period of economic success; there was talk of globalization and the new economy;[183] the cold war had ended, the end of history had been declared[184] and the shape of the future was written in the American (and Western) present. The East Asian Tiger economies came to be seen by American and European commentators as both creditably successful and regrettably authoritarian; the mainstream both celebrated the Asian economic miracle[185] and deplored the region's lack of political development.[186] These lines of criticism fused: East Asian political economies were mercantilist; East Asian capitalism was notable for its elite-level cronyism; and East Asian capitalism rested upon an unreasonable social and political authoritarianism.

Celebrants of the liberal-democratic market system were uninhibited in their advocacy of the merits of their model; this was a general phenomenon. In East Asia the end of the cold war had a region-specific aspect; during the long years of the cold war as the USA sought allies it had tolerated a variety of East Asian authoritarian regimes but the end of the cold war meant the end of such tolerance and American politicians began to voice criticisms. Longer-term anxieties about trade relations reinforced these criticisms. East Asian authoritarian regimes were now seen not only to be politically deficient (failing to measure up to liberal standards) but also to be deriving economic advantage from such arrangements, and a cry went up for more liberal democracy and more liberal markets.

A reply was made and three participants were notable: Ishihara Shintaro;[187] Mahtir Mohammed;[188] and Lee Kuan Yew.[189] These participants had in common that they rejected the criteria invoked by European and American critics and in their place asserted the vitality of Asian Values.[190] The foreign critics were answered directly: the claims to the universality of liberalism were rejected; it was pointed out that values were context bound; in East Asia the relevant political/ethic framework was not liberalism but – and here answers varied – community. In the great arc of the Chinese sphere the name of Confucius could be invoked. The name stood for elites, hierarchy, paternal concern, obedience, family, social discipline and the overriding priority of the needs of the community. A sharp counter-critique was made against the contemporary American and European examples of liberalism in practice: a series of social ills were cited; all were explained in terms of excessive liberalism; all were explained as evidence of the costs of forgetting the community in favour of unbridled individualism. In all this, Lee's version of Asian Values can be read as a species of communitarianism[191] – elite paternalism and collective endeavour. It has deep roots in his core beliefs; it has been used to discipline the population but the beliefs are sincerely held; and these beliefs also constitute a coherent set. The Pacific Asian model of development is distinctive; it embodies a distinctive set of ideas/practices;[192] Asian communitarianism is not simply a convenient confection called into being to justify authoritarian polities.

Much hot air was generated. However, there is a real debate buried in the rhetoric and it concerns the nature of modern industrial capitalism: does the system act to homogenize all those cultures which it draws into its orbit or does the system blend with extant cultures in order to produce a multiplicity of local hybrid variants?[193] The case of Singapore suggests the global system is home to numerous hybrids; or, more strongly, that as change is fundamental to the system, shifting hybrid forms are all that is on offer.

128 *Locating Singapore*

Multiple agents

The foregrounding of one agent from the many involved has provided the political-cultural project of the PAP with an ideological capstone. The National Past advertises and obscures the logic of the system. Multiple agents were involved in building contemporary Singapore: first, multiple groups were associated with the colonial power; second, many agents were involved in the process of decolonization; third, many agents were involved in the unexpected independence of Singapore; and, finally, many agents were involved in animating the distinctive political-cultural project of the PAP.

Politics: debating the first generation

Elites use the power of the state machine to pursue political projects which reflect not merely domestic class interests but also their understanding of enfolding global system structures. The Singapore state regime mobilized its population; the subtle exchanges of constraint and opportunity shaped unfolding political life. The original commitments of the core group of professionals, all of whom had made colonial pilgrimages, were social democratic; their early programme embraced demands for an end to colonial rule, the formation of a unitary Malayan state and social and economic development; subsequently, their position changed towards a technocratic authoritarianism as they responded to events in the global system; but there were signs of a softening in the use of state power with the retirement from the premiership of Lee Kuan Yew the accession of Goh Chok Tong.

Received traditions and social democracy in Singapore

European political philosophy distinguishes liberalism from democracy; in turn, these could be distinguished from liberal democracy, social democracy and communitarian democracy.[194] The delimited-formal ideology of the early PAP was social democratic;[195] the objectives of the party were stated at the November 1954 inaugural meeting;[196] the essence of the position comprised the goals of an end to colonialism, the formation of a unitary Malayan state and the pursuit of development. The PAP deployed the contemporary variant of social democracy to theorize the circumstances of a peripheral capitalist formation in the context of the disintegration of European colonial empires; the elite actively responded to a colonial legacy of circumstances and ideas; and as subsequent events unfolded the elite made further responses.

The PAP led by Lee Kuan Yew assiduously pursued national development.[197] Singapore in the official view is lacking natural resources, exposed and vulnerable,[198] crucial elements of a hegemonic ideology; yet there is a grain of truth in this; Singapore is lodged within the global capitalist system; economic, social and cultural changes flow through the system; and the intermixing of internal/external dynamics conditions elite responses. The image of vulnerability is misdirection; the state is an institutional membrane whereby global system flows can be controlled; constraint and opportunity offer occasions for state regime action, elite-ordered action in the first instance, other groups act insofar as they may; following independence events bear upon the Singapore elite, which having affirmed social-democratic goals slides towards a technocratic authoritarian mode of securing a niche for Singapore within the global capitalist system.[199] Over the period 1954–68 the PAP ran a series of overlapping and cross-cutting political struggles: to secure independence, its own power and the mobilization of their population in the search of growth and welfare goals; it lodged the territory in the global system; this was the success/ambiguity of dependent capitalist development.

The political struggles for independence were ostensibly against the colonial power but the issue was who would inherit power: communist allies in the anti-Japanese resistance were excluded,[200] notions of federation awoke latent Malay nationalism[201] and in Singapore the PAP forged an alliance with left-wing trades unions and Chinese students. The party was regarded initially with apprehension by the local establishment but on assuming internal power after the 1959 election it struggled with its erstwhile allies whilst addressing the issue of relations with Malaysia.[202] Barisan Socialis was formed in 1961 as left-leaning figures split from the PAP. A broad power struggle followed. The Barisan leadership were gaoled in the 1963 Operation Cold Store and a manipulated election secured power for the PAP.[203] The PAP secured union with Malaysia and this ran from September 1963 to August 1965. The Malaysian elite dissolved the union. In Singapore, PAP hegemony was established by late 1965 in what was now an independent country.[204] The machinery of the state was utilized; an official ideology was disseminated. There were characteristic state regime actions: the relentless promulgation of the idea of economic growth, taken as a non-ideological pragmatic course of action requiring a disciplined population; the design of social institutions to express and channel this mobilization for growth (schools, urban planning, ethnic identities, language policy, industrial planning and so on); alternative messages were blocked through control of the media and the co-option or suppression of alternative centres of political thinking; and care was shown in controlling incoming cultural messages, which expressed itself in direct controls of the media to exclude unwanted material and deploy desired messages, as well as the typical Singapore state campaigns (for clean streets, against long hair, against cigarettes, for politeness and so on).

The pursuit of development was central to the political project and involved diversifying the economy through industrialization and providing health care, schooling, housing and employment. Goh Keng Swee's policies involved fiscal incentives to business, provision of infrastructure, development banks and forced saving;[205] after separation from Malaysia and independence there was a shift from import-substituting to export-oriented strategies; success followed. The state has been committed to national

130 *Locating Singapore*

development; it invited in the multinational corporations in order to broaden its role within the global capitalist system; this fitted Singapore ever more tightly into the global capitalist system; the state fostered welfare and established an authoritarian political system; but success is generating increasing problems, such as how to continue the success of dependent capitalism whilst controlling the socio-political habits current in the modern world. The achievement of social democracy was attained at some cost; Lee took the legacy of the colonial power and secured employment, schools, housing and health care; the population acquiesced in an increasingly authoritarian polity; the deeper ambiguity was that the achievement of autonomy apparently entailed simultaneously discarding it as the territory was lodged more firmly within the global system.[206]

Characterizing the political culture

Reviewing the modern history of the political culture of Singapore there is shift from social democracy to technocratic authoritarianism; this slide is cognitively available within legislative doctrines;[207] and there was a rapid move from political reform to state management. The 1968 Employment Act shifted power to the state; the act was part of the response to the failure of federation, the decision to invite in the multinationals and the adoption of an export-oriented strategy. In political-cultural matters the end of federation meant a major shift in PAP thinking about nation building.

The elite had overlapping ideological dilemmas. First, internally, there was the development of the colonial port function or the pursuit of socialism which they had espoused and which implied a break with their colonial legacy, and they chose the former, called it the latter and suppressed dissent on the grounds of the vulnerability of the country. Then, second, circumstances constrained the state with regard to ideologies of development;[208] a largely Chinese population in a predominantly Malay region plus Western anti-communism meant Singapore could not celebrate Chineseness or invoke socialism and so nation building took the form of a non-ideological ideology. Thereafter the commitment to economic growth is presented as natural;[209] the exposed vulnerable position could only be tackled by the pursuit of economic growth; it was a technical matter; counter-readings were blocked; criticism was either dreaming or disruptive; the former was no problem, the later was removed. Inside the circle it all did make sense.

The strategy of inviting in the multinationals built on available strengths; it marked the end of the social-democratic period; the population of the island was made available to the multinationals; an official ideology was constructed, with the central focus on economic growth and celebrating pragmatism and the pursuit of rugged self-reliance. It is an ideology of demobilization.[210] Various machineries of control were deployed: routine manipulation of the electoral system;[211] bullying directed towards the electorate;[212] control of the media;[213] and the hounding of political opponents.[214]

An official ideology presented approved understandings and secured mass acquiescence. The official ideology presents an evolutionary story of the achievement of nation-statehood; the myth of the founder Raffles obscures the historical sequence of identifiable forms of life; the claim to vulnerability obscures the depth of the history of the territory; and the assertion of rugged self-reliance disguises the linkages to the wider system. Thereafter a positive image is presented in the New Singaporean;[215] the construct comprises a premier set of ideals which celebrate technocratic efficiency and obedience and a secondary set which identify what must be avoided, and here we find symbols of dissent.[216]

Singapore has been characterized as an administrative developmental state,[217] where meaningful political life was reserved for the world of the party elite, bureaucracy and business. Yet increasing inequality and a diminution of political freedom looks problematical; if all power is centred on an elite, then political renewal is difficult.[218] But political life does not stop;[219] the overriding goal of economic growth dominates the government's thinking and this goal establishes criteria of evaluation for all of Singaporean life; all other criteria are dismissed as not relevant; the official view is concerned with securing order; it reaches into the lives of ordinary citizens;[220] however, it may be that increasing affluence and generational change will challenge this pervasive-informal ideology.[221]

Singapore and Singaporeans are constructs of the post-colonial period;[222] making the new nation-state entailed demobilizing the ethnic aspect of life, promoting the idea of a national interest, prioritizing the economic (at state and individual levels), fashioning a suitable social order (language, discipline, education) and restructuring the community from one that was ethnic based to a disciplined multicultural population.[223] This has been successful; but the population is now outgrowing the paternalistic repressive polity; the state has responded too late with a programme of reinforcing Asianness; the pattern of economic activity is the key to the culture and the trends seem to be in the direction of more change.

The state intervenes routinely, extensively and deeply in the lives of all Singaporeans: with regard to ethnicity (definitions and relationships), language (the stress on English plus mother tongue), housing policy (the extensive social, economic and political role of the Housing Development Board (HDB)), education (often cited as social engineering), health, the position of women (via family policies), savings and pensions (via CPF), workplace and labour law (via law and co-opted unions), community centres a vehicle of social engineering), and campaigns and press control(the better to appropriately mobilize the population).

Subsequent changes in political life

After independence in the 1950s the elite sought the survival of an exposed country; along with the pragmatics of economic growth went repression;

economic success kept most people inside the official ideological frame. However, after the 1981 by-election which saw Jeyeratnam elected in Anson a new political phase was in prospect;[224] pressure was reinforced in the 1984 election. By the mid-1980s it was clear that a series of changes were in process: the increasing political maturity of the electorate was evidenced in the rejection of the PAP in elections; there was increasing affluence (and with it changes in social mores, summed up by the government as 'Westernization'); demographic change as the old generation which lived through the independence period died off; and, finally, a new generation of political leaders began to emerge.[225] In this new phase, the response of the PAP has been to cultivate the middle ground via changes in political style and organizational and institutional changes with feedback units, special MPs, group representation constituencies and an elected presidency. However, this reform tendency was not smooth; the late 1980s involved a mixture of reform (which involved, in additional to institutional changes, a year-long exercise in participation oriented to producing the National Agenda) and repression (including the nonsense of the alleged Marxist conspiracy and the expulsion of an American diplomat for interfering in Singapore's internal affairs).[226]

Singapore celebrated twenty-five years of independence in 1990; history was celebrated, national myths reaffirmed and the second-generation leader Goh Chok Tong took power.[227] A measure of change in the polity was mooted; some liberalization in the government's manner certainly, and maybe moves towards a less restricted democracy; it was suggested that the government was being forced into liberalization from above.[228] A measure of liberalization was clearly on Goh's agenda.[229]

Politics: foreign policy

Political elites deploy the machineries of the state in order to locate their polity advantageously within global structures of power; a political project entails both a domestic agenda and a foreign policy. The PAP ran through a series of broad positions: anti-colonialism and the pursuit of independence; unification with Malaysia and the formation of an independent state where an independent foreign policy was required.

The early party stance of the PAP was cast in then current terms of opposition to colonialism, affirmation of the non-aligned movement and the United Nations coupled to the central drive for independence. As the final collapse of the British Empire in Southeast Asia was drawn out over a period of years, there were extensive debates on the proper political form which post-colonial British Southeast Asia could take: economic anxieties figured amongst many participants as these territories were rich; ethnic anxieties figured as these colonized territories were home to mixed populations as a result of inward migration; and political anxieties figured as the decision of the Malayan Communist Party for armed struggle was both echoed within Singapore (mostly non-violently) and came to be subsumed by the departing authorities within the East Asian variant of the US-sponsored cold war. A solution to these manifold problems was perceived in the unification of Singapore with Malaysia. The proposal was greeted warmly by the PAP, opposed by local left groups (who correctly saw it was aimed in part at them) and distinctly cold-shouldered by the majority of the Singapore population. The PAP ran a drive to assimilate the population of Singapore island with the wider country; the proposal was not popular; the PAP manoeuvred against its left-wing opponents and after a dishonest referendum entered the union having first declared independence from Britain; much similar manoeuvring followed, all to no avail as the union was unsuccessful.

Once the PAP formed an independent government it faced a familiar trio of problems: security, order and development. Security means external borders (neighbours) and internal stability (minorities). Order means law, citizenship, political system and national identity. Development means growth (domestic/international) and welfare. In respect of the first, the Singaporean government's pursuit of security has often been remarked upon:[230] the PAP borrowed from the model of other small states, introduced conscription, built a citizen-based military, equipped it and adopted a defence posture which centred upon making the territory too expensive to be worth attacking. Some[231] have argued that the elite have taken a realist approach to foreign policy, representing themselves as uniquely vulnerable, a small Chinese city located within an area with a majority Malay population. The newly established government borrowed Swedish security ideas (total defence), and techniques and advisors from Israel, where Lee Kuan Yew implausibly compared Singapore to Israel in respect of its security concerns.[232] The government sought a balance of power within Southeast Asia, encouraging dialogue, joining multilateral bodies, in particular ASEAN, and encouraging the involvement of extra-regional powers, in particular the USA.[233] Others suggest that the Singaporean government paid rather more attention to 'norms and values' – that is, it embraced the ASEAN project,[234] it participated in the regional search for peace and stability.[235] Then, second, the Singaporean government's pursuit of order has often been remarked upon and the relevant notion here is that of vulnerability: as the territory was vulnerable to outside threats beyond direct control, so the future was vulnerable to indulgent domestic politics (communalism, party politicking or indulgent media activities) and so the PAP demobilized opposition groups and co-opted the population. And, finally, the Singaporean government's pursuit of development (growth and welfare) has also been noted: the local variant of a familiar post-colonial deal – the elite seek popular support in exchange for providing better material lives. Chong[236] characterizes the package as the Singaporean Model of Development (SMD) and two broad phases are identified. The first is the post-independence phase of establishing an independent state, which entailed accommodating the demands of non-aligned movement (that is, the context for Singapore as a third world state), the demands of ethnicity (that is, being a Chinese city in a Malay region and moreover not being a 'third China'), the demands of the cold war (repudiating earlier alliances with communist groups and accommodating the demands of the West), and which feeds into the non-ideology of vulnerability and pragmatism. Second, the success produces a Singaporean model of development which is not much remarked upon at first, but after the end of the cold war the situation changes as American post-cold war celebrations of liberal democracy reduce the public inclination to tolerate authoritarian polities, thereby generating pressures for adoption of the American model (presented as universal). But, amongst others, Singapore resists and promulgates an alternative idea of Asian Values. The debate turns bad tempered (with the 1993 UN World Conference on Human Rights, the Michael Fay episode and the 1997 Asian financial crisis). The upshot is that the notion of Asian Values has weight. Singapore successfully asserted soft power and the country is now more accepted at its own valuation: a regional trading hub with its own distinctive communitarian democratic system – something of a model in other parts of East Asia.

The PAP now maintains membership of a multiplicity of regional and global organizations: ASEAN, the various ASEAN spin-offs, APEC, ASEM and the United Nations. It asserts the importance of international law. It maintains good relations with its neighbours, where the crucial vehicle has been ASEAN. It maintains good relations with China yet it seeks to draw the USA into the region as a security balance to China. In all, it is the familiar stuff of diplomacy. It might be added that conventional foreign policy is subordinate to the elite's overriding goal of material advance. Singaporean foreign policy seeks contacts where it can find them; it is an omni-directional foreign policy appropriate to the optimistic 'flow-through five-star hotel Singapore' scenario.[237]

Changing dynamics

Singapore is not a newcomer to significance within the global capitalist system; post-colonial industrialization should not be seen as the start of a global economic role; rather, it is the latest in a long line of such roles. The political project of the PAP state regime was oriented towards securing a prosperous niche in the global division of labour; the strategy was technocratic, outward oriented; dependent capitalist development entails the omnipresence of the state; it makes available a depoliticized population for outward-oriented development. The upshot is ambiguous as the PAP came to power as a social-democratic party and has presided over the increasingly authoritarian incorporation of Singapore within the global capitalist system; yet pressures for democratization exist domestically with higher levels of living and internationally within the global capitalist system.

Politics: expectations of second-generation reforms

The PAP came to power within a particular context; a mix of factors shaped its efforts: the disintegrating British Empire, which opened up future politics; the drive for independence, democracy and development, evident in both the colonial and metropolitan territories, which both facilitated and shaped its political agenda; and the nascent cold war, which provided an external environment both unhelpful, in the guise of conflicts, and helpful, in the form of the provision of resources from extra-regional powers. There were multiple agents involved in the political process of decolonization; those leaving, those staying; together they had multiple anxieties: protecting metropolitan economic interests; reassuring locally based expatriates that their interests were secured; mollifying local supporters of metropolitan powers; and negotiating the make up of the replacement elite. It was an untidy, fraught business; only in the official world of agreements signed, receptions held and flags lowered or raised was the process orderly; only in retrospect could any of the arrangements be represented as inevitable. The old guard of the PAP operated within this environment of fluid politics, played for high stakes, and they secured power through a mixture of guile, violence, talent and luck. Thereafter, their project was successful; however by the 1980s the days of decolonization had fallen into the past and new generations of Singaporeans had come of age in business and the social realm; and change had run through the party as personnel had been turned over. However, the elite group still centred on Lee Kuan Yew and the PAP still presented a hard face to its citizenry; in a series of elections through the 1980s its support fell; the party sought renewal; not dramatic change but re-presentation. It seems that Lee anticipated the problem and following the shock of the 1984 election changes have been made:[238] non-elected MPs have been appointed (in order to buttress the opposition); group representative constituencies have been established (ostensibly to ensure mixed ethnic representation, though the procedure does handicap the opposition); an elected presidency has been established (with extensive blocking/oversight powers); a set of core shared values have been identified. In time a new prime minister was installed.[239]

Goh Chok Tong: second-generation leader

Singapore celebrated twenty-five years of post-colonial independence in 1990; the official history was celebrated, national myths reaffirmed and the second-generation leadership moved into place.[240] Goh Chok Tong became prime minister in November 1990; his style was characterized in the local press as open and consultative.[241] Informed commentary suggested that reform was on Goh's agenda;[242] domestic and international circumstances were conspiring to force a measure of democratization from above;[243] and the economic and institutional bases for reform were in place.[244] A number of themes cropped up in these discussions: the declining role of Lee Kuan Yew; domestic change, including both demographics (a younger population with different life experiences to the old guard) and material advance (the country was comparatively poor but it is now rich); and elite reconstruction and repositioning (a new updated PAP project). Goh's premiership ran from 1990 through until 2004.

Goh became leader in 1990 and assumed greater control within the core executive slowly.[245] He faced external problems and internal pressure for reforms. Goh initiated changes in economics, foreign policy and social policy. First, in economic policy there is growing debate about the direction of Singaporean economy and economic policy. Commentators[246] note that the early successes have not been sustained (for example growth rates, new manufacturing sectors) and they note that the economy is mature; that is, it behaves like that of other highly developed economies. They suggest that the early success might not be repeated. The cold war-protected niche is no longer available. But economic policy making does not seem to have changed. The PAP elite seek to guide the economy. The response is to look for new high-tech manufacturing sectors and to cut costs to industry (but inequality is growing, there are signs of class division and resentment, unemployment is growing and there is resentment towards foreign workers). Suggestions range from more marketization through to regionalization. One theme is the difficulty of generating new ideas when the PAP insists on setting all frames of debate. All these long-term problems were exacerbated by the 1997 Asian financial crisis, the 2001 attacks on the USA and global downturn and the 2003 SARS epidemic. Second, in foreign policy the region has been acknowledged more, free trade agreements (FTAs) have been signed and WTO global commitments are still in place. After 2001 Singapore broke with neighbours and supported the USA, an error now maybe acknowledged.[247] Third, in social policy the consultative style was pursued and commentators confirm this as marginal but welcome.[248]

However, Goh made no significant changes to the political system;[249] indeed, the electoral system in some respects became more rigged against the opposition. The Group Representation Committee (GRC) system introduced in 1988 was extended; shortly before the 1991 election further GRCs were constructed;[250] shortly before the 1997 election further changes to GRCs were made;[251] and shortly before the 2001 election further changes to GRCs were made. Commentators record that the PAP arguments about ethnic representation were plausible in 1988 and 1991, but not thereafter.[252] On the other hand, there was some slackening of elite intolerance of public criticism and debate.[253]

Goh addressed the issue of values. He first mooted a national ideology in October 1988. This was picked up by Lee Hsien Leong in January 1989 and he identified a number of core values, and in January 1991 the government issued a White Paper formalizing discussion on Shared Values.[254] Official ideologies are top-down affairs. In Singapore the early PAP project centred on the pursuit of material advance and an elaborate repertoire of ideas carried the project (economic, social and political). In the political sphere a hegemonic ideology was established (vulnerability, discipline and pragmatism, with the terms further unpacked so as to inform policy). But the PAP project is in part a victim of its success. The country is rich – vulnerability is an implausible claim; however, the PAP is not inclined to democratize and so a new revamped official ideology has been sought; one formulation has been found in the notion of Shared Values. It is a culturalist response to changing circumstances;[255] other responses were rejected. What have to be fixed are sets of ideas as values are failing in the face of materialism and Westernization. The restatement of core values will fix the problem. However, the population has diverse historical roots; it has its own form of life; it is distinct; it is its own place.[256] The values of the population don't need fixing. Change is a given and the elite cannot evade the consequences of their own success. The PAP are looking to manage or arrest change, and the Shared Values display an elite preference for a conservative, paternalist statist ideology.[257]

Goh sparked a related debate: communitarianism.[258] The party first came to power in 1959,[259] took control of independent Singapore in 1965, demobilized the opposition and ran its own EOI project, thereby linking power and ideological hegemony. The ideology embraces a clutch of ideas: external vulnerability entailed a concern for survival, which in turn required an overriding pragmatism in respect of necessary means. The domestic population is disciplined through a clutch of ideas, the 'five Ms',[260] and the project in its own terms has been very successful. The PAP is now the victim of its own success as it invites individualism. An early response invokes Confucianism and other religions, whereas the later version picks up from talk about the success of East Asia and the idea of communitarianism emerges. It is presented as the key to the distinctiveness of East Asia, the key to affirming shared values. American neo-conservatives post-1960s saw East Asia as stable and successful.[261] They attributed this to Confucianism. The PAP embraces these materials. The PAP argues that Singapore is successful because of Asian Values: a collectivist ethic, not individualist; the state is central, not minimal; and the key issue is how the state is legitimized. The PAP collapses the party, the government and the state.[262] However, institutional structures are crucial:[263] in this light, a communitarian democracy in Singapore would require significant changes; the minimum conditions are clean elections and open debate, and whilst the former condition is partially met, the later is not and so communitarian democracy has not yet arrived in Singapore.[264]

Managing changes: further demands

Structural change runs through the Singapore polity and agents read and react. The political system is distinctive. The elite 'core executive' comprises

138 *Locating Singapore*

the network of agents located within the institutional structures of state, market and society;²⁶⁵ it revolves around the prime minister and cabinet office; it is not established by formal institutional responsibilities (organization diagrams etc.); rather, it is a shifting network of power relationships; and the prime minister sits at the heart of this network, in total a few hundred people.²⁶⁶ The core executive works through this network; in the case of Singapore reference to the orthodoxies of liberal-democratic theory make little sense;²⁶⁷ it is the Westminster system; club government;²⁶⁸ it is an oligarchic system.²⁶⁹ The core executive has made its project hegemonic; power runs through its hands; economy, society and polity are thereby ordered. The elite have disciplined the population they inherited upon the dissolution of empire; they have pursued an overriding goal of material advance; they have suppressed internal critics; they have produced material advance. The system is effective but popular support is shallow. And the elite must continue to deal with change.

Demographic change means that younger generations of Singaporeans have no direct memory of the confused period of decolonization and national independence. This feeds an elite anxiety: Lee Kuan Yew has cast the matter in the backward-looking terms of younger Singaporeans lacking any experience of struggle and hardship; the theme reappeared in the run-up to the 2006 elections, when it was cast in terms of the particular experiences and concerns of the 'post-'65ers'²⁷⁰ who have grown up with independent Singapore, inheriting the successes. And if the young are a problem, so too are the established middle classes, as the middle class have embraced a consumerist lifestyle²⁷¹ and show signs of resentment of the heavy-handed PAP.²⁷² Also, the working class are aware of their comparatively poor position; inequality²⁷³ has grown and seems to have shown up in voting patterns.²⁷⁴ In brief, class differentiation, consumerism (underscoring class differences) and external models (consumer fashions, intellectual and professional ideas plus large numbers of middle-class guest workers) generate a demanding mix for agents inclined to a managerialist response.

Lee Kuan Yew has made himself the central figure in an elite project;²⁷⁵ the PAP has been described as a hollow shell,²⁷⁶ an occasionally useful vehicle for the core executive;²⁷⁷ and the distinctions between state, party and person have become blurred. Singapore politics has its own logic centred on the PAP monopoly of power but the system cannot be sustained unchanged. Although Goh Chok Tong became prime minister in 1990 and Lee Hsien Leong in 2004, Lee Kuan Yew's final departure will be significant²⁷⁸ – retirement or death. Lee has sought to manage future change; this is impossible; further changes will take place; their nature is at issue. Lee cannot institutionalize continuity or succession. The paradox is his core role: patronage and control run through his hands; all dissolve away on his retirement or death; and the core elite will then have to reorder their relationships.

Politics: debating the third generation

Lee Hsien Leong succeeded to the premiership in 2004; the succession had been widely trailed;[279] Lee Hsien Leong held an election in May 2006 and whilst the PAP vote went down a little he can now claim his own mandate. The issue now is how his premiership will develop: some commentators[280] construe external pressures in such a way as to imply the inevitability of change, whilst others, reading the external pressures less dramatically, and looking to the domestic scene, are sceptical about rapid change.

International and domestic pressures

The global system transmits pressures to which the Singapore state regime must respond; the external environment has to be managed. A series of elements have been debated: (1) there are structural pressures on Singapore's manufacturing role as others look to replicate East Asian success (that is, export-oriented industrialization and the off-shoring of low-tech manufacturing are now widely practised, and Singapore no longer looks special so its attraction to investors is fading); (2) there is competition from China (because in the low-tech cheap-labour manufactures it is difficult to compete against Chinese labour costs); and (3) the costs of picking high-tech areas for government investment are high, as recent high-tech investment has been very expensive (some electronics plants are not as advanced as the more numerous plants being built in China and the cost per job created is high).

The Singapore government response has been energetic, producing a series of reports which offered various recommendations comprising a mix of continuity and upgrading: continue with established policy; upgrade the business environment (regulation, incentives and labour); identify key high-tech sectors for state involvement; encourage local companies to work outside Singapore; and act similarly with government-linked companies (GLCs). A further theme was to pay more attention to linkages with neighbours in Southeast Asia: more economic links and better political links.[281] A series of familiar phrases are used: hub economy; regional hub; and platform economy.

In considering the global context it might be noted that the end of the cold war[282] – nominally 1989–91 – was significant in East Asia. US policy changed and it was no longer tolerant of authoritarian governments running mercantilist policies (developmental states or crony capitalism, depending on perspective). Globalization and liberalization were the new mantras. There were reforms within the region and the financial crisis of 1997 ensured further liberalization at the behest of the IMF. The Singapore government faced a dual dilemma: managing change and securing creativity through copying. The goal of becoming a regional knowledge industry hub – a rational upgrade policy – entailed some social and political liberalization, thereby threatening the elite control that had accompanied the earlier successes of the regime; and the goal seemed to be a variant of the economy of the USA, the elite wished to copy an imagined dynamism in order to generate dynamism at home (whilst worrying about importing democracy (although external pressures moderated after 2001)).[283]

Mainstream commentators often diagnose a dilemma between the putative demands of the global system – which imply the rational response of a movement towards a knowledge based economy, which in turn implies the local production or importation of knowledge professions, in turn suggesting a perhaps sharp diminution of the disciplinary regime run by the state over the years, in turn implying the risk of popular demands for further social and political liberal reform – and the state's heavy investment in machineries of discipline and mobilization. The Singaporean government has enthusiastically embraced new electronic media; the internet and so on; it has made them available to the corporate world it seeks to serve whilst actively regulating them within the domestic sphere in order to forestall an overtly critical internet-based civil society or the use of the internet to circumvent the tight controls on parties and election processes. The corporate world is content; so too, it seems, most Singaporeans.[284]

In the domestic sphere the elite face quite specific problems, some measurable, others more imponderable: demographics, inequality, unemployment and generational change. First, there is significant demographic change, thus the population is getting older and demands are being placed on the society to adapt and to care for its elderly.[285] Second, there is increasing inequality. There is increasingly evident inequality between the patterns of life of educated professionals and those of the less well educated – the elite speaks of 'heartlanders', the bedrock of PAP support; that the elite picks them out and thus labels them indicates elite-level doubts about their support.[286] Third, there is unemployment; the impact of 1990s liberalization and the desire of the elite to upgrade – the knowledge-based economy – means that many older and less well-educated workers are likely to experience difficulties in finding employment, one of the motivations for the 2006 decision to build casino resorts on Sentosa.[287] Fourth, the generational shift flagged in the notion of the 'post-'65ers'; a generation has grown to maturity in Singapore since independence; they have no memory of the struggles invoked by the first-generation leaders – including the still politically visible Lee Kuan Yew. The post-'65ers grew up in a relatively wealthy city; decolonization, cold war and domestic political conflicts form no part of their experience; new agendas are implied.[288]

The pressures of demography, inequality and unemployment all imply greater welfare spending on the part of the state; an early elite reluctance to provide 'subsidies' began to be revised as Goh Chok Tong took power;[289] and there will be further revisions. The emergence of a post-'65 generation might imply wider changes as their life experiences are not those of first- or second-generation leadership; a wealth of commentary[290] attests a clear if inchoate desire for social and political change.

Elite responses and the likelihood of change

In public politics, commentators have low expectations of significant change:[291] the core ideology of PAP will be sustained, their hostile attitude to opponents will remain and thereafter there might be some softening of their public stance, a more sophisticated control,[292] plus a disengaged population.[293] The core ideology of elitism plus progress plus merit is protected; other parts of the ideology can be adapted or revised; the second generation made some changes (they removed some of the policy excesses of Lee Kuan Yew in the areas of welfare and ethnicity as more tolerant policy stances were adopted)[294] and further changes might be anticipated with the third generation.

The elite designed system is not fixed. It is a contingent achievement. There are available speculations about sources of change:[295] first, there could be intra-party factionalism following the departure of the remnants of the old guard; second, given that the regime's legitimacy rests in significant measure on material success a prolonged economic downturn would be problematic; and, third, a new educated media-savvy generation might emerge. However, these commentaries run along conventional lines, looking to identify emergent pressures and problems; it is true that the PAP has to read and react to change but this demand is not new, and quite why they might suddenly lose an ability their record attests to is not clear.[296] The elite have demonstrated their nimble-mindedness on more than one occasion; emerging generations may be unsettled[297] but the PAP will respond. The recent utilization of the notion of civic society is one example; the party has taken to speaking of civic society and it seems to have in mind civic responsibility (a mix of caring for family, hard work and contributions to the community); the terms 'civic society' and 'civil society' are used interchangeably, presumably deliberately;[298] it is a strategy of demobilization coupled to co-option and any independent civil society is pre-empted; the elite's assertion of control is veiled (perhaps) but not significantly relaxed.

The elite is self-conscious.[299] It has broadened down the years through co-option. Today the elite mixes politicians, business, civil service, statutory boards, state-owned enterprises and the higher levels of the armed forces. There is a small coterie of key players. The elite has few rules but relies on elite socialization: personnel are recruited, tested and promoted upwards. The spheres noted interlink and personnel move freely amongst these spheres. The system has allowed the elite to mobilize its population for rapid development. The elite may be inherently fragile (instrumental commitments and factions); however, those who lose in elite-level disputes leave the elite, they do not organize oppositions. The third generation is now moving into power; earlier generations have revolved around the Lee family but a post-Lee Kuan Yew elite will form, perhaps as a new balance of elite forces as continuity is as likely as change. It might also be noted that the elite are adept at recruiting, albeit narrowly and in their own image,[300] and signs of decay are not evident.

142 *Locating Singapore*

Looking to the future, Low[301] records that the Singaporean developmental state has been successful in securing development (a sometimes brutal exercise in marginalizing local Chinese business groups in favour of an elite-sponsored reordering of the economy in concert with overseas capital) but now faces novel demands from the global system. The answer is to embrace the inevitability of globalization and move towards a knowledge-based economy. A slew of reforms is needed: privatization and liberalization (and these are likely to entail some social and political pressures for liberal reform); and whilst some work has been done, more needs to be done. Low offers three scenarios for the future.[302] In the first, economic, social and political reforms all mesh cleanly and there are no problems – Singapore is reordered and a new developmental state fitted to the new global situation is established. Low notes this is unlikely and offers two further visions: (1) Hotel Singapore – the place continues to be efficient and is used by foreigners and locals as a base, but there is no particular commitment to the place and ideas of nation, community and development slowly subside until Singapore Inc. fades; (2) 'flow-through five-star Hotel Singapore' – the place continues to be a base but the users and stakeholders retain a commitment to its success and the city-state becomes a 'business hub par excellence'. In this version Low envisages a more cosmopolitan Singapore as talent moves in and through; the island's 'Chinese' character perhaps becomes less evident and less problematical in the eyes of its neighbours; Singapore might even move ahead of its northern competitor, Hong Kong, whose elite are not masters in their own house (and have to cope with flows of low-skilled migrants from the mainland); and the means to the realization of this scenario are available in the habits of creative reform routinely embraced by the Singapore elite; they should take the lead.

Overall, the third generation must, as with earlier generations, read and react to change; external pressures flow through the global system, recently popularly cast in terms of the idea of globalization; internal pressures mount as the population ages and as new generations come onto the scene. It is difficult to envision failures, but success could take various forms; further scenarios can be sketched.

Politics: inscribing and naturalizing the project

Cities are human constructions, literal and figurative: collections of buildings and streets, places where people make their lives; they seem massive yet they are transient, made and remade down the years. The cities of East Asia were reconstructed in the years following the Pacific War; amongst the detritus of war, the chaos of dissolving empires and nascent cold war indigenous elites looked to build for the future; novel contingent political projects created new urban patterns; the cities and the lives of their inhabitants were remade, their politics inscribed in their shifting forms.

Contemporary Singapore emerged from the wreck of the British Empire; it did so in stages through internal self-government, union with Malaysia and finally an unanticipated independence; the elite mobilized its available population; it created both state and nation. The country's niche within the international division of labour has continued to change: in Singaporean elite terms, the fruits of necessary 'upgrading'; in social scientific terms, the results of changing elite policies as circumstances changed. The elite have been nimble; advantages have been pursued; there has been elite/policy/niche change, yet there are core aspects to the experience; the Singaporean polity is elite led, its population mobilized; the elite have built and rebuilt the city; urban redevelopment has embraced virtually all the city; hitherto rural areas have been similarly treated; new towns bead the island; what is true on the macro is repeated on the micro scale. These are planned and ordered[303] areas; the elite's contingent vision is inscribed in the patterns of life of the population and the form of the city they inhabit.

The political project: making selves and society

The state intervenes in the lives of all Singaporeans; such interventions bear upon the individuals' sense of themselves and upon their patterns of social life within the community. The interventions are routine, extensive and effective. In respect of their private selves: with regard to ethnicity (stipulative definitions and managed relationships); language (the stress on English plus mother tongue); and social mores (the stress on meritocracy and aspiration). In respect of their social selves: housing policy (the extensive social, economic and political role of the HDB); education (often cited as social engineering); health; the position of women (via family policies); savings and pensions (via CPF); workplace and labour law (via the law and co-opted unions); community centres (a vehicle of social engineering); and participation (campaigns and press control, the better to appropriately mobilize the population).

These multiple interventions have varied expression: law, institutions, social practices and so on. They also have expression in the urban form of the polity, its buildings, streets and spaces. The urban form of Singapore has been made and remade down the years; it has been extensively self-consciously reconstructed since independence; the political cultural project of the PAP has been inscribed in the urban form of the city.

Inscribing the project

Land use in Singapore has always been planned;[304] a layout for the settlement was sketched in the 1820s;[305] in broad terms it was followed; however, the settlement grew rapidly; the characteristics of colonial cities[306] elsewhere in Asia were repeated; the city was a link within a wider economic system; the functions of the city were therefore structurally prescribed; these structural

144 *Locating Singapore*

forces found local expression; colonial cities were made. There were a multiplicity of local agents; multiple economic roles; multiple ethnic groups; multiple cultural resources; discrete patterns of life; confused interactions; elaborate processes – direct and indirect – of reaching a shifting, always provisional modus vivendi; contested compromises.[307] Between 1819 and 1887 the settlement developed in a largely ad hoc fashion; there were multiple players; multiple objectives were pursued; much provision of urban capital was private. There was very rapid population growth in the later nineteenth century and whilst this fuelled the growth of the economy it produced a low-quality urban environment; overcrowding and disease were commonplace. An important step was taken with the promulgation of the 1887 Municipal Ordinance; it provided for urban regulation and reforms; it was the basis of government efforts in respect of the urban environment up until the Pacific War; its establishment was contested, so too its activities. There was early action in the areas of health and sanitation; the urban areas were overcrowded, underserviced and riddled with disease; however, the perceptions of colonial officials and local people differed; urban reforms were implemented against opposition; official concerns for hygiene could be and were read by local people as intrusive, unnecessary and costly. Parallel drives to upgrade housing conditions, waste collections and water supplies were similarly contested. The links made by colonial officials between overcrowding, settlement designs and disease were not readily granted by local populations; there were numerous campaigns of improvement; but the results were often meagre. At the turn of the twentieth century rapid population growth had produced very poor living conditions; however, around this time the earliest ideas of urban planning emerged in the metropolitan centre and these made their way to Singapore; by the 1920s ideas of urban planning were in place; reforms were to be large scale; and improvements to the lives of communities were to be engineered on a large scale.[308]

Notwithstanding these changes, the slow pace of change and the dislocations of war and decolonization meant that the urban inheritance of the PAP was poor: overcrowding; multiple uses; run-down facilities; outside the urban areas there were villages, kampungs, small-scale enterprises and farming. These other areas have been drawn into the planning process. There has been a series of urban master plans:[309] the 1958 Master Plan, after the style of United Kingdom planning, a core plus radial routes; the 1969 Ring Concept Plan, shaped by United Nations consultants after the style of Dutch urban planning, a ring city with settlements strung along; the 1970 Singapore government plan, a ring plus a core axial corridor running west to east; and the 1991 Revised Concept plan, encompassing all the land area of Singapore, involving a core plus two rings plus radial routes. The country is now a comprehensively planned settlement.[310]

Amongst the range of planning activities, housing is crucial to the PAP; it is a 'covenant'[311] between the people and the government. The HDB dominates all aspects of provision and management and it is well funded (via its

Figure 1 Singapore, boat quay.

own income streams and government transfers). The population is bound into the PAP project; it is disciplined; it does benefit; it does support the PAP; and thus housing underpins the legitimacy of the PAP project. The depoliticization thesis is wrong, as politics does not go away, it goes somewhere else; the political project of the PAP is inscribed in the routines of Singaporeans (hegemony/discipline)[312] and remade day by day. The PAP

146 *Locating Singapore*

Figure 2 Singapore, Yishun North Point Shopping Centre.

official ideology centres on material advance; it is presented as realistic and practical; and housing is the major material good provided to the population.[313] The PAP took possession of the land; the owners were minimally compensated; and the island was reworked; in pursuit of export-oriented industrialization, spaces and the population were made available for MNC-centred development; industrial development sites were established; and the population was drawn in via the provision of flats (both rented and owned (leased)).[314] The HDB is financed via the government, the CPF and its own income streams; the forced savings have funded infrastructure and contributed to housing costs. The available accommodation is not a welfare right; users pay and there is marginal welfare subsidy for the very poor. Complex rules govern ownership and occupancy as other policy goals are served; the ideological focus is on the putative normal family;[315] and ethnicity is managed.[316]The housing unit becomes the major material resource of Singaporeans; estates are routinely upgraded; the population is rewarded and government promises redeemed.

Underpinning the success are key structural features: in provision and management. At the outset inequalities in market economies generate a need for public housing; it is a familiar issue and provision is a political issue; there are various forms of subsidy available (mortgages and rents may be underpinned, tax breaks for developers given and inexpensive land

Figure 3 Singapore, Holland Avenue.

provided) and the choice is local politics: liberal-market systems prioritize the private market and public housing is a residual; and socialist systems prioritize society, housing is a right and bureaucracies control access.[317] The provision of residual social housing has often proved to be unsatisfactory; in the USA social housing has become an expensively subsidized dumping ground for social failures; in socialist Europe housing was decommodified but bureaucratically regulated provision and access proved inefficient;[318] in liberal-market Europe the situation resembled in some respects that of the USA.[319] The Singapore government has an alternative; they own all the land;[320] and they monopolize provision. The HDB runs the estates, both housing and commercial; the HDB has significant rental income plus government subvention; thereafter there are various tenure modes (rental, lease/buy); the HDB is not a stigmatized dumping ground as it houses 90 per cent of the population.[321] Housing is state provided; access is controlled; users pay; leasers and buyers can profit in the marketplace; and the system combines market and bureaucracy. Overall, the estates are carefully managed; the ethnic mix is monitored; family patterns are preferred; estates are policed; management treats problems of adjustment rationally; and estates are routinely upgraded. The task of assembling the stock of housing has not been without problems;[322] the estates have not escaped all problems;[323] but everyone has a stake[324] – it works.[325]

148 *Locating Singapore*

Figure 4 Singapore, upgraded apartment blocks, Holland Avenue.

Naturalizing the project: landscapes of sentiment and place

Declarative official ideologies are restrictedly useful; state projects have to be driven down into the ordinary patterns of life of subject populations; imposition works; naturalizing works better – inserting the state line into common practice, inscribing the state project in the urban environment.[326] State and nation are social constructs, not given; their contemporary forms are not inevitable; their construction is contested and entails necessarily

Locating Singapore 149

Figure 5 Singapore, hawker centre, Yishun.

routine reconstruction. In established polities this is likely done quietly; in the context of dissolving empires it was done more directly; in Singapore a series of steps can be identified: ideas, actions and reflections.[327]

The interlinked elements of the official ideology can be unpacked. In the first place, the discourse of survival, discipline and pragmatism offered a distinctive narrative: neighbouring countries were presented as latently hostile; the survival of the country depended upon domestic discipline; and the country had to eschew ideology in favour of pragmatism (a effective sleight of hand which placed the entirely ideological goal of material advance at the heart of the polity's elite-specified endeavours).[328] Second, the domestic political and policy principles of multiracialism, multiculturalism, multilingualism, multi-religions and meritocracy (the 'five Ms') have informed elite domestic actions. Kong and Yeoh locate the occasion of the principles in the mid-1950s when reports into high school riots diagnosed communalism and recommended policies to ameliorate such problems; the 'five Ms' are routinely affirmed or enforced:[329] multiracialism affirms the existence of distinctive races (definitions are stipulative) and manages their relations; multiculturalism offers a related specification of the cultures associated with the specified races; multilingualism offers a related specification of the languages that carry these cultures; multi-religions links races, cultures and languages to particular religions; and the state specifies performance criteria for individual competitive behaviour, that is, meritocracy is affirmed.

150 *Locating Singapore*

Finally, the third element[330] of the package enables the elite to assert that the Singaporean form of life is distinctive; it is informed by Asian Values and a communitarian ethos; it cannot be judged according to commonplace Western ideals; in the event, these defensive moves coincided with scholarly interest in the development trajectories of the Asian Tigers; a wider debate has developed and whilst some of the Singaporean elite apologetics would be widely rejected, that there was something worth discussing would be granted. The contemporary discourse[331] presents the country as modern, wealthy and gracious; or, in brief, Singapore is a part of the advanced modern world – it has 'arrived'.

The project carried by these ideas has been inscribed in routine action and the urban forms that carry such action; such construction is contested; elite demands are most powerful when unremarked upon, when they become part of common sense, when they become 'part of the landscape'; Kong and Yeoh review the practical expression of these core elite demands; they write of 'landscapes of sentiment and place';[332] they instance landscapes of death, religion, housing and art.[333] Thus, first, the landscapes embracing the rites of passage surrounding death have changed; important for all cultures, the Chinese in Singapore traditionally used burial; no longer – the state cited land-use efficiency and promoted cremation; this was reluctantly accepted by Chinese (as it undercut a role hitherto played by clan associations) and others. The landscape of death has been disciplined and ordered. Then, second, the sacred sites which mark landscapes of religious adherence have become controlled. The religious practices of adherents revolve around these sites; they are also centres for community life; they are sites of power (sacred or profane); they accumulate over time, reflecting the shifting patterns of community life. The Singapore state has ordered the provision of religious buildings; town planning rules specify the numbers of population required to support a given type of religious building; these significant social sites are thereby disciplined and ordered. Some key sites have also been designated as heritage and protected whilst at the same time being made available to tourism. Third, there is the important landscape of housing, where the realm of small-scale, familiar and ordinary social life has been radically remade by the Singapore elite and an inheritance of slums, squatter camps and kampungs has been removed by the state provision of housing; the HDB was established in 1960 (replacing the Singapore Improvement Trust (SIT), founded in 1927) and it has built housing, community facilities and numerous entire new towns; the agency has shaped the environments within which Singaporeans live; it has in part shaped their identities. The 1964 Housing Ownership Scheme (HOS) allowed occupants to use their mandatory provident funds to purchase their apartments. These new towns are, for ordinary people, the key evidence of the PAP project; they are functional, modernist-style 'workers' housing'. Architectural determinism looks to community but its not clear how successful this is as an instrumental view sees apartments as a resource that could be cashed; the state monitors the ethnic mix, sales are monitored; policies in respect of housing reflect the government's views (favouring extended families, not favouring singles or single mothers). Then, fourth, there is the landscape of art; the Singapore state has built infrastructure (concert halls and museums) but otherwise seems short of ideas; major facilities seem oriented to tourism and imported culture shows; and the local arts community seems relatively neglected.

Reflection offers a way of grasping these dynamics. Yeoh and Kong[334] note that places are filled with multiple meanings; state interventions – as with heritage – cut into these accumulated bodies of meanings; place records the marks of history; it reveals the actions of the powerful and is amenable to multiple readings; place is the location of community; there are dense networks running through the territory; and place is identity – people identify with place, and place shapes their identities. These concentrations of meaning are accumulated over time through routine human social interaction and become a point of conflict with the state as it seeks to impose (through rebuilding the urban environment according to its plans) its vision of Singaporean life – disciplined, ordered and regular. The project embraces the National Past[335] as it reaches into the sphere of heritage. There have been a series of exercises in conservation, new building and reinvention;[336] the expectations of the state have intermingled with local responses; the exchanges exemplify the asymmetries of power typical of Singapore, but local residents remain active in their responses (sometimes negatively, sometimes positively).[337] These are landscapes of heritage;[338] they represent self-conscious collective memory; selection is sensitive (what is remembered, what forgotten), political (which groups get to do the selection, which do not) and routinely contested (before the event, what to do with an area, and afterwards how the completed project is received). Kong and Yeoh[339] analyse a number of projects: China Town (which has been gentrified), Kampong Glam (whose arbitrary boundaries have caused surprise) and the Merlion (a confected symbol liked by tourists). It is suggested that heritage in Singapore is rather banal, touristy and quietly ignored (or contested) by the locals.

The production of heritage is highly contested:[340] there is the business of remembering, where official or commonsensical versions of Singapore are liable to criticism (the official ideological discourse of the evolutionary achievement of rugged nation-statehood is full of gaps and omissions); the business of recreating tradition, where the claims of the powerful are asserted and contested (the annual National Day procession is an exercise in 'inventing tradition', so too the growing collection of museums); the business of place making, where the urban environment is subject to relentless reconstruction in pursuit of national upgrading (thereby routinely overwriting the density of meaning accruing to place through routine experience – either with new building or heritage); and the language-related issue of sharing, as between the Chinese and English speaking (where colonial legacies, contemporary popular anxieties and government policy coincide unhappily). Conflicts over memory are likely to continue; what is at issue is the nature of the National Past, is meanings, its production and control.

152　*Locating Singapore*

Kong and Yeoh[341] conclude by recalling that nations are constructed, and that Singapore has been constructed since 1965. They add that all such constructions are contested and that this is the case in Singapore. What is perhaps somewhat unusual in this particular case is that the domestic patterns of power overwhelmingly support the elite; dissent is thus muted, indirect and understated; the population usually acquiesces quietly.

Urban renewal in practice: the Singapore river

The population has acquiesced in the face of extensive state-sponsored urban renewal; such renewal has been sweeping in its impact upon the lives of local people; acquiescence cannot be confused with contentment; living communities have been swept aside in these elite-sponsored programmes of renewal. These processes of elite-sponsored urban renewal (and social engineering) have been familiar within the developed industrial-capitalist world during the post-Second World War period; they were quite routine in the early post-war years; European and American cities were extensively reconstructed. The Singaporean government adopted a strategy which was already familiar to state-level policy makers. One area subject to extensive urban redevelopment – in pursuit of the elites goals for Singapore – was the river which had since the founding of the settlement served the function of the key port.[342]

The Singapore river served as the key economic resource of the island for around one hundred and fifty years; it was the key port; the port lay at the geographical heart of the settlement; to the south and west were commercial, trading and residential areas; to the north and east were government areas and further residences; the river served this purpose from 1819 through to 1983. Three phases in the river port's history can be identified. The first was 1819–69, the period of consolidation of the settlement, during which time the river was a base for lighters and the bay was used for ships, the trading role involved multiple small firms organized along ethnic and clan lines and run according to locally determined rules – a folk economics. In the period extensive work was done to upgrade the river and there were familiar conflicts in respect of funding such work. In the second period 1869–1972, the years after the opening of the Suez Canal and the introduction of steam-powered ships, these were larger and could not access the bay alongside the river. Keppel Harbour was developed to the south of the centre of the settlement and the lighters continued to work the river, which now served the local regional trade. Debates about upgrading the river continued as before. In the third period, 1972–83, the PAP government drove forwards the development of Singapore. Its vision of the settlement's future revolved around global commerce and high-tech goods and services. Keppel Harbour was remodelled and the docks at Pasir Panjang were developed so as to work with container ships; the lighters in the river were outmoded. The government saw the river as a misused asset at the heart of what is now a financial, commercial, government and tourist area. All the lighters were removed in

1983 and their role more or less disappeared. In this phase of the river's history extensive urban reconstruction took place; numerous small businesses, squatters and hawkers were progressively relocated; those affected protested to no avail. The removal of the lighters was not the final upgrade – these continued – but this reconstruction marked the end of the river as a port. It was now an area of offices, condominiums, museums and so on – the shophouses of Boat Quay were renovated as the river became 'heritage'.

Upgrading in sentiment: local spaces recalled

The Singapore elite is committed to 'upgrading'; the economy, organizations and people are subject to routine managerial attention oriented towards performance improvement. The commitment is evidenced in the routine remaking of the urban form; it has been radically remade over the last forty years; the remaking is sometimes ambiguous as established uses are changed, inhabitants displaced and spaces remade; there are benefits and costs. Two places are recalled here:[343] the old canteen at the World Trade Centre and the old Empress Place hawker centre. My recollections are built around specific experiences; images are presented; each image offers an illustration of the place (project and people); each image is limited (to a time and place), restricted (it offers a quite particular insight, not a general view – whatever that might be) and partial, shaped by the observer (expectations, ideas, values and aesthetic sensibilities – or not); and in both cases, for me, as it happens, improvement has entailed loss.

Tanjong Pagar is the main container terminal of Singapore. It is an energetic place, with multiple giant stacks of shipping containers, ranks of yellow cranes and an endless procession of trucks arriving at and departing from the dock gates. Adjacent to all this activity is the downtown area of high-rise offices, active during the day, quiet in the evenings. And also lying close by is Keppel Harbour. It used to be busy, but the area is changing its character and in recent years major shipping activity has been moved away. What had been a key port, a resource which helped underpin the territory's global trading role, one of those facilities which had been the bedrock of Singaporean wealth down the generations, has been changed into a modern service centre. The World Trade Centre is located in Keppel Harbour. It is separated from the container complex to the east by a new bridge that runs to Sentosa Island; once a military base and occasional holiday destination, it is now a pleasure park with a scatter of hawker centres, some reconstructions of war-time fortifications, a long beach and a couple of hotels. It is an oddly unattractive place and Singaporeans use the name as an acronym: 'so expensive and nothing to see'. To the west there are some shipyard repair facilities, a spreading collection of condominium buildings grouped around no longer used dockyard basins, and further away on a narrow strip of land between the roadway and the sea is the Keppel Club golf course. The World Trade Centre is housed in an imposing solid block of a building.

It is several stories high and emphatically cube shaped. A cable car links the highest floors to Sentosa Island and the nearby Mount Faber Park. The World Trade Centre is surrounded by exhibition halls, the familiar giant sheds of modern commercial architecture. The building houses shops and offices. There is a ferry terminus, from which fast ferryboats serve the nearby Indonesian islands. There is a centre for holiday cruise ships. There was also a canteen.

The canteen occupied the side of the building adjacent to the harbour in the early 1980s when I first visited. The space was plain. Along one wall was a long serving counter. It had a rail along which a tray could be manoeuvred. A series of dishes, drinks and snacks were on offer. The room was filled with simple tables and chairs; as the space was quite large there were a lot of these tables. Along one side, a glass wall offered an uninterrupted view of the harbour and, a few hundred metres away, Sentosa Island. At either end of this huge window with its delightful view hung large black speakers. In the late afternoon, on one visit, around six, as the sun went down, a few people gathered: some children, occupying a scatter of tables, their surfaces covered with school exercise books; a table of four businessmen, resting presumably from their work in the exhibition halls, drinking a jug of beer; and a couple of youngish women with children, eating snacks. It was an unhurried scene – the homework, the beer drinking and the snack eating proceeded quietly. And from the two large speakers adjacent to the window – now opening onto the rapidly gathering dusk of a tropical evening – came the offerings of Radio Heart, a string of pop songs, with one a firm favourite. I can recall the chorus: 'We built this city, We built this city on rock and roll'.[344] It seemed like an anthem. At the end of the day, at the end of a period of nation building, one can take one's ease, work quietly and enjoy undoubtedly beautiful surroundings. Yet the building and rebuilding continue and the old canteen is now gone, its floor space now occupied, it would seem, by the shops and restaurants servicing the new cruise terminal facilities; it is much more modern, and tawdry in its banal, rather seedy commercialism.

The Singaporean elite pursuit of development is attended by incessant change, manifest in upgrading and the endless anxiety for competitiveness and urban renewal. It can be thought of in terms of winners and losers, or, more subtly, the displacement of the poor, or, one further step further, the curious process of 'losing as you win'.[345] There are many instances. The old Empress Place hawker centre lay alongside the Singapore river. In 1982 the last of the old lighters which moved goods from ships lying offshore to the town's warehouses, and which used to fill the Singapore river, were moved to new anchorages. The curve of the river adjacent to the commercial centre and civic heart of the city was left free from commercial traffic. A long process of upgrading began: a line of shop-houses along Boat Quay was retained and renovated, and is now a string of restaurants; further upriver new hotels and condominiums were built. On the shore opposite, around this time, there was a hawker centre, Empress Place, dating from the 1960s and 1970s. It was not an original construction but rather an instance of early upgrading, one of the vast spread of urban renewal projects undertaken by the PAP.[346] The hawker centre sat on the banks of the river adjacent to the parliament building and a rather grand colonial concert hall. The centre comprised around fifty stalls, each offering one or two local dishes, fixed tables with equally fixed small stools. Customers ordered food, picked a table and paid as the food was served. There was also a beer stall. At this time it was run by an old couple, man and wife. They served Tiger beer and Anchor beer. Lemonade might also have been available. Regular customers were given special plastic chairs, preferable to the uncomfortable stools adjacent to the tables near their stall. In the evening local people gathered; the stalls nearby sold Chinese food and Malay food. The Malay stall was popular: long-haired young Malay boys would gather, rake combs in their back pockets, pretty girls in attendance, and they would stand around their motorcycles talking whilst along the river Chinese boys would fish. As the light fell the restaurants along the opposite shore were illuminated with strings of coloured lights; it was pleasant to sit, drink a beer and watch the world go by as ordinary Singaporeans took their ease. And, inevitably, the whole area was upgraded in the 1990s. The parliament building was extended and reoriented, no longer looking towards the river and the sea, but instead sitting square to a commercial road running parallel. The old colonial concert hall has been extensively reconstructed, and is now a Museum of Asian Culture. And the hawker centre? It has been swept away; adjacent to the new museum (celebrating Asian culture), the site is now graced by the presence of sterile international-style cafes.

The Singaporean elite project has unfolded down the years; the goals of the first generation were clear, so too those of the second, but the current project is unclear; the elite speak of a regional hub and a gracious city yet the city form resembles the politics – an internationalized elite and a firmly controlled domestic (and domesticated) population, the out-turn of an odd mixture of socialist planning and corporate capitalism. Down the years I have marvelled at Singaporean development but in 2003 for the first time I was unsettled. The visible nature of money and power was still there – so too the inequality, so too the good level of living of ordinary Singaporeans – but the elite were speaking about 'home-landers', those who lived in the HDB estates. To me this signalled their loss of contact (else why pick them out as a group). The elite continue with the theme of vulnerability, self-reliance and hard work; they continue to preach upgrading, but to what end? One often gets the feeling that ordinary Singaporeans are pushed aside when it suits the developers, and they lose these familiar stylish places; the new facilities are there for all, one can visit the new cafes, and buy the lattes, but what costs 80 cents in the hawker centres now costs $3 or $4. Ordinary Singaporeans are relocated in the ever-expanding system of new towns – out of the way – making their lives in the HDB flats, the local schools, leisure facilities and shopping centres.

156   *Locating Singapore*

You don't know what you've got till it's gone[347]

The pace of change in Singapore can be disconcerting. The island has been made and remade in the nearly fifty years of PAP rule. The first generation's project was shaped by the experience of inter-war and post-war political radicalism, the collapse of colonial empires and the cold war. It was shaped by the socialism of the Fabian Society and conditioned by the legacy of the colonial era and recent war; their arena was a colonial sea port with a shifting population, all the disruption of occupation and all the difficulties of post-war reconstruction. The PAP looked to union with the Malay peninsula, as this had been its hinterland; Singapore had developed along with British Malaya; the Straits Settlements were integral to this colonial sphere; an independent Singapore was not on anyone's mind in 1945. Yet the difficulties of the crystallization of prospective new nations from the disintegrating territories of colonial empires were severe; Lee Kuan Yew wept on TV as Singapore emerged in 1965 as an independent nation-state. The PAP development project involved a deal: the population was invited to support the party and in turn the party undertook to provide growth and welfare, a familiar post-colonial political arrangement. In Singapore the party was ruthless and effective; it suppressed local dissent and invited in the multinationals, becoming an offshore export-processing zone. Yet the key to progress, rather than processing for others, was the continual drive to upgrade the economy: better skills, better infrastructure, more advanced industry and ever more sophisticated linkages with the wider global economy. It worked. Singapore evidenced all the traits of an Asian Tiger. The second generation continued on the established path: more upgrading; now finance, now science-based industry; and sometime in the 1980s in terms of the familiar indices Singapore became 'developed'. Thereafter advance continued; by the twenty-first century Singapore was as rich as Europe or America or Japan. In 2004 the third generation moved into power, but a radical change of direction, the pursuit of new projects, seems for the present unlikely. In all this the urban form of Singapore has been continually made and remade: huge areas of land are cleared of forest, plantations or small-scale settlements and row upon row of apartment blocks appear in yet another new satellite town; land is reclaimed from the sea; old districts are torn down or, more recently, renovated and reused; new roads are built; new subways are cut through; the rebuilding seems continuous; the changing urban form of the city mirrors the vigour of the elite as they read and react to enfolding global structures.

Politics: consumerism

Singapore is not a fixed unit; there is no available single history; there is only the currently recoverable record of the island's various embeddings within enfolding circumstances; there have been several polities, each with its own state form or footprint, its place within the relevant wider scheme. The overall tale is of change. The Singapore of the PAP is no different; the PAP's project was cast in terms of national development (elite coherence, a disciplined population and a clearly delineated place in the world) and the paradox is that as they pursue material advance they lodge themselves ever more deeply within global structures. The elite manage their niche actively, they are agents, but as the polity deepens its linkages with the wider global system so it deepens its dependence on those linkages and on those wider systems; Singapore, examined closely, dissolves away into trans-state flows of people, goods and ideas.[348]

During the colonial period the flow of people through Singapore was largely unregulated; migrants from southern China or the archipelago or the Indian sub-continent moved in and through Singapore; diaspora communities were established throughout Southeast Asia, in particular Chinese people. In Singapore, at the moment of independence, the replacement elite inherited a diverse population – both settled and sojourners – the raw material for the PAP project. The PAP disciplined its population and pursued national development; it was successful; it created a rich city; it created Singaporeans. In recent years flows of inward and outward migration have attracted renewed attention. There has been a steady loss of educated people; and now there is a Singapore International to keep contacts as reports suggest 100,000 Singaporeans are resident overseas.[349] Now politicians distinguish stayers from quitters, the latter being the educated middle classes who vote with their feet.[350] A new programme is encouraging inward migration of professionally skilled people; it has had modest success, but there has been a local backlash as inward migration makes the local job market more competitive.[351] There are long-established flows of labourers from the region. A novel inward flow has involved maids, in particular young women from the Philippines or Indonesia. The Singapore government treats them as short-term workers making private contracts. There have been numerous cases of maid abuse, and whilst the government has made criminal law it has not adopted familiar strategies of regulating their employment.[352] Such flows of people are not likely to diminish; nor will the flows of ideas and goods.

After 1965 the PAP mobilized the population around the drive for economic growth; the state reached into the patterns of life and habits of thought of its population; practice and understanding were disciplined. The project has been successful but anticipated results, the goal sought, have proved ambiguous in their realization. The country is rich and consumerism has grown. Yet consumerism cuts against the task of inscribing the PAP project in the routine lives of the population; it presents the population with new spheres of expression (probably overstated); and it presents the state with problems of discipline. Grasping consumption is awkward[353] and as Singapore becomes richer the elite worry[354] about excess and Westernization, but Singapore was always a modern city, always part of the global system, and importing goods and ideas is not new. Singapore was never underdeveloped so there is no pristine indigenous culture to destroy. The elite are picking out a specific target; the elite object to Westernization. Japanese imports are unproblematic, as they are read as technical. American imports are problematic as liberal individualism is seen to be attached. But examination of consumption practices reveals that imports do not work on locals mechanically; the experiences they offer are read into local culture, and examination of practices suggests imports are both inevitable and unproblematic. It is not the imports per se; it is how they call into prominence some features of life in Singapore, in particular inequalities and changing social mores.

Class has been read out of Singaporean experience in favour of race sensitivity associated with the ideology of multiracialism, but consumption stresses display and class inequalities become clearer. Thus HDB housing is unfashionable for the middle classes and popular culture involves the figures of Ah Beng and Ah Lian, who exemplify lower-class lack of sophistication. The local provision of shopping malls has grown rapidly in recent years and these are spaces for consumption and display.[355] Class division is evident. The pursuit of material advance within a global capitalist system brings consumption into the heart of routine social practice (people become 'consumers'), feeds into the structural patterns of society (some consume more than others and inequality grows) and becomes more visible (consumption is always in part conspicuous consumption and choosing lifestyle entails differentiation – it has to be visible to achieve its objective). Such class division can feed through into politics and routine class oppositions. The PAP argue that merit should be the basis for advance (not family or communal or other ascribed status); but the elite specify what is or is not merit worthy, and individuals thereafter succeed or fail depending on their given talent and effort. In a growing economy this can be read as fair (whether it is or not depends on the criteria for and nature of competition), whereas in a static or restructuring economy this is less likely to be read as fair. For the PAP the emergence of class division and class-consciousness is unwelcome as it cuts against the social harmony desired by the elite.

In Singapore, individualism and privatism are evident. The Singaporean middle classes are wealthy and they can disengage and turn to family. Contemporary capitalism invites the creation of consumer societies and consumerism becomes a novel social practice or culture. The consumer marketplace offers consumers choices and consumers are invited to select. The portfolio of consumption practices generates a species of individualism through differentiation from others within the confines provided by the available consumption goods. Contemporary capitalism is also a global system; there is extensive trade and goods and ideas are exchanged. In the years following the Pacific War consumerism in East Asia has had a number of local creative sources (Japan, South Korea, Hong Kong, Taiwan) and one external creative source, the USA. Goods and ideas (popular cultural) originating in the USA carry a particular cultural baggage, an ideal (however absurd in practice) of individual freedom, and for the PAP the emergence of such individualism is problematic because it cuts against the social discipline desired by the elite.

Singapore is embedded within global flows of goods and ideas. The traffic is not simply from the USA and the West to Singapore. There are East Asian regional flows of great significance,[356] and popular culture is imported from Japan, Taiwan,[357] Korea and Hong Kong. It becomes part of the blend of contemporary Singaporean cultural practice.[358] Singapore is rich; like all rich cities it borrows ideas and practices from elsewhere and makes them its own. C. J. W. L. Wee[359] notes that whilst capitalist modernity might homogenize, capitalist modernity might be variously indigenized; Singapore is its own place but the business of indigenization is subtle and the self-conscious efforts of the state can look like pastiche (once upon a time Singapore marketed itself as 'instant Asia'). These comments perhaps find confirmation in the realm of scenarios of the future. One purportedly optimistic scenario is available: the city will become a major business hub, a site for a full range of high-value activities; ideas, goods and people will flow through the city. The image is of a 'flow-through five-star hotel Singapore', a centre for cosmopolitan talent serving regional and global networks.[360]

Changing state forms

The post-independence replacement elite inherited a rich city, deeply lodged within the global industrial-capitalist system. The English-educated elite read and reacted to the circumstances in which they found themselves; they allied themselves discreetly with the West, suppressed local political opponents, disciplined society and pursued growth and welfare. The elite have propelled contemporary Singapore along a distinctive trajectory; they have created a species of dependent capitalist development. But dependency does not entail either co-option or passivity on the part of the local elite, rather the reverse: the elite is active; the state is active. The Singaporean elite are assiduous in seeking out ways to upgrade the niche which they occupy within the context of the unfolding logics of the global industrial-capitalist system.

7 Trading cities

Human social interactions constitute the social world, formal institutions order these relationships and the familiar habit of reification presents such institutions as fixed, solid and thing-like; the exchange of social relationships and institutions is inverted as the latter are taken to determine the former. But the truth of the matter is that social relations are primary; human social life is thoroughgoingly social; this is true on the micro and macro scales. The empires of the modern world have been read in this reified fashion; empire has been presented as an institutional apparatus ordering a defined geographical territory; thereafter scholarly, political and popular discourses of empire would unfold, producing Orientalist scholarship,[1] informal stereotypes, memoirs,[2] collections[3] and daydreams.[4] But this inverts reality: empire was accumulated piecemeal; it was acquired by war, manoeuvre and elite-level accommodations; it was untidy;[5] it was accumulated around key cities; and the extent of territorial holdings was always in flux and the reach of any formal colonial apparatus within the peoples nominally controlled was always contested.[6]

The expansion of the British Empire was fuelled by a militaristic nationalism which reached into the lives of its domestic population in sharp class conflict and those of other communities through expansion; these overseas communities were subjugated. The process was often extraordinarily violent; the incoming power cooperated, competed and fought with local elites; the British elite invented themselves as they accumulated the territories of empire. The elite were the key; from 1600 to 1800 they were routinely violent; as the nineteenth century unfolded their position became more secure, the violence less emphatic and the business of empire was reimagined; a violently acquired collection of territories was remade as a coherent ordered empire.[7]

Read institutionally (or geographically), for simplicity, a distinction can be made between formal empire and informal empire;[8] the former points to those acquired territories which were delimited and rationally ordered (more or less), whilst the latter points to those areas drawn into the colonial sphere where for one reason or another the familiar apparatus of control was not constructed and where colonial interests could be secured indirectly through influence in key institutions or organizations.[9] British activities in East Asia found expression in both styles of expansion; the major base area was the Indian sub-continent, which was slowly ordered; thereafter the eastward expansion rested on trading ports, in particular Singapore and Hong Kong; the Malay peninsula was semi-ordered late in the nineteenth century; the west coast was brought into a close economic/political relationship;[10] and other interests in the archipelago, Indo-China and China were pursued in the context of informal empire, which grew through trading links with Bangkok and Shanghai. The further east the British travelled the more the simple concern for trade came into the foreground; trade required access, not territory.

Trade was the central preoccupation;[11] access was crucial; the keys to all these activities were the relationships established with local groups (country power elites, official servants, merchants and maybe villagers or other small local groups); these relationships enabled the trade; and without these relationships there could be no trade. It was trade that underpinned the colonial empires; the trade volumes were significant; people, goods and money flowed between South Asia, Southeast Asia and China; and the trading links were multiple, with local trades, sub-regional trades and global trades. All these trading links were ordered; treaties between the incoming powers outlined spheres of influence; exchanges with local powers through treaties were used to set up trading settlements; the trading settlements were crucial; they were bases for the incomers; they were linkages to the modern world set down within the spheres of extant civilizations; they sustained the overall network; and they also drew their surrounding hinterlands into the sphere of the modern world. The cities of the informal empire offered a variant of a familiar role; they prospered; they provided local elites with the impetus to reform; these cities joined the modern world; they did so just as distinctively as other locations; they were not sites of local economic, political and cultural passivity, rather the reverse.

Locating Hong Kong

Territory and polity can be distinguished. Hong Kong island has been home to a number of communities; in the pre-modern period there were a number of successful, locally trading, settled farming and fishing communities located on the southern periphery of the Qing Empire; in the period of the expansion of European and American colonialism the island was absorbed into the far eastern fringes of the British Empire, where a complex exchange between the now mixed population produced a distinctive, internationally important colonial trading port; in the period of general crisis the politics of declining empire, violent mainland national reawakening, war and cold war spilled across the borders, in time producing a distinctive city, Hong Kong as 'its own place'.

The 1997 transfer of sovereignty, over the heads of the local people, from London to Beijing, has opened a new phase in the development history of the

162 *Trading cities*

territory; the agreed formula of 'one country, two systems' enshrined in the Basic Law promises continuity in the local form of life, but this is in doubt; structural arguments would imply change (new structures, new agent projects) and local commentary[12] reveals awkwardness in adjusting agent relationships to new circumstances (lack of agent clarity, lack of project clarity); local commentary has identified a number of possible futures; and pessimistic scenarios seem to outnumber the more optimistic.[13] Against this, it is worth noting that Hong Kong is a rich, sophisticated, highly developed city; it has been embedded within the modern world for around 160 years.[14]

Hong Kong – the shift to the modern world

The standard version of the development history of Hong Kong makes a set of claims: the island was a barren rock until the British occupied it, introduced laissez-faire capitalism, ordered inward migration and through a wise policy style of extensive consultation and minimal intervention guided the territory so that its hardworking population could enjoy stability and great prosperity. As with other official ideologies, this one contains a mix of truth and misdirection: the island was not a barren rock, it was a remote rural part of the southern lands of the Qing dynasty;[15] the preference for consultation is true, but largely only amongst elites;[16] the putative policy of laissez faire has in fact been an elite preference for the concerns of the elite;[17] and the claim to anti-welfare spending is misleading as provision has always been made, but perhaps slowly.[18] It might be better to begin by noting that Hong Kong island has been home to various forms of life and that historians mention long-established communities of farming, fishing and trade. Hong Kong island has been lodged within various wider forms of life, economic, social and political. It was a part of the southern Pearl River Delta region of the Qing Empire, a trading port linking the Qing and British empires, a commercial centre within a global trading network linking southern China to Southeast Asia and North America, a cold war era conduit linking the People's Republic to wider economic spheres and lately one of East Asia's newly industrialized economies. It is clear that the island has played distinctive roles, but commentators report that it has been 'its own place' since the late nineteenth century.[19] On a macro scale the following periods can be specified: pre-contact (the form of life shaped over several centuries of settlement); impact/response (the incoming modern world – demands/opportunities); general crisis (as the metropolitan heartlands of industrial capitalism dissolved into systemic confusion, East Asia experienced a parallel breakdown); and (quasi-)national development (the default project of elites after the Pacific War).

The pre-contact form of life developed over centuries, a trajectory shaped by unfolding circumstances of forms of life untouched by the modern world. In the pre-contact period Hong Kong island was a remote part of the southern lands of the Qing Empire; there were numerous villages, many long established; the social pattern was that of rural China – family, clan and language group governed relationships, and temples, clan halls and perhaps schools provided the institutional structures for these communities; the local economy revolved around farming and fishing and there was a quarrying industry; the island communities exported stone and preserved fish; there was a subsistence economy and trading activity; the island communities had a recognized absentee landlord; and the island communities were taxed by the local Qing official. These were settled, ordered, established communities.[20] Early nineteenth-century Hong Kong island had a population of several thousand, farmers, fishermen and local traders, but it was not a significant site; nor did it contain significant settlements; however, it was not underdeveloped; in the early nineteenth century the empire was still strong and in preceding centuries China had been a major economic power within the global system.[21]

The modern world placed new demands on extant forms of life. The colonial incomers worked at the edge of empire remote from their metropolitan bases and received bodies of law and power; local initiative was imperative. The local agents with whom the incomers dealt were not passive; they were on their home ground; they commanded the resources of extant civilizations.[22] A process of mutual adjustment ensured that the nominally colonial holding developed through extensive collaboration between incoming British elites and the local elites which formed within the rapidly expanding Chinese population. It is true that there were asymmetries of power within the colonial holding but there was also routine and extensive collaboration; the development of Hong Kong – or any other colonial trading port – was impossible without such mutual cooperation. In Hong Kong the British and Chinese newcomers quickly outnumbered the established local population.[23] Around 7,500 people lived on Hong Kong island when the British took control in 1841;[24] the population grew as migrants moved in from the Pearl River Delta; these incomers were vital to the success of the settlement; the population reached 22,000 in 1847 and 85,000 in 1859; of that number only 1,600 were non-Chinese.[25]

Hong Kong was extracted from the Qing Empire in order to serve as a trading port for British trading interests; there was a complex exchange between the local population, inward migrants and the British, and it produced a layered economy: local, regional and global. The British were sojourners; they came for trade; in time local Chinese merchants settled; the colony received inflows of migrants from mainland China; the territory was divided by race; there was a small resident European population plus a rapidly growing Chinese population; it was at first a colonial trading port. The local population were active players and success rested upon the development of global capitalism and an outflow of people from unsettled China; the migrant or coolie trade made an obscure port linking two empires into a global commercial nexus. The local British and Chinese elites collaborated in order to build a prosperous settlement; stability did not mean an absence of political conflict;[26] a local balance was maintained; it was its own place.[27] In the 1918–41 inter-war period Chinese capital invested was equal to that of British;[28] the territory came to be secondary to Shanghai in the 1930s. But the Japanese invasion of China underscored its vulnerability; the territory was not militarily defensible and extant patterns of life were engulfed by the confusions of the Pacific War.

During the general crisis the region collapsed into civil strife, inter-state warfare and nationalist revolt (peaceful/violent). The crisis ran from 1911 to 1975 and in its early phases – running up to the end of the Chinese Civil War in 1949 – there was great loss of life and destruction of accumulated capital. In the early period Hong Kong became an island of relative calm. China, whose land border with the territory lay only a few miles to the north of the heart of the colony around Hong Kong harbour, suffered extensive civil warfare and then inter-state invasion. It was inevitable that mainland politics spilled over into Hong Kong, but the colonial authorities, with the assistance of the local Chinese elites, managed the problems.[29] It was not until the Pacific War that Hong Kong was fatally embroiled. The Imperial Japanese invasion in 1941 saw the territory occupied within a few days; the city was re-Asianized, with street names changed, a new currency and a much reduced population; foreigners were interred; and the local elite adapted.[30]

At the end of the Pacific War locally interred civil servants reasserted their authority within hours of receiving the news; and the colonial power, fearful of the intentions of the Chinese Nationalists, rushed to reoccupy the territory.[31] The civil war in China provided a space for the reoccupation. The war in China also produced a flow of refugees and the population quickly recovered and surpassed pre-war levels. The victorious Communist Party did not challenge directly the status quo with regard to Hong Kong; but the cold war added further complications as the outbreak of the Korean War in 1950 led to United Nations sanctions against China. Hong Kong became a link between China and the global system; there was covert trade with the People's Republic, as well as flows of migrants. If the war years had been destructive, recovery was quick and advance fortuitous.[32]

The city developed rapidly; economic growth was rapid, social reform slow.[33] The cold war had direct implications for Hong Kong; links with China were reworked and as the trading role diminished, manufacturing prospered; American war expenditures benefited the region and American policy benefited the region, for example by permitting access to US domestic markets, and this also helped Hong Kong.[34] The territory became one of the four Asian Tigers; up until 1967 these developments were ad hoc; in 1967 the Cultural Revolution spilled over into Hong Kong with riots and bombings; the local population rallied to the colonial government; the trouble was managed; economic, social and political reforms were instigated[35] and a distinctive Hong Kong form of life began to emerge[36] – the rise of a popular idea of Hong Kong.[37]

The first period of quasi-national development was 1967–97. A local elite had formed in the late nineteenth century; it collaborated with the colonial power; the territory became rich; but the success was ordered in terms of groups and networks; there was little explicit commitment to the future of city of Hong Kong itself. Local organizations were established; local charities were formed; successful Chinese businessmen played the role of philanthropists. All this was to the good; however, there was no overarching provision. The colonial state did not explicitly systematize the pursuit of development; an elite oligarchy pursued a project centred on commerce and trade; the British were sojourners, the Chinese elite focused on commerce and the local Chinese population used family, relatives and clan networks to order their lives. But with further outward migration from China there were accumulating welfare problems in housing, health and schooling; the colonial authorities were reluctant to act, but from the 1960s onwards the familiar apparatus of a modern welfare state appeared; the elite eschewed other than a minimal responsibility and blocked calls for democracy; it was a restricted development project.

An important prerequisite of this first phase of quasi-national development was the unplanned establishment of a closed border. Prior to the Pacific War, the Hong Kong population intermixed with the mainland, as there were more or less open borders.[38] However, in the context of the 1950s cold war, restrictions were imposed and the border was sealed. It became one more borderline between the two cold war camps; the realm of state socialism, with its uneasy double centre in Moscow and Beijing, and the realm of liberal markets ordered from Washington. In the absence of other choices, the Hong Kong population became settled. The new situation had implications for patterns of life – Hong Kong developed in new ways – and for patterns of self-identification; thus those who were born and raised locally had no experience of the mainland and they came to understand themselves in local terms. An important factor in the construction of this novel identity was that the local situation contrasted with that on the mainland. The end of the civil war had driven refugees to Hong Kong; further illegal migrants moved into Hong Kong; in the 1960s Maoist-inspired development mistakes culminated in the launch of the Cultural Revolution – a curious mix of elite-sponsored coup, political theatre and widespread social breakdown. It spilled over the border into Hong Kong as local anti-colonial groups took up the cause (such as it was). There were riots and bombings. A number of Hong Kong people were killed. The colonial government responded to the 1967 riots by modernizing itself; it became less evidently colonial; it became more like a modern city government; a number of welfare reforms were accelerated; the problems of endemic corruption amongst police, civil servants and local business were addressed; illegal migration was curbed; and the localization of jobs began such that Hong Kong people could move up the career ladder and rule their own city. Hong Kong emerged as an East Asian Tiger. Economic take-off

166 *Trading cities*

had begun in the 1950s,[39] when existing small-scale industries were joined by migrant textile entrepreneurs, but now, with some help from American cold war expenditures, manufacturing became an important economic sector.[40] In later years, following 1978, subsequent mainland reforms allowed Hong Kong entrepreneurs to become the major investors in the new export-processing zones. It was the first period of quasi-national development; a local Hong Kong form of life took shape and residents thought of themselves as 'Hong Kongers'.

A second period of national development followed. In 1984 the British and Chinese governments had negotiated the reversion of sovereignty of the territory to China. The agreement was recorded in the 1984 Sino-British Joint Declaration. The substance of this agreement was later enshrined in the Basic Law, which was written and promulgated by Beijing as a part of Chinese law. The Basic Law was the mini-constitution provided for Hong Kong by Beijing; it was the juridical outcome of Deng Xiaoping's 'one country, two systems' political formula. However, the people of Hong Kong were not official participants in the reversion talks and nor was there any exercise of soliciting popular approval;[41] one colonial power handed the territory to a successor colonial power and in 1997 Hong Kong became a Special Administrative Region of China.

Thereafter a process of mutual adjustment unfolded; local elites were split with respect to the relationship with Beijing, with some advocating working directly for the city whilst others insisted that Beijing must give the lead. Local elites evidenced widespread uncertainty about the future lines of development of Hong Kong. So far as might be judged, Beijing's views are unformed; other than saying no to any effective liberal-democratic local public politics, matters seem unclear. The first post-handover administration of Tung Chee Hwa (1997–2005) faced considerable difficulties as the Asian financial crisis, international terrorism, SARS and a series of local disputes about development policies proved overwhelming. In 2003 and again in 2004 the city saw mass demonstrations against the local government and its backers in Beijing. The second post-handover administration of Donald Tsang (2005–) was both more popular and luckier; there were no external crises, but lack of clarity with respect to the political future of the territory continued when a restricted electoral reform package was met with further large demonstrations and was rejected in the Legislative Council. The issue of domestic politics is intertwined with questions of relationships with Beijing and the attitudes of mainland elite leaders; and estimations of how these issues might be resolved colour the expectations which commentators have for the future.

Contemporary Hong Kong

The handover process marked the first step in a new direction for Hong Kong. The 1997 reversion of sovereignty replaced one distant colonial power with another; the people of Hong Kong were not represented in the handover negotiations; the Chinese government was explicit in rejecting their presence; and the departing colonial power acquiesced. The formal handover completed, a complex spread of adjustments are in prospect: local agents must settle how they wish to deal with their Pearl River Delta neighbours (a reciprocal process); local agents must settle how they wish to deal with Beijing (a reciprocal process); and local agents must settle how they wish to deal with regional and global partners (a reciprocal process). In brief Hong Kong must locate itself.

One aspect of these interlinked processes of location is the lack of clarity of local agents with respect to the crucial matter of ordering their domestic discussions: the formal political structure bequeathed to them by Anglo-Chinese discussions and the Basic Law is dysfunctional, as evidenced in exchanges between a partially elected legislature, a semi-appointed chief executive and an important civil service unclear about its role;[42] the substantive political community is divided in its opinions, as evidenced in opinion polling, numerous street demonstrations, the fragmented results of elections to local representative bodies and the often rather angry tone of contributors to the letters pages of local newspapers;[43] the substantive political community is also divided in its interests, as evidenced in the fact that Hong Kong has become more unequal economically since 1997.[44]

If regular political life within a community requires a contested compromise, an arrangement more or less balancing competing interests, then in Hong Kong, at the present time, the colonial contested compromise is in question, for the long-familiar colonial power is no longer present, yet no clear replacement has been secured, there is no new contested compromise and moreover, notwithstanding encouraging preliminary signs, it is not clear that one is locally available; it may be that a domestic settlement waits on the dynamics of the politics of Beijing. In the meantime, however, dynamics of change continue; these may be recorded and the possibilities for the future noted.

(i) Changing economics

Hong Kong's history can be characterized as a series of phases of development; in each phase there would be a domestic pattern of economic activity interacting with regional and global patterns; local actors would have particular links with overseas partners; in the ongoing shift to the modern world Hong Kong's footprint within the global system has thus far expanded; its role has deepened.

First, from 1841 there is an early colonial economy. The territory is extracted by war from the Chinese sphere, and the locally established state asserts itself and the colony is organized with a mix of co-option and repression; British traders are key players but the local merchants and people are active agents. The colonial focus is the China trade but the territory

Figure 6 Hong Kong, Argyle Street, Kowloon.

is also a base for local-area trade (foodstuffs, manufactures and some primary products such as fish and stone) and it also develops a commercial role to finance the port and its trade. The ideology of laissez-faire is invoked in order to justify the pattern of activity of the traders; and down the years it also serves to justify elite-level neglect of other economic activities. Then, second, from 1900 there is a mature colonial economy. The established trade and other activities continue, but by 1900, in addition, there is some light

Trading cities 169

Figure 7 Hong Kong, Shatin Village, New Territories.

industry and this is financed by Chinese capital. In the 1918–41 inter-war period, Chinese capital invested in Hong Kong becomes as important as that of the British. A Chinese-dominated industrial sector develops. It is a large employer but it does not get any direct help or acknowledgement from colonial rulers. A dual-sector economy develops, involving trade and commerce on the one hand and industry on the other. The former activities tend

170 *Trading cities*

Figure 8 Hong Kong, Shatin New Town, New Territories.

to be the preserve of colonialists and allies, whilst the latter tends to be organized by Chinese entrepreneurs. The Imperial Preferences system gives Chinese business access to a wider market but in the global system there is mercantilist competition. The depression damages local industry, which looks for protection and support, but the traders invoke laissez-faire and argue against protecting local industry. Shortly thereafter the 1941–45 occupation brings disaster to the economy; the population falls from 1,500,000 to 500,000 and the city comes to near collapse. But with the end of the Pacific War in 1945 a new phase opens up with the creation of a reformed colonial economy. The first moves are rebuilding and this is initially rapid but the 1949 UN embargo on trade with China is awkward and US hostility and restrictions hurt Hong Kong business. On the other hand, there is also flight capital coming in as Shanghai textile industrialists relocate to Hong Kong and these entrepreneurs link up with local banks and help to revive the local textile industry. Other light manufactures develop or recover. As before the war, these are small firms and they adapt to circumstances very flexibly; they make a range of low-tech goods including plastics, toys, electrical goods, watches and textiles. Labour is cheap as there are many refugees from the civil war in China, organized labour is fragmented (KMT/CCP) and the labour market is very competitive. The colonial authorities do not try to grow the industrial sector, but slowly they get more involved and there is some industrial assistance and some overseas promotion

Figure 9 Hong Kong, Ma On Shan, New Territories.

of Hong Kong, and later still there is some provision of welfare, but it is not until after 1997 that anything like an East Asian developmental state appears. Under the first chief executive it is not too successful, with confusion between projects of national development and government–business collusion. The proper role of the local state in formulating economic policy remains an open issue, now arguably more awkward, as the concerns of Beijing must be accommodated.

172 Trading cities

Figure 10 Hong Kong, Tolo Harbour, New Territories.

Overall, Hong Kong has a highly developed economy with a number of distinctive sectors. The territory is a major financial centre. The territory has a significant industrial sector although much of the manufacturing element has relocated to Guangdong Province as wage rates are much lower on the mainland and regulative regimes are more permissive. Hong Kong businesses are variously estimated to employ between 5 million and 10 million in Guangdong Province, which is now a world centre for the production of low-tech light consumer goods with large flows of exports to North America and the European Union. The territory is a key base for shipping, as it is a major container port for transhipment, export and re-export.[45] The port is experiencing competition with aspiring mainland ports and Hong Kong firms are relocating some activities. More generally, Hong Kong cannot compete in low-tech production any longer, but it can compete where human capital and links to the wider global economy are important: services, management functions, business planning and research and design. It can act as a leisure centre and now receives large numbers of mainland tourists. Hong Kong has a thriving arts scene, including local popular music and local film. There is also a local economy which serves a city of 6 million: houses, schools, shops, transport, services and so on. Public services are being upgraded; the housing market is important, is expanding and upgrading; transport infrastructure is being upgraded; and shopping complexes are being upgraded (to cater for the demands of the mainland tourist service industry). However, as noted, there are ongoing debates which revolve around the nature of the state and the proper spread of its responsibilities.

A first strategic issue revolves around the nature of the state. The idea of laissez faire has been the official doctrine of economic policy. The ideal of laissez faire dates from early in the nineteenth century and it was embraced by the colonial government and served as an excuse to favour the powerful and avoid wider responsibilities. Remarkably, it endured until the 1960s. At this time the idea of 'positive non-intervention' was advanced; the government agreed that it would pay minimum attention to monetary, financial and social services whilst offering only information and training encouragements to industry. It was a minimal acknowledgement that there were elements to the Hong Kong economy other than those trading and commercial activities controlled by the established colonial elite. Local commentators debate matters. Some claim that Hong Kong has a genuine minimally regulated free market, whilst others point to the extensive linkages between the business elite and the government. At the same time, others wonder about the quality of life of ordinary Hong Kong people. The debate continues. However, it is possible to distinguish between the character of the state and the project pursued by the state. In Hong Kong, as in other East Asian countries, the character of the state is clear; it is central to the economic, social and political life of the territory (thus the state certainly does exist, it is powerful and it does act). However, the state project has been narrowly targeted; the state has served the interests of a colonial/local elite (primarily traders). Trade with China has been facilitated to the satisfaction of these elites, and those on the mainland. However, after 1997 there have been signs of a new project, a variety of pursuit of national development where the state acts more energetically to build up the local economy. But, thus far, the results are ambiguous.

Second, a closely related issue centres on alleged collusion. It has been widely asserted by local commentators that in the absence of a democratic system elite politicians and business collude to secure mutual benefits, with the interests of the general population taking second place.[46] Commentators argue that collusion has been extensive and is still prevalent. The British colonial authorities colluded with local business and the Chinese comprador capitalists in order to sustain the colony. British and Chinese businesses have had good access to the colonial authorities as a matter of routine. Collusion has overlapped with extensive corruption and whilst the Independent Commission Against Corruption (ICAC) dealt successfully with the latter the former will need a more open democratic system.

Local commentators suggest that the close relationship between the state and the private sector has negative consequences. The environment is polluted and the rewards accruing to grassroots citizens are in question. First, the environment: the whole of the Pearl River Delta is very badly polluted – land, water and air; some of the pollution is from Hong Kong (in particular traffic and power stations), some is from Guangdong (the consequences of years of very rapid urbanization and industrialization) and some is from Hong Kong industry relocated to the mainland. The pollution is severe and impacts human health. The issue is only very slowly moving up the political agenda. And, second, there is an issue about the status and social condition of grassroots citizens. Colonial Hong Kong was an unequal society and wealth was concentrated in the hands of an elite. Since 1997 the society has become more unequal. The situation of ordinary Hong Kong people has been long debated. For example, the colonial authorities were very slow to provide the facilities most developed countries take for granted and the official ideology of laissez faire worked against such provision; indeed it still does. Contemporary citizen-based political groups argue that the territory is rich enough to provide better lives for its people; however business-linked parties continue to resist such claims.

(ii) Changing politics[47]

The colonial system of Hong Kong was organized around the person of the governor; all political power revolved around this office. The governor was assisted by two bodies: (1) the Executive Council (Exco), which was made up of key figures within the colony (army chief, security, civil service head and in time representatives from the business world) and which functioned as the key decision-making body; and (2) the Legislative Council (Legco), which was made up of a wider group of people who were broadly representative of the people living in the colony (businessmen, church leaders, civic leaders and so on). This system allowed the governor to co-opt the key figures and influential groups into the governing machinery of the colony. It was a top-down system. It was not a democratic system. It excluded the

Chinese. The decisions of the governor and the two councils were translated into practice via a civil service bureaucracy, backed up by colonial armed forces.

This system provided the colonial authorities with a mechanism for ordering the colony, and around this structure other groups ordered themselves. There was a division between the formal colony and the Chinese population (both resident, for example the original 6,500 residents of Hong Kong island and the villagers of the New Territories and the inward migrants who came to work and live in the rapidly expanding settlements of Hong Kong island and Kowloon). The Chinese organized themselves via family networks, clan groups, economic spheres, temples and welfare organizations. The two systems intersected in routine practice in the economic sphere – it was one city – but formal linkages were much slower to develop. The first Chinese person only joined Legco in 1880. An official responsible for the Chinese population joined Exco in 1883. A Chinese person was not appointed to Exco until 1926.

The system continued in the early part of twentieth century. However, a series of new factors emerged: the rise of Chinese nationalism associated with Sun Yat-sen's 1911 republican revolution in China; the rise of the economic power of the Chinese in Hong Kong (both rich capitalists and organized poor workers); and thoughts of reform amongst the colonial authorities (who had begun to think that maybe the system of empire was not sustainable in the long run and that sooner or later reforms would have to be introduced). All this meant that the formal colonial system of government was under pressure from new patterns of political forces but change was very slow.

After the Pacific War the colonial regime resumed. But there were new patterns of political forces: the end of the civil war in China meant that Hong Kong Chinese were split in their political allegiances between PRC and ROC sympathizers; the start of the cold war meant that the colonial authorities and ROC sympathizers were anti-communist; and the economic situation of Hong Kong was unstable (periods of rapid growth were followed by periods of recession and refugees swelled the population).

In the 1950s and 1960s the colonial authorities faced problems of strikes and civil disorder as the politics of the mainland and ROC spilled over into Hong Kong, where in addition there was intermittent strong resentment directed towards the colonial authorities. Then in the 1970s and 1980s the situation changed again; there was stability in China, the cold war in East Asia eased and there were sweeping changes in Hong Kong. These were important: first, the economy grew rapidly; second, the authorities became involved in the provision of basic services such as housing, schooling and welfare; and third, a generation grew up who had been born and raised in Hong Kong – they thought of themselves as Hong Kongers. It is in this period that 'modern Hong Kong' took shape as a rich, sophisticated Chinese city.

The 1984 Joint Declaration between the colonial authority and the government of the People's Republic of China agreed the return of Hong Kong to China in 1997. A new Basic Law for Hong Kong was established (as part of the law of China), the governor became the chief executive, the Executive Council was reformed to look more like a cabinet and the Legislative Council was reformed and became an elected body (partly functional constituencies and partly geographical). These are significant changes.

The government structure (chief executive, Exco and Legco) now has an elective element. This will get bigger. There are now new political parties which have been formed in the last decade and these are a growing influence on Legco and wider politics. There are three main parties: the Democratic Party, which is supported by the middle classes and professionals, argues strongly for a liberal-democratic system and has poor relations with Beijing; the Liberal Party, which draws support from the middle classes and is business oriented; and the Democratic Action for the Betterment of Hong Kong (DAB), which draws support from a wider 'grassroots' grouping, is sympathetic to Beijing and argues for slow and steady practical progress. As regards the internal politics broadly the polity has had a distinct historical trajectory and has developed its own internal logic (that is, key players, institutional vehicles and ways of understanding what is going on): the government machine revolves around the chief executive and the civil service; Exco and Legco are important but not central; the tycoons and big business are also important; there is rule of law but it is subject to Beijing's oversight; civil society is very vigorous but relatively weak. It was a top-down system in colonial days; it remains a top-down system; but, to recap, it is a rich and sophisticated city.[48]

The contemporary politics of Hong Kong are dominated by the relationship with Beijing; the two political systems are quite different; the two political cultures are quite different; and the economies are quite different. It would be a difficult task anywhere. There is a widespread view that the first chief executive, Mr Tung, was not up to the job despite being a very hardworking and nice man (and it might be noted that he came to power in 1997 just as the Asian financial crisis began). His government was the target of large public demonstrations in 2003 and 2004. He resigned unexpectedly in 2004 following the arrival of a new leadership in Beijing. There is widespread domestic support for his Beijing-chosen successor Mr Tsang, who was a long-serving colonial civil servant. Beijing speaks of 'executive-led government' – the state should be in charge, and in Hong Kong that means the chief executive and the civil service. Beijing speaks of its desire that Hong Kong should continue to be an 'economic city' and not become a 'political city'. However, there is an expectation of further democratization – it is in the Basic Law – and the city is politically sophisticated and there is no reason to suppose that the Hong Kongers are going to become politically quiescent. The city has a distinctive pattern of players, institutions and ways of understanding. The elite remain very much in charge, the formal system is top-down and the middle classes and grass roots continue to press for further change (roughly, democratization). Much will depend in the near future on the attitude of those in power in Beijing.

(iii) Hong Kong's futures

It is nearly ten years since the sovereignty of Hong Kong was transferred to Beijing; shortly after the handover the territory experienced economic/financial crisis, health scares and a series of major public demonstrations voicing opposition to SAR government policies. Beijing has shown little sign of understanding the internal social or political dynamics of Hong Kong; the relationship is uneasy; Beijing has to find a way of dealing with an important distinctive political unit;[49] Hong Kong has to find a mechanism to formulate a coherent political voice; the two are intertwined and local commentators specify Beijing as the block to the local democratization which is a necessary condition of securing political consensus and policy coherence. The future as the Hong Kong SAR remains open; it is difficult to see failure; it is difficult to see simple continuity (success); reorientation is likely; the issue is the precise nature of any reorientation. Five scenarios can be identified.[50]

- Scenario 1, Continuation of the Present Model: Beijing has selected the new leadership; the Beijing elite values stability; the local Hong Kong elite manage Beijing as they managed the British[51] and the territory maintains its global role, deepens its linkages with the mainland (economic, social and political), maintains its special status (juridical, administrative and political) and continues much as it has been in recent years; that is, sophisticated, prosperous and broadly content with itself and its unfolding trajectory/role. This is an optimistic scenario which requires Beijing not to interfere but there are signs that this is unlikely.
- Scenario 2, Adoption of the Singapore Model: Hong Kong gains effective local leadership; there is rapid economic advance; there are no public liberal-democratic-style politics; the territory maintains its special status but local leadership moves to compete energetically within the global system, seeking to follow Singapore in upgrading its global footprint or niche. This is a fairly optimistic scenario; however, the Beijing version relies on a distinction between 'political city' and 'economic city' which is neither tenable nor evidences any understanding of Singapore (whose development trajectory has been suffused with politics) or Hong Kong (whose development trajectory has been attended by a thoroughly sophisticated elite politics), and a non-Beijing version would require an absence of interference from Beijing, an optimistic assumption.
- Scenario 3, Deep Integration: Hong Kong becomes the key element of the Pearl River Delta region; there is deeper economic integration, cross-border investment and trade, cross-border flows of people; such integration extends

178 *Trading cities*

not merely to immediate neighbour cities but throughout the delta region; and the deepening integration is complemented by further delta region coordination (for example major infrastructural development or environmental regulation). Hong Kong keeps its juridical, administrative and political independence and it thus sustains its global role. This is a fairly optimistic scenario: developing the Pearl River Delta region offers new possibilities and whilst it requires an absence of interference from Beijing it posits the existence of local Southern China allies.

- Scenario 4, Slow Dissolve: deeper integration is driven by Beijing's anxieties and local elite short-termism; economic opportunism plus political timidity drives deeper integration but neglects to maintain juridical, administrative and political independence; mainland practices are imported; there is ineffective instruction from Beijing coupled with extensive corruption; Hong Kong becomes just another Pearl River Delta town; there is long-term relative decline but the territory continues to be just as prosperous as the rest of the delta region, which is now a global manufacturing site. This is a pessimistic scenario which tracks the slow reabsorption of Hong Kong into Southern China.[52]
- Scenario 5, Rational Authoritarianism Hong Kong: deeper integration is ordered in line with the policy styles and political agendas of Beijing; the integration draws in the Hong Kong elite as one more group of provincial/capital city players; it also draws in the broad mass of the people of Hong Kong has whether they wish it or not; the latter are disciplined; Hong Kong is a sophisticated modern city; the mix is interesting with rational authoritarianism plus great social discipline; the local elite and the mass diverge; the success of the mix depends on Beijing's ability not to interfere in the day-to-day running of Hong Kong; the future could be that of a disciplined Chinese city.

Hong Kong in prospect

Hong Kong Island was extracted by violence from Qing Dynasty China; it was ceded to the British after the Opium War in 1842. It prospered as colonial entrepot linking local to regional and global networks; as a trading city accessing China; its development was skewed as the colonial elite attended to their interests whilst paying scant attention to those of the local community.[53] The political economy involved a series of discrete groupings: the original local farming and fishing communities; the newly arrived colonial traders, administrators, armed forces and assorted camp followers; inward migration from southern China, both comprador merchants and large numbers of poorer people finding work in the burgeoning port city. This political economic pattern evolved; the inward migration generated a large internally divided Chinese population (family, clan, language), which in turn produced its own business community, that is, rich local Chinese families, and by 1900 Chinese capital equalled that of the British.

The East Asian general crisis of 1911–75 impacted upon Hong Kong in various ways. In the years prior to 1911 it was a site for Sun Yat-sen's revolutionaries and a base for multiple failed attempts at fermenting revolution in Southern China. From 1911 onwards it was a site for mainland Chinese political activity and both the KMT and CCP used it as a base whilst competing locally for support. From 1937 onwards it was a site for anti-Japanese agitation. And from 1941 to 1945 it was occupied by the Imperial Japanese; the local expatriate community were interned, local Chinese capitalists reluctantly cooperated and guerrilla groups operated in the rural areas. In 1945 Hong Kong experienced a second colonization as the British returned, and reconstruction was at first rapid but in 1949 the situation changed as the UN embargoed trade with China. The loss of the trading links with China was serious but a turn to export-oriented development began, aided by incoming flight capital from Shanghai, and light manufactures developed or recovered.[54] From 1949 to 1971 the territory was caught up in the American-sponsored cold war and Hong Kong grew along with East Asia. The situation changed in 1978 when special economic zones were located in Guandong Province, and commerce, industry and trade expanded rapidly and Hong Kong businesses invested heavily in Southern China.

Quasi-national development was pursued from the late 1960s onwards; on the back of a successful economy further successes were recorded. The current situation is unclear. In 1997 formal sovereignty over Hong Kong reverted to China; the central government established the Basic Law, a 'mini-constitution'; groups within the territory had perforce to deal with Beijing; the relationship between Hong Kong and Beijing became crucial to the future of the territory. The broad orienting policy/slogan had been enunciated by Deng Xiaoping – 'one country, two systems'; it now had to be translated into practice; the first SAR government undertook a series of activities, together constituting a second project of quasi-national development.

It may be that the collective pursuit of an affluent lifestyle will help local and mainland elites fashion a new contested compromise, a Hong Kong version of the familiar East Asian pattern of a developmental state; but that is an open question; the developmental state has been effective in the service of clear political projects, but for Hong Kong where is the project? It may be that 'to be rich is glorious', but in the context of an already rich city and in the absence of an effective domestic politics it might seem to be a narrow, impoverished and finally unpersuasive goal.

Informal empire: the trajectories of Bangkok and Shanghai

The British accumulated an empire in East Asia through the late eighteenth and nineteenth centuries; the process of expansion involved manoeuvring, opportunism and violence; these were colonies of trade rather than settlement;

and any settlement was transitory or incidental.[55] The first requirement was access and the institutional mechanism was the trading base; the early factories were small; they were exposed;[56] they were impermanent; and they were accumulated, exchanged and discarded at will.[57] Some succeeded whilst others failed. However, the trading relationship deepened: the factories became permanent; soldiers, administrators, adventurers and families joined the groups of traders; local merchants moved in to embrace new commercial opportunities; and the early bases grew into larger permanent settlements. In the formal empires, the great trading cities were the keys to maintaining these growing colonial accumulations, whilst in the informal empires settlements of traders were established and became influential. The cities and international settlements served two functions: they were crucial in sustaining a global network centred upon the metropolitan capital; and they drew their own particular hinterlands into the system oriented towards the metropolitan centre. They were links in a chain, but links with valuable hinterlands. The territorial holdings, the areas on the maps which were coloured pink, were secondary to the great trading cities; territory could be adjusted, or lost or acquired, but without the cities there could be no colonial holdings; economic, social and political power was concentrated in these urban settlements; global, regional and local trade flowed through; the local region might have plantations or mines up-country, but their prosperity rested upon the wider linkages forged by the cities.

Singapore and Hong Kong were acquired in order to serve as bases for trade-centred colonial expansion; the former was a quite unimportant part of the local Johor–Riau Sultanate, whilst the latter was a remote part of the vast Qing Empire; the former was extracted through guile, negotiation and bribery, whilst the latter was taken only after the 1842 Opium War. The two settlements were quickly remade; there were inflows of people, new institutional arrangements and rapid economic advance; and both became significant regional trading centres. The British, however, did not stop there; they sought further trade within the archipelago and deeper within China; important contacts were established with Bangkok and Shanghai, and whilst the contexts and characteristics of both settlements were quite different, both developed into major port cities within the European-dominated East Asian sphere.

Bangkok and Shanghai have had different trajectories, different routes into the modern world; but both run through an exchange with the British, other Europeans and Americans. Bangkok had a resident elite; the elite revolved around the Chakri Dynasty; the elite and their city were the inheritors of earlier polities which had been located further inland on the Chaophraya river; the elite ruled a mandala[58] state based in the Chaophraya river basin but extending north, east and south; it was a pre-modern state.[59] The response of the Bangkok-based elite to the incursions of the British was to modernize; the elite sought to absorb the lessons of the modern world in order to sustain their rule; Japan provided something of a model and the practices and procedures of French and British colonial neighbours offered further lessons. The Siamese elite were nimble footed and lucky, as their neighbours redrew their boundaries more than once but left them a territory in which to make their own modern nation-state.[60] Shanghai too had a local elite; it was a large city in the early nineteenth century; the British arrived in the 1840s and established a base; other Europeans followed, so too Americans; the British Settlement became the International Settlement.[61] The role of the British increased, as local authority was slowly displaced; later, when China dissolved into confusion, as did Shanghai, the International Settlement became more important. The International Settlement linked central China to the global system; the city became a major trading centre; the system was sustained through the domestic upheavals of Qing collapse, warlordism and civil war; in the 1930s Shanghai was the premier international city of China; and its wealth and influence eclipsed Hong Kong and Singapore. The catastrophe of the Pacific War overwhelmed the city. Shanghai's Europeans and Americans left. The civil war victory of the Communist Party was followed by a further exodus as the local bourgeoisie fled, many to Hong Kong. The city lost its international role as the new Beijing government pursued autarchic state-socialist policies.

After the collapse of empire, in their post-colonial guise, Singapore and Hong Kong have developed along lines that might have been expected as they have been and are trading ports. Singapore is now an independent city-state. It has been built on the legacies of the colonial era. The colonial era lasted some 140 years and in this time Singapore became an integral part of the modern world; its status shifted and changed; it has shifted and changed subsequently; but the city-state remains a key centre in Southeast Asia. It is a key site in the global liberal-capitalist system, a key link in East Asian regional economic networks and a key centre for trade within the archipelago; there are local doubts about the future, but they are those of a rich country. In Hong Kong a similar situation holds. The colonial era lasted around 150 years and established Hong Kong within the modern world; the territory's role and status changed during this period; and its role and status have changed subsequently. Hong Kong is not an independent city-state; its nominal colonial ruler withdrew but sovereignty reverted to the successor state of the Qing, that is, the People's Republic of China. The relationship between Beijing and Hong Kong is governed by the political doctrine of 'one country, two systems' and juridically by a Beijing-written Basic Law; it is an unusual arrangement but it has to be made to work; a process of mutual adjustment seems to be underway and in the meantime Hong Kong continues to be a rich, sophisticated, modern city.

After the Pacific War Bangkok was subject to significant externally directed change; the familiar informal empire of Britain had disappeared during the war years and it did not return; a strong American presence developed; cold war spillover and domestic militarism generated a slow

182 *Trading cities*

development trajectory; but after the end of the Indo-China wars the country emerged as a second tier Asian Tiger; and the informal colonial period faded into history. After the Pacific War Shanghai was absorbed into an autarchic state-socialist system; the international city was eclipsed; the linkages to the colonial powers were removed; and the international city that had existed until the war was recreated only after the 1978 inauguration of domestic reforms. Both cities are now embedded in the modern world just as both countries are now part of the modern world. The colonial powers resident in the International Settlement are a remote part of history, an available story for tourists. The British role in the growth of Bangkok is similarly a matter pursued only in history books. The trajectories of these two cities of the informal empire are quite distinctive: they are shaped by the exchange with colonial incursions; they read and react to these demands; as the colonial systems – formal and informal – collapse, they move forwards along distinct trajectories; local elites continue to read and react to enfolding circumstances; but they are now firmly lodged within the modern world; their trajectories are new variants of modernity.

The unfolding trajectory of Siam/Bangkok

A political economic history identifies groups forming, reading and reacting to enfolding complex change, prospering and declining; it is a contingent process; arguments for an immanent logic of progress cannot be read off the surface of changing social arrangements; the historical experience of the West does not offer a model. The trajectories of individual groups of people are shaped by the exchange of internal and external pressures. In the nineteenth century asymmetries of power within the global system allowed the outside world to impact a sophisticated pre-modern form of life centred on the basin of the Chaophraya river; the community reacted and, via particular domestic dynamics and within a quite particular international context, a country emerged (other, similarly impacted communities went under). A series of discrete phases can be identified in the trajectory that produces the contemporary nation-state of Thailand.[62]

In the first phase, the period 1822–55, there were early exchanges with incoming colonial powers; contacts were made, some official conversations were held and the first mutual adjustments begun; the incomers sought trade; the established elite sought to understand, survive and later to profit. The local political pattern comprised mandala states[63] located within the four river basins of Indo-China (Irrawadi, Chaophraya, Mekong and Red rivers); the power of these states waxed and waned in relation to the success of the local economy, the vigour of local royal families and the vagaries of warfare. A number of settlements became important as their resident royal family prospered; by the sixteenth century there were eight principal ethnic or political groupings in the region;[64] the city of Ayutthaya emerged as an important centre in the fifteenth century; it became rich. Ayutthaya was

Figure 11 Bangkok, downtown skyline.

Figure 12 Bangkok, Ramkamhaeng, suburban street scene.

184 *Trading cities*

Figure 13 Bangkok, Ramkamhaeng, informal housing area.

destroyed by the Burmese in 1767; the remnants of the city's population moved south; a local figure re-established the city in 1782 as Bangkok; shortly afterwards a royal figure displaced him to found a new dynasty, styling himself Rama I. The city thereafter reasserted its territorial reach and powerful families allied to the centre developed in the provinces; Buddhist ideas were used to legitimate kingship. There was significant inward Chinese migration, powerful Chinese families developed and foreigners added impetus to the market economy from the late eighteenth century.

Figure 14 Bangkok, Ramkamhaeng Road.

Thus the modern world arrives in the late eighteenth century and whilst the elite are interested they are also cautious; the incoming modern world, in the guise of colonial traders, constitutes both opportunity and threat. The British have a base in Singapore from 1818; their central concern is with trade; they use this base to reach out into the archipelago and into the various territories of Indo-China. Singapore is the base from which they

Figure 15 Bangkok, coffee shop, Ramkamhaeng.

make contact with Bangkok. The early contacts involve only small numbers of Europeans. At this time Bangkok is oriented towards China as a trade and political partner; China is the undisputed regional leader, the core of the long-established Sino-centric system. The 1842 Opium War sharply alters elite perceptions in the region, including Bangkok, and the incoming colonial traders are treated with a new caution/respect. In 1822 John Crawfurd travelled from Singapore to Bangkok and sought to establish trade links with Siam; he was not successful. However, the British were extending their reach within the peninsula and the 1826 Gurney Treaty delineated the British and Siamese spheres in the Malay peninsula; it granted British trading rights in these northern Malay states;[65] it was a first move. The British persisted; in 1850 James Brooke made a further attempt to establish trading relationships but the Siamese elite were undecided and the approach was rebuffed.[66] However, the elite had only bought time; King Mongkut (r.1851–68) responded to the incomers' challenge more directly; the old mandala structures of loose hierarchies of allegiance were adapted and a more centralized authority was asserted; it was the first positive response to the demands of the incoming modern world.

A second phase runs from 1855–1932, a period of significant impacts and major elite-level responses which together place the polity on a new historical trajectory. It is an entirely elite-driven project. There are deepening contacts with outsiders, the British and French in particular, and major domestic reforms; it is the period of the construction of an absolutist monarchy and a preliminary Thai nation-state. There are two key factors driving these changes: the 1885 the Bowring Treaty; and the reform-minded rule of Mongkut and later Chulalongkorn (r.1868–1910). The former is significant; it was the third British attempt to secure trade relations with the Siamese elite in Bangkok and it was successful. In 1855 John Bowring signed a treaty with Mongkut, the Siamese monarch.[67] Mongkut was a reformer and the treaty was a significant step. Signing the treaty had the effect (or marked the new reality) of reorienting Siamese elite thinking away from China towards the incoming Europeans; a new model was acknowledged. The treaty governed trade; it allowed the importation of opium; and it granted the British extra-territorial rights. The British involvement centred on trade; the treaty opened up Bangkok and Siam to the influences of global trade; rice turned out to be an important crop and as the elite modernized, trade drew them into the process. The outside provided models; the outside also agreed for its own reasons to acknowledge the emergent Siamese state, which provided a buffer between rival European empires, thus the 1896 Anglo-French Agreement guaranteed Siamese autonomy. Thereafter, it was the energetic efforts of Chulalongkorn which altered fundamentally Siamese elite responses; it was no longer a matter of modifying a mandala state; rather the task was to build a modern polity. The schedule of reforms were familiar: centralizing tax gathering; beginning a standing army; obtaining new armaments; and creating a new trained and competent bureaucracy. The

188 *Trading cities*

bureaucracy and army moved out from Bangkok throughout the former mandala territory in order to secure and organize the defined territory of Siam; maps were made and boundaries drawn. Inside the defined boundary a nation was specified: in the late nineteenth century the Siamese elite learned the discourse of race from the French and constructed an idea of a Thai race compounded of language, ethnicity and place; the inhabitants of the defined territory were members of the Thai Kingdom, which revolves around the central figure of the king. At the same time the economy grew through peasant rice cultivation; in Chaophraya basin land was brought into cultivation; land rights went to cultivators, creating a mass of small farmers; there were comparatively few estates and thus restricted landlordism; rice was a staple; it was an export crop; small farmers were often linked by Chinese traders to the global market; rice was shipped out to Singapore and Hong Kong; this was an element of the Southeast Asian regional food trade.[68] The late nineteenth century was a period of rapid change. Chulalongkorn shaped the distinctive domestic trajectory of Siamese development; he was an active reformer and created an elite bureaucracy in order to pursue modernization from above. This was a distinctive shift to the modern world; it created the outline of a modern nation-state; the ideal was celebrated in arts and letters;[69] but the project was centred upon an absolute monarch, with the Siamese elite thereafter borrowing from available colonial models. Siam can be seen as a colony of the Bangkok elite: elite factions, a strong bureaucracy, a powerful army and a demobilized mass with ethnic divisions internal to the territory, plus inward migration from Southern China.

Bangkok became a colonial port city;[70] the impact of the modern world deepened; at the time of the European Great War the city was dominated by foreigners, in particular the British; it was cosmopolitan, diverse, but with an effective local elite.[71] The British Borneo Company had established itself in Bangkok shortly after the Bowring Treaty was signed; an American firm built a rice mill; a British firm built a sugar mill; by 1880 there were twelve rice mills; in the 1920s there were more than eighty; rice was by now a key export, shipped via Singapore; teak mills were also established. On the back of these primary product trades further traders arrived, so too service industries; the city became cosmopolitan; it was a part of the colonial world, albeit not colonized by one particular power. The Siamese elite controlled the impetus of economic change; the schemes of outsiders for rubber, tin and railways were not accepted; the social impact of economic change refocused Siamese attention – away from China towards Europe and America – and some of the great local Chinese enterprises did not survive these changes; others moved into the important rice trade. The Siamese elite adjusted to these demands; their project was legitimated through ideas of nation, religion and monarchy. It was successful as they secured development plus continued independence from incoming colonial powers.

The reforms begun by Chulalongkorn are continued by his royal successors: Vajiravudh (r.1910–25) creates early official nationalism; and Prajadhipok (r.1925–33) affirms these ideas until his abdication in 1935.The complex shifting exchange between the incoming Europeans, who were carried on the resources and machineries of the modern world, the incoming Chinese merchants, traders and farmers and the rulers/peoples of the Siamese mandala state remade the extant society: economic change; social change; cultural change; and political change. Over time elite groups create a Thai nation-state;[72] however, it is an elite project; the elite is also growing more sophisticated in the ways of the modern world and the Royal Absolutism established by Chulalongkorn comes under criticism from elements within those modern institutions he established, and arguments for reform begin.

A third phase running from 1932 to 1945 encompasses general crisis;[73] in this period the accumulated complaints about royal absolutism finally precipitate dramatic change; in 1932 a group of democratic-minded figures announce the overthrow of the monarchy and confusion reigns; the reformers withdraw but a second coup in 1933 settles the matter and the revolt succeeds. However, there is internal dissent amongst the new leaders as to how to proceed; there is a liberal line and a military nationalist line within the reform movement; Pridi, a liberal looking to the model of France, looks to democracy; Phibun, a military figure looking to the model of Japan favours an authoritarian top-down strategy of change; they struggle for dominance and Pridi begins as leader, but in 1938 Phibun assumes the leadership. Phibun is very much more in tune with the times; the military come to the fore; politics are corporatist, nationalist and influenced by gathering war. It is a quasi-fascist period, a period of nationalism and aggressive nationalism; the break with the royal order of Siam is signalled when in 1939 the country is renamed Thailand. Phibun launches a war against the French in Indo-China and cooperates, partly by choice, partly of necessity, with Imperial Japan. The dalliance with a quasi-fascist project ends in 1944 as elite factions come to realize that Imperial Japan is going to be defeated by the United States.

A further phase can be marked out, running from 1945 to 1992: a continuation of general crisis as the future of the country remains unclear. The end of the Pacific War was followed by a host of domestic problems, made worse by the effects of a catastrophic period of war in Indo-China. The wartime leader Phibun withdrew from power in 1944 as the fate of Imperial Japan became clear; he was replaced by the more acceptable figure of Pridi; further confusions followed and a 1947 coup returned Phibun to power; a five-year period of low-level civil war followed, until Pridi lost and fled the country. Thailand became a military dictatorship. The elite affirmed an anticommunist stance and spoke of development; in the meantime, generals manoeuvred for power and profit. The long period was politically chaotic; politics went inside the military; generals manoeuvred for power; they enjoyed the spoils of power; there were cycles of plotting and coup making interspersed with short-lived attempts to establish liberal-democratic institutions and communist rebellions. These domestic dynamics were reinforced by events in the region. The determination of the USA to resist what its elites saw as international communism inclined them to support conservative groups around the region and Thailand was no exception. The Americans quickly lent support to the Thai military and tolerated a lengthy period of military dictatorship. Successive military governments haphazardly pursued economic development; there were experiments in democratic reform; a movement for democracy flourished briefly in the period 1973–76 but it was violently suppressed – shock provoked some reforms in army rule; General Prem ruled from 1980 to 1988, a period of reform and guided democracy. A further experiment in democracy eventually began; it was short lived. A 1991 coup put the army back in power; there was further violence but King Bhumibol (r.1946–) intervened and commentators suggest Thailand – by now spoken of as a new East Asian Tiger – has turned its back on military coups and become a liberal-market economy with an appropriately liberal-democratic polity.

Phase five could be dated 1992–2006 and characterized as a period of national development with economic growth, social reform and political advance. The characterization is somewhat ambiguous. There are two elements: the period 1992–2001 was shaped by a succession of coalitions of new businessmen and it was an economic boom period, but the economy overheated and the episode came to an end in the Asian financial crisis of 1997; the period 2001–06 was dominated by the political leadership of the business tycoon Thaksin, who sought to upgrade the economy and drive economic development forwards after the style of Malaysia and Singapore. However, the project sketched by this provincial Sino-Thai businessman cut across the interests of the established elite surrounding the palace; in 2006 a palace coup removed the thrice-elected prime minister and returned Thailand to the cycle of constitution writing and coup making.

The coup provoked surprise; most commentators had become accustomed to reading Thailand as a democracy. Since the end of military involvement in the late 1980s, there had been economic and political advance. In the 1990s there was a drive for export-oriented industrialization; local elites embraced the fashionable ideas of liberalization and foreign money flowed into the economy; it produced a bubble economy along with new business-linked politicians (Chatchai, Chuan, Banharn, Chavalit and later Thaksin). The bubble burst when speculation against the Thai currency overwhelmed government policy makers; the exchange rate crisis spilled over into the financial system, then the real economy, then society and finally into the political world. The crisis also spread throughout East Asia. Numerous explanations have been offered for the 1997 crisis: the Washington Consensus favoured 'crony capitalism', whereas political economists have looked to the particular interests of the players involved. Phongpaichit and Baker[74] discuss the key social groups, note their interests and how they influenced policy. The background was that the Thai economy from 1959 to 1976 had seen an ISI strategy; GDP growth averaged 7 per cent; it was a local version of the East Asian focus on national development with local banks, high savings and informal lending. There was little state direction, but with cheap rural labour and FDI from Japan a number of Thai corporate groups developed. The turning point was mid-1980s when there was a minor economic/financial crisis. It had four consequences: expansion of the role of technocrats; financial liberalization; the reorientation of Thai conglomerates; and the rise of new business groups. An informal coalition emerged involving technocrats, new business groups, reoriented conglomerates and Washington; the upshot was the drive to liberalize and develop rapidly. The liberalization was begun by the technocrats, supported by Washington and enjoyed by new business groups, reoriented conglomerates and newly influential politicians (urban and rural bosses). The process ran out of control; when foreign exchange market sentiment turned against the local currency, local businesses were over-borrowed; the sharp increase in the costs of debt servicing coupled with a lack of new credit tipped them into default and bankruptcy; the crisis then unfolded within Thailand and spread around the region.

The recovery was painful; economic distress spilled over into social distress as many urban workers returned to the countryside. A new constitution was prepared. A local business tycoon formed a new party and in 2001 he was elected. Thaksin sought to reinvigorate the Thai economy; he was successful; debts were paid off, rural development projects initiated and the urban economies restarted. The government was re-elected in 2005. It continued with its pursuit of national development; again successfully. However, in early 2006 a political crisis developed, ostensibly over the prime minister's business dealings; it became a battle for power between progressive business groups and a reactionary elite clique of military personnel linked to the palace. Thaksin called a snap election, which his party won; however, a popular opposition boycott technically invalidated the election, which was subsequently voided. Confusions continued, with elite manoeuvring, street demonstrations and hysterical press commentary; further elections were scheduled for the autumn, which commentators reported Thaksin was expected to win comfortably. However, in October 2006 the army staged a coup; the king indicated his support;[75] and the old elite took power. The Bangkok population welcomed the coup; rural Thai's did not; however, in reality, both sections of the population are now once again powerless as the long-familiar metropolitan politics of elite-level manoeuvring are resumed.

Overall, in sum, Bangkok was a colonial port city in the late nineteenth and early twentieth century; the city was the base of an elite which responded creatively to the demands and opportunities opened up through trade and participation within the modern world; the Bangkok elite ordered an hitherto mandala territory into a modern nation-state; it has been successful; it has made its own place in the world; nineteenth-century colonial powers are long forgotten; so too the episode of adjusting to Imperial

192 *Trading cities*

Japan; the key power in the years after the Pacific War was America; it too has softened its presence; no longer articulated via cold war violence, its influence runs through the trading patterns of the Pacific Rim; however, long-established tensions remain. The Bangkok elite seems not to have settled its sense of its place in the world. Two variants of Thai nationalism are available: one places the monarchy within the confines of a constitution, with the monarchy as the head of state; whilst the other places the monarchy centrally within Thai social life, where the monarch embodies the wisdom of the Buddhist sage; but in both cases the official ideology of the polity continues to be the trinity of nation (Thais), religion (Buddhism) and monarchy (Chakri Dynasty). It is a distinctive accommodation to the demands of the modern world – a synthesis of inherited cultural resources and the demands of the modern global system; it is a distinctive domestic structure; and it has sketched out a distinctive historical trajectory.

The unfolding trajectory of China/Shanghai

The 1842 Treaty of Nanking settled the Opium War; one aspect of the treaty allowed that five treaty ports were open to Europeans and Americans; Shanghai was one of these treaty ports. The British acted promptly; their representative George Balfour arrived in Shanghai in November 1843. Uncertain of his welcome he moved cautiously; his demeanour met with the approval of local officials; and the incoming colonial representative, together with the local bureaucracy, began the negations which inaugurated the process of building what was to become the Shanghai International Settlement.[76] It became a great colonial trading centre. A number of phases in the historical trajectory of the city can be identified.

Shanghai was an established city prior to the arrival of Europeans; it had a large population as a result of its role within the local areas of the Chinese economy, and merchants in the city had begun some trade with Europeans before 1842; thus the city was known to the Europeans. Balfour rented a house to serve as a consulate inside the city walls; this was against the wishes of the local authorities, who wished the foreigners and traders to be outside their city wall; for this same reason Balfour insisted, but, as he had been advised, accommodations within the city were cramped and expensive; in time, the British representative's office was moved to the settlement.[77] The British Settlement was built on land outside the city leased from local peasant landowners; accumulating the land was a drawn-out business. A grid of streets was laid out and firms constructed buildings; collective facilities were also laid out (wharves, the Bund, cemeteries, a race course and so on). The British brought Cantonese compradors with them, so links to locals were at first limited; Balfour worked closely with the local authorities to establish procedures for trade; they were giving practical effect to the Treaty of Nanking. The settlement prospered, the British thinking in terms of quasi-colony, the Chinese thinking in terms of the familiar pattern of the trading guild.[78] The first moves in Shanghai's shift to the modern world were read by the local authorities in terms of long-established practices; Confucian officials ruled; merchants followed these rules.[79]

Shanghai as a treaty port was successful.[80] Many Chinese merchants came to the city; foreign traders were also attracted. There were successes in exporting tea and silk, along with disappointments with regard to imports of cotton piece goods. The new trading economy served foreigners, local merchants and the chains of suppliers and distributors along the Yangtze river; it interacted with the existing economy, where there winners and losers. An important trade good was opium; it was an unofficial trade, carried out in China in the company of local producers and distributors;[81] it was also intimately related to the growth of the local banking industry as it required lines of credit;[82] more generally, it was crucial to British trade in the East.[83] Other traders came, in particular French and American, and both established settlements; the French Concession remained separate, whereas the British Settlement embraced American interests and in 1852 became the International Settlement.[84] The settlement prospered; in time it covered a large area measuring some seven by two miles alongside the Huangpu river, adjacent to the Chinese city; and it developed into a quasi-colonial enclave. Much of the development was secured in agreement with the local Chinese authorities; the early settlement boasted a population of a few dozen at a time when the city of Shanghai had grown to around 250,000.[85] It was a complex situation involving foreign traders, local traders, traders from other parts of China and Qing officials. A brief 1853–55 occupation of the city by Small Sword rebels added further confusions.[86] As the wider Taiping Rebellion continued its course during 1851–64 refugees from the warfare came to the city; trade in Shanghai advanced.[87] The confusions allowed the foreigners to advance their control within the settlement; and it became a quasi-colonial port city, a dual city comprising foreigners and locals.[88]

The high tide of imperialist advance ran from 1864 to 1911. After 1864 the city grew; it was a major centre for trade with a powerful local textile industry. After the 1894–05 Sino-Japanese War foreign investment was allowed;[89] it flowed in and the already prosperous city grew further. Shanghai became the key port gateway to central China. The city developed, as did other colonial settlements; there was economic, social and cultural separation; the city was densely populated, the economy finely divided; the elite prospered, whilst others made their livelihoods in the mix of available trades; the city was cosmopolitan; conservative critics castigated the pattern of life as degraded;[90] but the city was also open to imported ideas and became a centre of political opposition to the Qing and the colonial occupation. But the 1911 revolution was partial; it marked the start of a long period of chaos; China experienced a long drawn-out general crisis.

Shanghai continued to advance economically; business thrived; so too gangsterism; so too radical politics. Yet in Shanghai the established historical trajectory which had been shaped by treaty port activity was remade; Shanghai entered the modern world in concert with foreign traders but from then on its trajectory was shaped by domestic political factors. After 1911 Shanghai was a major site of conflict between the KMT and the CCP; the latter, in particular, looked to Shanghai, as unusually in China at that time it had a large urban working class. After 1920 it was a major industrial and commercial city; local power was shared between the KMT, CCP, local merchants, trades unions and gangsters. Chiang Kai-Shek's Northern Expedition advanced towards Shanghai in early 1927; local nationalist sympathizers confronted and massacred the local Communist Party members; it was the first move in the long drawn-out Chinese Civil War. From 1927 to 1937, the Nanjing decade, it was the key city of nationalist China; the city became a major trading city within the global system; the International Settlement and French Concession were home to many foreign business concerns; these reached along the valley of the Yangtze river into the heartlands of central China. Shanghai was successful and fashionable; it eclipsed Hong Kong and Singapore.

The Imperial Japanese had involved themselves in Chinese affairs since the Sino-Japanese War; the Imperial Japanese alliance with the British, French and Americans during the European Great War both gave them more status within the world community and encouraged their demands on China. Japanese involvement paralleled that of the Europeans and Americans; it was economic and involved military force. However, the Imperial Japanese deployed their armies rather freely. In 1932 there were conflicts in Manchuria and an attack on part of Shanghai; the locals resisted and a drawn-out battle ensued. In 1937 the Japanese invasion of China inaugurated a long drawn-out war; the city of Shanghai was occupied; yet the city continued to function; there were complex adjustments made to the demands of the Japanese; business continued; so too the life of the city.[91] However, the outbreak of the Pacific War meant that the International Settlement was occupied;[92] the European and American foreign occupation was terminated; the general condition of the city slowly declined thereafter as conditions worsened in China and as international war intermeshed with actions relating to the unfinished civil war.[93]

The Japanese surrendered in 1945; Shanghai was occupied by American troops and Nationalists; the latter were spectacularly corrupt; in time the combatants resumed their civil war; the communists defeated the KMT; and there was massive capital flight. The People's Republic was inaugurated in 1949, marking a sharp change in the fortunes of the city. After the communist takeover the city's links with the outside world were severed; domestic communist agendas ran together with cold war tensions; the new government adopted an autarchic state-socialist development strategy which was unhelpful to a trading city. Capital flight had taken place; most foreigners left; and Hong Kong received some inward textile industry resources which helped spur the growth of the city. In Shanghai the party made the city into a major industrial centre and redistributed the resources generated throughout the country. The party controlled inward migration and encouraged outward relocation. The city grew slowly.[94] However, as in other parts of China, the 1978 reforms were significant. Shanghai was not at first an SEZ but it was granted open-port status in 1984; the economy grew; the Pudong area was developed from 1990; and there was subsequent rapid growth. The fortunes of the city are bound up with Beijing's personnel and policy; the very rapid growth in recent years was targeted for reductions in 2006; there were fears of local economic overheating; there were also significant elite-level personnel changes associated with the new leadership of Wen and Hu in Beijing; together these are elements of the new official policy of building a 'harmonious society' whereby the negative aspects of the growth-at-any-price policies of recent years can be addressed: inequality, rural poverty and catastrophic pollution.

Contingent trajectories

In East Asia the Pacific War radically remade domestic and international relations; familiar patterns of economic linkages and associated social and political relationships were broken; European influence was not sustained; the trading cities that had sustained the British sphere in the region were reoriented; the linkages amongst them and with the wider global system were redirected. America became the pre-eminent outside power within the region; new replacement elites emerged; the political mixture was quite different; and so too the trajectories sketched out by these replacement elites within the context of contemporary East Asia.

In Hong Kong the colonial reoccupation was anachronistic; the action belonged to the past; it was sustained in the quite peculiar circumstances of the cold war: a closed border with China, now seen as a communist opponent by the hegemonic Western power; local prosperity forming behind the historically novel barrier; and with local upheavals and belated colonial acknowledgment, the slow pursuit of a quasi-national development in the service of the emerging community of those who made their homes in Hong Kong. With the retrocession to China the future, once again, becomes rather opaque; there is likely to be continued success but there could be relative decline. Then in Bangkok the war-time period removed the influence of the Europeans and after the conflict the USA became the key foreign contact of the Bangkok elite; the relationship prospered within the context of the cold war; it became closer as the wars in Indo-China unfolded. Bangkok's politics revolved around the military, the bureaucracy and the monarchy; a cycle was established in which military coups succeeded one another (a constitution was written, elections held, charges of corruption would be made and a new coup would be held); the economy advanced fitfully. However, by the 1990s a liberal-democratic system seemed to be in place and the economy was advancing; Thailand was characterized as a new Asian Tiger; but the 1997 Asian financial crisis undermined that characterization; yet recovery was rapid. Thailand seemed to be part of an increasingly affluent and democratic East Asia; however, the 2006 coup turned the clock back as the cycle was evidenced once again. Finally, in Shanghai the war-time period removed the influence of Europeans and Americans; after the civil war the country pursued an autarchic state-socialist path within the context of cold war division; the city developed within the confines of China; it was not until the 1978 reform programme was inaugurated that the city began to recover something of its pre-war international role. At the present time the city once again has aspirations to be the premier economic and financial centre of China.

Hong Kong and the cities of the sometime colonial periphery have sketched out diverse trajectories. In the former case, the colonial power was in retreat for decades before the final retrocession to China; the handover presented local elites with a new configuration of structures to which they must accommodate themselves; the demands of Beijing loom large; more optimistically, the opportunities of the Pearl River Delta are available; but so far little seems clear. In the latter case, the cities of the sometime colonial periphery broke with inherited patterns of regional and global relationships in the later part of the regional general crisis. Entering the modern world through an exchange with colonialism might shape the subsequent trajectory but it does not determine it and nor does it identify any inherent implied end-point. The shift to the modern world does not entail replicating the experience of the Europeans or Americans. Change is routine; patterns of development shifting; trajectories contingent; Bangkok and Shanghai have gone their own ways. In Hong Kong and the cities of the sometime colonial periphery, colonial days are long past, consigned to the history books.

8 Unfolding trajectories

Recently, globalization has been presented as a series of interlinked processes which are uniquely problematical for contemporary states/polities;[1] however, this is an implausible line of argument because states/polities have always had to deal with structural change; against the dramatic claims of the proponents of globalization it could be asserted that the system is always in flux and states/polities are always adjusting. If we view matters in an historical and contextual perspective, then it is clear that the trajectories of development followed by contemporary states/polities are not smooth but are marked by discontinuities, reconfigurations and relatively stable phases.[2] All these are intrinsic to the process of industrial-capitalist intensification and expansion.[3] One might speak of a series of interlinked routes to the modern world; in each case a series of patterns of response by elite groups to changing enfolding structural circumstances can be identified. As the circumstances which constrain the patterns of action of relevant agents change, agents must respond; these responses will involve necessary elements, flowing from the simple recognition of change, and contingent elements, as agents self-consciously identify new routes to novel futures; and over time accumulating contingent decisions will mark out a track, an historical development trajectory.

The long process of the shift to the modern world established the trajectories of Singapore and Hong Kong; the demands of mercantile capitalist expansion prompted their extraction from established contexts and relocation within the modern world; the new elites struck a variety of bargains with local agents and on the basis of these alliances both territories became colonial port cities; they linked their respective hinterlands to the modern world; they became exchange points within the global network of the British commercial empire and more broadly the global capitalist system; both cities prospered, developed distinctive colonial societies and established effective colonial polities. The general crisis in East Asia impacted the two cities; independence movements spilled into the territories; domestic Chinese, Indian and Malay politics found expression in the cities; the crisis found direct expression in Singapore in the period 1941–65 as the colonial system dissolved away leaving an independent state; the crisis found different

198 *Unfolding trajectories*

expression in Hong Kong in the period 1941–97 as the dissolution of empire was long, drawn-out and ambiguous in outcome, neither an independent state nor an integral part of China; instead there was retrocession to the successor state of the Qing Dynasty in the guise of the curious status of a special administrative zone. In Singapore a replacement elite were quickly in place; they have been active in carving out a niche within the modern global capitalist system; they have deepened their role within the global system; and the early role as exchange point has been sustained/advanced. In Hong Kong a replacement elite was not put in place; a shifting alliance of elite groups have pursued their own advantage; the colonial authorities affirmed a policy of laissez-faire and later the disingenuous notion of positive non-intervention. Colonial activity was slow (thus housing, health care, schooling – key elements of NIC development); local civil society groups were present but weak;[4] manoeuvring between domestic groups and the external power – now Beijing – seems set to continue; economic and social success seem both somewhat fortuitous and well established; but expectations for the future are unclear. Nonetheless, the trajectories of Singapore and Hong Kong record great success; both are rich, cosmopolitan, modern cities. However, now they face difficulties: in Singapore the costs of success and the difficulties of reform within an oligarchic system; and in Hong Kong the dilemma of how to sustain established habits of success as a deeply conservative local elite endeavour to adjust to Beijing. Local commentators in both territories are uneasy; neither is going to collapse, but domestic stasis attended by slow relative decline is a possibility; in Singapore's case this would be awkward; in Hong Kong's potentially more damaging.

Complex change enfolds these polities, as it does others in the modern global system; this perspective offers a way of conceptualizing the changes found in the discontinuous, episodic and uneven historical development experiences of the countries of East Asia: analysis centres on the business of livelihood; the social construction of social life; the historical development experiences of communities can be tracked, with communities of agents together sketching out a contingent historical trajectory.[5] Agents animate the overall tale. In the long process of the shift to the modern world of the territories of East Asia the key players were the incoming Western traders, manufacturers, financiers and thereafter the whole extensive apparatus of colonial rule. The place of indigenous elites was marginal, except in the case of Japan, and everywhere the ordinary people saw their lives remade over the generations. However, the expansion of the Western industrial-capitalist system generated the intellectual and political means whereby the formal colonial system could be resisted, and in the confusions attendant upon the Pacific War indigenous nationalist groups attained a measure of influence and eventually secured independence for their prospective countries. In contemporary East Asia the key players are state regimes, multinational corporations and other commercial operations, international organizations and the groups of peoples involved in the region, the newly prosperous, the weak, the marginal and so on.

Phases mark the discontinuous nature of development for any particular area. The historical development experience of any particular region will involve both periods of relative stability and episodes of more or less rapid complex change. It is clear that there have been discrete phases in the development experiences of the various parts of the East Asian region. Within the frame of any one phase we would expect to find a specific and continuing pattern of economic, social and cultural life, a more or less settled way of doing things. The settled form of life could be characterized in terms of both its internal dynamics and the linkages which it had with the relevant wider system. Relative stability is familiar; a particular historical developmental phase embraces a specific political-economic, social-institutional and cultural pattern within the territory plus definite linkages with the wider global system. Within the confines of these broad frameworks the people of the territory make their ordinary lives, pursue their several projects and elaborate their cultural self-understandings. When these settled patterns are disturbed, either as a result of the logics of internally secured advance or as the enfolding global structural pattern shifts, with consequent internal implications, the business of orchestrating coherent responses is difficult and the resultant period of rapid complex change can be traumatic for elite and mass alike.

Breaks in the historical development trajectories of particular parts of the region can occur either as a result of internal developments or as the enfolding global or regional system is reconfigured and offers the particular territory a new route to the future. For many cultures the impetus to radical change came with shifting patterns within the global system. Change has been impressed upon many cultures. The routes to the modern world taken by non-European territories have depended upon the ways in which local elites have read and reacted to shifting patterns within the enfolding global capitalist system. More broadly, shifts in patterns of development within a region will occur as particular areas advance relative to others. The historical development experience of a particular territory can be described directly, that is, as a history of that territory; but these individual patterns are always lodged within the context of wider systems. The dynamics of change within territories will not be equivalent. Against the modernization/globalization-theory-inspired expectations of a single logic repeating itself in diverse contexts, such that all territories might expect equal advance in the absence of accidental inhibitions to progress, political economic argument acknowledges the fundamentally uneven nature of progress. The patterns made by global structures of power are not regular, and different territories will advance (or retreat), relative to the fundamental expectations of progress lodged within the classical social-theoretic tradition, at different rates. There will also be shifts in the patterns of relationships between the particular region and the wider developing global system; these will occur as patterns of development advance unevenly at the global system level. In the case of East Asia it is clear both that the region has undergone a recent period of rapid relative advance within the global system and that within this general pattern particular countries within the region have advanced more rapidly than others.

Viewed in historical and contextual perspective, the trajectories of Singapore and Hong Kong have similarities and differences: they were founded as colonial trading cities; their prosperity flowed from strong, somewhat veiled alliances with local elites; they produced diversified economies, plural societies and idiosyncratically democratic polities; today they link relatively poor regions with the richer global system; and both have recently experienced problems in engineering domestic reform in order to confront contemporary challenges in their trading environments.

Locating Singapore

It is clear that Singapore island has been home to a number of discrete polities; these have made their livelihoods, ordered their societies and managed their politics in similarly discrete ways; elites and masses have read and reacted to enfolding structural circumstances. A sequence can be retrospectively identified, a series of ways in which the people based on the island have made their lives within the world that they inhabited. The contemporary form of life is but one of a number; change is not atypical; it is given.

In Southeast Asia the pre-contact Malay world was characterized by the rise and fall of a succession of maritime trading empires. The economies of these maritime empires were in the main based on seaborne trade, and extensive networks of trade were established. The internal politics of these sultanates were beset with intra-familial manoeuvrings for power in a fluid political system ordered around the person of the sultan, with patterns of loyalty personalized rather than formalized. Thereafter the political extraction of the island itself from the Johor–Riau Sultanate's grasp by the British involved a period of intense political manoeuvring which centred on inventing a sultan of Singapore by promoting a weak member of the ruling family. The newly invented sultan signed an agreement with Raffles that gave the British a claim against both the indigenous ruler in Riau and the Dutch. Thereafter, on a wider stage the survival of this new polity was dependent on arguments between Penang, the East India Company, London and the Dutch. Then, as the nineteenth century drew towards its close, a crucial change took place within the capitalist heartlands of Europe with the rise of industrial production and a mass market for consumption goods. The impact upon Southeast Asia was in terms of a new schedule of goods demanded, with a movement away from agricultural specialist crops and miscellaneous handicrafts towards those goods required by an industrial mass economy: tin, rubber, sugar, oil and so on. There were related new political arrangements both in the peninsula and on Singapore island itself. And after the Pacific War there have been two main episodes: the early attempt to submerge Singapore within a federation with the peninsula and the subsequent effective establishment of a dependent capitalist economy and society which was drawn into the Japan-centred Pacific Asian region and more recently confronts the implications of the peaceful rise of China.[6]

After independence the original ideological commitments of the PAP core group of English-educated professionals, all of whom had made what have been called colonial pilgrimages,[7] are best regarded as social democratic, thus their early programme embraced demands for an end to colonial rule, the formation of a unitary Malayan state and a spread of social and economic development ideas which may be summed up as the pursuit of national development. The circumstances and future of a peripheral capitalist formation are theorized by a group of English-educated professionals; and so the shift to independence entails a significant measure of intellectual, as well as political-economic, continuity. Subsequently, as the elite respond to events in the wider world system the ideology undergoes a series of adjustments.[8] Commentators have stressed the role of the state machine in contemporary Singapore; the state has been active in fashioning the particular pattern of economic, social and cultural development. Having come to power in alliance with a Chinese-speaking socialist mass movement, the technocratic, professional English-educated core of the PAP then ran a series of battles with the mass elements in order to secure total control of local politics. Their control was complete very early on and has remained free from effective challenge ever since. The support of the masses was sought and achieved via export-oriented economic development policies that relied on providing a base for multinational manufacturing companies and supplying basic welfare in the form of housing, schooling and health services. It is an extensively interventionist system; decisions are made at the top and passed down.[9] Local commentators have spoken of depoliticization, or an administrative society, or, recently, an Asian communitarianism.[10] The PAP has used an interventionist state machine to make the population and resources of the state (its geography and the history of linkages to the capitalist centres) maximally involved with the wider currents of the world capitalist market.

The official ideology comprises accurate summation and misdirection. The elite has read its circumstances in particular ways: an inherited condition of third world underdevelopment is affirmed; the uncertain situation of the first generation of PAP leaders stressed; an official discourse promulgated comprising ideas of vulnerability, discipline and pragmatism; and a track record identified which is characterized by domestic stability and material advance.[11] The elite assert that reforms made since independence to broaden the economic base, advance welfare provision and unify an ethnically plural population have made Singapore a strong sovereign nation-state competing widely in the global marketplace; in all, they assert the successful management of success.[12]

The discourse of vulnerability, discipline and pragmatism offered a distinctive narrative:[13] neighbouring countries were presented as latently hostile;[14] the survival of the country depended upon domestic discipline; and the country had to eschew ideology in favour of pragmatism (an effective sleight of hand which placed the entirely ideological goal of material advance at the heart of the polities elite-specified endeavours). The domestic political and policy principles of multiracialism, multiculturalism, multilingualism, multi-religions and meritocracy – the 'five Ms' – have informed elite domestic actions. The ideas were established in the mid-1950s when reports into high-school riots diagnosed communalism and recommended policies to ameliorate such problems.[15] The 'five Ms' are routinely affirmed/enforced:[16] multiracialism affirms the existence of distinctive races, stipulatively defined, and manages their relations; multiculturalism offers a related specification of the cultures putatively associated with the specified races; multilingualism offers a related identification of the languages that ostensibly carry these cultures; multi-religions links particular religions to races, cultures and languages; and the state specifies performance criteria for individual competitive behaviour, that is, meritocracy is affirmed. And in this package a related element enables the elite to assert that the Singaporean form of life is distinctive; it is informed by Asian Values and a communitarian ethos; it cannot be judged according to commonplace Western ideals. In the event these defensive moves coincided with scholarly interest in the development trajectories of the Asian Tigers;[17] a wider debate has developed and, whilst some of the Singaporean elite apologetics would be widely rejected, that there was something worth discussing would be widely granted. The contemporary discourse recently expressed in the *Next Lap* and the *Singapore 21 Vision* can be summed up: Singapore is a modern, wealthy and gracious nation. Or, in brief, Singapore is a part of the advanced modern world – 'it has arrived'.[18]

The official ideology summarizes Singapore's domestic and international environment from the perspective of the PAP party/state's commitment to economic advance, to upgrading and an upmarket niche within the global system. But, domestically, what is presented as realistic description (the first four Ms) is better understood as the disciplinary project of the PAP, whilst the fifth M veils the source of the evaluative criteria (determined by the elite's project), represents the occasion for failure or success as individual (not class-structural) and undergirds the package by insisting on the natural givenness of talent. Similarly, externally, with regard to national independence, what are represented as uniquely problematical (elite confusion, boundary disputes and domestic tensions) were common issues amongst dissolving foreign empires. More generally, the official ideology is curiously context-less; it is as if the island has no history and no location. It is true that the practical problems, as defined by the elite, are noted (vulnerability etc.), but the positive legacy of around 150 years as part of the British Empire – that is, that Singapore was highly developed in 1965 precisely because of its history – is not flagged up, and nor are the established linkages, that is, that Singapore was an integral element of the global system in 1965 because of its history, and was not, as the elite claim, a part of the underdeveloped third world.

Against the elite's official ideology, with its evolutionary achievement of success,[19] it is clear both that Singapore island has played a number of roles within enfolding structural patterns and, more importantly, that in 1965 the island was a highly developed integral part of the global capitalist system. The state integrates the local polity into the global system. States are transmission mechanisms. They are formal mechanisms for the integration of a given population or territory into a wider system of power relationships. The resultant pattern will be distinctive. Singapore island has seen not one state form, but several; each of these can be seen to represent a particular occasion of the integration of the population of the island into the wider embracing system; each of these occasions of integration can be seen to have characteristic economic, social and cultural forms; and each has its own self-understanding. Thus we move from Malay maritime empire, where political and cultural life centred on the person of the sultan, through to the construction of a formal colony, to a dependent capitalist state which vigorously promotes a notion of nation-statehood as it operates within the East Asian region of the global system. Further, the shifting patterns of structural power which enfold the Singaporean polity have been reconfigured in recent years: the context within which Singapore operates is sub-regional (ASEAN), regional (centred on Japan but with a rising China altering these balances) and thereafter global (now multipolar). It is the given pattern of structural circumstances to which agents must necessarily respond. It may be said that these are old problems. It might also be said that the elite is utilizing familiar strategies to address its schedule of contemporary problems: read and react to enfolding structural circumstances; adjust intelligently; and adjust prospectively. A number of themes have emerged in elite discussion, such as upgrading, going global and attaining success as a regional hub, and a number of scenarios can be sketched; the future is both constrained and open.

Locating Hong Kong

The standard version of the development history of Hong Kong makes a set of claims: the island was a barren rock until the British occupied it, introduced laissez-faire capitalism, ordered inward migration and through a wise policy style of extensive consultation and minimal intervention guided the territory to a situation whereby its hardworking population could enjoy stability and great prosperity. As with other official ideologies, this contains a mix of truth and misdirection: the island was not a barren rock, it was a remote rural part of the southern lands of the Qing Dynasty;[20] the preference for consultation is true, but largely only amongst elites;[21] the putative policy of laissez faire has in fact been an elite preference for the concerns of the elite;[22] and the claim to anti-welfare spending is misleading as provision has always been made, but perhaps slowly.[23]

Hong Kong island has been home to various forms of life and historians mention long-established communities of farming, fishing and trade. Hong Kong island has been lodged within various wider forms of life, economic, social and political. It was a part of the southern Pearl River Delta region of the Qing Empire, a trading port linking the Qing and British empires, a commercial centre within a global trading network linking Southern China to Southeast Asia and North America, a cold war era conduit linking the People's Republic to wider economic spheres and lately one of East Asia's newly industrialized countries. It is clear that the island has played distinctive roles, but commentators report that it has been 'its own place' since the late nineteenth century.[24] On a broad macro scale the following periods can be specified: pre-contact (the form of life shaped over several centuries of settlement); impact/response (the incoming modern world – demands/opportunities); general crisis (as the metropolitan heartlands of industrial capitalism dissolve into systemic confusion, East Asia experiences a parallel breakdown); and (quasi-)national development (the default project of elites after the Pacific War).

The pre-contact form of life developed over centuries, a trajectory shaped by unfolding circumstances of forms of life untouched by the modern world. In the pre-contact period Hong Kong island was a remote part of the southern lands of the Qing Empire. There were numerous villages, many long established. The social pattern was that of rural China; family, clan and language group governed relationships and temples, clan halls and perhaps schools provided the institutional structures for these communities; the local economy revolved around farming and fishing and there was a quarrying industry; the island communities exported stone and preserved fish; there was a subsistence economy and trading activity; the island communities had a recognized absentee landlord; and the island communities were taxed by the local Qing official. These were settled ordered established communities.[25] Early nineteenth-century Hong Kong island had a population of several thousand, farmers, fishermen and local traders, but it was not a significant site, nor did it contain significant settlements; however, it was not underdeveloped.[26] In the early nineteenth century the empire was still strong as in preceding centuries China had been a major economic power within the global system.[27]

The modern world placed new demands on extant forms of life; the colonial incomers worked at the edge of empire and local agents were not passive;[28] accommodative adjustments and prospective responses ensured that the nominally colonial holding developed through extensive collaboration between incoming British elites and the local elites who formed within the rapidly expanding Chinese population. British and Chinese newcomers quickly outnumbered the established local population:[29] around 7,500 people lived on Hong Kong island when the British took control in 1841;[30] the population reached 22,000 in 1847 and 85,000 in 1859 (1,600 were non-Chinese).[31] Hong Kong was a base for British trade with China. The British were sojourners; they came for trade; in time local Chinese merchants settled; and the colony received inflows of migrants from mainland China. The territory was divided by race; there was a small resident European population plus a rapidly growing Chinese population; it was at first a colonial trading port but later it became a key commercial city within the global economy.

The European/American-centred modern world was expansionary; Europeans and Americans sought trade relations with the Qing Empire and these were secured by war. Hong Kong was extracted from the Qing Empire in order to serve as a trading port for British trading interests; there was a complex exchange between the local population, inward migrants and the British and it produced a layered economy: local, regional and global. The local population were active players and success rested upon development of global capitalism and an outflow of people from unsettled China; the migrant or coolie trade made an obscure port linking two empires into a global commercial nexus. The local British and Chinese elites collaborated in order to build a prosperous settlement; stability did not mean an absence of political conflict;[32] a local balance was maintained; hence it was its own place.[33] In the 1918–41 inter-war period Chinese capital invested was equal to that of the British;[34] the territory came to be secondary to Shanghai in the 1930s. The Japanese invasion of China underscored its vulnerability; the territory was note militarily defensible and extant patterns of life were engulfed by the confusions of the Pacific War.

General crisis in East Asia[35] was signalled by breakdowns of inherited established systems, failures of accommodations with empire and drives for an autonomous locations within the modern world. East Asia collapsed into civil strife, inter-state warfare and nationalist revolt (peaceful/violent); and there was great loss of life and destruction of accumulated capital. Hong Kong became an island of relative calm as China suffered extensive civil warfare and then inter-state invasion; mainland politics spilled over into Hong Kong but the colonial authorities and local Chinese elites managed the problems.[36] It was not until the Pacific War that Hong Kong was embroiled. The Imperial Japanese invasion in 1941 saw the territory occupied within a few days; the city was re-Asianized, with street names changed, a new currency and a much reduced population; foreigners were interred; the local elite adapted.[37] The colonial power rushed to reoccupy the territory in 1945; the civil war in China provided a space for the reoccupation; the war in China produced a flow of refugees and the population quickly recovered and surpassed pre-war levels. The victorious Communist Party did not challenge directly the status quo with regard to Hong Kong; the cold war

206 *Unfolding trajectories*

added further complications as the outbreak of the Korean War in 1950 led to United Nations sanctions against China. Hong Kong became a link between China and the global system; there was covert trade with the People's Republic and flows of migrants; if the war years had been destructive, recovery was quick and advance fortuitous. The city developed rapidly; economic growth was rapid, social reform slow. The cold war had direct implications for Hong Kong; links with China were reworked and as the trading role diminished manufacturing prospered; American war expenditures benefited the region and American policy benefited the region, for example by permitting access to US domestic markets, and these also helped Hong Kong.[38] The territory became one of the four Asian Tigers; up until 1967 these developments were ad hoc; in 1967 the Cultural Revolution spilled over into Hong Kong with riots and bombings; the local population rallied to the colonial government and the trouble was managed; economic, social and political reforms were instigated[39] and a distinctive Hong Kong form of life began to emerge;[40] this marked the rise of a popular idea of Hong Kong.[41]

The first period of quasi-national development was 1967–97; the local elite had formed in the late nineteenth century; it collaborated with the colonial power; the territory became rich. The state did not explicitly systematize the pursuit of development; an elite oligarchy pursued a project centred on commerce and trade. The British were sojourners; the Chinese elite focused on commerce and the local Chinese population used family, relatives and clan networks to order their lives. But with further outward migration from China there were accumulating welfare problems in housing, health care and schooling; the colonial authorities were reluctant to act but from the 1960s onwards the familiar apparatus of a modern welfare state appeared; the elite eschewed other than a minimal responsibility and blocked calls for democracy; it was a restricted development project.

Prior to the Pacific War, the Hong Kong population intermixed with that of the mainland; there were more or less open borders.[42] In the context of the 1950s, cold war restrictions were imposed and the Hong Kong population became settled; those who were born and raised locally had no experience of the mainland and they came to understand themselves in local terms. Crucially, the local situation contrasted with that on the mainland, where Maoist-inspired development mistakes culminated in the launch of the Cultural Revolution; the colonial government responded to the 1967 riots by modernizing itself; it became less evidently colonial and more a city government; welfare reforms were accelerated; endemic corruption addressed; illegal migration curbed; and there was localization of jobs. Hong Kong emerged as an East Asian NIC; economic take-off had begun in the 1950s,[43] when existing small-scale industries were joined by migrant textile entrepreneurs; manufacturing became an important economic sector. American cold war expenditures and policies helped.[44] Subsequent mainland reforms allowed Hong Kong entrepreneurs to become the major investors in the new export-processing zones. This was the first period of quasi-national development; a local Hong Kong form of life took shape; residents thought of themselves as 'Hong Kongers'.

A second period of national development followed. The 1997 reversion of sovereignty to China was accomplished by the British and Chinese governments; the population of Hong Kong were not consulted; nor were they official participants in the reversion talks; one colonial power handed the territory to a successor colonial power. Hong Kong became an SAR; the Sino-British Joint Declaration 1984 was enshrined in the Basic Law, which is the mini-constitution provided for Hong Kong by Beijing, the outcome of Deng Xiaoping's 'one country, two systems' formula. A process of mutual adjustment is unfolding; local elites are split in respect of their relationship with Beijing; local elites are unclear about lines of development for Hong Kong; Beijing's views are unformed: no to local public politics, otherwise unclear. The first post-handover administration of Tung Chee Hwa (1997–2005) faced considerable difficulties (Asian financial crisis, international terrorism, SARS and a series of local disputes about development policies). The second post-handover administration of Donald Tsang (2005–) was both more popular and luckier; there were no external crises, but lack of clarity with respect to the political future of the territory continued. The issue of domestic politics is intertwined with questions of relationships with Beijing and the attitudes of mainland elite leaders; estimations of how these issues might be resolved colour the expectations commentators have for the future.

Scenarios: local elites, changing circumstances and possible futures

Characterizing historical development experiences in terms of trajectories invites an obvious line of speculation: how might these trajectories continue into the future? Commentators[45] suggest that Singapore and Hong Kong face problems; past strategies cannot be relied upon to deliver further successes; and local political dynamics inhibit necessary domestic change. Singapore has distanced itself from its regional hinterland but now faces problems competing as a global hub; the elite seem unable to renew themselves, but new policy initiatives are needed. Hong Kong faces the daunting problems attendant upon the transfer of sovereignty to Beijing; this relationship must work if Hong Kong's success is to continue. The signs are ambiguous as neither the local elite nor Beijing seem clear about the future; but local success requires local elite leadership, which seems to be beyond their reach and in any case is anathema to Beijing.[46] Contrariwise, in the medium term Beijing could accept Hong Kong's slow absorption but the price tag for the territory would be its effective eclipse.[47] A number of scenarios can be drawn, but the political default setting, in both cases, seems to be continuity plus hope that it all turns out well.

208 *Unfolding trajectories*

Singapore scenarios debated

Singapore island has been lodged within a number of wider encompassing social systems; the island has been a site where multiple systems intersected; these co-existing intersecting systems have secured particular political relationships, allowing the participants to secure their diverse objectives. Singapore island has played a number of different roles in line with dominant elite interests: Malay settlement/trade, British trade/empire and Chinese trade/settlement. In each set of structures there were different actors and institutions; and between agents within each sphere there were complex exchanges. These forms of life have interacted on Singapore island; at any one time a particular mix of elements could be found ordered according to shifting political relationships. It is now around fifty years since Singaporeans secured internal self-government; the PAP national development project distanced the island from its familiar archipelagic hinterland and a deeper role within extant global capitalism was secured as industry, commerce and government-linked companies supplemented the inherited port and service activities. The local population was disciplined and their reward was significant material advance. The mobilizing/legitimating official ideology spoke of a vulnerable island, disciplined work, a dedicated elite and great success. But in the early years of the twenty-first century the elite confront novel international and domestic problems: the rise of Chinese and other similar industrial manufacturing centres will undercut local production, whilst domestic wealth, individualism and familial quietism threaten the ability of the government to provide a disciplined workforce/environment. The dilemma of the elite is that whilst they can rehearse familiar strategies there is growing doubt that they will work, and the local political system militates against the emergence of novel alternatives; the default setting seems to be continuity plus hope that things will work out.

Interpretive-critical social science is ill suited to the task of making predictions about the future; that likely futile task is more usually associated with the positivist mainstream. However, a number of speculative scenarios could be sketched; one grouping revolves around an idea of continuity, another group centres on strategies of globalization and a final group looks to the possibilities of greater links to the region. It can be assumed that all are likely to fail the test of unfolding events, but they can help unpack the possibilities lodged in the present. In respect of Singapore, five scenarios can be sketched.

Scenario 1, Muddle Through Alone: the PAP party-state continues unreformed whilst the elite endeavours to replicate the recipe of earlier success (vulnerability requires economic advance, which in turn demands a disciplined population). The territory continues to be presented as a base for global capitalist business, where this entails upgrading the population/labour, upgrading the administration, upgrading fiscal incentives, upgrading government-linked companies, further state investment in key industries/

technologies and state investment in key service sectors. This is a mutedly optimistic scenario; the lack of domestic political/cultural reform militates against domestically generated new initiatives and the multiplicity of external competitors – financial/commercial hubs and export production sites – shrinks the field of possible opportunities.

An alternative formulation is Air-con Plus (or Cosy Singapore):[48] in this scenario the elite/expatriate community looks to the USA (and maybe the EU); the elite inhabit a social world set apart from the masses; the elite continue to run and upgrade the established paternalistic social system; the middle classes continue their private lives; and the local people service the needs of the outward-oriented economy. However, Singaporeans turn inwards and build their lives in the pleasant well-designed new towns; amongst the local people some leave, with those who can and do live and work overseas merely calling in to Singapore from time to time (the PAP make a pejorative distinction between 'stayers' and 'quitters').

Scenario 2, Globalization (American sphere): the PAP party-state continues unreformed, whilst the elite endeavours to replicate the recipe of earlier success with particular focus on East Asian NICs, Japan and the USA. The territory continues to be presented as a business hub (upgrading etc.) but a preference for trading partners becomes clearer (vulnerability requires economic advance etc., but also veiled security linkages, and as the desired ally is the USA the East Asian network of the USA becomes attractive as a rebalanced location for Singapore). This is a mutedly optimistic scenario: again, similar domestic and international problems are present; it is unclear that the recipients of the policy tilt would find it particularly advantageous.

An alternative formulation is Regional Base (USA): in this scenario the territory builds on its historically established trajectory and regional linkages in order to deepen its role within the US East Asian sphere (Globalization (American sphere)) but also seeks to become a key ally or base for the USA. There is a long-established trading relationship;[49] the Singaporean elite look to the USA as a model;[50] there is an established security self-understanding as an alien vulnerable territory within its region;[51] and there is a modestly developing military linkage. This is a mutedly optimistic scenario: domestic and international problems are present and the extent of consistent US interest is moot.

Scenario 3, Globalization (General): the PAP party-state continues unreformed, whilst the elite endeavours to replicate the recipe of earlier success but now grants that the global system is extensively integrated, therefore business opportunities can be exploited around the globe. Singaporean government-linked companies (GLCs) expand overseas operations. This is a mutedly optimistic scenario: the territory continues to be presented a business hub (upgrading etc.) but the Singapore economic footprint is reworked. The Singaporean niche within the global capitalist system is dispersed and deepened. Again, similar domestic and international problems are present; however, an outward-looking strategy might discover new opportunities.

Scenario 4, Regional Hub (East Asia): the PAP party-state is partially reformed as the elite reads and reacts to changing enfolding circumstances. The elite discontinues its long-established habit of defining itself against its neighbours. A number of key decisions are made: the territory cannot compete with low/medium-tech Chinese production; the NICs, Japan and the USA are remote partners; the local area was the environment within which Singapore prospered prior to 1965 and it could be once again, therefore a new partnership could be forged. This is a tentatively optimistic scenario: the domestic reforms open up new possibilities; the reforging of regional linkages also opens up new possibilities; the characterization of established partners as distant is accurate but does not militate against continuing links.

An alternative formulation is Regional Hub (ASEAN): in this scenario the territory builds on its historically established trajectory and regional linkages to become a key centre within a vibrant ASEAN region; the elite embrace a regional leadership role; the ASEAN countries assume a quasi-flying geese pattern; Malaysia, Indonesia and Brunei become closely linked; the Philippines, Thailand and Vietnam form a second-tier group and the poor periphery is made up of Myanmar, Laos and Cambodia. This is a radically optimistic alternative: intra-ASEAN trade involving Singapore is significant but political legacies militate against it.

Another alternative formulation is Regional Hub (Port City): in this scenario the territory builds on its historically established trajectory and regional linkages to become a base for regional and global business operations; as a platform economy it prospers through an updated version of the role of a port city, providing a base for sophisticated manufacturing and trading activities; and the local population service the needs of this international business platform. This is a modestly optimistic alternative: intra-ASEAN trade involving Singapore is significant and could provide the basis for deepening sub-regional cooperation.

Scenario 5, Hotel Singapore:[52] the city-state has always been open to the wider flows within the global system; at the present time there are pressures for greater trade; at the present time new communications technologies have made possible the formation of ever more sophisticated trans-state networks (as with, for example, logistics); the Singaporean developmental state must respond to the demands for greater liberalization; liberalization plus political reform would be fine but it is unlikely; more likely is that the territory is used as a base for business and ideas of nation and so on slowly fade. This is the Hotel Singapore future. More optimistically, the city can become a global business hub with a loyal clientele and happy stakeholders. This is the 'five-star business hub'. In either case, the city-state dissolves itself ever more deeply within trans-state networks; the local population emigrate, or withdraw or become happy stakeholders. It is a curiously optimistic view of one possible future – a post-national, post-state business hub.

Overall, against local pessimisms, variously expressed, it is difficult to see the city-state being other than successful; it is embedded not merely within the modern world but also within a very dynamic region; it is true that history offers no guarantees – one of the claims of the present text – however, radical breaks are few. The noted diagnoses of possible futures offer no predictions of such breaks; the general expectation would be further success (one way or another).

Hong Kong scenarios debated

Hong Kong is a city of around 6 million; it has a highly sophisticated first world economy. The domestic economy is highly developed: houses, schools, shops, transport, administrative services and so on. It has highly competitive international trading sectors: finance; industry;[53] logistics;[54] and urban services.[55] There are a number of critical debates surrounding its character and regional/global role. Hong Kong elites have embraced the idea of laissez faire, claiming the territory as a genuine free market. However, the state is central as in other East Asian countries; the machinery has been turned to the interests of a colonial or local elite; commentators argue that collusion has been extensive and is still prevalent;[56] the colonial authorities colluded with Chinese comprador capitalists to sustain the colony; British and Chinese business had access to the colonial authorities; collusion has overlapped with extensive corruption; the ICAC dealt successfully with the later but the former will need a more open democratic system. And there is an issue about the condition off the grass roots;[57] colonial Hong Kong was an unequal society; since 1997 it has become more unequal; the official ideology militates against welfare actions yet citizen groups argue that the territory is rich enough to provide better lives for its citizens.

The domestic agenda is full; a series of political initiatives are required; however, in Hong Kong the situation is complicated by the looming political presence of Beijing; it is true that economic, social and cultural linkages with the mainland, in particular Guangdong Province, are good and are deepening, but linkages with Beijing are clouded with uncertainty. Local agents jockey for position; the position of the central government is unclear; and such political uncertainty impacts speculations about the future of the territory. Beijing recovered sovereignty in 1997; shortly after the handover the territory experienced financial and economic crisis, health scares and a series of major public demonstrations voicing opposition to SAR government policies. Beijing has shown little sign of understanding the internal social or political dynamics of Hong Kong; yet Beijing has to find a way of dealing with an important distinctive political unit;[58] similarly, Hong Kong has to find a mechanism to formulate a coherent political voice; the two are intertwined.[59] The future as the Hong Kong SAR remains open; it is difficult to see failure; it is difficult to see simple continuity (success); reorientation is likely; but the issue is the precise nature of any reorientation. In respect of Hong Kong, it is possible to identify five scenarios.

212 Unfolding trajectories

Scenario 1, Securing Continuation of the Present Model: Beijing has selected the new leadership; the Beijing elite value stability; the local Hong Kong elite manage Beijing as they managed the British[60] and the territory maintains its global role, deepens its linkages with the mainland (economic, social and political), maintains its special status (juridical, administrative and political) and continues much as it has been in recent years; that is, sophisticated, prosperous and broadly content with itself and its unfolding trajectory/role. It is an optimistic scenario which requires Beijing not to interfere but there are signs that this is unlikely.[61]

An alternative formulation is Quasi-Colonial Continuation: in this scenario there are relatively few changes; domestic elite fractions variously accommodate the presence of a new external authority; London is exchanged for Beijing; local economic elites value their positions; the Beijing authorities are wedded to the idea of economic growth; there is a coincidence of interest; and slow success continues under Beijing's benign distant leadership.

Scenario 2, Adoption of the Singapore Model: Hong Kong gains effective local leadership; there is rapid economic advance; there is no public liberal-democratic style politics;[62] the territory maintains its special status but local leadership moves to compete energetically within the global system, seeking to follow Singapore in upgrading Hong Kong's global footprint or niche. This is a fairly optimistic scenario; however, the Beijing version relies on a distinction between 'political city' and 'economic city' which is neither tenable nor evidences any understanding of Singapore (whose development trajectory has been suffused with politics) or Hong Kong (whose development trajectory has been attended by a thoroughly sophisticated elite politics), and a non-Beijing version would require an absence of interference from Beijing, an optimistic assumption.

An alternative formulation is Developing Economic Global City: in this scenario Hong Kong advances economically whilst remaining politically quiescent; this is Beijing's preference, sometimes tagged the Singapore option; the SAR state actively pursues economic growth; there is government intervention in market at the time of the 1997 crisis; there are major development projects (Cyber Port, Science Park, Macau Bridge, West Kowloon Project); and an SAR-centred (sub-)national development strategy emerges; the territory deepens/upgrades its role as an exchange point within local, regional and global networks.

Scenario 3, Deep Integration:[63] Hong Kong becomes key element of the Pearl River Delta region; there is deeper economic integration, cross-border investment and trade, and cross-border flows of people; such integration extends not merely to immediate neighbour cities but throughout the delta region; and the deepening integration is complemented by further delta region coordination (for example major infrastructural development or environmental regulation). Hong Kong keeps its juridical, administrative and political independence and it thus sustains its global role. This is a fairly optimistic scenario: developing the Pearl River Delta region offers new possibilities and whilst it requires an absence of interference from Beijing it posits the existence of local Southern China allies.

Scenario 4, Slow Dissolve: deeper integration is driven by Beijing's anxieties and local elite short-termism; economic opportunism plus political timidity drive deeper integration but neglect to maintain juridical, administrative and political independence; mainland practices are imported; there is ineffective instruction from Beijing coupled with extensive corruption; Hong Kong becomes just another Pearl River Delta town; and whilst there is long-term relative decline, the territory continues to be just as prosperous as the rest of delta region, which is now a global manufacturing site. This is a pessimistic scenario which tracks the slow reabsorption of Hong Kong into Southern China.[64]

An alternative formulation is Rapid Dissolve: Hong Kong has played a major role in China's development, as trade partner, as source of direct investment, as source of human capital; Hong Kong plays a role as a transhipment centre for Chinese trade; it is argued that 'deep integration' of the Hong Kong and mainland economies would benefit both; however, this must be on Hong Kong's terms; if integration involves absorbing mainland third world practices (partial rule of law, extensive corruption, social indiscipline and political interference), then the territory will become just one more town in the Pearl River Delta.[65]

Scenario 5, Rational Authoritarianism: Beijing continues to support Hong Kong but slowly draws it into the mainland system; Hong Kong's form of life does not change dramatically; rather, it slowly fuses with that of the mainland; both polities are oligarchic. The political culture of the mainland comprises the legacies of Chinese history overlain by the serial ideological and policy experiments of some fifty years of state socialism; little of this impacts Hong Kong directly because the border stays in place (one country, two systems), but Beijing's policy orientation does and that has been characterized as rational authoritarianism. The political culture of Hong Kong comprises the legacies of Chinese history plus some 150 years of a distinctive embedding within the modern world; colonial rule produced an inward-looking, disciplined and somewhat parochial city. The interaction of oligarchic rule, central state policy style and local culture could produce a distinctive scenario – Beijing blocks democratic reforms, elites build networks to Beijing's power structures, the local population remains disciplined and the city prospers as a disciplined Chinese city.

As with Singapore, local pessimism is sometimes difficult to comprehend; the city is rich, sophisticated and deeply embedded within the global system; its immediate neighbour is the Pearl River Delta, a global centre for manufacturing. Nevertheless, there is one area of doubt – the exchange between the local elite and Beijing; both have their own understandings and interests; the domestic political system of Hong Kong is oligarchic; a narrow elite shape the territory and their interests are commercial; Beijing is remote and its interests are with the stability and development of a continental country of 1.3 billion. The exchange between Hong Kong and Beijing within the confines of 'one country, two systems' as enshrined in the Basic Law is crucial. It has to work. However, confidence amongst local Hong Kong commentators in the local elite, the national elite and the linkages between them is weak. But, incompetence and mutual confusions aside, neither side has any interest in breakdowns – the general expectation would be further success (one way or another).

Contingent pasts, unfolding futures

The expansion of British capitalism in the eighteenth and nineteenth centuries impacted extant civilizations in Asia; the Indian princes of the sub-continent were subject to numerous aggressive wars;[66] by 1800 most of India was controlled by the British; expansion towards the east continued in the nineteenth century; Singapore was occupied in 1818; Hong Kong in 1841; Shanghai was drawn into the system in 1842; Bangkok in 1855; and the high-watermark of British expansion revolved around Shanghai and the Yangtze river valley.[67] The expansion saw winners and losers. Singapore was drawn into the modern world in the early nineteenth century; it became a key nexus within the British-centred sphere of the global capitalist system; it developed for some 140 years in the context of empire; and it also enjoyed significant linkages with the USA. Over this long period of time local elites have ordered trans-territory structures and the island has been home to a series of polities: a colony at the edge of empire; a stable element within a global empire; a backwater; then occupied in war before being decolonized and becoming independently lodged within regional and global networks. Today commentators suggest reforms are needed but there are problems of domestic political inflexibility; thus the future is unclear. And Hong Kong, too, was drawn into the modern global capitalist system in the early nineteenth century; it provided a base for agents variously engaged in local, regional and global trading networks; it developed for some 150 years in the context of empire. Here the high point of empire was interrupted by the Pacific War, before recolonization misdirected domestic energies that might otherwise have fed aspirations to nation-state status. In the post-war period there were sweeping reforms; but the territory was retroceded to the People's Republic of China in 1997; confusions followed; and so the future is unclear.

Yet the general situation is familiar; agents must always read and react to enfolding structural change. This is true of the leaderships of large powerful countries; it is also true of the leaderships of relatively small countries; and Singapore and Hong Kong are rich and powerful. The modern world was shaped by industrial capitalism; industrial-capitalist expansion drew these cities and countries into the modern world; and the exchange involved cooperation, exploitation and development. Singapore as an independent nation-state was created through the colonial episode. Hong Kong as 'its own place' was created through the colonial episode. All these are contingent outcomes of unfolding dynamics of complex change; there is no essential unfolding of national presence or identity; there is no process of the nation awakening to take finally its place in the world; there is no teleology; there is no end of history and there is no socialist utopia; there is only the currently observable pattern; it is the contingent out-turn of the intermingled historical trajectories of numerous socially constituted groups.

Change is given, elites must read and react, mobilizing their populations, legitimating their projects and managing unfolding change. This requires effective local leadership, yet in Singapore commentators identify problems consequent upon the inability of an oligarchic system to satisfactorily renew itself, whilst in Hong Kong commentators identify problems consequent upon the absence of an effective local political centre, in turn consequent upon the inability of local elites to manage the anxieties and concerns of the new imperial centre in Beijing. However, both cities are rich, sophisticated and confront problems attendant upon success, which is, at the very least, a comfortable starting point. Their past records are contingent, so too their contemporary problems; trajectories are discrete; and the futures of Singapore and Hong Kong will unfold at their own pace and with their own particular logics.

Notes

1 Singapore contexts

1 Nationalist politicians project the existence of their countries back into history. The existence of the nation is given and ahistorical; it has always existed; the history can then be tracked back into the mists of time. The Singaporean state looks back to a founding myth of 'Temasek', a putative thirteenth-century trading port. History can then be rolled forwards up to the present. The social-scientific truth is more interesting – the social construction of the idea of nation, state and, as an instance, 'Singapore'. For the myth investigated as fact, see M. N. Murfett, J. N. Miksic and M.S. Chiang 1999 *Between Two Oceans: A Military History of Singapore from First Settlement to Final British Withdrawal*, Oxford University Press, ch. 1.
2 The best history centred on the colonial experience is M. Turnbull 1977 *A History of Singapore 1819–1975*, Oxford University Press.
3 The term comes from P. J. Cain and A. G. Hopkins 1993a *British Imperialism: Innovation and Expansion 1688–1914*, London: Longman; P. J. Cain and A. G. Hopkins 1993b *British Imperialism: Crisis and Deconstruction 1914–1990*, London: Longman; see also R. E. Dumett (ed.) 1999 *Gentlemanly Capitalism and British Imperialism: The New Debate on Empire*, London: Longman, in particular the introductory essay by Dumett and the essay by Akita Shigeru on the informal empire in East Asia before the Pacific War. A good map is provided by Patricia Buckley Ebrey 1996 *The Cambridge Illustrated History of China*, Cambridge University Press, p. 241.
4 A. Acharya 2000 *The Quest for Identity: International Relations of Southeast Asia*, Oxford University Press.
5 Regions are constructs, not simply given, so the terminology matters. It is also difficult to use precisely, so in this text I use the following terms as outlined here:
- East Asia is used as a general term to point to the area encompassing the Chinese cultural sphere and the Malay sphere of Southeast Asia. They are extensively linked today and were linked by trade in the past.
- East Asia is the more specific area encompassing the Chinese cultural sphere.
- Southeast Asia is the more specific area encompassing the Malay world.
- Indo-China is arguably an outmoded term but is used here to point to mainland Southeast Asia.
- South Asia is used to point to present-day India, Bangladesh and Sri Lanka. It is mentioned in this text only as a source of cultural influence plus trade links reaching into Southeast and East Asia.

6 The expression comes from Patrick Wright 1985 *On Living in an Old Country*, London: Verso, and points to the elite/popular version of the history of a political

community. The national past tells a community where they have come from, what sort of people they are and where they are going. Wright points out that the national past is contested – it is a a highly political construction. One version of the Singapore national past is available in corporate video style in the Discovery Channel series.
7 A rather polemical term – it hints at a wide-ranging debate about the nature of social science – it serves to distinguish Anglo-Saxon traditions of empiricist positivism from the philosophically informed work of continental thinkers. It serves also to recall the materials of European thinkers against the recent intellectual hegemony of the USA. With regard to the philosophical debate, see Simon Critchley 2001 *Continental Philosophy: A Very Short Introduction*, Oxford University Press. With regard to the materials of the European tradition, see, for example, S. Pollard 1971 *The Idea of Progress*, London: Penguin; Raymond Aron 1968 *Main Currents in Sociological Thought*, London: Pelican; Z. Bauman 1987 *Legislators and Interpreters*, Cambridge: Polity; or in the philosophy of social science, see G. Delanty and P. Strydom (eds) 2003 *Philosophies of Social Science: The Classical and Contemporary Readings*, Maidenhead: Open University Press.
8 A sketch is offered in Chapter 2.
9 The term 'global (non)system' is awkward but it points to the contingent nature of contemporary patterns. There is no system. The familiar talk of economists, international relations theorists and, in recent years in particular, globalization theorists in respect of the putative single integrated global system are in my view false. Better to track the accumulated patterns. However, the phrase 'global system' is convenient and will be used in that fashion in this text.
10 P. Worsley 1984 *The Three Worlds: Culture and World Development*, London: Weidenfeld.
11 C. Bayly and T. Harper 2004 *Forgotten Armies: The Fall of British Asia 1941–45*, London: Allen Lane.
12 Recent work (see, for example, Linda Colley) has reminded us that colonial empire building was not neat and tidy. Rather the reverse: empire was only ever contingently present on the territory of other peoples, sometimes heavily (colonial centres), sometimes only lightly, as in the informal empire spheres.
13 L. Colley 2002 *Captives: Britain, Empire and the World 1600–1850*, London: Jonathan Cape, reminds us of the detail of empire advance: accidental, unplanned, fortuitous, combining advances and defeats. The resultant pattern is historically contingent.
14 These cities mapped the British Empire in East Asia; France looked to Saigon; the Dutch to Batavia; America to Manila; later Japan would look to Taipei and Seoul. On colonial cities, see A. D. King 1990 *Urbanism, Colonialism and the World Economy, Cultural and Spatial Foundations of the World Urban System*, London: Routledge.
15 An overview of the life of the city of Bangkok is given by M. Askew 2002 *Bangkok: Place, Practice and Representation*, London: Routledge; an overview of Thai development trajectory is given by C. Baker and P. Phongpaichit 2005 *A History of Thailand*, Cambridge University Press. Both make it clear that one element in the rise of Bangkok/Thailand was the presence of an outward trading port.
16 See Linda Cooke Johnson 1995 *Shanghai: From Market Town to Treaty Port 1074–1858*, Stanford University Press; Bryna Goodman 1995 *Native Place, City and Nation: Regional Networks and Identities in Shanghai 1853–1937*, University of California Press.
17 The idea of a sequence of phases is fairly readily available in the literature. The awkward term is 'post-colonial national development' because, contrary to the

development literature's imputation to replacement elites of the pursuit of effective nation-statehood (which assimilated their futures to a model serving the continued interests of departing colonial powers and the new hegemon, the business of 'modernization'), the first concern of replacement elites was their own survival and thereafter East Asian replacement elites pursued a variety of projects ranging from national development (Lee Kuan Yew's Singapore), through elite self-protection (the Bangkok elite's version of Thailand, unexpectedly and absurdly reasserted in the 2006 coup) to simple elite theft (Ferdinand Marcos's Philippines). In the post-colonial context, the pursuit of national development was only one available goal and its pursuit was context dependent.

18 Acharya 2000.
19 A. G. Frank 1998 *Re-Orient: Global Economy in the Asian Age*, University of California Press; or Chris Patten 2005 *Financial Times*, 26 September, who remarks that 'China has been the world's largest economy for 18 of the last 20 centuries'.
20 The American civil war and the drive to control the continent delayed overseas expansion. See Bruce Cummings 1999 *Parallax Visions: Making Sense of American–East Asian Relations at the End of the Century*, Duke University Press.
21 The Thai elite adjusted, absorbing the demands and lessons of the British and organizing their own essentially defensive shift to the modern world; so too more prospectively the Japanese. However, the Chinese elite resisted until it was too late to change and then they were swept away. In the Malay world some kingdoms disappeared, whilst others became pensioners of the new colonial powers and became fixed in place (British Malaya).
22 W. G. Beasley 1990 *The Rise of Modern Japan*, Tokyo: Tutle.
23 G. Barraclough's argument on India. See G. Barraclough 1967 *An Introduction to Contemporary History*, Harmondsworth: Penguin.
24 A term taken from Arno Mayer, derived from Antonio Gramsci and denoting the collapse into confusion of a pattern of life. See A. Mayer 1988 *Why Did the Heavens Not Darken*, New York: Pantheon.
25 Other dates could doubtless be chosen. The start date seems appropriate as it marks the collapse of China into a series of interrelated wars and conflicts which came to an end only in 1978 with the inauguration of Deng Xiaoping's reforms. The end date also seems appropriate: the crisis was more than China's and the end of the Vietnam War did mark the end of aggressive US imperialism (the Europeans having been ejected long before), notwithstanding its continued military presence (residues of the Pacific and cold wars).
26 Recently, Tony Payne 2004 *The New Regional Politics of Development*, London, Palgrave.
27 P. Lawson 1993 *The East India Company: A History*, London: Longman, notes that the first Royal Charter was granted in 1600 with the Spice Islands in mind; the organization evolved and the later date is the formation of a joint stock company.
28 The global scope of the changes in the eighteenth century is discussed by Bayly.
29 L Colley 1992 *Britons: Forging the Nation 1707–1837*, Yale University Press.
30 A rag-tag of agents plus a rag-tag of motives: the 1787 impeachment of Warren Hastings encapsulated the early phase of the Raj; the 1857 Indian Mutiny the mid-period; the twentieth-century career of Ghandi the end time.
31 A list is available at www.zum.de/whkmla/military/india/milxbrindia.htmla (accessed 27 January 2006); lists of Dutch, French, Portuguese and American wars of colonial expansion are also available. Wars of colonial retreat are not listed.
32 First Anglo-Burmese War 1824–26; Second 1852–53; and Third 1885–86.

Notes 219

33 M. Jasanoff 2005 *Edge of Empire: Conquest and Collecting in the East 1750–1850*, London: Fourth Estate.
34 Now Kolkata and Chennai.
35 Acharya 2000.
36 Steve Tsang 2004 *A Modern History of Hong Kong*, Hong Kong University Press.
37 The British made a series of efforts to establish trade links with Siam: John Crawfurd 1821; Henry Burney 1825; and John Bowring 1855. See Kullada Kesboonchoo Mead 2004 *The Rise and Decline of Thai Absolutism*, London: RoutledgeCurzon, pp. 25–37.
38 Linda Cooke Johnson 1995 *Shanghai: From Market Town to Treaty Port, 1074–1858*, Stanford University Press, chs 7–9.
39 Contentious. See Brian Inglis 1979 *The Opium War*, London: Coronet; Carl Trocki 1999 *Opium, Empire and the Global Political Economy: A Study of the Asian Opium Trade 1750–1950*, London: Routledge. For an alternate view of opium, see Frank Dikkoter, Lars Laamann and Zhou Xun 2004 *Narcotic Culture: A History of Drugs in China*, Hong Kong University Press.
40 Bayly and Harper 2004; N. Tarling 1993 *The Fall of Imperial Britain in Southeast Asia*, Oxford University Press.
41 Bayly and Harper 2004.
42 Comprising, tin, rubber and petroleum. See W. G. Huff 1994 *The Economic Growth of Singapore: Trade and Development in the Twentieth Century*, Cambridge University Press.
43 Turnbull 1977, ch. 6.
44 1965–90 Lee Kuan Yew; 1990–2004 Goh Chok Tong; from 2004 Lee Hsien Leong.
45 Linda Low 2001 'The Singapore Development State in the New Economy and Polity', *The Pacific Review* 14.3.
46 J. M. Carroll 2005 *Edge of Empire: Chinese Elites and British Colonials in Hong Kong*, Harvard University Press, conclusion.
47 This rests on a quite specific reading of the historical experience and present make-up of Singapore; a species of neo-liberal reading which sees social discipline as key to growth; but what this misses is the thoroughly political project of the PAP.
48 Sung Yung-Wing 2005 *The Emergence of Greater China*, London: Palgrave; M. J. Enright *et al.* 2005 *Regional Powerhouse: The Greater Pearl River Delta and the Rise of China*, London: Wiley; and L. Goodstadt 2005 *Uneasy Partners: The Conflict between Public Interest and Private Profit in Hong Kong*, Hong Kong University Press.
49 Sung 2005, p. 217.
50 Zhao Chenggen, 'Rational Authoritarianism and Chinese Economic Reform', in P. W. Preston and J. Haacke (eds) 2003 *Contemporary China: The Dynamics of Change at the Start of the new Millennium*, London: RoutledgeCurzon.

2 Complex change

1 Reflexive self-embedding is a necessary condition of scholarship. A series of frameworks of analysis inform the argument presented in this text; a series of domains; a particular quartet of 'windows'. In the foreground is the discussion of the unfolding historical development trajectory of Singapore; the immediate background is provided by the discussions of the comparative trajectories of related colonial cities; standing behind these substantive concerns is a formal area of reflection, the matter of the idea of complex change; and, finally, standing in the deep background is a related formal area of reflection, the business of

the nature of social theorizing per se, the territory of the philosophy of social science. Putting these 'windows' in sequence we have: (1) the text is lodged within the classical European tradition of social theorizing; that is, formally, it is philosophically interpretive critical; (2) the text is lodged within the classical European tradition of social theorizing; that is, it is substantively concerned with elucidating the dynamics of complex change; (3) the text is centred upon the dynamics of the shift to the modern world in East Asia, where this in particular entails focusing on the role of colonial cities, the links in the global chains of empire which drew in particular peripheral territories; and (4) the text deals with the historical development experience of a number of cities within the sometime sphere of the British Empire, in particular the city-state of Singapore.
2 Z. Bauman 1987 *Legislators and Interpreters*, Cambridge, Polity.
3 An idea sketched elsewhere; see P. W. Preston 1985 *New Trends in Development Theory*, London: Routledge; P. W. Preston 1996 *Development Theory*, Oxford, Blackwell, chs 1 and 18; P. W. Preston 1998a *Pacific Asia in the Global System*, Oxford, Blackwell, ch. 1. This section is derived from Preston 1998a, ch. 2.
4 N. Long (ed.) 1992 *Battlefields of Knowledge*, London: Routledge.
5 M. Watson 2005 *Foundations of International Political Economy*, London: Palgrave.
6 The dynamics of change within territories will not be equivalent; against the modernization-theory-inspired expectations of a single logic repeating itself in diverse contexts, such that all territories might expect equal advance in the absence of accidental inhibitions to progress, structural international political economy recognizes the fundamentally uneven nature of progress.
7 Beijing's phrase – indicating its appreciation of the destabilizing effects of China's rapid growth for regional and global systems – flags a diplomatic wish to avoid the conflicts that have in the past attended such rebalancing.
8 Work compatible with a formally interpretive-critical and substantively materialist approach would include A. G. Frank, I. Wallerstein, E. Meskins Wood, R. Brenner, these locate the assumptions of this text within the (ever-widening) literature.
9 E. Gellner 1983 *Nations and Nationalism*, Cambridge University Press (elite); J. C. Scott 1985 *Weapons of the Weak*, Yale University Press (masses); H. D. Evers and H. Schrader (eds) 1994 *The Moral Economy of Trade*, London: Routledge (groups).
10 A. Gamble and T. Payne 1996 *Regionalism and World Order*, London: Macmillan; M. Shibusawa *et al.* 1992 *Pacific Asia in the 1990s*, London: Routledge; C. Mackerras (ed.) 1995 *Eastern Asia*, London: Longman; T. Payne (ed.) 2004 *The New Regional Politics of Development*, London: Palgrave.
11 These early debates about regions were reviewed in Shaun Breslin and Richard Higgot (eds) 2000 *New Political Economy Special Issue: Studying Regions* 5.3.
12 The Atlantic slave trade and the East Asian opium trade were debated at the time. With regard to the former there was a long campaign for abolition. In East Asia the British state authorities and traders knew full well what they were doing; see Brian Inglis 1979 *The Opium War*, London: Coronet; C. Trocki 1999 *Opium, Empire and the Global Political Economy*, London: Routledge.
13 A. Reid 1988/93 *Southeast Asia in the Age of Commerce*, Yale University Press. The Chinese elite turned away from long-distance trade in the mid-sixteenth century. This created a space for the Europeans; see A. G. Frank 1998 *ReOrient: Global Economy in the Asian Age*, University of California Press.
14 A. Acharya 2000 *The Quest for Identity: International Relations of Southeast Asia*, Oxford University Press.
15 P. Worsley 1984 *The Three Worlds: Culture and World Development*, London: Weidenfeld.

16 H. Furber 1976 *Rival Empires of Trade in the Orient 1600–1800*, University of Minnesota Press.
17 P. Lawson 1993 *The East India Company: A History*, London: Longman; C. R. Boxer 1990 *The Dutch Seaborne Empire 1600–1800*, Harmondsworth: Penguin.
18 The Amsterdam Company had sponsored a voyage in 1596–97 to Bantam.
19 Furber 1976.
20 Furber 1976.
21 D. J. M. Tate 1971/79 *The Making of Southeast Asia*, Oxford University Press.
22 A. Reid, 'Indonesia: Revolution without Socialism', in R. Jeffrey (ed.) 1981 *Asia: The Winning of Independence*, London: Macmillan; J. Pluvier 1977 *Southeast Asia from Colonialism to Independence*, Oxford University Press, ch. 1.
23 Pluvier 1977, ch. 1.
24 Pluvier 1977, ch. 1.
25 Pluvier 1977, ch. 1.
26 Reid, in Jeffrey 1981.
27 Reid, in Jeffrey 1981.
28 Acharya 2000.
29 K. C. Tregonning 1965 *The British in Malaya: The First Forty Years 1786–1826*, University of Arizona Press.
30 M. Borthwick 1992 *Pacific Century: The Emergence of Modern Pacific Asia*, Boulder, CO: Westview, ch. 2.
31 S. Tsang 2004 *A Modern History of Hong Kong*, Hong Kong University Press.
32 The British sent trade missions: John Crawfurd, 1821; Henry Burney, 1825. King Mongkut agreed the 1855 Bowring Treaty.
33 M. Osborne 1995 *Southeast Asia: An Introductory History*, St Leonards: Allen and Unwin, ch. 5.
34 J. L. S. Girling 1981 *Thailand: Society and Politics*, Cornell University Press, ch. 1.
35 S. Piriyarangsan 1983 *Thai Bureaucratic Capitalism 1932–1960*, Bangkok: Chulalongkorn University Social Research Centre.
36 W. J. Duiker 1995 *Vietnam: Revolution in Transition*, Boulder, CO: Westview, ch. 2.
37 Pluvier 1977, ch. 1.
38 Osborne 1995, ch. 5.
39 Osborne 1995, ch. 5.
40 A. W. McCoy, 'The Philippines: Independence without Decolonization' in Jeffrey 1981.
41 Pluvier 1977, ch. 1.
42 Worsley 1984.
43 A. D. King 1990 *Urbanism, Colonialism and the World Economy: Cultural and Spatial Foundations of the World Urban System*, London: Routledge.
44 E. Hobsbawm 1994 *The Age of Extremes: The Short Twentieth Century*, London: Michael Joseph.
45 Arno Mayer 1988 *Why Did the Heavens Not Darken: The Final Solution in History*, New York: Pantheon. The notion points to systemic collapse.
46 The names add up to a roll call of reformers and activists – Yukichi Fukuzawa, Sun Yat Sen, Luang Wichit, Ghandi, Aung San, Sukarno, Chin Pin, Lee Kuan Yew, Ho Chi Minh.
47 As a list: 1911–13 Revolution; 1913–16 Yuan Shikai; 1916–26 Warlord period; 1926–27 Northern Expedition; 1931–33 Invasion of Manchuria; 1930–36 Encirclement/Long March; 1937–45 Sino-Japanese War; 1927–49 Civil War; 1950–53 Korean War; 1966–69 Cultural Revolution; and 1976–78 post-Mao elite transition.
48 Jonathan Fenby 2005 *Generalissimo: Chiang Kai Shek and the China He Lost*, London: Free Press; see also R. J. Rummel 1991 *China's Bloody Century*, London: Transaction.

49 The country was devastated; to give an idea of the scale of this devastation, from 1916 to 1949 around 35 million died, and from 1949 to 1978 around a further 30 million. See Fenby 2005; Rummel 1991.
50 Unpacking the tale for Europe is awkward. The collapse of the old regime in Europe ushered in fascism and an autarchic party-state Marxism–Leninism. Division/occupation allowed significant reforms. Arguably a new phase of recovery is in process following the 1989/91 end of the cold war. This is not a straightforward issue; see P. W. Preston 2004 *Relocating England*, Manchester University Press.
51 A. Mayer makes the point with respect to Europe – the shift was slow. See A. Mayer 1981 *The Persistence of the Old Regime*, New York: Croom Helm.
52 In earlier work I criticized orthodox development theorists for imputing to replacement elites the goal of the pursuit of effective nation-statehood. It ignored the context of new states and the political problems of elites; it assumed a uni-directional process that recapitulated the historical experience of the West. I suggested that replacement elites were interested in many objectives. The key to their futures was dealing with the demands of complex change and circumstances would produce a variety of projects. In the event those parts of the world that have 'developed' have done so in terms of various projects of national development – the elite political drive to carve out a niche within the global division of labour. The projects were local. Elites were successful in East Asia, where circumstances were propitious; they were less so in Latin America; and they were unsuccessful in Africa and the Middle East.
53 J. Clammer 1995 *Difference and Modernity*, London: Kegan Paul International.
54 In Korea at the end of the Pacific War the Imperial Japanese authorities handed power to a local nationalist grouping who established a provisional government. However, the Great Powers decided to divide Korea into two occupation zones divided by the 38th parallel – the Soviet Union controlled the north and the USA the south. These developed into the two Koreas. The Democratic People's Republic of Korea (DPRK) turned inwards, the Republic of Korea (ROK) eventually joined the Tigers. Syngman Rhee's regime held power from 1948 to 1960: US assistance provided a large percentage of the state budget; it encouraged rent seeking as business and the state machine looked for access to aid flows; Rhee used access to buttress his position in a period of very slow ISI-style growth. His successor Park Chung Hee's regime ruled from 1961 to 1979 and laid the foundations of the contemporary South Korean economy: the state was in charge; technocrats became influential; the state controlled credit and licences for investment (credit for favoured firms whose performance is monitored); and the economy developed conglomerates (chaebol) with close relations to the state and nationalized banks. The 1979–87 Chun Doo Hwan and Roh Tae Woo regime, followed by Roh Tae Woo (1987–92), established a dual programme of reforms: economic liberalization made credit more freely available and the chaebols were targeted for reform; also political reforms led to a freely elected president – Kim Young Sam from 1992. Whilst overall direction is not too clear, by now Korea has a very sophisticated modern high-tech economy.
55 In Taiwan the KMT sought local legitimacy via economic advance; thus there was a strong political drive towards economic development. The state has been central in Taiwan's development. In the 1950s import-substituting industrialization focused on low-tech manufactures: the state allocated foreign exchange, set tariffs, enjoyed an overvalued currency and there was routine corruption. The economy advanced rapidly in textiles, petroleum and metals, but by 1954 there were problems with small domestic market. The KMT was pressured to shift to export-oriented industrializaton (EOI) by both the USA and the technocrats (often trained in the US). In the 1960 and 1970s EOI encouraged small firms to

compete in export markets and in the 1980s a high-tech economy emerged. A secondary ISI strategy of industrial deepening occupied the period 1973–80: the oil crisis suggested vulnerability; the US rapprochement with China encouraged state-developed heavy industry in the strategic areas of steel, ships and petrochemicals. Thereafter, from 1980 the economy became more internationalized, with investments in China and Southeast Asia.
56 1967 ASEAN 5, Malaysia, Singapore, Indonesia, Thailand, Philippines; 1984 ASEAN 6 with Brunei; 1995 ASEAN 7 with Vietnam; 1997 ASEAN 9 with Laos and Myanmar; and 1999 ASEAN 10 with Cambodia.
57 Strongly committed to development; intermittently and only recently concerned.
58 Acharya 2000.
59 Huang Xiaoming 2005 *The Rise and Fall of the East Asian Growth System, 1951–2000*, London: RoutledgeCurzon; a related critique of the idea of the developmental state as an oversimplified non-Asian construct is made by Richard Boyd and Ngo Tak Wing 2005 *Asian States: Beyond the Developmental Perspective*, London: RoutledgeCurzon.
60 Worsley 1984.
61 King 1990.
62 Worsley 1984.
63 King 1990.
64 Hobsbawm 1994.
65 H. C. Chan, 'Democracy: Evolution and Implementation', in R. Bartley *et al.* 1993 *Democracy and Capitalism: Asian and American Perspectives*, Singapore: Institute for Southeast Asian Studies; B. H. Chua 1995 *Communitarian Ideology and Democracy in Singapore*, London: Routledge.
66 J. M. Carroll 2005 *Edge of Empire: Chinese Elites and British Colonials in Hong Kong*, Harvard University Press.
67 The post-Second World War concern on the part of departing colonial powers and replacement elites to grasp the changes enfolding them issued in the discourse of development, where one idea became central: 'underdevelopment', an unsatisfactory condition in need of remedy, that is, development. That material circumstances were in need of improvement is not in question, but the notion was in one respect pernicious: it made the days before independence or before colonialism into a phase of life outside history, an original condition where nothing had happened. But there were long-established coherent forms of life long before colonial incursions, and the territories attaining independence did have histories; in particular they had histories of colonial development and exploitation. Hong Kong easily escapes characterization as underdeveloped if its history is pointed out. However, in Singapore the official national past has embraced an idea of underdevelopment (thus Lee Kuan Yew titles one volume of his autobiography *From Third World to First: The Singapore Story 1965–2000* (Lee 2000, New York, Harper Collins), an untenable claim on the slightest acquaintance with Singapore's history), which makes grasping the truth a little more awkward.
68 See, for example, A. G. Frank 1998; J. M. Hobson 2004 *The Eastern Origins of Western Civilization*, Cambridge University Press.
69 James Hayes, 'Hong Kong Island Before 1841', in David Faure (ed.) 2003 *Hong Kong: A Reader in Social History*, Oxford University Press.
70 Tsang 2004, p. 16.
71 Tsang 2004, p. 59.
72 Carroll 2005.
73 Historians mention the established population – 6,000 to 7,500 – and note the rapid increase in population (mostly incoming Chinese – the colonial British were always a small minority). Carroll (2005) argues that Hong Kong developed only slowly until Chinese merchants moved to Hong Kong – rather like in Singapore

(but here the numbers are larger) the original inhabitants are supplanted, partly ignored and partly absorbed within the expanding confines of a novel dynamic form of life.
74 Ngo Tak Wing 'Colonialism in Hong Kong Revisited', in Ngo Tak Wing (ed.) 1999 *Hong Kong's History: State and Society Under Colonial Rule*, London: Routledge.
75 Carroll 2005.
76 Ngo Tak Wing, 'Industrial History and the Artifice of Laissez Faire Colonialism', in Ngo 1999.
77 Tsang 2004, ch. 8.
78 Carroll 2005, pp. 182–86.
79 R. Stubbs 2005 *Rethinking Asia's Economic Miracle*, London: Palgrave, ch. 4.
80 Tsang 2004, ch. 13.
81 Tsang 2004, ch. 13.
82 Carroll (2005) argues that the elite had an idea of themselves as Hong Kong Chinese by the late nineteenth century; Tsang 2004 titles ch. 13 'The Rise of Hong Kongers'.
83 Tsang 2004, ch. 13.
84 Tsang 2004, ch. 12.
85 Stubbs 2005, pp. 108–12.
86 Carroll 2005, conclusion.
87 This perspective rests on a quite specific reading of the historical experience and present make-up of Singapore – a species of neo-liberal reading which sees social discipline as key to growth. What this misses is the thoroughly political project of the PAP. It is the politics that Beijing's version of Singapore wants to lose – but what would be the Hong Kong project? Economic growth alone is not what they had in Singapore.
88 Sung Yung-Wing 2005 *The Emergence of Greater China*, London: Palgrave; M. J. Enright *et al.* 2005 *Regional Powerhouse: The Greater Pearl River Delta and the Rise of China*, London: Wiley; and L. Goodstadt 2005 *Uneasy Partners: The Conflict Between Public Interest and Private Profit in Hong Kong*, Hong Kong University Press.
89 Edward Said – one example – late-nineteenth-century French ideas of race used to pick out peripheral peoples within the Siamese sphere to designate them as races deserving nationhood and thus extraction by enlightened French from the Siamese sphere; see C. Baker and P. Phongpaichit 2005 *A History of Thailand*, Cambridge University Press, ch. 3.
90 D. Canadine 2001 *Ornamentalism: How the British Saw Their Empire*, London: Allen Lane.
91 The idea is used in P. J. Cain and A. G. Hopkins 1993a *British Imperialism: Innovation and Expansion 1688–1914*, London: Longman, pp. 6–9, where it adds to discussions of formal machineries of empire the business of trade – conducted partly within delimited terrirories but also outside them, hence informal.
92 Kedah, Kelantan, Trenganau and Pattani. The Burney Treaty of 1826 was superseded by the Anglo-Siamese Treaty of 1909 (Bangkok Treaty), which drew the border to the advantage of the British. Siam only slowly moved from a mandala state to a bounded state in the nineteenth and early twentieth century. It was squeezed between the British and French; see Baker and Phongpaichit 2005.
93 Baker and Phongpaichit 2005, ch. 2.
94 On these matters, see Linda Cooke Johnson 1995 *Shanghai: From Market Town to Treaty Port 1074–1858*, Stanford University Press.
95 By his successor, Rutherford Alcock in 1849; Cooke Johnson 1995, ch. 9.

Notes 225

96 Cooke Johnson (1995) records two main types of association: native place and commercial activity. Outsiders called both guilds; the Chinese distinguished them but native place organizations could be formed around commercial activities; see ch. 5.
97 Cooke Johnson 1995, ch. 7.
98 Rutherford Alcock, Balfour's successor from 1846 to 1855, vigorously encouraged developments; see Cooke Johnson 1995, ch. 9.
99 Cooke Johnson 1995, ch. 8.
100 Cooke Johnson 1995, ch. 8; see Trocki 1999.
101 In respect of Shanghai, Trocki (1999, p. 119) mentions the local competition; with respect to Singapore, see C. A. Trocki 1990 *Opium and Empire: Chinese Society in Colonial Singapore 1800–1910*, Cornell University Press; the domestic British debate is nicely reviewed in Inglis 1979.
102 The twists and turns of European and American relationships in Shanghai reflected different home government views, as well as the opinions of officials and traders on the ground; see Cooke Johnson 1995, pp. 243–47.
103 Characterized as a coup by Bryna Goodman – a coalition of multiple groups within the Chinese population including merchants and secret societies, native place groups and officials seized the town; see B. Goodman 1995 *Native Place, City and Nation: Regional Networks and Identities in Shanghai 1853–1937*, University of California Press, ch. 2.
104 Cooke Johnson 1995, ch. 12.
105 Zhang Wei Bin, 'Shanghai: a Gateway to China's Modernization', in A. E. Andersson and D. E. Andersson 2000 *Gateways to the Global Economy*, Cheltenham: Edward Elgar.
106 Zhang, in Andersson and Andersson 2000.

3 Impact and reply

1 An historian would correctly point out that European contacts long pre-dated any European domestic system that was 'industrial capitalist'. True, but the shorthand lets the detail be kept under control; otherwise the discussion of change in Asia would require a parallel detailed discussion of change in Europe (and America). It has recently been attempted: the historical experience of the West is presented in softened form as a general experience of all countries – an upmarket euro-centrism – but the discussion is marvellous; see C. A. Bayly 2004 *The Birth of the Modern World 1780–1914*, Oxford, Blackwell.
2 A list of wars is available at www.zum.de/whkmla/military/india/milxbrindia.htmla (accessed 27 January 2006); on European violence, see also V. G. Kiernan 1982 *European Empires from Conquest to Collapse 1815–1960*, London: Fontana. It might also be noted that local violence was also familiar. In Indo-China Burmese, Thai, Khmer and Vietnamese fought wars; in the archipelago Acharya reports warfare, maybe somewhat ritualized, over people rather than land. The early European incomers were just one more group. Later, as Kiernan makes clear, their military superiority was obvious.
3 On Europe at this time, see N. Davies 1997 *Europe: A History*, London: Pimlico, ch. 7, on the Renaissance.
4 See M. Osborne 1995 *Southeast Asia: An Introductory History*, St Leonards: Allen and Unwin; B. N. Pandy 1980 *South and Southeast Asia 1945–79: Problems and Policies*, London: Macmillan; N. Tarling (ed.) 1992 *The Cambridge History of Southeast Asia*, Cambridge University Press; Bayly 2004; C. Bayly and T. Harper 2004 *Forgotten Armies: The Fall of British Asia 1941–45*, London: Allen Lane.
5 The British trimmed and adjusted their position as players around them adjusted their positions. Finally the British, with the permission of the American

226 Notes

military, reoccupied the territory; see P. Snow 2003 *The Fall of Hong Kong: Britain, China and the Japanese Occupation*, Yale University Press, chs 5 and 6.

6 In conversation, at the Australian National University (ANU), David Goodman remarked that 'China isn't a country, it's a continent' – and, it might be added, it has a population of some 1.3 billion.

7 C. Baker and P. Phongpaichit 2005 *A History of Thailand*, Cambridge University Press.

8 Linda Cooke Johnson 1995 *Shanghai: From Market Town to Treaty Port 1074–1858*, Stanford University Press; Bryna Goodman 1995 *Native Place, City and Nation: Regional Networks and Identities in Shanghai 1853–1937*, University of California Press.

9 A. G. Frank 1998 *Re-Orient: Global Economy in the Asian Age*, University of California Press.

10 The American Civil War and the drive to control the continent delayed overseas expansion; see B. Cummings 1999 *Parallax Visions: Making Sense of American–East Asian Relations at the End of the Century*, Duke University Press.

11 The Thai elite adjusted, absorbing the demands and lessons of the British and organizing their own shift to the modern world; so too the Japanese; the Chinese elite resisted until they were swept away. In the Malay world some kingdoms disappeared, whilst others became pensioners of the new colonial powers and became fixed in place (British Malaya).

12 Their reach into local extant forms of life varied; a simple distinction between formal and informal empire is made in P. J. Cain and A. G. Hopkins 1993a *British Imperialism: Innovation and Expansion 1688–1914*, London: Longman.

13 Simple stories of Westerners overcoming the passive East or alternatively of the harmonious stable East being overcome by aggressive outsiders are false, as expansion was an exchange involving multiple agents. In general terms, agents can and do act, circumstances provide constraint and opportunity, and few are wholly without power.

14 There is a wealth of literature on this, starting with the ideas of 'plural society' produced by the colonial civil servant and reformer; see J. S. Furnivall 1939 *Netherlands India: A Study of Plural Economy*, Cambridge University Press.

15 A. Acharya 2000 *The Quest for Identity: International Relations of Southeast Asia*, Oxford University Press.

16 C. Trocki 1999 *Opium, Empire and the Global Political Economy*, London: Routledge.

17 M. Yahuda 2004 *The International Politics of the Asia-Pacific*, London: Routledge; R. Stubbs 2005 *Rethinking Asia's Economic Miracle: The Political Economy of War, Prosperity and Crisis*, London: Palgrave.

18 In P. Lawson 1993 *The East India Company: A History*, London: Longman, Lawson notes that the first Royal Charter was granted in 1600, with the Spice Islands in mind; the organization evolved and the later date of 1657 is that of the formation of a joint stock company.

19 The global scope of the changes in the eighteenth century is discussed by Bayly 2004.

20 L. Colley 1992 *Britons: Forging the Nation 1707–1837*, Yale University Press.

21 S. Tsang 2004 *A Modern History of Hong Kong*, Hong Kong University Press.

22 First Anglo-Burmese War 1824–26; Second 1852–53; and Third 1885–86.

23 A fuller treatment is given in P. W. Preston 1998a *Pacific Asia in the Global System*, Oxford, Blackwell, pt 2.

24 Acharya 2000.

25 A. Reid 1988/93 *Southeast Asia in the Age of Commerce*, Yale University Press; Frank 1998.

26 Frank 1998.

Notes   227

27 P. Worsley 1984 *The Three Worlds: Culture and World Development*, London: Weidenfeld.
28 See G. Barraclough 1967 *An Introduction to Contemporary History*, Harmondsworth: Penguin; B. Anderson 1983 *Imagined Communities*, London: Verso.
29 The Congress of Berlin divided the world amongst the rival Western powers; Worsley (1984) remarks that Asia 'seemed to have gone under for good' (p. 15) but adds that what in retrospect is surprising in the light of its technological and scientific superiority is the brevity of Western rule. An explanation is available in the social upheaval which attended the entire episode. As the peoples of Asia made their shift to the modern world in the context of colonial rule, they learned how to operate within the system, how to become autonomous agents in the shifting structural patterns of the now global industrial-capitalist system.
30 H. Furber 1976 *Rival Empires of Trade in the Orient 1600–1800*, University of Minnesota Press.
31 There were three major trading areas – trade goods could be associated with ethnic groups, the British producing opium, Chinese bringing in coolies, Malays and Bugis trading archipelago products and so on – and marketplaces differed. There was long-distance trade to Europe, regional trade to India or China and local trade around the archipelago.
32 Lawson 1993; C. R. Boxer 1990 *The Dutch Seaborne Empire 1600–1800*, Harmondsworth: Penguin.
33 It lay within the Bantam Sultanate and in 1619 the Dutch annexed the area. This was the first of many Dutch wars in the archipelago. They they claimed the spice trade and tried to block their rivals the British.
34 Furber 1976.
35 Baker and Phongpaichit (2005) have a series of maps of mainland Southeast Asia.
36 J. L. S. Girling 1981 *Thailand: Society and Politics*, Cornell University Press.
37 Acharya 2000.
38 The political forms in the region were various: see D. J. M. Tate 1971/79 *The Making of Southeast Asia*, Oxford University Press.
39 Acharya 2000.
40 In C. Mackerras 1999 *Western Images of China*, Oxford University Press, Mackerras tracks the 'regimes of truth' whereby Europeans and Americans have apprehended and dealt with China – from medieval European notions of exotic Cathay, through missionary optimism, to imperialist characterizations of an old moribund degenerate civilization, and through twentieth-century American optimism and, after 1949, doubts. The general view of China now seems to be one of cautious optimism in the face of a recovering or rising power.
41 E. Moise 1994 *Modern China*, London: Longman. The Han Chinese originated in the Yellow River region; recorded history details rulers from about 2700 BC; archaeological evidence can confirm these materials to 1300 BC. City-states controlled areas of agricultural land; there were shifting patterns of power; the Han Chinese slowly expanded. The core areas of China have been the valleys of the Yellow river, Yangtze river and Pearl river; there are peripheral areas, including Manchuria, Mongolia, Sinkiang and Tibet, where central control has waxed and waned.
42 B. Moore 1966 *The Social Origins of Dictatorship and Democracy*, Boston: Beacon.
43 Moise 1994.
44 B. Inglis 1979 *The Opium War*, London: Coronet; Trocki 1999.
45 Moore 1966.
46 Frank 1998.

228 Notes

47 M. Borthwick 1992 *The Pacific Century: The Emergence of Modern Pacific Asia*, Boulder, CO: Westview, ch. 2.
48 Moise 1994.
49 Moore (1966) argues that the Qing Dynasty system comprised five key groupings: (1) the central authorities, who dispensed laws of property, but whose power was relatively weak; (2) the powerful scholar-bureaucrats who administered the regions of the country; (3) the powerful local gentry, who were landowners; (4) the peasantry, who had little scope for independent action; and (5) merchant groups, whose activities were not encouraged. The system worked in a quite particular way. The scholar-bureaucrats administered the dynastic system of law, tax gathering and public works. They were recruited by merit in examination but their activities overlapped with the family- and clan-based networks of the landowning gentry. The country was very large and central control was always relatively weak, so that local scholar-bureaucrats could establish mutually beneficial relationships with local powerful landowners. The system was designed to extract resources from the peasantry. However, the merchant, manufacturing and trading groups were not directly involved in this political-economic system. They existed, so to say, off to one side. The scholar-bureaucrats acted to keep them in check and they did not establish themselves as an independent socio-economic grouping (as had been the case in Europe).
50 J. Fenby 2005 *Generalissimo: Chiang Kai Shek and the China He Lost*, London: Free Press.
51 Cummings 1999.
52 R. Bowring and P. Kornicki (eds) 1993 *The Cambridge Encyclopedia of Japan*, Cambridge University Press.
53 W. G. Beasley 1990 *The Rise of Modern Japan*, Tokyo: Tuttle.
54 Beasley 1990.
55 K. Sheridan 1993 *Governing the Japanese Economy*, Cambridge: Polity, suggests that the period did contribute to later post-Meiji success by establishing: (1) low birth and death rates; (2) urban growth and commercialization in villages; (3) ethnic uniformity; (4) irrigation systems; (5) commercial and financial systems; and (6) systems of land tenure and taxation. Sheridan notes that prosperity grew steadily if slowly over the whole period. However, people were still poor and lived hard lives. Sheridan also notes what the period did not produce: no capital for industrialization; no technology for industrialization; and no entrepreneurs to run the system.
56 A new state was constructed by an oligarchic group based on the Choshu and Satsuma diamyos which had made the revolution in the name of the emperor. It included a series of elements: (1) a modern pattern of central and local government was instituted and the domains were transformed into prefectures within a modern state centred on Tokyo; (2) the caste system was abolished; (3) the daimyo and samurai retainers were paid off; (4) landownership and taxation were reformed to provide state revenues; (5) a centralized bureaucracy was formed; (6) the state theory of Germany and the constitutional law of France were studied in order to write and promulgate in the name of the emperor a new constitution in 1889; (7) a political structure involving emperor, parliament and cabinet was formed, and the oligarchy or genro remained outside as a group of 'elder statesmen advising the emperor', although in practice they both held all the power and held the system together; (8) political parties formed; and (9) the system of State Shinto, which stressed the role of the emperor, was inaugurated and Buddhism repressed. Thereafter, under the slogan 'rich country – strong army' the Meiji government adopted an industrialization programme in parallel with its political reforms. The key to the industrialization drive was the state-sponsored construction of modern industry. A Ministry of Industrial Development

was set up to oversee heavy industry. In the agricultural sphere, which was important as a foreign exchange earner with silk, the Ministry of Home Affairs was established. In addition to direct state involvement the Meiji government co-opted persons whom it thought could become successful industrialists. And in the social sphere the Meiji oligarchy looked to draw on the legacies of the Tokugawa period in order to fashion a mobilized corporate society. The key institution was the continuing family, which was reworked and enshrined in the new civil code as the principal agent of development. Thereafter the role of education was crucial in inducting citizens into the 'family-state' oriented to the pursuit of development.

57 Barraclough 1967.
58 A process detailed for the third world by Worsley 1984.
59 S. Tanaka 1993 *Japan's Orient: Rendering Pasts into History*, University of California Press.
60 A. D. King 1990 *Urbanism, Colonialism and the World Economy*, London: Routledge.
61 For a general history, see M. Turnbull 1977 *A History of Singapore 1819–1975*, Oxford University Press; S. S. Bedlington 1978 *Malaysia and Singapore: The Building of New Nation States*, Cornell University Press.
62 The Malay world was characterized by the rise and fall of a succession of maritime trading empires. Loose in their extent, expanding and contracting with the ebb and flow of the power of the central sultanate, the empires were based on trade. Political power/authority required control of a key port; see Tate 1971/79.
63 C. Trocki 1979 *Prince of Pirates: The Temmenggongs and the Development of Johor 1784–1885*, Singapore University Press, argues that the key concerns of the rulers of the Riau Sultantate were the trade routes which passed through the Straits of Malacca – control over a key trade nexus was the key to these mandala states.
64 K. F. Pang 1984 'The Malay Royals of Singapore', unpublished dissertation, Department of Sociology, National University of Singapore.
65 Trocki 1979.
66 C. Trocki 1990 *Opium and Empire*, Cornell University Press.
67 Robert Hughes 1988 *The Fatal Shore*, London: Pan.
68 H. C. Brookfield 1972 *Colonialism, Development and Independence: The Case of the Melanesian Islands in the South Pacific*, Cambridge University Press.
69 K. C. Tregonning 1965 *The British in Malaya: The First Forty Years 1786–1826*, University of Arizona Press.
70 K. H. Lee, 'Malaya: New State and Old Elites' in R. Jeffrey 1981 *Asia: The Winning of Independence*, London: Macmillan.
71 Lee, in Jeffrey 1981.
72 J. M. Carroll 2005 *Edge of Empires: Chinese Elites and British Colonials in Hong Kong*, Harvard University Press.
73 Carroll 2005, introduction.
74 Carroll 2005, ch. 2.
75 Carroll 2005, ch. 3.
76 Carroll (2005) comments 'Indeed, Hong Kong's legendary economic success perhaps has less to do with its status as a British colony than because, at least at crucial points in Chinese history, it was not part of China' (p. 57).
77 Carroll 2005, ch. 3.
78 Carroll 2005, ch. 4.
79 Carroll 2005, ch. 5.
80 Carroll 2005, ch. 6, discusses the 1925/25 strike/boycott, arguing both that the local elite supported the colonial power and also that events marked the beginning of the end of British imperial power in China.

81 The theme of the 'ragged edge' of empire – the multiple agents involved, the contingent nature of these exchanges, the difficulties of those involved, the great scope for personal loss, the elision of these truths in the official history of empire, where hindsight uncovers a coherent accumulative tale – is pursued by Linda Colley 2002 *Captives: Britain, Empire and the World 1600–1850*, London: Jonathan Cape; see also Maya Jasanoff 2005 *Edge of Empire: Conquest and Collecting in the East 1750–1850*, London: Fourth Estate.

82 Carroll (2005, pp. 191–94) adds that the local elite managed the incoming British successfully. Hong Kong was developmentally far ahead of the mainland for most of the colonial era. Post-1997 the local elite must manage the demands of Beijing.

83 A wonderful series of maps is given in Baker and Phongpaichit 2005.

84 Osborne 1995; Girling 1981; Baker and Phongpaichit 2005.

85 It may be that Siam became a quasi-colony of the British – see Marc Askew 2002 *Bangkok: Place, Practice and Representation*, London: Routledge.

86 S. Piriyarangsan 1983 *Thai Bureaucratic Capitalism 1932–1960*, Bangkok: Chulalongkorn University Social Research Centre.

87 Askew 2002, ch. 2.

88 Baker and Phongpaichit 2005.

89 Furber 1976. In all, the number of Europeans involved was fairly small compared to the local populations, maybe 75,000 towards the end of the pre-industrial mercantile period. Indeed, Barraclough (1967) argues that one reason for the collapse of the empires in the wake of the Pacific War was the simple demographics of the relationship.

90 The East India Company traded piece goods (cottons, calicos and silk), teas and spices; and later opium in consort with country traders.

4 General crisis

1 In Singapore and Hong Kong the resident European populations were a few per cent of the population, the overwhelming majority were local people, in particular Chinese (M. Turnbull 1977 *A History of Singapore, 1819–1975*, Oxford University Press; S. Tsang 2004 *A Modern History of Hong Kong*, Hong Kong University Press, p. 59).

2 The disruption created local losers and winners. The latter prospered. In Hong Kong the arrival of British opened up possibilities for merchants (J. M. Carroll 2005 *Edge of Empire: Chinese Elites and British Colonials in Hong Kong*, Harvard University Press, ch. 2; Singapore's status as a free port (in contrast to local ports or Dutch, where dues had to be paid) drew in many traders. Overall, however, the disruption contributed to the reception amongst locals of new ideas, in respect of political organization, for example independence.

3 Minority – but Dutch came up with 'ethical policy' – British talked about eventual independence (J. Pluvier 1977 *Southeast Asia From Colonialism to Independence*, Oxford University Press). Colonial officials participated – for example, George Orwell on his experiences (*Burmese Days*) or J. S. Furnivall working with nationalists in Burma (C. A. Bayly and T. Harper 2004 *Forgotten Armies: the Fall of British Asia 1941–45*, London: Allen Lane). It was difficult to imagine anything much happening. The Pacific War was crucial to the dissolution of empire.

4 Recall Ernest Gellner 1964 *Thought and Change*, London: Weidenfeld, on the nature of crisis (radical lack of clarity in respect of the nature of problems and the nature of possible solutions) and on minimum demands for intelligibility and legitimacy of contemporary polities (industrial or industrializing plus co-cultural elite).

5 Any dating of the start of sweeping change is arbitrary. In two places change was inaugurated by established elites – Siam and Tokugawa Japan. Neither was directly colonized; both had later shorter 'general crises', Japan in 1937–51 and Siam/Thailand in 1932–45. All the territories in East Asia had their own trajectories; they participated, so to say, in the region's general crisis in different ways and at different times.

6 Somewhat arbitrarily; other dates could doubtless be chosen. The start date seems appropriate as it marks the collapse of China into a series of interrelated wars and conflicts which came to an end only in 1978 with the inauguration of Deng Xiaoping's reforms. The end date also seems appropriate – the crisis was more than China's and the end of the Vietnam War did mark the end of aggressive US imperialism (the Europeans having been ejected long before), notwithstanding their continued military presence (residues of the Pacific and cold wars).

7 A. Iriye 1997 *Japan and the Wider World*, London: Longman; A. Iriye 1987 *The Origins of the Second World War in Asia and the Pacific*, London: Longman.

8 B. Cummings 1999 *Parallax Visions: Making Sense of American–East Asian Relations at the End of the Century*, Duke University Press.

9 The British situation is discussed by Shigeru Akita 'British Informal Empire in East Asia, 1800–1939' in R. E. Dumett 1999 *Gentlemanly Capitalism and British Imperialism: The New Debate on Empire*, London: Longman.

10 P. Buckley Ebrey 1996 *Cambridge Illustrated History of China*, Cambridge University Press, p. 241.

11 E. Hobsbawm 1994 *The Age of Extremes: The Short Twentieth Century*, London: Michael Joseph.

12 For example, Malay Royals became participants in empire, Thai Royals sought development, Japanese elites sought development, Philippines elites came to collaborate and the Qing elite tried to respond.

13 Thus Serekat Islam in the Dutch East Indies in the early twentieth century.

14 C. Thorne 1978 *Allies of a Kind*, Oxford University Press; C. Thorne 1986 *The Far Eastern War: States and Societies 1941–45*, London: Counterpoint.

15 B. J. Kerkvliet 1977 *The Huk Rebellion: A Study of Peasant Revolt in the Philippines*, University of California Press.

16 The international relations are described in M. Yahuda 2004 *The International Politics of the Asia-Pacific*, 2nd edn, London: Routledge; the paradoxical economic impact is described in R. Stubbs 2005 *Rethinking Asia's Economic Miracle*, London: Palgrave.

17 The American Civil War was an industrial war, so too the Russo-Japanese War of 1904–05, and both recorded very high casualty rates.

18 S. Lindqvist 2002 *A History of Bombing*, London: Granta.

19 There is a particular inspiration for these lists. Norman Davies 1997 *Europe: A History*, London: Pimlico, entitles an annex 'Europe's Wars: A Selection' (p. 1,282) and makes a list. Philosophically, lists are poor social science (thus 'the emperor's list' of miscellaneous objects or Sai Shonagon's similar lists) but, after Davies, they make the point – there have been too many wars. The same can be done for East Asia; the list is long and a rough estimate of the war casualties is around 30 million; a rough estimate of famine/politics-related deaths in Maoist China is around 20 million (estimates here vary widely). This is information taken from web pages so it is only a guide. Information on Europe is given by Davies.

20 Two examples: it is clear reading J. Fenby 2005 *Generalissimo: Chiang Kai Shek and the China He Lost*, London: Free Press, and P. Short 1999 *Mao: A Life*, London: John Murray, that both Mao Zedong and Chiang Kai-Shek lived through a period of Chinese history marked by sustained violence. It marks

232 Notes

their biographies. Violence was familiar; it is clear that the dissolution of the British Empire in Southeast Asia was attended by much confusion. It is the period Lee Kuan Yew refers to when he berates younger Singaporeans for being soft. Again the period was highly fluid.

21 T. Hasegawa 2005 *Racing the Enemy: Stalin, Truman and the Surrender of Japan*, Harvard University Press.
22 P. Buckley Ebrey 1996, pp. 262 et seq.
23 B. Moore 1966 *Social Origins of Dictatorship and Democracy*, Boston: Beacon, p. 181.
24 E. Moise 1994 *Modern China: A History*, London: Longman.
25 Moise 1994, ch. 3.
26 Fenby 2005.
27 Short 1999.
28 Short 1999.
29 A revolt by subordinates obliges Chiang to abort a sixth encirclement campaign: the Xian incident of December 1936. See Short 1999, pp. 345–50.
30 J. Hunter 1989 *The Emergence of Modern Japan*, London: Longman.
31 S. Tanaka 1993 *Japan's Orient: Rendering Pasts into History*, University of California Press.
32 M. Borthwick 1992 *Pacific Century: The Emergence of Modern Pacific Asia*, Boulder, CO: Westview, ch. 1.
33 The peace accord between China and Japan was made with the Treaty of Shimonoseki. Japan received an indemnity and acquired Taiwan and areas of influence in Korea and Manchuria. However Russia, Germany and France then intervened diplomatically and the Japanese government was obliged to relinquish its gains in Manchuria. This caused public dismay in Japan. The government's reaction was to reaffirm the ideas of 'strong economy, strong army' and to increase armaments spending the better to resist any future impositions. The Anglo-Japanese Treaty was signed in 1902 and this signalled the Japanese government's preference for involvement with the British and US notions of the Open Door in respect of China trade such that all were to have access.
34 P. W. Preston 2000 *Understanding Modern Japan: A Political Economy of Development, Culture and Global Power*, London: Sage, chs 3 and 4.
35 Borthwick 1992, ch. 4.
36 Borthwick 1992, ch. 4.
37 W. G. Beasley 1990 *The Rise of Modern Japan*, Tokyo: Tutle, ch. 11.
38 Preston 2000, ch. 4.
39 E. Wilkinson 1991 *Misunderstanding: Europe versus Japan*, Harmondsworth: Penguin.
40 Iriye 1997.
41 J. Hunter 1989 *The Emergence of Modern Japan*, London: Longman, argues that the hitherto key powers in East Asia – China, Korea and Japan – were all weak at this point in time.
42 Tanaka 1993.
43 On the fall of Hong Kong, see P. Snow 2003 *The Fall of Hong Kong: Britain, China and the Japanese Occupation*, Yale University Press.
44 Iriye 1987 and Beasley 1990 both note that Tokyo had less than full control over the army in China and that the army seems to have had little clear idea about its strategy.
45 Iriye 1987.
46 Iriye 1987, ch. 5.
47 N. Tarling 2001 *A Sudden Rampage: The Japanese Occupation of Southeast Asia 1941–45*, Singapore: Horizon Books; Bayly and Harper 2004.
48 C. Baker and P. Phongpaichit 2005 *A History of Thailand*, Cambridge University Press, ch. 5.

49 Bayly and Harper 2004 record that the Japanese stopped on the borders of India only as a result of running out of men/supplies. They suggest that had they continued British India might have collapsed. Local nationalists were active and wanted independence.
50 The damage and deaths were extensive: see R. Bowring and P. Kornicki (eds) 1993 *The Cambridge Encyclopaedia of Japan*, Cambridge University Press, pp. 95–104; on the bombing, see Cummings 1999, ch. 2.
51 Hasegawa 2005
52 J. Dower 1999 *Embracing Defeat: Japan in the Aftermath of World War II*, London: Allen Lane.
53 C. Thorne 1986 *The Far Eastern War*, London: Counterpoint.
54 C. Thorne 1978 *Allies of a Kind*, Oxford University Press.
55 For general reviews of the experiences of Southeast Asia, see J. Pluvier 1977 *Southeast Asia From Colonialism to Independence*, Oxford University Press; B. N. Pandy 1980 *South and Southeast Asia 1945–1979: Problems and Policies*, London: Macmillan; M. Osborne 1995 *Southeast Asia: An Introductory History*, St Leonards: Allen and Unwin.
56 Bayly and Harper 2004.
57 Chin Peng 2003 *My Side of History*, Singapore: Media Masters.
58 Kerkvliet 1977.
59 W. J. Duiker 1995 *Vietnam: Revolution in Transition*, Boulder, CO: Westview.
60 Snow 2003.
61 The cold war was confected in America. Action and inevitable reaction generated the division of the global system into competing blocs; see G. Kolko 1968 *The Politics of War: US Foreign Policy 1943–45*, New York: Vintage.
62 R. C. Thompson 1994 *The Pacific Basin since 1945*, London: Longman; Fenby 2005.
63 See P. W. Preston 1998a *Pacific Asia in the Global System*, Oxford: Blackwell, ch. 5.
64 The republic of Korea (ROK) was established on 15 August 1948; the Democratic People's Republic of Korea (DPRK) on 25 August 1948.
65 B. Cummings 1997 *Korea's Place in the Sun*, New York: Norton.
66 A general overview is given by Fred Halliday 1989 *Cold War Third World*, London: Radius.
67 Overview is given by Duiker 1995.
68 Baker and Phongpaichit 2005.
69 The sequence mirrors the experience of Europe; general crisis unfolded over the period 1914–45; partial resolution was accomplished; the final step was not taken until the events of 1989–91; the current situation revolves around the uneven dynamics of the project of European unification.
70 G. G. Gong (ed.) 2001 *Memory and History in East and Southeast Asia*, Washington, DC: Centre for Strategic and International Studies.
71 Two examples: in Japan, the debates between nationalists and leftists; in China, the exchange between official truths – century of humiliation, Japanese wickedness, etc. – and independent debate, about the Pacific War or Mao for example.
72 There are national pasts, there are sharp public disagreements, there seem to be only occasional ad hoc attempts by scholars or activists or peace campaigners to seek broad understanding of the common history. Europeans and Americans are implicated; for the former the issues are remote (one might say that Europeans disappeared from East Asia in 1945), whilst for the later it is still awkward (witness the Smithsonian row). In this matter the European experience is more optimistic. Post-nationalism allows official truths to be revisited (even if slowly).
73 P. W. Preston 1997 *Political-Cultural Identity: Citizens and Nations in a Global Era*, London: Sage.

234 *Notes*

74 The principal empire considered in this text with its focus on Singapore and Hong Kong is the British Empire, but there were in total four major extra-regional foreign players – France, the Netherlands, the USA and Britain.
75 For example 1930s Shanghai – 'Paris of the East'.
76 Fenby 2005.
77 Ian Buruma 1994 *Wages of Guilt*, London: Jonathan Cape.
78 Cummings 1999.
79 This happened quickly. Formal colonial rule was brief. The British conquered the Indian princely states by around 1800; the Mutiny took place in 1857; Congress was founded in 1885; in 1949 they were gone. The Dutch conquest of Aceh ran on until the early twentieth century and by 1948 they were gone. American conquest of Philippines took place in 1900 and by 1945 they were gone. French invasions of Vietnam took until late nineteenth century and by 1954 they were gone.
80 See Barraclough (1967) for an argument on India.
81 A term taken from Arno Mayer (A. Mayer 1988 *Why Did the Heavens Not Darken*, New York: Pantheon, p. 18); the term was originally used by Hugh Trevor-Roper 1959 'The General Crisis of the Seventeenth Century', *Past and Present* 16 and characterized the collapse of economic, social and political order in the seventeenth century attendant upon the emergent power of the modern state in conflict with the extant dispersed landed powers, part of the shift to the modern world. It was accepted by Eric Hobsbawm, who stressed the economic and social rather more than the political. The notion is also available from Antonio Gramsci, denoting the collapse into confusion of a pattern of life as the state loses its hegemonic power and authority (A. Gramsci 1973 *Selections from the Prison Notebooks* (edited and translated by Quintin Hoare and Geoffrey Nowell Smith), London: Lawrence and Wishart, pt 11.2.
82 Presented thus it seems smooth. It was not: the violence was extensive, the resolution contested; there were subsequent wars in Indo-China; there are hangover problems in North Korea and Beijing/Taipei; there are low-level conflicts in other parts of the region. All these are comparatively minor. The region is at peace; its elites are wedded to national development.
83 Carroll 2005.
84 Tsang 2004, ch. 13: in 1967 there were Maoist riots, bombs and the population supported the Hong Kong colonial government. This was the key to the 'rise of Hong Kongers'.
85 Hong Kong was returned in the absence of the consent of the population not to the state from which it had been extracted but to its radically different successor state.
86 Hong Kong has been part of the modern world for over 150 years, whereas China is in major respects still a third world country.

5 New trajectories

1 For an example, see I. Miao 2004 *A Social Constructivist Approach to the Sovereignty of the Republic of China on Taiwan*, PhD, University of Birmingham.
2 P. W. Preston 2000 *Understanding Modern Japan: A Political Economy of Development, Culture and Global Power*, London: Sage, ch. 5; see also John Dower 1999 *Embracing Defeat: Japan in the Aftermath of World War II*, London: Allen Lane.
3 Comments here derived from B. Moore 1966 *The Social Origins of Dictatorship and Democracy*, Boston: Beacon Press; C. Johnson 1995 *Japan: Who Governs?*, New York: Norton; K. Sheridan 1993 *Governing the Japanese Economy*, Cambridge: Polity; P. Katzenstein and T. Shiraishi (eds) 1997 *Network Power: Japan*

and Asia, Cornell University Press; R. Bowring and P. Kornicki (eds) 1993 *The Cambridge Encyclopaedia of Japan*, Cambridge University Press; W. G. Beasley 1990 *The Rise of Modern Japan*, Tokyo: Tutle; K. Henshall 1999 *A History of Japan*, London: Macmillan; A. Waswo 1996 *Modern Japanese Society*, Oxford: Opus; G. Hook et al. 2001 *Japan's International Relations*, London: Routledge.
4 Dower 1999.
5 R. Stubbs 2005 *Rethinking Asia's Economic Miracle: The Political Economy of War, Prosperity and Crisis*, London: Palgrave, ch. 3.
6 C. Johnson 1982 *MITI and the Japanese Miracle*, Stanford University Press; Johnson 1995.
7 Some have focused on the role of politics. The iron triangle links bureaucracy, business and politicians, and they adopt responsibility for the family of Japanese people, who in turn affirm the ideal of harmony. The nature of the state is debated, along with the power of the various elements; the ministries are powerful and independent minded; there are numerous parties (communist, socialist, liberal and those associated with religious groups); and ministries and parties link up with business. Some have argued that the key to the developmental state was the Ministry of International Trade and Industry (MITI). The state machinery has been the vehicle for an alliance of elite bureaucrats, elite politicians and elite business. The key organization was MITI and the country was mobilized for rational pursuit of economic growth.
8 Some have focused on the nature of firms and the market. A dual economy has developed, which has allowed competitive international companies to thrive and an inclusive domestic economy to prosper. First, there are the conglomerates (keiretsu), a network of related companies that support each other, each company as family, with flat hierarchies, mission statements, continual improvement and just-in-time production; the conglomerate sector includes big name companies, as well as construction companies which are notorious for money politics, are influential and a vehicle for state Keynesian-style development. Second, there is a high-quality small-family-firm sector, which includes suppliers to the big companies, with long-term relationships; it also includes a large retail sector with many small family-run shops; it is heavily protected from open competition by the local authorities; the small-firm sector also includes farms, which are small and heavily protected, with prices much higher than the world market, as the small-firm sector creates employment.
9 Some have focused on the nature of society, arguing that religion/culture fosters harmony and obedience; thus the 'Confucian work ethic' mirrors the Western 'Protestant work ethic'. There is an indigenous literature – *Nihonjinron* – that celebrates the racial/ethnic specialness of the Japanese. However, the relationship between culture and economic activity is interesting but difficult: the relationship is not causal. Culture shapes understandings and interests. If agents must read and react to structural change, then they read and react in terms of the ideas available to them, the ideas passed down in tradition and reinforced and amended in practice; in other words, ideas count, but how they count depends on local circumstances.
10 B. Cummings 1997 *Korea's Place in the Sun*, London: Norton.
11 A. Acharya 2000 *The Quest for Identity: International Relations of Southeast Asia*, Oxford University Press.
12 W. Case 2002 *Politics in Southeast Asia*, London: RoutledgeCurzon, considers the elite fractions which jostled for power in these new states; development patterns were in part the out-turn of these labyrinthine struggles. Analysed in Case's distinctly Western-centric terms, Southeast Asia displays a series of regime types: Indonesia, pseudo-democracy; Singapore, stable semi-democracy; Malaysia, semi-democracy; Thailand, unconsolidated democracy; and the Philippines, stable low-quality democracy.

13 Acharya 2000.
14 Jonathan Rigg 1997 *Southeast Asia: The Human Landscape of Modernization and Development*, London: Routledge.
15 Acharya 2000.
16 An issue of regional definition – Myanmar was included so as to 'complete the project'. O. Rattanachot 2005 *Pressures for Change in ASEAN: Lessons from the Admission of Burma and the Economic Crisis*, PhD, University of Birmingham.
17 Dates on which countries joined ASEAN:
 - 1967 ASEAN5, Malaysia, Indonesia, Thailand, the Philippines, Singapore;
 - 1984 ASEAN6, plus Brunei;
 - 1995 ASEAN7, plus Vietnam;
 - 1997 ASEAN9, plus Laos and Myanmar;
 - 1999 ASEAN10, plus Cambodia.
18 Lists of comparative data can be compiled from, for example, World Bank's *World Development Report* or the United Nations Development Programme's *Human Development Report*; however, the quantitative lists seem to be of little analytical value and here qualitative work is preferable, but not just disconnected country studies (even where these are good). Acharya makes it clear that in Southeast Asia nation-state building was a matter of social relationships – elites within the region and elites within their territories – and the treatment here grants that these relationships underpinned events and tries to grasp the resultant outcome as a set.
19 This is a list-plus-characterization – it is a restrictedly useful intellectual strategy; like any list it serves to order reflection, not much more. The members can be grouped in terms of the nature of their emergence from colonialism: (1) mostly peaceful decolonization, plus a forgiving international situation coupled to a smooth pursuit of development; (2) conflict in decolonization, plus a problematical international situation coupled to an interrupted pursuit of development; and (3) relatively peaceful decolonization, plus a problematical international situation coupled to a confused pursuit of development.
20 Acharya 2000.
21 Case 2002.
22 Rigg 1997.
23 D. Held and A. McGrew 2002 *Globalization/Anti-Globalization*, Cambridge: Polity.
24 P. Hirst and G. Thompson 1996 *Globalization in Question*, Cambridge: Polity; A. Payne 2004 *The New Regional Politics of Development*, London: Palgrave.
25 Acharya 2000.
26 P. Short 1999 *Mao: A Life*, London: John Murray.
27 Deng Xiaoping, Jiang Zemin and Hu Jinta.
28 F. Christiansen and S. Rai 1996 *Chinese Politics and Society*, London: Prentice Hall, distinguish: (1) totalitarian – a system controlled by one ideologically motivated repressive party; (2) factionalism/clientism – elite control fissured by manoeuvring for position/advantage; (3) complex bureaucracy and state – the system is essentially bureaucratic, with power/decisions taken inside the system and handed down; (4) culturalist approach – appeals to the cultural resources of the Chinese, with the common practices of the Chinese, hierarchy and obedience ('Confucianism'); and (5) the idea of complex change – trajectories/phases, political system, exchange with modernity.
29 It may be that the project is also Beijing defined. This debate is ongoing; postcolonial reorganization is familiar but in other cases has been undertaken by a newly sovereign government, whereas this is not the case in Hong Kong, where the replacement elite must deal with Beijing.

Notes 237

30 C. George 2000 *Singapore: The Air Conditioned Nation*, Singapore: Landmark Books.
31 R. Stubbs 2005 *Rethinking Asia's Economic Miracle*, London: Palgrave.
32 More generally, see L. Weiss 1998 *The Myth of the Powerless State: Governing the Economy in a Global Era*, Cambridge: Polity.
33 Nationalism and memory – one way in which national identities are constituted is through memory, official and unofficial – and the issue of Imperial Japan's wars in East Asia remain. Critics argue that the Japanese elites and people have never fully appreciated the extent of the damage their wars caused in East Asia. It would seem these opinions are a mixture of genuine views and opportunistic nationalist posturing. However, the problem remains. In Japan there is a mixture of views. Nationalists take the view that the Japanese state has wars, Japan had a war and it happened to lose it (along with territory). The nationalists cannot see what there is to apologize for and they would like their territory back, please. Members of the peace movement, which is extensive in Japan, focus on the atomic bombing of Hiroshima and Nagasaki. They take the view that Japan was both an aggressor and a unique victim and say that it is peace which should be stressed. The political elite and the people plot a middle way: yes, the war was bad, but Japan has apologized and helped its neighbours rebuild. It is easy to see why most people would like to get on with their lives. Most Japanese were born long after the Pacific War ended. The generation that followed the war have worked hard to rebuild Japan; the younger generations have only known the modern rich consumer Japan.
34 Miao 2004.

6 Locating Singapore

1 An earlier version of the argument presented here, one with rather different preoccupations, was offered in P. W. Preston 1994 *Discourses of Development: State, Market and Polity in the Analysis of Complex Change*, Aldershot: Avebury, and some of the materials of that text have been taken and reworked here.
2 Amitav Acharya 2000 *The Quest for Identity: International Relations of Southeast Asia*, Oxford University Press.
3 The island's orientation is thus outward – the domestic sphere is either a product of this outward role (the ordinary domestic lives of those who lived and worked there) or a residue of earlier roles (the fishermen or agriculturalists, slowly displaced). This view cuts across the received view which reads history via the frame of nation-statehood and finds a coherent bounded unit – it wasn't: it was not coherent (many agents) and was not bounded (a nexus).
4 Linda Low 2001 'The Singapore Developmental State in the New Economy and Polity', *Pacific Review* 14.3.
5 There have been costs; for a sharp critique, see C. Tremewan 1994 *The Political Economy of Social Control in Singapore*, London: Macmillan.
6 E. Gellner 1983 *Nations and Nationalism*, Cambridge University Press; B. Anderson 1983 *Imagined Communities*, London: Verso.
7 D. J. M. Tate 1971/79 *The Making of Southeast Asia*, Oxford University Press; J. M. Pluvier 1977 *Southeast Asia from Colonialism to Independence*, Oxford University Press.
8 Acharya 2000.
9 P. W. Preston 1998a *Pacific Asia in the Global System*, Oxford: Blackwell, pp. 55–57, 73–74.
10 M. Turnbull 1977 *A History of Singapore 1819–1975*, Oxford University Press, pp. 1–13.
11 Lee Poh Ping 1978 *Chinese Society in Nineteenth Century Singapore*, Oxford University Press.

12 C. Trocki 1979 *Prince of Pirates: The Temmenggongs and the Development of Johor and Singapore 1784–1885*, p. xv.
13 Trocki argues that the 'Riau entrepot of 1784 was but the last in a succession of similar "urban" centres whose history stretches back to Srivijaya in the seventh century' (Trocki 1979, p. xv).
14 Trocki remarks: 'Power in this context was always sea power. Thus traditional political systems emphasized the control of a majority of sea peoples and the management of the trade. ... The traditional Malay maritime state was always a fragile entity. Its lines of control were the sea routes and its authority was strung out from island to island and from one river mouth to another' (Trocki 1979, p. xvii).
15 N. Tarling 1962 *Anglo-Dutch Rivalry in the Malay World 1780–1842*, Cambridge University Press.
16 Trocki 1979.
17 Johor in southern Malaya was virtually unpopulated except for Chinese gambier producers – part of a wider Chinese agricultural network; see Lee 1978.
18 C. Trocki 1990 *Opium and Empire: Chinese Society in Colonial Singapore 1800–1910*, Cornell University Press.
19 On this business generally, we can recall: (1) that eighteenth-century mercantile capitalism was trading-block minded and there was routine competition for access and control of areas within which trading patterns might be ordered; (2) that in this part of the world there were three major areas of concern, Indian trade, spice trade and China trade; and (3) that in Southeast Asia there was routine conflict between the British and Dutch for trade advantage, that is, wars and exchanges of territories, which manoeuvring routinely involved the indigenous powers. See H. Furber 1976 *Rival Empires of Trade in the Orient 1600–1800*, University of Minnesota Press.
20 Raffles is usually presented as the key but it is likely that Farquhar contacted the Temmengong on an earlier visit; see C. H. Wake 1975 'Raffles and the Rajas', *Journal of the Malaysian Branch of the Royal Asiatic Society*. Wake also makes the suggestion in respect of British/Malay 'condominium'.
21 See Tarling 1962; N. Tarling 1975 *Imperial Britain in Southeast Asia*, Kuala Lumpur: Oxford University Press.
22 Trocki (1979) argues the early success was precisely because the settlement was a traditional style trade port – i.e. it looked like another Malay maritime empire.
23 Trocki 1979. Agreeing an end to the practice of seeing tribute from passing ships, the British called it piracy and it was suppressed in 1835 in a brief gunboat campaign.
24 Trocki 1979. The Temmengong's move into Johor followed Chinese agriculturalists who had been displaced from Singapore island.
25 Lee 1978; critically reviewed by Wong Lin Ken 1980 'Review Article: The Chinese in Nineteenth Century Singapore', *Journal of Southeast Asian Studies*.
26 Lee 1978.
27 G. Woodcock 1969 *The British in the Far East*, London: Weidenfeld and Nicholson; Woodcock mentions traders, seafarers, soldiers, administrators, miscellaneous adventurers, later on planters and missionaries. See also K. C. Tregonning 1965 *The British in Malaya: The First Forty Years 1786–1826*, University of Arizona Press.
28 Lee 1978, p. 26.
29 Trocki 1990.
30 Thus 1858 saw the end of the EIC and the transfer of the official government of Singapore to London. In 1867 Crown Colony status was established. In 1874 we had the Pangkor Engagement, which conventionally marked the move of the British into the peninsula.

31 Lee 1978.
32 Trocki 1979; for an interpretive comparison, see the established text from Turnbull 1977.
33 Sometimes tagged the 'second industrial revolution' – machines plus science plus rising populations plus popular consumption, plus, for Singapore, the opening of the Suez Canal in 1869; see W. G. Huff 1994 *The Economic Growth of Singapore: Trade and Development in the Twentieth Century*, Cambridge University Press.
34 P. Regnier 1992 *Singapore: City State in Southeast Asia*, Kuala Lumpur: Abdul Majeed, pp. 17–20;.
35 Turnbull 1977, pp. 86–90.
36 J. F. Warren 1984 'Living on the Razor's Edge', *Bulletin of Concerned Asian Scholars* 16.4; the fuller treatment is in J. F. Warren 1986 *Rickshaw Coolie: A People's History of Singapore 1880–1940*, Oxford University Press.
37 On the collapse, see Christopher Bayly and Tim Harper 2004 *Forgotten Armies: The Fall of British Asia 1941–1945*, London: Allen Lane; see also N. Tarling 1993 *The Fall of Imperial Britain in South-East Asia*, Oxford University Press.
38 Malayan Union; Federation of Malaya – see Turnbull 1977.
39 Contrariwise, for the newly established Malaysia, continuing dominance by Singapore would have meant an economic pattern that carried with it a significant measure of Chinese primacy.
40 Regnier 1992, pp. 52–61: the period 1965–67, when hostility from neighbours called into question the viability of an independent state; 1967–79, when accelerated outward-directed industrialization succeeded; 1979–81, when the state attempted to shift the economy into a higher-value-added posture; 1985–86, when there was recession, and the aggressive response thereto; and from 1987, when the pursuit of high-tech industry, the status of regional service centre, and the shifting of low-wage production into the surrounding areas have continued.
41 Anderson 1983.
42 For an exposition of the official position, see M. Leifer 2000 *Singapore's Foreign Policy: Coping with Vulnerability*, London: Routledge.
43 In securing independence these political battles were ostensibly against the British but the detail reveals a more tangled situation. Crucially the British were leaving anyway, and through the late 1940s and early 1950s the only issue was how and to whom would power be bequeathed. It was quickly made clear that those communist members of the anti-Japanese resistance were not going to inherit power, and the resultant Malayan Emergency fixed this decision in place. General notions of federation, which seem to have been popular with the British, were discussed and latent Malay nationalism awakened. After a period of confusion as to the nature of constitutional arrangements, Malaysian independence with Malay rights entrenched came in August 1957. Singapore independence was more problematical – multiple local voices contended – Lee Kuan Yew and the core of the PAP were English-educated professionals and were discreetly supported by the British.
44 Lee Kuan Yew forged an alliance with left-wing trades unions and Chinese students; seemingly regarded with fear by the local establishment, the PAP achieved internal self-government in 1959 with their indigenized programme of social democracy; and thereafter securing the hegemony of the PAP was a similarly complex and drawn-out matter; in the run-up to the 1959 election the PAP fought against other pro-independence parties and they distinguished themselves by making a successful alliance with the left-wing unions and Chinese students.
45 After securing internal power there was a confused interval which involved two areas of manoeuvre: the Malaysian Federation issue and the PAP's struggle with

its erstwhile allies, the unions and students; the battle against the left unions and students, which had taken institutional form with the establishment in 1962 of Barisan Socialis, was tilted firmly in the direction of the PAP by the expedient of Operation Cold Store and the detention of some one hundred political opponents; the union with Malaysia lasted from September 1963 to August 1965 and PAP hegemony was established.

46 Goh Keng Swee's growth policies involved fiscal incentives and infrastructural development, and after independence there was a shift from ISI to EOI strategies so as to address the problems of withdrawal from Malaysia, Singapore's established trade area; see Lam Peng Er and Kevin Y. L. Tan (eds) 1999 *Lee's Lieutenants: Singapore's Old Guard*, St Leonards: Allen and Unwin.

47 P. Chen 1983 *Singapore: Development Policies and Trends*, Oxford University Press.

48 Chan Heng Chee and H. D. Evers, 'National Identity and Nation Building in Singapore', in P. Chen and H. D. Evers (eds) 1978 *Studies in ASEAN Sociology*, Singapore: Chopmen.

49 Chua Beng Huat 1995 *Communitarian Ideology and Democracy in Singapore*, London: Routledge.

50 N. Heyzer, 'International Production and Social Change: An Analysis of State, Employment and Trade Unions in Singapore', in Chen 1983; see also F. Deyo 1981 *Dependent Development and Industrial Order*, New York: Praeger.

51 Regnier 1992.

52 Schools, hospitals, leisure facilities and in particular housing – see Chua Beng Huat 1997 *Political Legitimacy and Housing: Stakeholding in Singapore*, London: Routledge.

53 Lam and Tan 1999; M. D. Barr 2000a *Lee Kuan Yew: The Beliefs Behind the Man*, London: Curzon. Most of these leaders had made their 'colonial pilgrimages' to the United Kingdom in the years immediately after the Pacific War.

54 Lam and Tan 1999.

55 Some see a species of neo-colonial regime; see Tremewan 1994.

56 T. L. S. George 1973 *Lee Kuan Yew's Singapore*, London: Andre Deutsch, identifies Israel as the PAP model at independence, with a militarized and hierarchical state that used routine political repression; Leifer 2000.

57 M. G. Asher 1985 *Forced Savings to Finance Merit Goods*, Canberra: Australian National University. The provident fund has been reviewed recently; see Linda Low and Aw Tar Choon 2004 *Social Insecurity in the New Millennium: The Central Provident Fund in Singapore*, Singapore: Marshall Cavendish.

58 The tendency is inherent; see Alasdair MacIntyre 1985 *After Virtue: A Study in Moral Theory*, London: Duckworth, ch. 8.

59 See C. George 2000 *Singapore: The Air Conditioned Nation: Essays on the Politics of Comfort and Control 1990–2000*, Singapore: Landmark; A. Ghani et al. 2006 *Struck by Lightning: Singaporean Voices Post-1965*, Singapore: SNP Editions.

60 K. Sandhu and P. Wheatley (eds) 1989 *Management of Success*, Singapore: Institute of Southeast Asian Studies.

61 Heyzer, in Chen 1983.

62 Chan Heng Chee, 'The Political System and Political Change', in R. Hassan (ed.) 1976 *Singapore: Society in Transition*, Oxford University Press.

63 K. Yoshihara 1988 *The Rise of Ersatz Capitalism in Southeast Asia*, Oxford University Press.

64 G. Rodan 1989 *The Political Economy of Singapore's Industrialization*, London: Macmillan, p. xv.

65 H. Mirza 1986 *Multinationals and the Growth of the Singapore Economy*, London: Croom Helm.

66 C. Hamilton 1983 'Capitalist Industrialization in East Asia's Four Little Tigers', *Journal of Contemporary Asia* 13; the argument has been revisited by R. Stubbs 2005 *Rethinking Asia's Economic Miracle*, London: Palgrave.
67 See, for example, W. Bello and S. Rosenfeld 1990a *Dragons in Distress: Asia's Miracle Economies in Crisis*, Penguin: London.
68 See Stubbs 2005.
69 See R. H. McLeod and R. Garnaut (eds) 1998 *East Asia in Crisis: From Being and Miracle to Needing One?*, London, Routledge; F. Gibney 1998 *Unlocking the Bureaucrat's Kingdom: Deregulation and the Japanese Economy*, Washington, DC: Brookings Institute.
70 See W. R. Nester 1992 *Japan and the Third World*, New York: St Martins Press; W. R. Nester 1990 *Japan's Growing Power over East Asia and the World Economy: Ends and Means*, London: Macmillan.
71 R. Steven 1990 *Japan's New Imperialism*, London: Macmillan.
72 R. P. Cronin 1992 *Japan, the United States, and the Prospects for the Asia-Pacific Century: Three Scenarios for the Future*, Singapore: Institute for Southeast Asian Studies.
73 Debate focused on Japan in the 1980s but the golden recession plus the emergence of China plus renewed American anxieties have clouded the debate – the regional future of East Asia seems both inevitable and unclear; see A. Payne (ed.) 2004 *The New Regional Politics of Development*, London: Palgrave.
74 See, for example, R. M. Orr 1990 *The Emergence of Japan's Foreign Aid Power*, New York: Columbia University Press; A. Rix 1993 *Japan's Foreign Aid Challenge*, London: Routledge.
75 L. Thurow 1994 *Head to Head: The Coming Economic Battle Among Japan, Europe and America*, London: Nicholas Brearly.
76 There is a core group which deploys the machinery of the state: see A. Sampson 2004 *Who Runs this Place: An Anatomy of Britain in the 21st Century*, London: John Murray; M. Bevir and R. A. W. Rhodes 2003 *Interpreting British Governance*, London: Routledge; and R. Worthington 2003 *Governance in Singapore*, London: Routledge Curzon.
77 The official ideological rhetoric has shifted: at first, in opposition to colonialists, socialist; in power, social democratic in opposition to communists, leftists and ethnic communalists; thereafter slowly drifting into a more technocratic authoritarian stance – the familiar rhetoric of Lee Kuan Yew. A new rhetoric is emerging which bends the foregoing plus ideas of globalization, upgrading and creativity.
78 The informal extension of these official rhetorics has sought to create a widespread informal understanding amongst the citizenry in respect of the circumstances of Singapore and its consequent duties as citizens: hard work, obedience, discipline, upgrading, gratitude. On social control, see Tremewan 1994.
79 My list. Others would offer somewhat different lists; see Chua 1995; see also Lily Kong and Brenda S. A. Yeoh 2003 *The Politics of Landscapes in Singapore*, New York: Syracuse University Press, in particular ch. 3.
80 Leifer 2000 records the elite's views of Singapore as uniquely vulnerable. It informs their international diplomacy. It also informs their official domestic ideology, where the vulnerability is that of a Chinese city-state in a Malay world. It is a world read in realist terms (power) and offers a highly partial view of the territory's history and situation as the territory is in fact long established and deeply embedded in the region (see Acharya 2000). There is also the matter of the antagonistic diplomatic relations which (as Leifer makes clear) are routinely provoked by Singaporean elite hostility.
81 Heyzer, in Chen 1983.
82 G. Benjamin, 'The Cultural Logic of Singapore's Multi-Racialism', in Hassan 1976.

83 P. Berger and T. Luckman 1967 *The Social Construction of Reality*, Harmondsworth: Penguin, speak of machineries of universe maintenance; citizens must dwell within specified conceptual realms; discipline maintains such structures. See also A. MacInyre, 'A Mistake about Causality in Social Science', in P. Laslett and W. G. Runciman (eds) 1962 *Politics, Philosophy and Society Series Two*, Oxford: Blackwell; MacIntyre discusses Stalin's ideology and his show trials where dissidents confessed – thereby protecting the system; inside the ideological circle it all makes sense – sustaining the circle is crucial.
84 Chua Beng Huat 1983 'Reopening Ideological Discussion in Singapore', *Southeast Asian Journal of Social Science* 11. See also Chua Beng Huat 1985 'Pragmatism of the Peoples Action Party Government of Singapore: A Critical Assesment', *Southeast Asian Journal of Social Science* 13.2.
85 Chen 1983; see also Sandhu and Wheatley 1989; Rodan 1989; for an introductory survey in orthodox vein, see R. S. Milne and D. K. Mauzy 1990 *Singapore: The Legacy of Lee Kuan Yew*, London: Routledge.
86 P. W. Preston 1982 *Theories of Development*, London: Routledge; P. W. Preston 1985 *New Trends in Development Theory*, London: Routledge.
87 Early analysis included G. White (ed.) 1988 *Developmental States in East Asia*, London: Macmillan; and R. P. Appelbaum and J. Henderson (eds) 1992 *States and Development in the Asian Pacific Rim*, London: Sage. The debate is reviewed by S. Haggard 1990 *Pathways from the Periphery: The Politics of Growth in the Newly Industrialized Countries*, Cornell University Press.
88 A major study appeared in the early 1990s which endeavoured to reconcile liberal-market theory with the state-centred record of the NICs; see World Bank 1993 *The East Asian Miracle: Economic Growth and Public Policy*, Oxford University Press.
89 Bello and Rosenfeld 1990a.
90 Tun-jen Cheng and S. Haggard 1987 'Newly Industrializing Asia in Transition', in *Policy Papers in International Affairs 31*, Institute of International Studies, University of California Berkeley.
91 J. Halliday 1980 'Capitalism and Socialism in East Asia', *New Left Review* 124.
92 H. C. de Bettignies, 'NIE-Japanese Strategic Interdependence in the Pacific Basin', in M. Kulessa (ed.) 1990 *The Newly Industrializing Economies of Asia*, Berlin: Springer.
93 Johan Saravanamuttu 1988 'Japanese Economic Penetration in ASEAN in the Context of the International Division of Labour', *Journal of Contemporary Asia* 18.
94 T. Leuenberger, 'A World Scenario: The Emergence of Three Main Trading Zones', in Kulessa 1990.
95 Yoshihara 1988, p. 131.
96 Huang, Xiaming 2005 *The Rise and Fall of the East Asian Growth System, 1951–2000*, London: RoutledgeCurzon, reviews debates in ch. 1 – the 'post' indicates the author's view that the period of rapid economic growth is coming to an end as economies 'mature'.
97 Lim, C.Y.,'Singapore's Economic Development: Retrospect and Prospect', in Chen 1983, p. 100.
98 Lim, C.Y., 'The Transformation of Singapore in Twenty-Five Years: A Glimpse', in You, P. S. and Lim, C. Y. (eds) 1984 *Singapore: Twenty Five Years of Development*, Singapore: p. 6.
99 Lim, in You and Lim 1984, p. 9.
100 Republic of Singapore 1986 *Report of the Economic Committee: The Singapore Economy New Directions*, Singapore: Ministry of Trade and Industry.
101 Republic of Singapore 1986.
102 Regnier (1992, p. 59) reports that the budget of 1986 introduced reforms that were in line with those suggested by Lee's report.

103 Regnier 1992, pp. 60–61.
104 Seah C. M., 'Political Change and Continuity in Singapore', in You and Lim 1984, p. 249.
105 L. Lim 1983 'The Myth of the Free Market Economy', *Asian Survey* 23.
106 Lim 1983, pp. 754–57.
107 Lim 1983, pp. 758–61, argues that the rhetoric of markets does not fit with its record and when the economic consequences are spelled out it is not likely to figure in the country's future.
108 Lim 1983, p. 762.
109 H. C. Rieger and W. Veit, 'State Intervention, State Involvement and Market Forces: Singapore and South Korea', in Kulessa 1990, p. 156.
110 P. W. Preston 1996 *Development Theory*, Oxford: Blackwell.
111 D. C. O'Brien 1972 'Modernization, Order and the Erosion of the Democratic Ideal', *Journal of Development Studies* 8.4.
112 F. Halliday 1989 *Cold War, Third World*, London: Hutchison Radius.
113 R. Higgot and R. Robison (eds) 1985 *South East Asia: Essays in the Political Economy of Structural Change*, London: Routledge.
114 R. Robison *et al.* (eds) 1987 *South East Asia in the 1980s: The Politics of Economic Crisis*, St Leonards: Allen and Unwin, p. 17.
115 Best exemplified in W. W. Rostow 1960 *The Stages of Economic Growth: A Non-Communist Manifesto*, Cambridge University Press.
116 Higgot and Robison 1985; see also Robison *et al.* 1987.
117 The general crises in Europe and East Asia dominated their respective twentieth centuries. Lee Kuan Yew is correct to start his reflections with a note on the poor condition of the island and its environment; Lee, K. Y. 2000 *From Third World to First World: The Singapore Story 1965–2000*, New York: Harper Collins.
118 M. Castells 1988 'The Developmental City State in an Open World Economy: The Singapore Experience', in *Berkeley Roundtable on International Economy Paper* 31, p. 39.
119 Castells 1988, p. 28.
120 D. J. Gayle 1988 'Singaporean Market Socialism: Some Implications for Development Theory', *International Journal of Social Economics* 15, p. 60.
121 J. Wong 1979 *The ASEAN Economies in Perspective*, London: Macmillan, p. 121.
122 Castells 1988, p. 74.
123 Castells 1988, p. 75.
124 Chan, in Hassan 1976.
125 Sandhu and Wheatley 1989; Chan, H. C., 'Politics in an administrative state', in Seah, C. M. (ed.) 1975 *Trends in Singapore*, Singapore: Institute of Southeast Asian Studies; Chen and Evers 1978.
126 Yoshihara 1988, pp. 115–17.
127 Rodan 1989, p. xv.
128 Rodan 1989, pp. 207–12.
129 G. Rodan, 'Industrialization and the Singapore State', in Higgot and Robison 1985.
130 G. Rodan, 'The Rise and Fall of Singapore's Second Industrial Revolution', in R. Robison *et al.* (eds) 1987 *Southeast Asia in the 1980s: The Politics of Economic Crisis*, Sydney: Allen and Unwin.
131 Mirza 1986.
132 W. Case 2002 *Politics in Southeast Asia*, London: RoutledgeCurzon.
133 Max Weber and Joseph Schumpeter are usually cited; see D. Held 1987 *Models of Democracy*, Cambridge: Polity.
134 Wilfredo Pareto, Gaetanao Mosca and Robert Michels; the 'new Machievellians' – see H. S. Hughes 1979 *Consciousness and Society: The Reorientation of European Social Thought 1890–1930*, Brighton: Harvester, ch. 7.

244 Notes

135 Contemporary democratic elite theory begins with the work on democratic transitions in Latin America; for commentary, see D. Rueschemeyer *et al.* 1992 *Capitalist Development and Democracy*, Cambridge: Polity.
136 Case 2002, ch. 3.
137 Worthington 2003.
138 J. L. Margolin, 'Foreign Models in Singapore's Development and the Idea of a Singaporean Model', in G. Rodan (ed.) 1993 *Singapore Changes Guard: Social, Political and Economic Directions in the 1990s*, Melbourne: Longmans. Other models could be added – Sweden in defence – but the point about borrowing is correct; the Singaporean elite still do it, now seemingly looking to the USA.
139 An available characterization of Japan; see C. Johnson 1995 *Japan: Who Governs?*, New York: Norton.
140 An idea I take from Patrick Wright 1985 *On Living in An Old Country*, London: Verso. It designates the official/hegemonic version of the history of a polity, the history that encapsulates the official/hegemonic claims about the essence of the people and polity; it is an ideological construct through and through.
141 J. Minchin 1990 *No Man Is an Island: A Portrait of Singapore's Lee Kuan Yew*, 2nd edn, Sydney: Allen and Unwin; Barr 2000a; and there are many others, hagiographic and critical.
142 Lam and Tan 1999.
143 Worthington 2003.
144 Lam and Tan 1999.
145 It is invoked in the title of Lee's autobiography – Lee Kuan Yew 2000 *From Third World to First: The Singapore Story 1965–2000*, New York: HarperCollins – but Singapore was never part of the third world; it was never underdeveloped and it was in 1818 part of the Malay Johor–Riau Sultanate and thereafter lodged variously within the modern world.
146 Preston 1996.
147 On the role of Lee Kuan Yew, see Barr 2000a; on the first-generation leaders, see Lam and Tan 1999.
148 On the role of the Singapore river as a port plus the various phases of its development, see S. Dobbs 2003 *The Singapore River: A Social History 1819–2002*, Singapore University Press.
149 Stubbs 2005.
150 Barr 2000a, ch. 2.
151 An overview of the political changes is given in Turnbull 1977, ch. 7; a flavour of the intense politics of the period are given in A. Lau 1998 *A Moment of Anguish: Singapore in Malaysia and the Politics of Disengagement*, Singapore: Times Academic Press; the early years are dealt with extensively in Lee, K. Y. 1998 *The Singapore Story: Memoirs of Lee Kuan Yew*, Singapore: Prentice Hall.
152 In Europe the general crisis of 1914–45 killed around 60 million and left the continent occupied, divided and ruined. In East Asia, the general crisis of 1911–75 caused similar problems and produced similar casualty figures. That Singapore was dilapidated in 1945 is unremarkable.
153 Barr (2000a, ch. 9) also adds that the whole edifice is psychologically grounded in a privileged elite conceit; the psychological characterization is recognizable, but it misleads; Lee's psychology is a minor matter in any elucidation of the historical development trajectory of Singapore. Barr notes a debt to James Michin, whose work has also considered Lee's psychology (see Minchin 1990). It might be noted that there are a multiplicity of books which work this same vein of speculation-cum-analysis – Minchin offers a list of titles in his introduction.
154 Barr 2000a, ch. 2.
155 Contrasting tales come from Minchin 1990, ch. 6; J. Drysdale 1984 *Singapore: Struggle for Success*, Singapore: Times, ch. 32; on the entire episode, see Lau 1998.

156 Barr (2000a, pp. 31, 75) mentions early elite figures recalling that Lee was advised not to attack the Malaysian elite but when confronted by a microphone and audience lost his self-control.
157 Barr 2000a, p. 31.
158 Barr 2000a, chs 3, 4 and 5.
159 In a later paper Barr amends his position – element three of the Lee Kuan Yew position is cited as 'racial essentialism'; see M. D. Barr 2003 'Perpetual Revisionism in Singapore: The Limits of Change', *Pacific Review* 16.1, p. 87.
160 Once in power, Lee Kuan Yew could assert that talent was the key to success – meritocracy – whilst defining what counted as talent and in practice advancement has required both talent and connections. These matters are pursued by M. D. Barr 2006 'Beyond Technocracy: The Culture of Elite Governance in Lee Hsien Leong's Singapore', *Asian Studies Review* 30.
161 Barr (2000a, ch. 2) sketches a familiar family dynamic – downward class mobility recovered through children.
162 Barr 2000a, ch. 2.
163 Huff (1994) makes it clear that from the turn of the twentieth century onwards Singapore was a major trading port firmly lodged within the global trading system and Singapore was one of the richest territories in Southeast Asia. The economy advanced up until the Imperial Japanese invasion; the PAP inherited a rich well-connected city.
164 Stubbs (2005) points to the 'long boom' plus a series of local American wars which entailed large financial expenditures in the region.
165 T. Nairn 1988 *The Enchanted Glass*, London: Hutchinson Radius; the notion of an ideological capstone comes from Nairn. Elizabeth II and the monarchy generally act as an ideological capstone of the residual British system: she/they exemplify an official nationalism; she/they exemplify an ideal form of life; she/they instance an official historical continuity; she/they represent an essentially oligarchic liberal (that is, non-democratic) institutional political apparatus (British state) within the popular public realm (she/they misdirect and disarm critics).
166 Summary taken from Chua 1995; Worthington 2003; Koh 2004; Mahizhnan 2005.
167 Chua 1995, pp. 187–89.
168 Worthington 2003, p. 40.
169 A European example might be General Franco, who was a key figure in the recent history of Spain; he was long lived, long serving, and tolerated by other European nation-state elites; tolerated by the mass of the population (Spain was a popular holiday destination) but reviled by most European intellectual elites. General Franco and Francoist Spain became an anachronism but Spain did not change; Franco's presence sustained the system. King Juan Carlos was groomed to ensure continuity; however, the Francoist system dissolved away after the general's death; a sophisticated country emerged quickly and joined mainstream Europe. See P. Anderson 1992 *English Questions*, London: Verso, ch. 6; W. Nicoll and T. C. Salmon 2001 *Understanding the European Union*, London: Longman, ch. 16.
170 Chan Heng Chee, 'Democracy: Evolution and Implementation. An Asian Perspective', in R. Bartley *et al.* 1993 *Democracy and Capitalism: Asian and American Perspectives*, Singapore: Institute of Southeast Asian Studies.
171 See American theoretical ideas of 'waves of democracy' or 'electoral democracy' or 'market democracy' or the indices of democracy produced by organizations such as the Heritage Foundation.
172 Chua 1995, ch. 1.
173 Kong and Yeoh 2003; see ch. 3.
174 Chua 1995.

175 Chua 1995, ch. 7.
176 Chua 1995.
177 Chua 1995, p. 187.
178 Chua 1995, p. 192.
179 Chua 1995, p. 201.
180 Thus nominated MPS, an elected presidency and GRCs insofar as they protect minority representation.
181 Chua 1995, ch. 8.
182 See Alan Chong 2004 'Singaporean Foreign Policy and the Asian Values Debate, 1992–2000: Reflections on an Experiment in Soft Power', *Pacific Review* 17.1; see also M. D. Barr 2000b 'Lee Kuan Yew and the Asian Values Debate' *Asian Studies Review* 24.3.
183 This aspect is celebrated by Low 2001.
184 Francis Fukuyama 1992 *The End of History and the Last Man*, London: Hamish Hamilton.
185 Notably in World Bank 1993.
186 See, for example, the journals *Foreign Affairs* and the *Economist*.
187 S. Ishihara 1991 *The Japan that Can Say No*, New York: Simon and Shuster.
188 In many speeches; see also Mohamad Mahathir and Shintaro Ishihara 1995 *The Voice of Asia: Two Leaders Discuss the Coming Century*, Tokyo: Kodansha.
189 Chua 1995, ch. 7, suggests the idea has a root in post-1960s American neo-conservatism: they looked to East Asia and saw order, attributed it to Confucianism and the idea then migrated back across the Pacific.
190 The debate was sharpened in the 1997 Asian financial crisis. More than a few American and European commentators were happy to be proved – as they saw it – correct in their criticisms of East Asian development models; see P. W. Preston 1998b 'Reading the Asian Crisis: History, Culture and Institutional Truths', *Contemporary Southeast Asia*, December.
191 Chua 1995, chs 7 and 9.
192 P. W. Preston 1998a; see part IV.
193 In respect of Singapore, see C. J. W. L. Lee 2000 'Capitalism and Ethnicity: Creating Local Culture in Singapore', *Inter Asia Cultural Studies* 1.1.
194 Against current popular and superficial usage of the notion of democracy, which points to liberal markets and electoral parliamentary systems, the point, to labour it, is that there are discrete traditions in political philosophy and practice. David Held gets this nicely – models (Held 1987). Thus (1) liberalism – which argues that the world is comprised of discrete individuals whose aggregate actions contractually constitute society ordered by the invisible hand of the marketplace plus the moral imperatives of tradition, and which may be understood only to a very limited extent; thus (2) democracy – which insists on the inevitably social nature of human life and on the necessity of collective wellbeing for individual wellbeing, such wellbeing being secured via the collective political actions of actors knowledgeable about an extensively intelligible social world; thus (3) liberal democracy – which attempts to compromise between these two positions such that the state, the agent which deploys the extensive but imperfect knowledge available, secures both a minimum collective provision and the framework for individual actions; thus (4) social democracy – which acknowledges the social nature of human life, insists that social life can be understood extensively, and proposes that a technically competent elite should secure and deploy such understanding; thus (5) communitarian democracy – which looks to the interests of the social totality and the flourishing of those who are members.
195 See Central Executive Committee, People's Action Party 1979 *People's Action Party 1954–79*, Singapore: People's Action Party; see also Pang Eng Fong, 'The Distinctive Features of Two City States: Hong Kong and Singapore', in P. L.

Berger and H. M. Hsiao (eds) 1988 *In Search of an Asian Development Model*, New Brunswick, NJ: Transaction, where the inspiration of the PAP is referenced back to Fabian socialism (p. 227) and is taken to have subsequently become centred on the managerialist pursuit of economic growth (p. 230); see also Barr 2000a.
196 Fong Sip Chee (1980) *The PAP Story – The Pioneering Years*, Singapore: Times Periodicals, p. 12, reports:

1. To end colonialism and establish an independent national state of Malaya comprising the territories now known as the Federation of Malaya and the Colony of Singapore; 2. To create a democratic unitary government of Malaya based on universal suffrage of all those who are born in Malaya or who adopt Malayan nationality; 3. To abolish the unjust inequalities of wealth and opportunity inherent in the present system; 4. To establish an economic order which will give to all citizens the right to work and the full economic returns for their labour and skill; 5. To ensure a decent living and social security to all those who through sickness, infirmity or old age, can no longer work; 6. To infuse into the people of Malaya a spirit of national unity, self respect and self reliance, and to inspire them with a sense of endeavour in the creation of a prosperous, stable and just society.

197 See Barr 2000a; for the first-generation leaders, see Lam and Tan 1999.
198 See Leifer 2000.
199 Chen and Evers 1978.
200 A tangled story as war-time alliance gave way to cold war; the standard story is a familiar one, but see also Chin Peng 2003 *Alias Chin Peng: My Side of History*, Singapore: Media Masters.
201 On these debates and the two constitutions, see Turnbull 1977.
202 Turnbull 1977, ch 8.
203 Turnbull 1977, pp. 285–86.
204 George 1973.
205 The Central Provident Fund welfare system was begun in 1955 by the colonial authorities. It has provided resources for government investments. Chua 1997, p. 22; see also Asher 1985; its future is discussed by Low and Aw 2004.
206 Chan, H.C. 1971 *Singapore: The Politics of Survival*, Oxford University Press.
207 Z. Bauman 1987 *Legislators and Interpreters*, Cambridge: Polity; MacIntyre 1981.
208 Chen and Evers 1978.
209 Chua 1985.
210 Chan H. C., 'The Political System and Political Change', in Hassan 1976.
211 Which being modelled on the British pattern was never very honest in the first place; on the Singaporean parliament, see Worthington 2003.
212 Thus, for example, eliding the distinction between state and party – constituencies voting for opponents have been threatened with the withholding of state money for housing upgrades.
213 Print, film and broadcast media were heavily controlled; on this in general, see G. Rodan 2003 'Embracing Electronic Media but Suppressing Civil Society: Authoritarian Consolidation in Singapore', *Pacific Review* 16.4.
214 Operation Cold Store produced political prisoners, some confined for decades; the PAP elite has made frequent use of courts in libel actions against opponents; foreign newspapers have been caught up in these activities; a knowledgeable discussion is offered by C. Lingle 1996 *Singapore's Authoritarian Capitalism*, Fairfax: The Locke Institute.
215 Heyzer, in Chen 1983.
216 N. Heyzer 1984/85 *Transnationalization, the State and the People: the Singapore Case*, Quezon City, Philippines: Third World Studies Centre, University of the Philippines.

248 Notes

217 Chan H. C., 'Politics in an Administrative State', in Seah 1975.
218 The theme is continued in later work: see Chan H. C., 'The PAP and the Structuring of the Political System' in Sandhu and Wheatley 1989.
219 Chua 1983; see also Chua, B. H. 1991b 'Not Depoliticized but Ideologically Successful: The Public Housing Programme in Singapore', *Journal of Urban and Regional Research* 15.1.
220 J. Clammer 1985 *Singapore Ideology, Society and Culture*, Singapore: Chopmen, p. 165.
221 Chua 1985.
222 Chua, B. H. and E. Kuo n.d. 'The Making of a New Nation: Cultural Construction and National Identity in Singapore', mimeo, Department of Sociology, National University of Singapore.
223 G. Benjamin, 'The Cultural Logic of Singapore's Multiracialism', in Hassan 1976.
224 Lew, E. F., 'Singapore in 1988: Uncertainties of a Maturing Polity', in K. S. Sandhu (ed.) 1989 *Southeast Asian Affairs*, Singapore: Institute of Southeast Asian Studies, notes that the PAP's response to the Anson 1981 and the general election of 1884 took the form of a tilt in the direction of political liberalization.
225 Chua 1991a.
226 J. S. T. Quah, 'Singapore in 1987: Political Reform, Control and Economic Recovery', in K. S. Sandhu (ed.) 1988 *Southeast Asian Affairs*, Singapore: Institute of Southeast Asian Studies.
227 Chua, B. H., 'Singapore 1990: Celebrating the End of an Era', in Sandhu 1991.
228 Chua 1991a.
229 See, for example, A. Chong 1991 *Goh Chok Tong: Singapore's New Premier*, Petaling Jaya: Pelanduk Publications: Shin Min Daily News Series 1991 *From Lee Kuan Yew to Goh Chok Tong*, Singapore: Shin Min Daily News. On the transition to the 'New Guard' and the ambiguities which abound in regard to liberalization, see G. Rodan 1992 'Singapore's Leadership Transition: Erosion or Refinement of Authoritarian Rule', *Bulletin of Concerned Asian Scholars*, and for a further commentary, see I. Chalmers 1992 'Weakening State Controls and Ideological Change in Singapore', *Asia Research Centre Working Paper*, Murdoch University; see also G. Rodan 1993.
230 Leifer 2000; on the security of the region, see M. Yahuda 2004 *The International Politics of the Asia-Pacific*, London: Routledge.
231 Leifer 2000.
232 Barr (2000a) cites somewhere Goh Keng Swee as remarking that the analogy was far-fetched; on Israel/Singapore, see Leifer 2000.
233 Critics of Leifer suggest his work within the English School is too pessimistic in respect of ASEAN – the key regional organization – and that he is too quick to find tensions and problems whereas the record shows that at least since the end of post-colonial confusions and cold war proxy conflicts, that is, since, say, 1975, now around thirty years, the region has been broadly stable; see Yuen Foong Khong 2005 'The Elusiveness of Regional Order: Leifer, the English School and Southeast Asia', *Pacific Review* 18.1; Amitav Acharya 2005 'Do Norms and Identity Matter? Community and Power in Southeast Asia's Regional Order', *Pacific Review* 18.1.
234 Acharya 2005; on ASEAN and the region, see Acharya 2000.
235 Yuen 2005.
236 Chong 2004.
237 Low 2001.
238 James Cotton, 'Political Innovation in Singapore', in Rodan 1993, pp. 5–7.
239 Rodan 1993, introduction.
240 Chua, in Sandhu 1991.

241 See, for example, Chong 1991; Shin Min Daily News Series 1991. On the transition to the 'New Guard' and the ambiguities which abound in regard to liberalization, see Rodan 1992; and for a further commentary, see Chalmers 1992; see also Rodan 1993.
242 See Review Publishing Company 1991 *Asia 1991 Yearbook*, Hong Kong: Review Publishing Company.
243 Chua 1991a.
244 Chua 1991a; see also Chua, B. H. 1993 'Beyond Formal Strictures: Democratization in Singapore', *Asian Studies Review* 17.
245 Worthington 2003.
246 Arun Mahizhnan (ed.) 2004 *Singapore Perspectives 2004: At the Dawn of a New Era*, Singapore: Marshall Cavandish.
247 Amitav Acharya, 'Waging War on Terror', in Mahizhnan 2004, pp. 45–49.
248 Mahizhnan 2004.
249 Barr (2003) argues that the second generation have adjusted some of Lee's more untenable policies – in welfare and ethnic relations, for example, – but the core ideas shaping the polity have not been reformed.
250 Worthington 2003, p. 41.
251 Worthington 2003, p. 43.
252 Derek da Cunha, 'Political Change and Continuity: The Near Term Outlook', in Gillian Koh (ed.) 2005 *Singapore Perspectives 2005: People and Partnerships*, Singapore: Marshall Cavandish, pp. 7–13.
253 Derek Da Cunha, in Koh 2005, p. 5.
254 J. Clammer, 'Deconstructing Values: The Establishment of a National Ideology and Its Implications', in Rodan 1993.
255 Clammer, in Rodan 1993, p. 37.
256 Clammer, in Rodan 1993, p. 41.
257 Clammer, in Rodan 1993, p. 45.
258 The term seems to have entered Singaporean debate via a speech given by Goh Chok Tong in 1998 entitle 'Our National Ethic'; Chua (1995, p. 31) reports that the term had been picked up from a book – G. Lodge and E. Vogel 1987 *Ideology and National Competitiveness: An Analysis of Nine Countries*, Boston: Harvard Business School – and Goh summarized the book's thesis in his speech; it is a species of the Western characterization of Asian Values.
259 Chua 1995, ch. 1.
260 Kong and Yeoh 2003; see ch. 3.
261 Chua 1995, ch. 7.
262 Chua 1995, p. 187.
263 Chua 1995, p. 192.
264 Chua 1995, p. 201.
265 Worthington (2002) remarks that accessing the detail of personnel is very difficult; a focus on institutions and policy networks can accomplish some useful work. Worthington also notes that he takes the idea of the core executive from Rod Rhodes (R. A. W. Rhodes 1995 'From Prime Ministerial Power to Core Executive' in R. A. W. Rhodes and P. Dunleavy (eds) 1995 *Prime Minister, Cabinet and Core Executive*, London: St Martins Press. In Singapore elite members are selected, recruited and assessed – elite group membership is not static as personnel change (thus new MPs are routinely selected and introduced via elections to parliament) and internal relationships change. The party recruits widely and it drops unsentimentally those deemed unsatisfactory. The procedure is managerialist; it is overseen by the prime minister's office; see Worthington 2003.
266 Worthington 2003, p. 37.
267 Worthington 2003, p. 11.

268 D. Marquand 1988 *The Unprincipled Society*, London: Fontana.
269 Worthington (2003) makes this point repeatedly. The Westminster system is oligarchic; in the United Kingdom this is decently veiled; in Singapore it is, if anything, flaunted by the PAP; the UK system can replenish itself as the oligarchy draws on a population of 60 million; some diversity of opinion is inevitable. Singapore is much smaller; the enduring core is small, potential recruits many fewer (Worthington argues that recruitment to the civil service, the judiciary and party is difficult) – managing change will always be awkward in such a system.
270 Ghani *et al.* 2006.
271 Chua Beng Huat 2003 *Life Is Not Complete Without Shopping: Consumption and Culture in Singapore*, National University of Singapore.
272 Chua 1995.
273 G. Rodan, 'The Growth of Singapore's Middle Class and Its Significance', in Rodan 1993, p. 53.
274 Rodan 1993, p. 67.
275 Lam and Tan (1999) suggest that Lee was only one of a core group – his pre-eminence was only secured over time. See also R. Worthington 2003: the core executive is constituted through power relations; Lee's dominance emerged through successive reconstructions of PAP and elite political actors (pp. 55–61); Goh Chok Tong took over power only slowly and used his own key bases within the shifting relationships of the core executive.
276 Cotton, in Rodan 1993, p. 11.
277 Worthington 2003; see also Ho Khai Leong 2000 *The Politics of Policy Making in Singapore*, Oxford University Press, who argues that the prime minister plays a crucial role in a hierarchical system with a politicized bureaucracy.
278 Cotton, in Rodan 1993, pp. 4–11.
279 Barr 2006.
280 Low 2001.
281 Koh 2005.
282 C. J. W.-L. Lee 2001 'The End of Disciplinary Modernization? The Asian Economic Crisis and the Ongoing Reinvention of Singapore', *Third World Quarterly* 22.6.
283 M. R. Thompson 2004 'Pacific Asia after Asian Values: Authoritarianism, Democracy and Good Governance', *Third World Quarterly* 25.5, points out that the attacks on New York and Washington changed the priorities of the US government: security came to the fore; the pressure on authoritarian regimes to reform slackened.
284 G. Rodan 2000 'Asian Crisis, Transparency and the International Media in Singapore', *Pacific Review* 13.2; Rodan 2003 – it seems that Singaporeans acquiesce in controls of political web sites out of a mix of fear, agreement and alienation (p. 518).
285 Barr (2003) mentions welfare where Lee Kuan Yew's 'self-help' preferences are being overturned to introduce, for example, medical benefits.
286 On social class, see S. R. Quah *et al.* 1991 *Social Class in Singapore*, Singapore: Times Academic Press; Tan, E. S. 2004 *Does Class Matter: Social Stratification and Orientations in Singapore*, Singapore: World Scientific.
287 Source – newspaper reports, various.
288 On this, see Ghani *et al.* 2006.
289 Barr (2003) mentions welfare and also ethnicity, where the state's rigid divisions are breaking down in practice.
290 Such desire is written all the way through contemporary Singaporean academic and popular commentary. It is routinely veiled but quite evident. The post-Lee period might see such ideas being more clearly expressed as many of the Singaporean scholars mentioned in this chapter argue discreetly that social and poli-

tical change is needed, with movement towards a less heavily disciplinized society/polity; or, as one local academic remarked in conversation a few years ago, 'twenty-five years of LKY is enough'.
291 Derek da Cunha, in Koh 2005.
292 Sylvia Lim, 'Constant in Substance, Changes in Style', in Mahizhnan 2004.
293 Chua Beng Huat, 'Political History: In an Arrested State', in Mahizhnan 2004.
294 Barr 2003.
295 Hussin Mutalib 2000 'Illiberal Democracy and the Future of Opposition in Singapore', *Third World Quarterly* 21.2.
296 Searching for sources of change extrinsic to the Singapore system – that is, shocks/breakdowns of one sort or another – seems unfruitful; the system is well embedded and has delivered extensive material benefits to the population; it may be that immanent lines of critique will have more purchase – that is, better grasp the unfolding logics and identify sites of possible change (for example the immanent critiques provided by Chua Beng Huat on the failures of Singaporean communitarianism); see Chua 1995, ch. 9.
297 See, for example, George 2000; Ghani *et al.* 2006.
298 The blurring of distinctions here recalls the Roman Catholic Church in the Philippines. Confronted with mass demonstrations against President Ferdinand Marcos they spoke of 'people power', the weight of the mass, rather than 'people's power', the political moral force of the citizenry – thus disabling the pressures for deep-seated reform.
299 N. Hamiton-Hart 2000 'The Singapore State Revisited', *Pacific Review* 13.2.
300 Barr (2006) notes that the core executive revolves around Lee Kuan Yew; it is a talented elite; advancement rests on talent and connections; the former is defined by Lee and his coterie, whilst the later simply revolves around Lee; the ideology of meritocracy is therefore misleading; the elite recruits in its own image. It might be noted that this is likely true of any elite. Barr grants that Singaporean elite recruitment is more than just cronyism – they are effective.
301 Low 2001.
302 Low 2001, pp. 436–37.
303 Clammer 1985, ch. 15.
304 Chua 1997, p. 29.
305 Lieutenant Jackson's town map is reproduced in Turnbull 1977, p. xvi; a simplified reproduction is offered in Chua 1997, p. 30.
306 Brenda S. A. Yeoh 2003 *Contesting Space in Colonial Singapore: Power Relations and the Urban Built Environment*, Singapore University Press, reviews debates about the special characteristics of these cities.
307 A. D. King 1990 *Urbanism, Colonialism and the World Economy*, London: Routledge.
308 Yeoh (2003) details the colonial-era record.
309 Chua 1997, ch. 2, pp. 32–47; Wong Tai Chee and Yap Lian Ho Adriel 2004 *Four Decades of Transformation: Land Use in Singapore 1960–2000*, Singapore: Marshall Cavendish, pp. 13–27.
310 A positive overview is offered by Wong and Yap 2004; see, in particular, the annexes of plans indicating the depth to which the territory is now planned.
311 Chua 1997, p. xi.
312 Chua 1997, p. 127; Tremewan (1994) describes the housing as 'working-class barracks'.
313 Chua 1997, pp. 131–32.
314 Chua 1997, p. 135.
315 Chua 1997, p. 142.
316 Chua 1997, p. 142.
317 Chua 1997, pp. 1–4.

318 Chua 1997, pp. 13–18.
319 European countries did/do provide social housing. Some is poor; much has been acceptable; in recent years moving stock into the private market has been popular.
320 Chua (1997) makes it clear that this is crucial. If the government buys in open property-company-dominated private market the prices are too high; betterment values created by government action go into private hands; owning the land or taking it into ownership at prevailing (i.e. pre-development) prices makes land cheap; the system can then function on rental income and subventions.
321 Chua 1997, pp. 4–5.
322 Brenda S. A. Yeoh and Lily Kong (eds) 1995 *Portraits of Places: History, Community and Identity in Singapore*, Singapore: Times Editions.
323 Kong and Yeoh 2003, ch. 6.
324 Chua (1997) notes that selling flats to occupiers has created stakeholders; on the legal implications of the policy, in particular what counts as ownership, see Tan Sook Yee 1998 *Private Ownership of Public Housing in Singapore*, Singapore: Times Academic Press.
325 Chua 1997, chs 3–6.
326 On identity, see P. W. Preston 1997 *Political Cultural Identity: Citizens and Nations in a Global Era*, London: Sage; in this context, scholars of cultural studies and urban geography have pursued these matters; the social construction of Singapore and the naturalization of the project can be analysed; one further arena of politics in Singapore is thereby critically illuminated; moreover, the critical debate is itself evidence that, notwithstanding the tireless efforts of the state to close down political discussion, debate will continue (politics does not go away; it appears somewhere else).
327 Kong and Yeoh 2003, ch. 1.
328 Kong and Yeoh 2003, ch. 3.
329 Kong and Yeoh 2003, ch. 3.
330 Kong and Yeoh 2003, ch. 3.
331 Kong and Yeoh 2003, pp. 45–50; recently expressed in the government's reports – Government of Singapore 1991 *Singapore: The Next Lap*, and *The Singapore 21 Vision* 1999.
332 Kong and Yeoh 2003, ch. 1.
333 Kong and Yeoh 2003, ch. 2.
334 Yeoh and Kong 1995.
335 P. Wright 1985 *On Living in an Old Country*, London: Verso.
336 Yeoh and Kong 1995.
337 Thus the civic district is not much liked; Tanjong Pagar is for yuppies; Orchard Road is widely enjoyed; Tiong Bahru is welcomed by locals; Katong is held to have a residual local identity; Holland Village has experienced 'expatriation'; Ang Mo Kio has a sense of community; plus there is nostalgia for some now demolished kampungs. The responses are subtle – locals are well able to judge.
338 Kong and Yeoh 2003.
339 Kong and Yeoh 2003, ch. 8.
340 Kwok Kian-Woon *et al.* (eds) 1999 *Our Place in Time: Exploring Heritage and Memory in Singapore*, Singapore: Singapore Heritage Society.
341 Kong and Yeoh 2003, ch. 10.
342 Dobbs 2003.
343 I first visited these sites in the period 1982–85; I visited them on a regular basis; over subsequent years they have been stopping-off points on many subsequent visits to Singapore; these descriptions are my own recollections – the style is deliberate.
344 The band was called Starship, the song 'We Built this City'.

345 Thus the work of local critics: see Kong and Yeoh 2003; see also Yeoh and Kong 1995 – the built environment is extensively remade, areas are swept away; for the critics a Singaporean instance of Joni Mitchell's 'you don't always know what you had till it's gone'.
346 Discussed by Dobbs 2003.
347 Lyric from Joni Mitchell, 'Big Yellow Taxi'; it is noticeable that a literature of nostalgia is now available from expatriates, local people and younger Singaporeans. See, for example, J. Davidson 2001 *One For the Road: Recollections of Singapore and Malaya*, Singapore: Topographica; J. Bertram van Cuylenburg 1991 *Singapore through Sunshine and Shadow*, Singapore: Heinemann; B. Lim 1994 *A Rose on My Pillow: Recollections of a Nyonya*, Singapore: Armour; D. Tessensohn 2001 *Elvis Lived in Katong: Personal Singapore* Eurasiana, Singapore: Dagmar; Koh Buck Song 2002 *From Boys to Men: A Literary Anthology of National Service in Singapore*, Singapore: Landmark; J. Chia Over 1993 *Isn't Singapore Somewhere in China Luv? Stories about Singaporeans Abroad*, Singapore: Angsana. It might also be added that there are local novelists and poets writing about life in Singapore; see, for example, the work of Edwin Thumboo or Philip Jeyaretnam.
348 The point at which globalization theory gets going and multiple surveys are available: see D. Held and A. McGrew 2002 *Globalization/Anti-Globalization*, Cambridge: Polity; see P. Hirst and G. Thompson 1999 *Globalization in Question*, 2nd edn, Cambridge: Polity. The notions of migration, diasporas and the realm of consumption offer better routes into these issues.
349 D. K. Mauzy and R. S. Milne 2002 *Singapore Politics Under the People's Action Party*, London: Routledge, p. 189.
350 Mauzy and Milne 2002, pp. 189–90.
351 Mauzy and Milne 2002, p. 190.
352 B. S. A. Yeoh *et al.* 2004 'Diasporic Subjects of the Nation: Foreign Domestic Workers, the Reach of the Law and Civil Society in Singapore', *Asian Studies Review* 28. There are agencies working for women, but running feminist arguments would be awkward; see L. Lyons 2000 'A State of Ambivalence: Feminism in a Singaporean Women's Organisation', *Asian Studies Review* 24.1.
353 Chua (2003) operates political sociology, urban sociology and popular consumption: the opening pair allow him to illustrate how the PAP project drives into the ordinary lives of citizens; the last noted reveals how the marketplace offers spaces for citizenry and how the elite worry (either needlessly, because they misunderstand the logic of consumerism, or hopelessly, because they cannot insulate the territory from the global capitalist system).
354 Chua 2003, pp. 18–37.
355 Chua 2003, pp. 4–14.
356 On the wider scene, see Chua Beng Huat (ed.) 2000 *Consumption in Asia: Lifestyle and Identities*, London: Routledge.
357 Chua (2003, ch. 9) notes that the state treatment of the Hokkien language in Singapore and Taiwan differed: it was suppressed in the former as a source of communalist anti-modernism and supported in the latter as the key to local non-mainland identity. Recently the PAP has allowed the import of films from Taiwan using Hokkien.
358 Chua (2003, ch. 5) notes that powerful women in Singapore have started wearing the Cheongsam – this parallels the rise of the Asian Tigers – part of the reassertion of political pride in Asia. At the same time the Malay Sarong-Kebaya has fallen out of use along with new importance of Islam, which enjoins modest dress for women.
359 Wee 2000.
360 Low 2001.

7 Trading cities

1 Edward Said is one example. Late nineteenth-century French ideas of race were used to pick out peripheral peoples within the Siamese sphere to designate them as races deserving nationhood and thus extraction by enlightened French from the Siamese sphere; see C. Baker and P. Phongpaichit 2005 *A History of Thailand*, Cambridge University Press, ch. 3.
2 On European childhoods in Shanghai and Hong Kong, see J. G. Ballard 1984 *Empire of the Sun*, London: Victor Gollancz; or Martin Booth 2005 *Gweilo: A Memoir of a Hong Kong Childhood*, London: Bantam.
3 Maya Jasanoff 2005 *Edge of Empire: Conquest and Collecting in the East 1750–1850*, London: Fourth Estate.
4 D. Canadine 2001 *Ornamentalism: How the British Saw Their Empire*, London: Allen Lane.
5 On this, see Linda Colley 2002 *Captives: Britain, Empire and the World 1600–1850*, London: Jonathan Cape.
6 Europe exported population to North America and South America. These were areas of early colonial settlement; later colonial acquisitions typically were not colonies of settlement. The numbers of colonialists were small – they were mostly sojourners. This is true of all the British colonies in South Asia, Southeast Asia and East Asia – the only significant exceptions in the region were New Zealand and Australia. Colonies of settlement and colonies of trade are quite different.
7 Colley 2002; see also Linda Colley 1992 *Britons: Forging the Nation1707–1837*, Yale University Press.
8 The idea is used by P. J. Cain and A. G. Hopkins 1993a *British Imperialism: Innovation and Expansion 1688–1914*, London: Longman, pp. 6–9, where it adds to discussions of formal machineries of empire the business of trade – conducted partly within delimited territories but also outside them, hence informal.
9 Cain and Hopkins (1993a) identify the role of economic activity in general and the power of financial linkages in particular.
10 In general, see M. Turnbull 1977 *A History of Singapore 1819–1975*, Oxford University Press; on the economic links, see W. G. Huff 1994 *The Economic Growth of Singapore: Trade and Development in the Twentieth Century*, Cambridge University Press, ch. 2.
11 The concern for trade was crucial to the early modern empires in East Asia – Portuguese, Dutch and British; later national pride loomed larger – France and America; and later still there were preoccupations with Malthusian population projections and living room was sought for ostensibly surplus populations, thus Imperial Japanese expansion in Northeast Asia.
12 The local English-language press *South China Morning Post*, spring 2003, then summer 2004 to summer 2006; also local English-language TV and radio broadcasts.
13 Sung Yung-Wing 2005 *The Emergence of Greater China*, London: Palgrave; see, in particular, the last chapter.
14 Local responses to 1997 are various; one anxious line of response is given analytical expression in J. M. Carroll 2005 *Edge of Empires: Chinese Elites and British Colonials in Hong Kong*, Harvard University Press, who argues that one key reason for Hong Kong's success has been its insulation from the mainland, now of course removed.
15 Steve Tsang 2004 *A Modern History of Hong Kong*, Hong Kong University Press.
16 Tsang (2004) is sympathetic to the colonial authorities, whom he describes as successfully Chinese, that is, responsibly paternalistic. Lam Wai Man 2004

Understanding the Political Culture of Hong Kong: The Paradox of Activism and Depoliticization, New York, M. E. Sharpe, presents case studies of assorted protests, riots and strikes.
17 L. Goodstadt 2005 *Uneasy Partners: The Conflict Between Public Interest and Private Profit in Hong Kong*, Hong Kong University Press.
18 R. J. Estes (ed.) 2005 *Social Development in Hong Kong: The Unfinished Agenda*, Oxford University Press.
19 Carroll 2005.
20 James Hayes, 'Hong Kong Island Before 1841' in David Faure (ed.) 2003 *Hong Kong: A Reader in Social History*, Oxford University Press.
21 See, for example, A. G. Frank 1998 *Re-Orient: Global Economy in the Asian Age*, University of California Press; J. M. Hobson 2004 *The Eastern Origins of Western Civilization*, Cambridge University Press.
22 Carroll 2005.
23 Historians mention the established population of 6,000 to 7,500 and note the rapid increase in population, mostly incoming Chinese. The colonial British were always a small minority. Carroll (2005) argues that Hong Kong developed slowly until Chinese merchants moved to Hong Kong, when, rather like Singapore, the original inhabitants were supplanted.
24 Tsang 2004, p. 16.
25 Tsang 2004, p. 59.
26 Ngo Tak Wing, 'Colonialism in Hong Kong Revisited', in Ngo Tak Wing (ed.) 1999 *Hong Kong's History: State and Society Under Colonial Rule*, London: Routledge.
27 Carroll 2005.
28 Ngo Tak Wing, 'Industrial History and the Artifice of Laissez Faire Colonialism', in Ngo 1999.
29 Tsang 2004, ch. 8.
30 There was little other choice, as returning British were to acknowledge (Carroll 2005, pp. 182–86).
31 Tsang 2004.
32 R. Stubbs 2005 *Rethinking Asia's Economic Miracle: The Political Economy of War, Prosperity and Crisis*, London: Palgrave, ch. 3.
33 An insight into the colonial world is given in Booth 2005.
34 Stubbs 2005, pp. 108–12.
35 Tsang 2004, ch. 13.
36 Tsang 2004, ch. 13.
37 Carroll (2005) argues that the *elite* had an idea of themselves as Hong Kong Chinese by the late nineteenth century; see ch. 13.
38 Tsang 2004, p. 180 et seq.
39 Tsang 2004, p. 161 et seq.
40 Stubbs 2005, pp. 108–12.
41 C. Patten 1998 *East and West*, London: Pan; J. Dimbleby 1998 *The Last Governor: Chris Patten and the Handover of Hong Kong*, London: Warner Books. The last noted is highly critical of the British government and colonial officials in the run-up to the handover, in effect accusing them of dishonestly manipulating the local people through spurious consultations whose results were further manipulated.
42 The legislature is elected – half by popular vote in geographical constituencies, half by so-called functional constituencies. Legislators scrutinize laws presented by the executive. The executive centres on the chief executive officer, who is elected through a closed-circle system. Functional constituencies elect a committee of 800, who elect the CEO; local commentators regard this as tantamount to a Beijing appointment system, thus a semi-legitimate legislative with powers of scrutiny has to deal with a more or less non-legitimate executive with

power of initiative. Finally, the sometime key colonial civil service is now unsure of its role – neutral, engaged or obedient to Beijing's man or what?
43 Political parties have only been around for some fifteen or so years; local people do not value politicians; numerous parties vie for votes in a legislature with limited power so the party scene is fragmented. Opinion polls reveal sharply divergent views on the political future – roughly democrats versus patriots versus economic pragmatists. There are also regular street demonstrations; the first CEO managed to get half a million onto the streets in 2003 and 2004 to oppose his policies.
44 Official data; source newspaper commentary.
45 Sung 2005.
46 See Goodstadt 2005.
47 See Tsang 2004; see also Sing Ming 2003 *Hong Kong Government and Politics*, Oxford University Press.
48 In the 1950s and 1960s a characteristic way of looking at the politics of Hong Kong was developed. Scholars pursued quantitative comparative studies and found relatively little formal democratic political action and it was said that Hong Kong people were family centred, politically indifferent and that the sphere of political life had been absorbed into the civil service administration. It is true that much politics revolved around the colonial government apparatus and that much debate was cast in narrowly practical terms, but doubt has been cast on the suggestion that somehow political life is absent. A qualitative perspective is available from Lam Wai Man, who suggests that Hong Kong people have been routinely politically active (strikes, letter writing campaigns, petitions, riots, demonstrations, pamphlets and debates in the press), not simply materialistic but principled (holding pro-socialist, pro-capitalist and social reformist positions), and that the talk of depoliticization is a mix of error (getting the story wrong) and colonial government policy (that is, they have deliberately portrayed the Chinese as depoliticized as a control strategy). Lam argues that there is extensive political activity in Hong Kong – formal and informal – adding that more needs to be done to achieve a fuller formal democratic system. But the key now is the attitude of Beijing.
49 It is an odd relationship: Hong Kong provided the bulk of foreign direct investment in the Pearl River Delta; it is the key city in one of China's major manufacturing areas; it is geographically remote from Beijing and its population in a continent of 1.3 billion is a mere 7 million.
50 The substance here is mostly derived from Sung 2005; M. J. Enright *et al.* 2005 *Regional Powerhouse: The Greater Pearl River Delta and the Rise of China*, London: Wiley; and Goodstadt 2005.
51 Carroll 2005, conclusion.
52 Sung 2005, p. 217.
53 Tsang 2004.
54 Ngo 1999.
55 People moved into these areas for economic purposes – plantations, mines, sea ports and so on. Few of the migrants intended to stay; the Europeans were sojourners, the Indian migrants were convicts or indentured labour and the Chinese were also transients who anticipated a return to their homelands. The populations of both Singapore and Hong Kong only became permanent after the Pacific War. The upheavals of the war years gave rise to the comparative stability of new nation-state building and cold war. Hitherto potentially mobile populations became ordered national populations. Many examples running counter to these generalizations could doubtlessly be found. In British Southeast Asia the oddest exception would be the Brook family – the White Rajah ruling in Sarawak.

56 An imaginative expression of the difficulties of these bases is given in Giles Milton 1999 *Nathaniel's Nutmeg: How One Man's Courage Changed the Course of History*, London: Sceptre.
57 N. Tarling's work makes this clear – drawing the archipelago into the modern world was a long drawn-out business.
58 Discussed in Amitav Acharya 2000 *The Quest for Identity: International Relations of Southeast Asia*, Oxford University Press.
59 Baker and Phongpaichit 2005, p. 55.
60 Baker and Phongpaichit 2005, pp. 60, 136, 200.
61 Local Chinese official cast the local British in the role of supervisor – the French maintained their own territory, the others folded into the British, now International, Settlement; see Linda Cooke Johnson 1995 *Shanghai: From Market Town to Treaty Port 1074–1858*, Stanford University Press.
62 The following material is taken mainly from Baker and Phongpaichit 2005.
63 Acharya 2000.
64 Baker and Phongpaichit 2005, p. 12, cite Burma, Mon, Lanna, Lanchang, Viet, Mueangnua, Siam and Khmer.
65 Kedah, Kelantan, Trenganau and Pattani. The Burney Treaty of 1826 was superseded by the Anglo-Siamese Treaty of 1909 (Bangkok Treaty), which drew the border to the advantage of the British. Siam moved only slowly from a mandala state to a bounded state in the nineteenth and early twentieth century – it was squeezed between the British and French; see Baker and Phongpaichit 2005.
66 K. K. Mead 2004 *The Rise and Decline of Thai Absolutism*, London: RoutledgeCurzon, pp. 25–30.
67 Baker and Phongpaichit 2005, ch. 2.
68 Singapore was a significant player in this regional food trade; see Huff 1994, ch. 3.
69 Baker and Phongpaichit 2005, ch. 3.
70 This paragraph is taken from Baker and Phongpaichit 2005, pp. 89–92.
71 Baker and Phongpaichit 2005, ch. 4.
72 The official nationalism moved through phases. A particular popular contribution was made in the 1930s by Luang Wichit Wathakan. Nation, religion and king were presented in top-down fashion as encompassing what it was to belong to the Thai nation through popular writings; see Scot Barme 1993 *Luang Wichit Wathakan and the Creation of a Thai Identity*, Singapore: Institute for Southeast Asian Studies.
73 Baker and Phongpaichit 2005, ch. 5.
74 P. Phongpaichit and C. Baker 2000 *Thailand's Crisis*, Singapore: Institute of Southeast Asian Studies.
75 On the 'restoration' of the monarchy, see P. M. Handley 2006 *The King Never Smiles: A Biography of Thailand's Bhumibol Adulyadej*, Yale University Press.
76 On these matters, see Cooke Johnson 1995.
77 In 1849, by his successor Rutherford Alcock (Cooke Johnson 1995, ch. 9).
78 Cooke Johnson (1995) records two main types of association – native place and commercial activity; outsiders called both guilds. The Chinese distinguished them but native place organizations could be formed around commercial activities; see ch. 5.
79 Cooke Johnson 1995, ch. 7.
80 Rutherford Alcock, Balfour's successor from 1846 to 1855, vigorously encouraged developments (Cooke Johnson 1995, ch. 9).
81 In respect of Shanghai, C. Trocki 1999 *Opium, Empire and the Global Political Economy: A Study of the Asian Opium Trade 1750–1950*, London: Routledge,

258 *Notes*

p. 119, mentions the local competition; in respect of Singapore, see C. A. Trocki 1990 *Opium and Empire: Chinese Society in Colonial Singapore 1800–1910*, Cornell University Press; the domestic British debate is nicely reviewed in Inglis 1979.
82 Cooke Johnson 1995, ch. 8.
83 Cooke Johnson 1995, ch. 8; see Trocki 1999.
84 The twists and turns of European and American relationships in Shanghai reflected different home government views, the opinions of officials and traders on the ground; see Cooke Johnson 1995, pp. 243–47.
85 Cooke Johnson 1995, ch. 7. The figures for population vary; the 250,000 figure is cited in Stella Dong 2000 *Shanghai: The Rise and Fall of a Decadent City*, New York: HarperCollins, p. 3.
86 Characterized as a coup by Bryna Goodman. A coalition of multiple groups within the Chinese population, including merchants and secret societies, native place groups and officials, seized the town; see B. Goodman 1995 *Native Place, City and Nation: Regional Networks and Identities in Shanghai 1853–1937*, University of California Press, ch. 2.
87 Dong 2000, pp. 15–18.
88 Cooke Johnson 1995, ch. 12.
89 Zhang Wei Bin, 'Shanghai: a Gateway to China's Modernization', in A. E. Andersson and D. E. Andersson 2000 *Gateways to the Global Economy*, Cheltenham: Edward Elgar.
90 Dong 2000, ch. 2.
91 Betty Peh-Ti Weh 1987 *Shanghai: Crucible of Modern China*, Oxford University Press, ch. 13, details the riches of the city and the multiplicity of actors involved – again, the Nationalists are noted as in alliance with corrupt business and gangsters.
92 Ballard 1984.
93 On actions and memory, see C. Henriot and Yeh W. H. (eds) 2004 *In the Shadow of the Rising Sun: Shanghai Under Japanese Occupation*, Cambridge University Press.
94 Zhang, in Andersson and Andersson 2000.

8 Unfolding trajectories

1 Claims to the unitary nature of capitalism are familiar: the 1950s produced modernization/convergence theory and the 1990s produced globalization, and both fail as they reduce the complexity of real-world social dynamics to a teleological recipe (as illustrations, on industrialism, see C. Kerr *et al.* 1973 *Industrialism and Industrial Man*, Harmondsworth: Penguin; on globalization, see D. Held and Anthony McGrew 2002 *Globalization/Anti-Globalization*, Cambridge: Polity).
2 The idea of change used here derives from the classical European tradition of social theorizing; the arguments are sketched in P. W. Preston 1994 *Discourses of Development: State, Market and Polity in the Analysis of Complex Change*, Aldershot: Avebury.
3 P. Worsley 1984 *The Three Worlds: Culture and World Development*, London: Weidenfeld.
4 Lam Wai Man 2004 *Understanding the Political Culture of Hong Kong*, London: M. E. Sharpe, offers case studies of political action.
5 The substantive background to this work, as noted, is the classical European tradition of social theorizing. Its concerns have been rehearsed, it seems to me, in recent international political economy; for a review, see M. Watson 2005 *Foundations of International Political Economy*, London: Palgrave.

6 Summary overview: see M. Turnbull 1977 *A History of Singapore 1819–1975*, Oxford University Press; G. Rodan 1989 *The Political Economy of Singapore's Industrialization*, London: Macmillan; and C. Trocki 2006 *Singapore: Wealth, Power and the Culture of Control*, London: Routledge.
7 B. Anderson 1983 *Imagined Communities*, London: Verso.
8 J. L. Margolin, 'Models in Singapore's Development and the Idea of a Singaporean Model', in G. Rodan (ed.) 1993 *Singapore Changes Guard: Social, Political and Economic Directions in the 1990s*, Melbourne: Longmans, identifies a series of borrowings: third worldism, social democratic, Nippo-Swiss.
9 Political science analyses are presented by Ho Khai Leong 2000 *The Politics of Policy Making in Singapore*, Oxford University Press; R. Worthington 2003 *Governance in Singapore*, London: RoutledgeCurzon.
10 Chua Beng Huat 1995 *Communitarian Ideology and Democracy in Singapore*, London: Routledge; Chan Heng Chee, 'Democracy: Evolution and Implementation, An Asian Perspective', in R. Bartley *et al.* 1993 *Democracy and Capitalism: Asian and American Perspectives*, Singapore: Institute of Southeast Asian Studies.
11 Exhaustively discussed by Chua Beng Huat 1997 *Political Legitimacy and Housing: Stakeholding in Singapore*, London: Routledge; Chua 1995; and Lily Kong and Brenda S. A. Yeoh 2003 *The Politics of Landscape in Singapore: Constructions of Nation*, New York: Syracuse University Press.
12 The title of a noted collection: K. S. Sandhu and P. Wheatley (eds) 1989 *The Management of Success*, Singapore: Institute of Southeast Asian Studies.
13 Kong and Yeoh 2003, ch. 3.
14 M. Leifer 2000 *Singapore's Foreign Policy*, London: Routledge, see ch. 1.
15 Kong and Yeoh 2003, ch. 3.
16 Kong and Yeoh 2003, ch. 3; all are problematic and have been extensively debated by Singapore-based scholars.
17 Kong and Yeoh 2003, ch. 3; Chua 1995, ch. 7.
18 Kong and Yeoh 2003, pp. 45–50.
19 Often the elite point to 1965, formal independence, but occasionally a more distant date is preferred, 1818 and T. S. Raffles; either way the history is read (wrongly) as evolutionary success.
20 Steve Tsang 2004 *A Modern History of Hong Kong*, Hong Kong University Press.
21 Tsang (2004) is sympathetic to the colonial authorities, whom he describes as successfully Chinese, that is, responsibly paternalistic; Lam 2004 presents case studies of assorted protests, riots and strikes.
22 L. Goodstadt 2005 *Uneasy Partners: The conflict Between Public Interest and Private Profit in Hong Kong*, Hong Kong University Press.
23 R. J. Estes (ed.) 2005 *Social Development in Hong Kong: The Unfinished Agenda*, Oxford University Press.
24 J. M. Carroll 2005 *Edge of Empire: Chinese Elites and British Colonials in Hong Kong*, Harvard University Press.
25 James Hayes, 'Hong Kong Island Before 1841', in David Faure (ed.) 2003 *Hong Kong: A Reader in Social History*, Oxford University Press.
26 The post-Second World War concern of departing colonial powers and replacement elites to grasp the changes enfolding them issued in the discourse of development and one idea became central, that of underdevelopment, characterized as an unsatisfactory condition in need of remedy, that is, development. That material circumstances were in need of improvement is not in question, but the notion was pernicious as it placed the days before independence or before colonialism outside history as an original condition where nothing had happened. But there were established forms of life long before colonial incursions,

and these colonial periods did mix development along with exploitation, and more particularly the territories attaining independence did have histories (in particular they had histories of colonial development or exploitation). Thus Lee Kuan Yew titles one volume of autobiography *From Third World to First: The Singapore Story 1965–2000* (2000, New York: HarperCollins) – an untenable claim on the slightest acquaintance with Singapore's history; so too, of course, the related familiar claim that the PAP enjoys sole responsibility for Singapore's current condition. Given Hong Kong's population of 7,500 in 1841, any claim to underdeveloped status is similarly foolish.

27 See, for example, A. G. Frank 1998 *Re-Orient: Global Economy in the Asian Age*, University of California Press; J. M. Hobson 2004 *The Eastern Origins of Western Civilization*, Cambridge University Press.
28 Carroll 2005.
29 Historians mention the established population of 6,000 to 7,500 and note the rapid increase in population, mostly incoming Chinese. The colonial British were always a small minority. Carroll (2005) argues that Hong Kong developed slowly until Chinese merchants moved to Hong Kong, when, rather as in Singapore, the original inhabitants were supplanted.
30 Tsang 2004, p. 16.
31 Tsang 2004, p. 59.
32 Ngo Tak Wing, 'Colonialism in Hong Kong Revisited', in Ngo Tak Wing (ed.) 1999 *Hong Kong's History: State and Society Under Colonial Rule*, London: Routledge.
33 Carroll 2005.
34 Ngo Tak Wing, 'Industrial History and the Artifice of Laissez Faire Colonialism', in Ngo 1999.
35 The idea comes from Antonio Gramsci. It usefully applies to Europe 1914–45 (89–91). It also usefully applies to East Asia from the 1911–75 Chinese Revolution through to the liberation from colonialism of Vietnam. The two regions had similarly catastrophic twentieth centuries.
36 Tsang 2004, ch. 8.
37 There was little other choice, as returning British were to acknowledge (Carroll 2005, pp. 182–86).
38 R. Stubbs 2005 *Rethinking Asia's Economic Miracle*, London: Palgrave, pp. 108–12.
39 Tsang 2004, ch. 13.
40 Tsang 2004, ch. 13.
41 Carroll (2005) argues that the elite had an idea of themselves as Hong Kong Chinese by the late nineteenth century; see ch. 13.
42 Tsang 2004, p. 180 et seq.
43 Tsang 2004, p. 161 et seq.
44 Stubbs 2005, pp. 108–12.
45 The view of many local scholars and commentators in the respective cities – it is from their commentaries that these scenarios are freely distilled.
46 But see Carroll (2005), who argues in his conclusion that local elites have managed imperial powers before and can do so again.
47 Sung Yung-Wing 2005 *The Emergence of Greater China*, London: Palgrave; see the conclusion.
48 C. George 2000 *Singapore: The Air Conditioned Nation: Essays on the Politics of Comfort and Control 1990–2000*, Singapore: Landmark.
49 Trocki 2006; J. Baker 2005 *The Eagle in the Lion City: America, Americans and Singapore*, Singapore: Landmark.
50 As an economic system, the linkages are long established; Americans traded in the archipelago around the time of Singapore's foundation; by 1900, with US

industrialization, America became a major trading partner of Singapore; see Baker 2005. As as a social/political model the relationship is more awkward; the PAP has railed against foreign culture, in particular Western, that is, American.
51 Leifer 2000.
52 Linda Low 2001 'The Singapore Developmental State in the New Economy and Polity', *Pacific Review* 14.3.
53 Hong Kong industry has a history reaching back to late nineteenth century; it grew in post-war years; in recent years it has relocated manufacturing plant to Guangdong Province, where wage rates are lower and regulative regimes more permissive and Hong Kong businesses are variously estimated to employ between 5 million and 10 million people; Guangdong Province is now a world centre for production of low-tech light consumer goods and exports to North America and the European Union.
54 Hong Kong is a major container port involved in transhipment, export and re-export (Sung 2005) and is in competition with aspiring mainland ports, where some Hong Kong firms are relocating some activities.
55 Hong Kong cannot compete in low-tech production but it can compete where human capital and links to wider global economy are important: services, management functions, business planning, research and design. It can act as a leisure centre; it now receives large numbers of mainland tourists. Hong Kong has a thriving arts scene: local popular music, local film.
56 Goodstadt 2005; however, after 1997 there were signs of a new approach, a variety of the pursuit of national development were the state acts more energetically to build up the local economy; the Tung Chee Hwa administration in the wake of the Asian financial crisis initiated several large projects – Sum Ngai Ling, '(Post-)Asian Crisis and Greater China: On the Bursting of the Bubbles and Hi-Tech (Re-)Imaginations', in P. W. Preston and J. Haacke (eds) 2003 *Contemporary China: The Dynamics of Change at the Start of the New Millennium*, London: RoutledgeCurzon; this preoccupation continued to resurface in public debate during the CEO-ship of Donald Tsang.
57 Estes (ed.) 2005.
58 It is an odd relationship: Hong Kong provided the bulk of foreign direct investment in the Pearl River delta; it is the key city in one of China's major manufacturing areas; it is geographically remote from Beijing and its population in a continent of 1.3 billion is a mere seven million.
59 The internal fissures within Hong Kong politics and the way Beijing's influence plays into these are discussed in Ma Ngok 2007 *Political Development in Hong Kong: State, Political Society and Civil Society*, Hong Kong University Press.
60 Carroll 2005, conclusion.
61 Sources local press 2003–07: (hard power) multiple instances of Beijing officials and allies seeking to influence local politics, plus three 'interpretations' of the Basic Law, plus extensive interference in the ostensibly local small-circle election of the CEO; (soft power) the periodic presentation of official gifts to Hong Kong (medical supplies during SARS, blocks of mainland tourists as travel permissions are given and the equestrian part of the 2008 Olympics) and official visits (China's spacemen).
62 This perspective rests on a species of neo-liberal reading which sees social discipline as key to growth, but what this misses is the thoroughly political project of the PAP; economic growth alone is not what they had in Singapore.
63 Sung 2005; M. J. Enright *et al.* 2005 *Regional Powerhouse: The Greater Pearl River Delta and the Rise of China*, London: Wiley.
64 Sung 2005, p. 217.
65 Sung 2005, pp. 217–18.

66 M. Jasanoff 2005 *Edge of Empire: Conquest and Collecting in the East 1750–1850*, London: Fourth Estate; for a list of wars visit *World History at KMLA* at www.zum.de/whkmla (accessed January 2006).
67 Maps of Qing Empire and European incursions are provided by P. Buckley Ebrey 1996 *Cambridge Illustrated History of China*, Cambridge University Press, pp. 223, 241.

Bibliography

Acharya, A. 2000 *The Quest for Identity: International Relations of Southeast Asia*, Oxford: Oxford University Press.
— 2005 'Do Norms and Identity Matter? Community and Power in Southeast Asia's Regional Order', *Pacific Review* 18.1.
Anderson, B.1983 *Imagined Communities*, London: Verso.
Anderson, P. 1992 *English Questions*, London: Verso.
Andersson, A. E. and Andersson, D. E. 2000 *Gateways to the Global Economy*, Cheltenham: Edward Elgar.
Appelbaum, R. P. and Henderson, J. (eds) 1992 *States and Development in the Asian Pacific Rim*, London: Sage.
Aron, R. 1968 *Main Currents in Sociological Thought*, London: Pelican.
Asher, M. G. 1985 *Forced Saving to Finance Merit Goods*, Canberra: Australian National University.
Askew, M. 2002 *Bangkok: Place, Practice and Representation*, London: Routledge.
Aw T. C. 1997 *Housing a Healthy, Educated and Wealthy Nation through the CPF*, Singapore: Times Academic Press.
Baker, C. and Phongpaichit, P. 2005 *A History of Thailand*, Cambridge: Cambridge University Press.
Baker, J. 2005 *The Eagle in the Lion City: America, Americans and Singapore*, Singapore: Landmark.
Balakrishnan, N. 1991a 'Numbers Test: Goh Campaigns for a Convincing Mandate', *Far Eastern Economic Review*, 29 August.
— 1991b 'Missed Mandate: Election Results Pose Dilemma for Prime Minister Goh', *Far Eastern Economic Review*, 12 September
Ballard, J. G. 1984 *Empire of the Sun*, London: Victor Gollancz.
Barme, S. 1993 *Luang Wichit Wathakan and the Creation of a Thai Identity*, Singapore: Institute for Southeast Asian Studies.
Barr, M. D. 2000a *Lee Kuan Yew: The Beliefs Behind the Man*, London: Curzon.
— 2000b 'Lee Kuan Yew and the Asian Values Debate', *Asian Studies Review* 24.3.
— 2003 'Perpetual Revisionism in Singapore: The Limits of Change', *Pacific Review* 16.1.
— 2006 'Beyond Technocracy: The Culture of Elite Governance in Lee Hsien Leong's Singapore', *Asian Studies Review* 30.
Barraclough, G. 1967 *An Introduction to Contemporary History*, Harmondsworth: Penguin.

Bibliography

Bartley, R., Chan, H. C., Huntington, S. and Ogata, S. 1993 *Democracy and Capitalism: Asian and American Perspectives*, Singapore: Institute of Southeast Asian Studies.
Bauman, Z. 1987 *Legislators and Interpreters*, Cambridge: Polity.
Bayly, C. A. 2004 *The Birth of the Modern World 1780–1914*, Oxford: Blackwell.
Bayly, C. A. and Harper, T. 2004 *Forgotten Armies: the Fall of British Asia 1941–45*, London: Allen Lane.
Beasley, W. G. 1990 *The Rise of Modern Japan*, Tokyo: Tutle.
Bedlington, S. S. 1978 *Malaysia and Singapore: The Building of New Nation States*, Ithaca, NY: Cornell University Press.
Bello, W. and Rosenfeld, S. 1990a *Dragons in Distress: Asia's Miracle Economies in Crisis*, Penguin: London.
— 1990b 'Dragons in Distress: The Crisis of the NICs', *World Policy Journal* 7.
Berger, P. and Luckman, T. 1967 *The Social Construction of Reality*, Harmondsworth: Penguin.
Berger, P. L. and Hsiao, H. M. (eds) 1988 *In Search of an Asian Development Model*, New Brunswick, NJ: Transaction.
Bertram van Cuylenburg, J. 1991 *Singapore through Sunshine and Shadow*, Singapore: Heinemann.
Bevir, M. and Rhodes, R. A. W. 2003 *Interpreting British Governance*, London: Routledge.
Booth, M. 2005 *Gweilo: A Memoir of a Hong Kong Childhood*, London: Bantam.
Borthwick, M. 1992 *Pacific Century: The Emergence of Modern Pacific Asia*, Boulder, CO: Westview.
Bowring, R. and Kornicki, P. (eds) 1993 *The Cambridge Encyclopaedia of Japan*, Cambridge: Cambridge University Press.
Boxer, C. R. 1990 *The Dutch Seaborne Empire 1600–1800*, Harmondsworth: Penguin.
Boyd, R. and Ngo, T. W. 2005 *Asian States: Beyond the Developmental Perspective*, London: RoutledgeCurzon.
Breslin, Shaun and Higgot, Richard (eds) 2000 *New Political Economy Special Issue: Studying Regions* 5.3.
Brookfield, H. C. 1972 *Colonialism, Development and Independence: The Case of the Melanesian Islands in the South Pacific*, Cambridge: Cambridge University Press.
Buckley Ebrey, P. 1996 *Cambridge Illustrated History of China*, Cambridge: Cambridge University Press.
Buruma, I. 1994 *Wages of Guilt*, London: Jonathan Cape.
Cain, P. J. and Hopkins, A. G. 1993a *British Imperialism: Innovation and Expansion 1688–1914*, London: Longman.
— 1993b *British Imperialism: Innovation and Expansion 1914–1990*, London: Longman.
Canadine, D. 2001 *Ornamentalism: How the British Saw Their Empire*, London: Allen Lane.
Carroll, J. M. 2005 *Edge of Empire: Chinese Elites and British Colonials in Hong Kong*, Cambridge, MA: Harvard University Press.
Case, W. 2002 *Politics in Southeast Asia*, London: RoutledgeCurzon.
Castells, M. 1988 'The Developmental City State in an Open World Economy: The Singapore Experience', *Berkeley Roundtable on International Economy Paper* 31, p. 39.

Central Executive Committee, People's Action Party 1979 *Peoples Action Party 1954–79*, Singapore: People's Action Party.
Chalmers, I. 1992 'Weakening State Controls and Ideological Change in Singapore', *Asia Research Centre Working Paper*, Perth: Murdoch University.
Chan, H. C. 1971 *Singapore: The Politics of Survival*, Oxford: Oxford University Press.
Chaponniere, J. R. 1985 'Industrial Development in Singapore and South Korea: A Challenge to Development Economics?', *Contemporary Southeast Asia* 7.
Chen, P. 1983 *Singapore: Development Policies and Trends*, Oxford: Oxford University Press.
Chen, P. and Evers, H. D. (eds) 1978 *Studies in ASEAN Sociology*, Singapore: Chopmen.
Cheng, T. J. and Haggard, S. 1987 'Newly Industrializing Asia in Transition', *Policy Papers in International Affairs 31*, Berkeley, CA: Institute of International Studies, University of California Berkeley.
Chia Over, J. 1993 *Isn't Singapore Somewhere in China Luv? Stories about Singaporeans Abroad*, Singapore: Angsana.
Chin, P. 2003 *Alias Chin Peng: My Side of History*, Singapore: Media Masters.
Chong, A. 1991 *Goh Chok Tong: Singapore's New Premier*, Petaling Jaya: Pelanduk Publications.
— 2004 'Singaporean Foreign Policy and the Asian Values Debate, 1992–2000: Reflections on an Experiment in Soft Power', *Pacific Review* 17.1.
Christiansen, F. and Rai, S. 1996 *Chinese Politics and Society*, London: Prentice Hall.
Chua, B. H. 1983 'Reopening Ideological Discussion in Singapore: A New Theoretical Discussion', *Southeast Asian Journal of Social Science* 11.
— 1985 'Pragmatism of the Peoples Action Party Government in Singapore: A Critical Assessment', *Southeast Asian Journal of Social Science* 13.2.
— 1991a 'Building a Democratic State in Singapore', paper presented to International Symposium, Institutions in Cultures: Theory and Practice, National University of Singapore, June.
— 1991b 'Not Depoliticized but Ideologically Successful: The Public Housing Programme in Singapore', *Journal of Urban and Regional Research* 15.1.
— 1993 'Beyond Formal Strictures: Democratization in Singapore', *Asian Studies Review* 17.
— 1995 *Communitarian Ideology and Democracy in Singapore*, London: Routledge.
— 1997 *Political Legitimacy and Housing: Stakeholding in Singapore*, London: Routledge.
— (ed.) 2000 *Consumption in Asia: Lifestyle and Identities*, London: Routledge.
— 2003 *Life Is Not Complete Without Shopping: Consumption and Culture in Singapore*, Singapore: National University of Singapore.
Chua, B. H. and Kuo, E. n.d. 'The Making of a New Nation: Cultural Construction and National Identity in Singapore', mimeo, Department of Sociology, National University of Singpore.
Clammer, J. 1985 *Singapore Ideology, Society and Culture*, Singapore: Chopmen.
— 1995 *Difference and Modernity*, London: Kegan Paul International.
— 2001 'The Dilemmas of the Over Socialized Intellectual: The Universities and the Political and Institutional Dynamics of Knowledge in Post Colonial Singapore', *Inter Asia Cultural Studies* 2.2.

266 Bibliography

Clements, K. P. 1980 *From Right to Left in Development Theory*, Singapore: Institute for Southeast Asian Studies.
Colley, L. 1992 *Britons: Forging the Nation 1707–1837*, New Haven, CT: Yale University Press.
— 2002 *Captives: Britain, Empire and the World 1600–1850*, London: Jonathan Cape.
Cooke Johnson, L. 1995 *Shanghai: From Market Town to Treaty Port 1074–1858*, Stanford, CA: Stanford University Press.
Critchley, S. 2001 *Continental Philosophy: A Very Short Introduction*, Oxford: Oxford University Press.
Cronin, R. P. 1992 *Japan, the United States, and the Prospects for the Asia-Pacific Century: Three Scenarios for the Future*, Singapore: Institute for Southeast Asian Studies.
Cummings, B. 1997 *Korea's Place in the Sun*, London: Norton.
— 1999 *Parallax Visions: Making Sense of American–East Asian Relations at the End of the Century*, Durham, NC: Duke University Press.
Davidson, J. 2001 *One For the Road: Recollections of Singapore and Malaya*, Singapore: Topographica.
Davies, N. 1997 *Europe: A History*, London: Pimlico.
Delanty, G. and Strydom, P. (eds) 2003 *Philosophies of Social Science: The Classical and Contemporary Readings*, Maidenhead: Open University Press.
Deyo, F. 1981 *Dependent Development and Industrial Order*, New York: Praeger.
Dikkoter, F., Laamann, L. and Xun, Z. 2004 *Narcotic Culture: A History of Drugs in China*, Hong Kong: Hong Kong University Press.
Dimbleby, J. 1998 *The Last Governor: Chris Patten and the Handover of Hong Kong*, London: Warner Books.
Dobbs, S. 2003 *The Singapore River: A Social History 1819–2002*, Singapore: Singapore University Press.
Dong, S. 2000 *Shanghai: The Rise and Fall of a Decadent City*, New York: HarperCollins.
Dower, J. 1999 *Embracing Defeat: Japan in the Aftermath of World War II*, London: Allen Lane.
Drysdale, J. 1984 *Singapore: Struggle for Success*, Singapore: Times Academic Press.
Duiker, W. J. 1995 *Vietnam: Revolution in Transition*, Boulder, CO: Westview.
Dumett, R. E. 1999 *Gentlemanly Capitalism and British Imperialism: The New Debate on Empire*, London: Longman.
Enright, Michael J., Scott, E. E. and Chang, K.-M. 2005 *Regional Powerhouse: The Greater Pearl River Delta and the Rise of China*, Chichester: John Wiley.
Estes, R. J. (ed.) 2005 *Social Development in Hong Kong: The Unfinished Agenda*, Oxford: Oxford University Press.
Evers, H. D. and Schrader, H. (eds) 1994 *The Moral Economy of Trade*, London: Routledge.
Faure, D. (ed.) 2003 *Hong Kong: A Reader in Social History*, Oxford: Oxford University Press.
Fenby, J. 2005 *Generalissimo: Chiang Kai Shek and the China He Lost*, London: Free Press.
Fong, S. C. 1980 *The PAP Story – The Pioneering Years*, Singapore: Times Periodicals.
Frank, A. G. 1971 'Asia's Exclusive Models', *Far Eastern Economic Review*, 25 June.
— 1998 *Re-Orient: Global Economy in the Asian Age*, Berkeley, CA: University of California Press.

Fukuyama, F. 1992 *The End of History and the Last Man*, London: Hamish Hamilton.
Furber, H. 1976 *Rival Empires of Trade in the Orient 1600–1800*, Minneapolis, MN: University of Minnesota Press.
Furnivall, J. S. 1939 *Netherlands India: A Study of Plural Economy*, Cambridge: Cambridge University Press.
Gamble, A. and Payne, T. 1996 *Regionalism and World Order*, London: Macmillan.
Gayle, D. J. 1988 'Singaporean Market Socialism: Some Implications for Development Theory', *International Journal of Social Economics* 15.
Gellner, E. 1964 *Thought and Change*, London: Weidenfeld.
— 1983 *Nations and Nationalism*, Cambridge: Cambridge University Press.
George, G. 2000 *Singapore the Air Conditioned Nation: Essays on the Politics of Comfort and Control 1990–2000*, Singapore: Landmark.
George, T. L. S. 1973 *Lee Kuan Yew's Singapore*, London: Andre Deutsch.
Ghani, A., Huei, P. S., Teo, L. and Lim, L. 2006 *Struck by Lightning: Singaporean Voices Post-1965*, Singapore: SNP Editions.
Gibney, F. 1998 *Unlocking the Bureaucrat's Kingdom: Deregulation and the Japanese Economy*, Washington, DC: Brookings Institute.
Giddens, A. 1979 *Central Problems in Social Theory*, London: Macmillan.
Girling, J. L. S. 1981 *Thailand: Society and Politics*, Ithaca, NY: Cornell University Press.
Gong, G. G. (ed.) 2001 *Memory and History in East and Southeast Asia*, Washington, DC: Centre for Strategic and International Studies.
Goodman, B. 1995 *Native Place, City and Nation: Regional Networks and Identities in Shanghai 1853–1937*, Berkeley, CA: University of California Press.
Goodstadt, L. 2005 *Uneasy Partners: The Conflict Between Public Interest and Private Profit in Hong Kong*, Hong Kong: Hong Kong University Press.
Government of Singapore 1991 *Singapore: The Next Lap*, Singapore: Government of Singapore.
Gramsci, A. 1973 *Selections from the Prison Notebooks*, edited and translated by Quintin Hoare and Geoffrey Nowell Smith, London: Lawrence and Wishart.
Hacohen, M. H. 2000 *Karl Popper: The Formative Years 1902–45*, Cambridge: Cambridge University Press.
Haggard, S. 1990 *Pathways from the Periphery: The Politics of Growth in the Newly Industrialized Countries*, Ithaca, NY: Cornell University Press.
Halliday, F. 1989 *Cold War Third World*, London: Radius.
Halliday, J. 1980 'Capitalism and Socialism in East Asia', *New Left Review* 124.
Hamilton, C. 1983 'Capitalist Industrialization in East Asia's Four Little Tigers', *Journal of Contemporary Asia* 13.
Hamiton-Hart, H. 2000 'The Singapore State Revisited', *Pacific Review* 13.2.
Handley, P. M. 2006 *The King Never Smiles: A Biography of Thailand's Bhumibol Adulyadej*, New Haven, CT: Yale University Press.
Harris, N. 1986 *The End of the Third World: Newly Industrializing Countries and the Decline of an Ideology*, London: I. B. Tauris.
Hasegawa, T. 2005 *Racing the Enemy: Stalin, Truman and the Surrender of Japan*, Cambridge, MA: Harvard University Press.
Hassan, R. (ed.) 1976 *Singapore Society in Transition*, Oxford: Oxford University Press.
Held, D. 1987 *Models of Democracy*, Cambridge: Polity.

Bibliography

Held, D. and McGrew, A. 2002 *Globalization/Anti-Globalization*, Cambridge: Polity.
Henriot, C. and Yeh, W. H. (eds) 2004 *In the Shadow of the Rising Sun: Shanghai Under Japanese Occupation*, Cambridge: Cambridge University Press.
Henshall, K. 1999 *A History of Japan*, London: Macmillan.
Hettne, B. 1995 *Development Theory and the Three Worlds*, London: Longman.
Heyzer, N. 1984/85 *Transnationalization, the State and the People: the Singapore Case*, Quezon City, Philippines: Third World Studies Centre, University of the Philippines.
Higgot, R. and Robison, R. (eds) 1985 *South East Asia: Essays in the Political Economy of Structural Change*, London: Routledge.
Hirst, P. and Thompson, G. 1996 *Globalization in Question*, Cambridge: Polity.
Ho, K. L. 2000 *The Politics of Policy Making in Singapore*, Oxford: Oxford University Press.
Hobsbawm, E. 1994 *The Age of Extremes: The Short Twentieth Century*, London: Michael Joseph.
Hobson, J. M. 2004 *The Eastern Origins of Western Civilization*, Cambridge: Cambridge University Press.
Hook, G., Gilson, J., Hughes, C.W. and Dobson, H. 2001 *Japan's International Relations*, London: Routledge.
Huang, X. 2005 *The Rise and Fall of the East Asian Growth System, 1951–2000*, London: RoutledgeCurzon.
Huff, W. G. 1994 *The Economic Growth of Singapore: Trade and Development in the Twentieth Century*, Cambridge: Cambridge University Press.
Hughes, H. S. 1979 *Consciousness and Society: The Reorientation of European Social Thought 1890–1930*, Brighton: Harvester.
Hughes, R. 1988 *The Fatal Shore*, London: Pan.
Hunter, J. 1989 *The Emergence of Modern Japan*, London: Longman.
Inglis, B. 1979 *The Opium War*, London: Coronet.
Iriye, A. 1987 *The Origins of the Second World War in Asia and the Pacific*, London: Longman.
— 1997 *Japan and the Wider World*, London: Longman.
Ishihara, S. 1991 *The Japan that Can Say No*, New York: Simon and Shuster.
Janik, A. and Toulmin, S 1973 *Wittgenstein's Vienna*, New York: Simon and Shuster.
Jasanoff, M. 2005 *Edge of Empire: Conquest and Collecting in the East 1750–1850*, London: Fourth Estate.
Jeffrey, R. (ed.) 1981 *Asia: The Winning of Independence*, London: Macmillan.
Jessop, J. 1990 *State Theory*, Cambridge: Polity.
Johnson, C. 1982 *MITI and the Japanese Miracle*, Stanford, CA: Stanford University Press.
— 1995 *Japan: Who Governs?*, New York: Norton.
Katzenstein, P. and Shiraishi, T. (eds) 1997 *Network Power: Japan and Asia*, Ithaca, NY: Cornell University Press.
Kerkvliet, B. J. 1977 *The Huk Rebellion: A Study of Peasant Revolt in the Philippines*, Berkeley, CA: University of California Press.
Kerr, C., Dunlop, J., Harbinson, F. and Myers, C. 1973 *Industrialism and Industrial Man*, Harmondsworth: Penguin.
Mead, K. K. 2004 *The Rise and Decline of Thai Absolutism*, London: RoutledgeCurzon.
Khoo, O. 2006 'Slang Images: On the Foreignness of Contemporary Singaporean Films', *Inter-Asia Cultural Studies* 7.1.

Kiernan, V. G. 1982 *European Empires from Conquest to Collapse 1815–1960*, London: Fontana.
King, A. D. 1990 *Urbanism, Colonialism and the World Economy: Cultural and Spatial Foundations of the World Urban System*, London: Routledge.
Koh, B. S. 2002 *From Boys to Men: A Literary Anthology of National Service in Singapore*, Singapore: Landmark.
Koh, G. (ed.) 2005 *Singapore Perspectives 2005: People and Partnerships*, Singapore: Marshall Cavendish.
Kolko, G. 1968 *The Politics of War: US Foreign Policy 1943–45*, New York: Vintage.
Kong, L. and Yeoh, B. S. A. 2003 *The Politics of Landscape in Singapore: Constructions of Nation*, New York: Syracuse University Press.
Kulessa, M. (ed.) 1990 *The Newly Industrializing Economies of Asia*, Berlin: Springer.
Kwok, K. W., Guan, K. C., Kong, L. and Yeoh, B. S. A. (eds) 1999 *Our Place in Time: Exploring Heritage and Memory in Singapore*, Singapore: Singapore Heritage Society.
Lam, P. E. and Tan, Y. L. K. (eds) 1999 *Lee's Lieutenants: Singapore's Old Guard*, St Leonards: Allen and Unwin.
Lam, W. M. 2004 *Understanding the Political Culture of Hong Kong: The Paradox of Activism and Depoliticization*, New York: M. E. Sharpe.
Laslett, P. and Runciman, W. G. (eds) 1962 *Politics, Philosophy and Society Series Two*, Oxford: Blackwell.
Lau, A. 1998 *A Moment of Anguish: Singapore in Malaysia and the Politics of Disengagement*, Singapore: Times Academic Press.
Lawson, P. 1993 *The East India Company: A History*, London: Longman.
Lee, K. Y. 1998 *The Singapore Story: Memoirs of Lee Kuan Yew*, Singapore: Prentice Hall.
Lee, K. Y. 2000 *From Third World to First: The Singapore Story 1965–2000*, New York: HarperCollins.
Lee, P. P. 1978 *Chinese Society in Nineteenth Century Singapore*, Oxford: Oxford University Press.
Leifer, M. 2000 *Singapore's Foreign Policy: Coping with Vulnerability*, London: Routledge.
Lim, B. 1994 *A Rose on My Pillow: Recollections of a Nyonya*, Singapore: Armour.
Lim, L. 1983 'The Myth of the Free Market Economy', *Asian Survey* 23.
Lindqvist, S. 2002 *A History of Bombing*, London: Granta.
Lingle, C. 1996 *Singapore's Authoritarian Capitalism*, Fairfax: The Locke Institute.
Lodge, G. and Vogel, E. 1987 *Ideology and National Competitiveness: An Analysis of Nine Countries*, Boston: Harvard Business School.
Long, N. (ed.) 1992 *Battlefields of Knowledge*, London: Routledge.
Low, L. 2001 'The Singaporean Developmental State in the New Economy and Polity', *Pacific Review* 14.3.
Low, L. and Aw, T. C. 2004 *Social Insecurity in the New Millennium: The Central Provident Fund in Singapore*, Singapore: Marshall Cavendish.
Lyons, L. 2000 'A State of Ambivalence: Feminism in a Singaporean Women's Organisation', *Asian Studies Review* 24.1.
Ma Ngok 2007 *Political Development in Hong Kong: State, Political Society and Civil Society*, Hong Kong: Hong Kong University Press.
MacIntyre, A. 1985 *After Virtue: A Study in Moral Theory*, London: Duckworth.
Mackerras, C. (ed.) 1995 *Eastern Asia*, London: Longman.

270 Bibliography

— 1999 *Western Images of China*, Oxford: Oxford University Press.
McLeod, R. H. and Garnaut, R. (eds) 1998 *East Asia in Crisis: From Being and Miracle to Needing One?*, London: Routledge.
Mahathir, M. and Ishihara, S. 1995 *The Voice of Asia: Two Leaders Discuss the Coming Century*, Tokyo: Kodansha.
Mahizhnan, A. (ed.) 2004 *Singapore Perspectives 2004: At the Dawn of a New Era*, Singapore: Marshall Cavandish.
Marquand, D. 1988 *The Unprincipled Society*, London: Fontana.
Mauzy, D. K. and Milne, R. S. 2002 *Singapore Politics under the People's Action Party*, London: Routledge.
Mayer, A. 1981 *The Persistence of the Old Regime*, New York: Croom Helm.
— 1988 *Why Did the Heavens Not Darken*, New York: Pantheon.
Miao, I. 2004 *A Social Constructivist Approach to the Sovereignty of the Republic of China on Taiwan*, PhD, University of Birmingham.
Milne, R. S. and Mauzy, D. K. 1990 *Singapore: The Legacy of Lee Kuan Yew*, London: Routledge.
Milton, G. 1999 *Nathaniel's Nutmeg: How One Man's Courage Changed the Course of History*, London: Sceptre.
Minchin, J. 1990 *No Man Is an Island: A Portrait of Singapore's Lee Kuan Yew*, 2nd edn, Sydney: Allen and Unwin.
Mirza, H. 1986 *Multinationals and the Growth of the Singapore Economy*, London: Croom Helm.
Moise, E. 1994 *Modern China: A History*, London: Longman.
Moore, B. 1966 *The Social Origins of Dictatorship and Democracy*, Boston: Beacon Press.
Murfett, M. N., Miksic, J. N. and Chiang M. S. 1999 *Between Two Oceans: A Military History of Singapore from First Settlement to Final British Withdrawal*, Oxford: Oxford University Press.
Mutalib, H. 2000 'Illiberal Democracy and the Future of Opposition in Singapore', *Third World Quarterly* 21.2.
Nairn, T. 1988 *The Enchanted Glass*, London: Hutchinson Radius.
Nester, W. R. 1990 *Japan's Growing Power over East Asia and the World Economy: Ends and Means*, London: Macmillan.
— 1992 *Japan and the Third World*, New York: St Martins Press.
Ngo, T. W. (ed.) 1999 *Hong Kong's History: State and Society Under Colonial Rule*, London: Routledge.
Nicoll, W. and Salmon, T. C. 2001 *Understanding the European Union*, London: Longman.
O'Brien, D. C. 1972 'Modernization, Order and the Erosion of the Democratic Ideal', *Journal of Development Studies* 8.4.
Orr, R. M. 1990 *The Emergence of Japan's Foreign Aid Power*, New York: Columbia University Press.
Osborne, M. 1995 *Southeast Asia: An Introductory History*, St Leonards: Allen and Unwin.
Overbeek, H. 1990 *Global Capitalism and National Decline*, London: Allen and Unwin.
Pandy, B. N. 1980 *South and Southeast Asia 1945–79: Problems and Policies*, London: Macmillan.
Pang, K. F. 1984 'The Malay Royals of Singapore', unpublished dissertation, Department of Sociology, National University of Singapore.

Patten, C. 1998 *East and West*, London: Pan.
— 2005 *Financial Times*, 26 September.
Payne, A. (ed.) 2004 *The New Regional Politics of Development*, London: Palgrave.
Phongpaichit, P. and Baker, C. 2000 *Thailand's Crisis*, Singapore: Institute of Southeast Asian Studies.
Piriyarangsan, S. 1983 *Thai Bureaucratic Capitalism 1932–1960*, Bangkok: Chulalongkorn University Social Research Centre.
Pluvier, J. 1977 *Southeast Asia from Colonialism to Independence*, Oxford: Oxford University Press.
Pollard, S. 1971 *The Idea of Progress*, London: Penguin.
Preston, P. W. 1982 *Theories of Development*, London: Routledge.
— 1985 *New Trends in Development Theory*, London: Routledge.
— 1994 *Discourses of Development: State, Market and Polity in the Analysis of Complex Change*, Aldershot: Avebury.
— 1996 *Development Theory*, Oxford: Blackwell.
— 1997 *Political Cultural Identity: Citizens and Nations in a Global Era*, London: Sage.
— 1998a *Pacific Asia in the Global System*, Oxford: Blackwell.
— 1998b 'Reading the Asian Crisis: History, Culture and Institutional Truths', *Contemporary Southeast Asia*, December.
— 2000 *Understanding Modern Japan: A Political Economy of Development, Culture and Global Power*, London: Sage.
— 2004 *Relocating England*, Manchester: Manchester University Press.
Preston, P. W. and Haacke, J. (eds) 2003 *Contemporary China: The Dynamics of Change at the Start of the New Millennium*, London: RoutledgeCurzon.
Quah, S. R., Chiew S. K., Ko Y. C. and Lee, S. M. 1991 *Social Class in Singapore*, Singapore: Times Academic Press.
Rattanachot, O. 2005 *Pressures for Change in ASEAN: Lessons from the Admission of Burma and the Economic Crisis*, PhD, University of Birmingham.
Regnier, P. 1992 *Singapore: City State in Southeast Asia*, Kuala Lumpur: Abdul Majeed.
Reid, A. 1988/93 *Southeast Asia in the Age of Commerce*, New Haven, CT: Yale University Press.
Republic of Singapore 1986 *Report of the Economic Committee: The Singapore Economy New Directions*, Singapore: Ministry of Trade and Industry.
Review Publishing Company 1991 *Asia 1991 Yearbook*, Hong Kong: Review Publishing Company.
Rhodes, R. A. W. and Dunleavy, P. (eds) 1995 *Prime Minister, Cabinet and Core Executive*, London: St Martins Press.
Rigg, J. 1997 *Southeast Asia: The Human Landscape of Modernization and Development*, London: Routledge.
Rix, A. 1993 *Japan's Foreign Aid Challenge*, London: Routledge.
Robison, R., Hewison, K. and Higgot, R. (eds) 1987 *South East Asia in the 1980s: The Politics of Economic Crisis*, St Leonards: Allen and Unwin.
Rodan, G. 1989 *The Political Economy of Singapore's Industrialization*, London: Macmillan.
— 1992 'Singapore's Leadership Transition: Erosion or Refinement of Authoritarian Rule', *Bulletin of Concerned Asian Scholars* 24.1.

272 Bibliography

— (ed.) 1993 *Singapore Changes Guard: Social, Political and Economic Directions in the 1990s*, Melbourne: Longman.
— 2000 'Asian Crisis, Transparency and the International Media in Singapore', *Pacific Review* 13.2.
— 2003 'Embracing Electronic Media but Suppressing Civil Society: Authoritarian Consolidation in Singapore', *Pacific Review* 16.4.
Rostow, W. W. 1960 *The Stages of Economic Growth: A Non-Communist Manifesto*, Cambridge: Cambridge University Press.
Rueschemeyer, D., Stephens, E. H. and Stephens, J. D. 1992 *Capitalist Development and Democracy*, Cambridge: Polity.
Rummel, R. J. 1991 *China's Bloody Century*, London: Transaction.
Sampson, A. 2004 *Who Runs this Place: An Anatomy of Britain in the 21st Century*, London: John Murray.
Sandhu, K. S. (ed.) 1988 *Southeast Asian Affairs*, Singapore: Institute of Southeast Asian Studies.
— (ed.) 1989 *Southeast Asian Affairs*, Singapore: Institute of Southeast Asian Studies.
— (ed.) 1991 *Southeast Asian Affairs*, Singapore: Institute of Southeast Asian Studies.
Sandhu, K. S. and Wheatley, P. (eds) 1989 *The Management of Success*, Singapore: Institute of Southeast Asian Studies.
Saravanamuttu, Johan 1988 'Japanese Economic Penetration in ASEAN in the Context of the International Division of Labour', *Journal of Contemporary Asia* 18.
Scott, J. C. 1985 *Weapons of the Weak*, New Haven, CT: Yale University Press.
Seah, C. M. (ed.) 1975 *Trends in Singapore*, Singapore: Institute for Southeast Asian Studies.
Sheridan, K. 1993 *Governing the Japanese Economy*, Cambridge: Polity.
Shibusawa, M., Atimod, Z. H. and Bridges, B. 1992 *Pacific Asia in the 1990s*, London: Routledge.
Shin Min Daily News Series 1991 *From Lee Kuan Yew to Goh Chok Tong*, Singapore: Shin Min Daily News.
Short, P. 1999 *Mao: A Life*, London: John Murray.
Sing Ming 2003 *Hong Kong Government and Politics*, Oxford: Oxford University Press.
Skinner, Q. 1985 *The Return of Grand Theory in the Human Sciences*, Cambridge: Canto South China Morning Post.
Snow, P. 2003 *The Fall of Hong Kong: Britain, China and the Japanese Occupation*. New Haven, CT: Yale University Press.
Steven, R. 1990 *Japan's New Imperialism*, London: Macmillan.
Strange, S. 1988 *States and Markets*, London: Pimlico.
Stubbs, R. 2005 *Rethinking Asia's Economic Miracle: The Political Economy of War, Prosperity and Crisis*, London: Palgrave.
Sung, Y. W. 2005 *The Emergence of Greater China*, London: Palgrave.
Tan, E. S. 2004 *Does Class Matter: Social Stratification and Orientations in Singapore*, Singapore: World Scientific.
Tan, S. Y. 1998 *Private Ownership of Public Housing in Singapore*, Singapore: Times Academic Press.
Tanaka, S. 1993 *Japan's Orient: Rendering Pasts into History*, Berkeley, CA: University of California Press.
Tarling, N. 1962 *Anglo-Dutch Rivalry in the Malay World 1780–1824*, Cambridge: Cambridge University Press.

—— 1975 *Imperial Britain in Southeast Asia*, Kuala Lumpur: Oxford University Press.
—— (ed.) 1992 *The Cambridge History of Southeast Asia*, Cambridge: Cambridge University Press.
—— 1993 *The Fall of Imperial Britain in Southeast Asia*, Oxford: Oxford University Press.
—— 2001 *A Sudden Rampage: The Japanese Occupation of Southeast Asia 1941–45*, Singapore: Horizon Books.
Tate, D. J. M. 1971/79 *The Making of Southeast Asia*, Oxford: Oxford University Press.
Tessensohn, D. 2001 *Elvis Lived in Katong: Personal Singapore Eurasiana*, Singapore: Dagmar.
Thompson, M. R. 2004 'Pacific Asia after Asian Values: Authoritarianism, Democracy and Good Governance', *Third World Quarterly* 25.5.
Thompson, R. C. 1994 *The Pacific Basin since 1945*, London: Longman.
Thorne, C. 1978 *Allies of a Kind*, Oxford: Oxford University Press.
—— 1980 'Racial Aspects of the Far Eastern War of 1941–45', *Proceedings of the British Academy*, Oxford: Oxford University Press.
—— 1986 *The Far Eastern War: States and Societies 1941–45*, London: Counterpoint.
Thurow, L. 1994 *Head to Head: The Coming Economic Battle among Japan, Europe and America*, London: Nicholas Brearly.
Tregonning, K. C. 1965 *The British in Malaya: The First Forty Years 1786–1826*, Tucson: University of Arizona Press.
Tremewan, C. 1994 *The Political Economy of Social Control in Singapore*, London: Macmillan.
Trevor-Roper, H. 1959 'The General Crisis of the 17th Century', *Past and Present* 16.
Trocki, C. A. 1979 *Prince of Pirates*, Singapore: Singapore University Press.
—— 1990 *Opium and Empire: Chinese Society in Colonial Singapore 1800–1910*, Ithaca, NY: Cornell University Press.
—— 1999 *Opium, Empire and the Global Political Economy: A Study of the Asian Opium Trade 1750–1950*, London: Routledge.
—— 2006 *Singapore: Wealth, Power and the Culture of Control*, London: Routledge.
Tsang, S. 2004 *A Modern History of Hong Kong*, Hong Kong: Hong Kong University Press.
Turnbull, M. 1977 *A History of Singapore 1819–1975*, Oxford: Oxford University Press.
United Nations Development Programme various years *Human Development Report*, New York: United Nations Development Programme.
Wake, C. H. 1975 'Raffles and the Rajas', *Journal of the Malaysian Branch of the Royal Asiatic Society* 48.1.
Warren, J. F. 1984 'Living on the Razor's Edge', *Bulletin of Concerned Asian Scholars* 16.4.
—— 1986 *Rickshaw Coolie: A People's History of Singapore 1880–1940*, Oxford: Oxford University Press.
Waswo, A. 1996 *Modern Japanese Society*, Oxford: Opus.
Watson, M. 2005 *Foundations of International Political Economy*, London: Palgrave.
Wee, C. J. L. 2000 'Capitalism and Ethnicity: Creating Local Culture in Singapore', *Inter Asia Cultural Studies* 1.1.

—— 2001 'The End of Disciplinary Modernization? The Asian Economic Crisis and the Ongoing Reinvention of Singapore', *Third World Quarterly* 22.6.
Weh, P. T. B. 1987 *Shanghai: Crucible of Modern China*, Oxford: Oxford University Press.
Weiss, L. 1998 *The Myth of the Powerless State: Governing the Economy in a Global Era*, Cambridge: Polity.
White, G. (ed.) 1988 *Developmental States in East Asia*, London: Macmillan.
Wilkinson, E. 1991 *Misunderstanding: Europe versus Japan*, Harmondsworth: Penguin.
Wong, J. 1979 *The ASEAN Economies in Perspective*, London: Macmillan.
Wong, L. K. 1980 'Review Article: The Chinese in Nineteenth Century Singapore', *Journal of Southeast Asian Studies* 11.1.
Wong, T. C. and Yap, L. H. A. 2004 *For Decades of Transformation: Land Use in Singapore 1960–2000*, Singapore: Marshall Cavendish.
Woodcock, G. 1969 *The British in the Far East*, London: Weidenfeld and Nicholson.
World Bank 1993 *The East Asian Miracle: Economic Growth and Public Policy*, Oxford: Oxford University Press.
—— various years *World Development Report*.
Worsley, P. 1984 *The Three Worlds: Culture and World Development*, London: Weidenfeld.
Worthington, R. 2003 *Governance in Singapore*, London: RoutledgeCurzon.
Wright, P. 1985 *On Living in an Old Country*, London: Verso.
Yahuda, M. 2004 *The International Politics of the Asia-Pacific*, 2nd edn, London: Routledge.
Yeoh, B. S. A. 2003 *Contesting Space in Colonial Singapore: Power Relations and the Urban Built Environment*, Singapore: Singapore University Press.
Yeoh, B. S. A. and Kong, L. (eds) 1995 *Portraits of Places: History, Community and Identity in Singapore*, Singapore: Times Editions.
Yeoh, B. S. A., Huang, S. and Devasaharyam, T. W. 2004 'Diasporic Subjects of the Nation: Foreign Domestic Workers, the Reach of the Law and Civil Society in Singapore', *Asian Studies Review* 28.
Yoshihara, K. 1988 *The Rise of Ersatz Capitalism in Southeast Asia*, Oxford: Oxford University Press.
You, P. S. and Lim, C. Y. (eds) 1984 *Singapore: Twenty Five Years of Development*, Singapore: Nan Yang Xing Zhou Lianhe Zaobao.
Yuen, F. K. 2005 'The Elusiveness of Regional Order: Leifer, the English School and Southeast Asia', *Pacific Review* 18.1.

Index

Arrow War (1856–60) 6, 44
Asian Tigers *see* Tiger economies
Asian Values 126–27, 137, 150
Asia-Pacific Economic Cooperation (APEC) 112
Association of Southeast Asian Nations (ASEAN) 23, 84–87, 91–92, 111–12, 134

Balfour, George 37, 44, 192
Bangkok: and British empire 9, 180–81; development of 95, 180–82, 188; elite 180–81; history 34–37, 182–92
Barisan Socialis 109, 129
Batavia 16, 17
Bowring Treaty (1855) 6, 34–35, 44, 187
Bretton Woods system 97, 112
British East India Company 5–6, 7, 16, 44
British Empire: elites 160; end of 7, 71–72; extent of 3, 44–45, 160–61, 214; history in Asia 5–6, 17–18, 100, 179–80; Malay peninsula 41, 52–53, 100, 103–6
Brunei 89
Burma 17, 90–91

Cambodia 74–75, 90
casualties: East Asian crisis 62–63, 70
Chiang Kai-Shek 20, 38, 49, 65–66, 72–73, 76, 194
China: British imperialism 37–39, 192–94; civil war (1946–49) 72–73; Communist Party 38, 65–66, 205–6; crisis 20, 60–61, 64–66, 76; Cultural Revolution 31, 32, 41, 92, 164; development trajectories 97; economic development 92–93; and Hong Kong 31–33, 54–55, 165–66; Japanese involvement 20, 49, 66–69, 194; national development 23–24; Qing Dynasty 29–30, 38, 48–49, 64; Revolution (1911) 4, 19–20, 44, 49, 57, 64; warlords 64–65
Chulalongkorn, King of Siam 18, 35, 42, 55, 187–88
cities: development of 25
cold war 14, 73–75, 76, 96
colonialism: collapse of 19–22, 58, 71–72, 76–78; East Asia 15–19, 40–44; social relations 59–60, *see also* British Empire
communism: American opposition to 73–74; China 38, 65–66, 194, 205–6
communitarianism 27, 125–26, 128, 137
conflicts: casualties 62–63; East Asia 19–22, 30–31, 60–63
Crawfurd, John 34, 187
crises: East Asia (1911–75) 19–22, 30–31, 60–63

Deng Xiaoping: market reforms 20, 92–93, 96; 'one country two systems' 32, 166, 179, 207; Southern Tour 24, 93
Dutch: end of colonialism 71; imperialism 16–17, 21
Dutch East Indies Company (VOC) 16, 46–47

East Asia: cities 25; cold war 96; crises (1911–75) 19–22, 30–31, 60–63; economic development 5, 126–27; European imperialism 4, 5–6, 15–19, 40–45, 47, 51–52; historical development 198–200; indigenous civilizations 3–4, 15–16, 45–47, 56–57; national development 22–25, 98–99, 198; Pacific War 69–71; regional development 111–12

Elliot, George 6, 44
Europe: Asian imperialism 4, 5–6, 15–19, 40–44, 47, 51–52; imperialism collapse 21
European Union: influence of 98

financial crisis (1997) 36, 88, 96–97, 111, 190–91, 196
France: end of empire 72; imperialism 16, 18

George Town 1, 6, 41, 44
Goh Chok Tong 128, 132, 135–37
Goh Keng Swee 109, 129
Great Depression 59, 68
Greater East Asian Co-Prosperity Sphere 14, 112
Group Representation Committee (GRC) system 136
Gurney Treaty (1826) 34, 187

Hong Kong: British control 6, 8–9, 30–32, 41, 53–55, 163–66; and China 31–33, 41, 54–55, 165–66; collusion 174, 211; crisis 60–61, 77–78, 164, 197–98, 205; development history 29–33, 162–66, 178–79, 196, 203–7; economic development 93–95, 164, 165–66, 167; elite 163, 165, 204–5; future scenarios 10–11, 33–34, 177–78, 211–14; laissez faire ideology 95, 162, 168, 170, 173, 203–4, 211; politics 174–77; pollution 174; post-handover 32–33, 166–74, 207; Qing period 29–30, 53–54, 162–63, 203–4; Sino-British Joint Declaration (1984) 32, 41, 78, 166, 207
Huk Rebellion (1946–51) 20, 21

imperialism *see* colonialism
India: British imperialism 5–6
Indian Mutiny (1857) 6, 44, 57, 105
Indo-China War, First (1946–54) 74
Indo-China War, Second (1960–75) 20, 21, 74
Indo-China War, Third (1978–91) 74–75
Indonesia: Dutch imperialism 17, 21; elites 89; independence 71
industrial revolution 16, 47
International Monetary Fund (IMF) 96

Japan: Asian conflicts 21, 76; and China 20, 49, 66–69, 76, 194; crisis 60–61; economy 22–23, 59, 97, 111; elites 80–82; European involvement 50–51; history 49–51; imperialism 16, 20, 66–69; Meiji restoration 50–51, 59; Pacific War 69–71; post-War development 80–82
Johor-Riau Sultanate 52, 102–3, 200

Korea: elites 82–84; Japanese involvement 66, 67, 83
Korean War (1950–53) 20, 21, 22, 73–74
Kuomintang (KMT): China 49, 194; Taiwan 84

Laos 90
Lee Hsien Leong 138, 139
Lee Kuan Yew 118–27, 138
Light, Francis 6, 17, 44, 53

Malacca 17, 41
Malay peninsula: British imperialism 17, 41, 52–53, 100, 103–6; pre-colonial 102–3
Malaysia: crisis 60–61; elites 87–88; independence 71–72, 108–9, 119–20
Manchuria 20, 67, 72
Mao Zedong 66, 76, 92
Mongkut, King of Siam 18, 35, 41, 55, 187
Myanmar *see* Burma

Nanking, Treaty of (1842) 37, 192
newly-industrialized countries (NICs) 115

Opium Wars 6, 44, 48, 56, 187

Pacific War (1941–45) 20, 69–71, 76, 106
Pangkor Engagement (1874) 52–53, 105
People's Action Party (PAP): English-educated professionals 27, 106–7, 110, 117, 122, 159, 201; foreign policy 132–34; and Goh Chok Tong 135–37; housing projects 144–45; ideology 27, 201–3; and Lee Kuan Yew 119–25; Singapore development 8, 108–10, 157, 201; social democracy 128–30
Phibun, General 35–36, 189
Philippines: American involvement 18, 72; elites 89–90; independence 72
Plaza Accord (1985) 22, 82, 96, 111

political change: colonial era 59–60

Raffles, Stamford 6, 26, 44, 113, 200
Russia: Russo-Japanese War (1904–5) 51, 67

Second World War 7, 63, 65, 111, *see also* Pacific War
Shanghai: British influence 37–38, 56, 192; development of 95, 180–82; elite 181; history of 10, 37–39, 192–95; politics 194; trade 38, 193
Shared Values 136–37
Siam *see* Thailand
Singapore: British imperialism 7–8, 41, 52–53, 100–101, 103–6; consumerism 156–59; core executive 137–38; crisis 60–61, 77–78; development of 156; economic development 93–94, 109–10, 114–18; elites 27, 88–89, 118, 123, 126, 141–42, 155, 159, 201; Empress Place hawker centre 153, 154–55; 'five Ms' 120, 126, 137, 149, 202; foreign policy 132–34; founding of 6, 26, 44; future scenarios 10, 28–29, 208–11; heritage 151; historical development 26–28, 100–101, 113, 197–98, 200–203; housing 144–47, 150; Housing Development Board (HDB) 131, 144–47, 150; independence 106–7; international relations 139–41; Japanese control 8; Lee Kuan Yew leadership 118–27; National Past 118–19, 120–21, 128, 151; official ideologies 148–52; political developments 108–9, 128–42; political reforms 135–38; pre-colonial 102–3; regional networks 111–12; settlement of 143–47; Singapore river 152–53; state forms 101–2, 113–14; state intervention 143; World Trade Centre 153–54, *see also* People's Action Party (PAP)
Singaporean model of development 133–34
Sino-Japanese War (1894–95) 51, 67
Sino-Japanese War (1931–45) 20, 76
social relations: colonialism 59–60
Sun Yat-sen 49, 64, 175, 179
Supreme Commander Allied Powers (SCAP) 70, 80–81

Taiping Rebellion 38, 54, 193
Taiwan 67, 72–73, 84
Thailand: Anglo-French agreement 18, 187; British imperialism 34–35, 41–42, 55–56, 185–89; crisis 60–61, 189–90; economy 190–91; elites 88, 187–89; politics 189–90, 195–96; pre-colonial states 182–84
Thaksin Shinawatara 37, 88, 190–91
Tiger economies 5, 23, 111–12, 126–27
trade: British Empire 5–6; European imperialism 16
Tsang, Donald 32, 166, 207
Tung Chee Hwa 32, 166, 207

United States: cold war 73; East Asian involvement 5, 20–21, 81, 97–98; imperialism 16, 18–19; influence of 14; Japan involvement 81; Pacific War 69–71; Thailand involvement 35–36

Vietnam: elites 89; war 72, 74

Washington Consensus 36, 96, 98, 190
World Trade Organization (WTO) 98

Yuan Shikai, General 49, 64

eBooks – at www.eBookstore.tandf.co.uk

A library at your fingertips!

eBooks are electronic versions of printed books. You can store them on your PC/laptop or browse them online.

They have advantages for anyone needing rapid access to a wide variety of published, copyright information.

eBooks can help your research by enabling you to bookmark chapters, annotate text and use instant searches to find specific words or phrases. Several eBook files would fit on even a small laptop or PDA.

NEW: Save money by eSubscribing: cheap, online access to any eBook for as long as you need it.

Annual subscription packages

We now offer special low-cost bulk subscriptions to packages of eBooks in certain subject areas. These are available to libraries or to individuals.

For more information please contact webmaster.ebooks@tandf.co.uk

We're continually developing the eBook concept, so keep up to date by visiting the website.

www.eBookstore.tandf.co.uk

For Product Safety Concerns and Information please contact our EU representative GPSR@taylorandfrancis.com
Taylor & Francis Verlag GmbH, Kaufingerstraße 24, 80331 München, Germany

www.ingramcontent.com/pod-product-compliance
Lightning Source LLC
Chambersburg PA
CBHW070555300426
44113CB00010B/1262